W9-AFE-813

Business Strategy in a Semiglobal Economy

Business Strategy in a Semiglobal Economy

Panos Mourdoukoutas

M.E.Sharpe
Armonk, New York
London, England

Copyright © 2006 by Panos Mourdoukoutas.

All rights reserved. No part of this book may be reproduced in any form
without written permission from the publisher, M.E. Sharpe, Inc.,
80 Business Park Drive, Armonk, New York 10504.

Library of Congress Cataloging-in-Publication Data

Mourdoukoutas, Panos.
Business strategy in a semiglobal economy / Panos Mourdoukoutas.
    p. cm.
Includes bibliographical references and index.
ISBN 0-7656-1341-7 (hardcover : alk. paper) ISBN 0-7636-1342-5 (pbk. : alk. paper)
  1. Strategic planning. 2. Globalization. 3. International business enterprises.
4. Competition, International. I. Title.

HD30.28.M684 2006
658.4′012—dc22

2005021259

Printed in the United States of America

The paper used in this publication meets the minimum requirements of
American National Standard for Information Sciences
Permanence of Paper for Printed Library Materials,
ANSI Z 39.48-1984.

∞

BM (c)	10	9	8	7	6	5	4	3	2	1
BM (p)	10	9	8	7	6	5	4	3	2	1

To Mei

Contents

List of Figures and Tables

Figures

Tables

Preface

As has been the case with new shoes, clothes, Barbie dolls, and teenage drinks, emerging economic trends generate fashion and faddism among business executives, strategy consultants, and the academic community racing to grasp their implications for business and society. In the 1980s and the 1990s, globalization, the increasing integration and interdependence of local and national markets, drew the attention of scores of business executives and academicians. Dozens of books on *Total Quality Management* and *Re-engineering,* for instance, advised businesses to streamline their operations by cutting costs, improving product quality, and becoming more responsive to changes in market conditions. In *Re-engineering the Corporation,* business strategists Michael Hammer and James Champy argue for a new business strategy that replaces Frederick W. Taylor's system of the division of labor by tasks with the division of labor by processes. In *The Virtual Corporation,* Davidow and Malone argue for a new breed of corporate organization, a network of corporate alliances of producers, suppliers, and customers that provide the theoretical underpinning for outsourcing. In the *Innovator's Dilemma,* Christensen discusses the trade-off between sustained innovations that improve the operational effectiveness of core business, and disruptive innovations that create new products that compete directly against such business. In *Managing Across Borders,* Bartlett and Ghoshal outline the concept of the transnational corporation and the importance of efficiency, local responsiveness, and organizational learning in competing in global markets.

In *The Global Corporation: The Decolonization of International Business,* the author of this book discusses the growing integration of world markets and the decolonization of international businesses, the "liberation" of the multinational corporation subsidiaries from the tyranny and control of the headquarters. In *Collective Entrepreneurship in a Globalizing Economy,* the author addresses the shift of the focus of business strategy from the managerial to the entrepreneurial function of the firm, outlining a new concept of business strategy, "collective entrepreneurship," which is further explored in a third book, *Nurturing Entrepreneurship in a Globalizing Economy: Institutions and Policies.* In "Bundling in a Semiglobal Economy," published in *The European Economic Review,* the author and his coauthor, Pavlos Mourdoukoutas, examine how the bundling of highly globalized and highly localized product characteristics can improve pricing power in highly globalized industries.

Updating and expanding this work, this book begins with the basic premise that in the first decade of the new millennium the world economy has come under the crosscurrents of globalization and localization that create an unsettled, a fluid world business environment. In some industries, globalization is assuming the upper hand, creating "pure" global market environments. In other industries, localization is assuming the upper hand, producing "pure" local market environments, while in a third group of industries no clear winner is emerging, creating semiglobal market environments, which include two segments: a highly globalized segment, characterized by high degree of integration of local and national markets, rapid technological advances and product obsolescence and imitation, intense competition, and price and profit swings; and a highly localized segment, characterized by a low degree of integration of local and national markets, slow technological advances, product obsolescence and imitation, limited competition, and steady prices and profits.

The rise of the semiglobal market means that international business must compete both in highly globalized and in highly localized markets at the same time, which has challenged a number of popular notions in international business strategy. First, it has challenged the notion that "one strategy fits all," that international business can apply the same strategy in every national and local market around the world. Second, it has challenged the notion of "think global, act local," the localization of products through domestic marketing campaigns, cozy relations with government bureaucrats, and generous philanthropy. Third, it has challenged the notion that horizontal-network-like business organizations are more suitable to competing in international markets than conventional hierarchical organizations.

Addressing these challenges requires a new business model, the semiglobal corporation, which organizes its operations according to the global/local content of its value propositions. Highly localized value propositions are placed under a conventional hierarchical multinational organization, while highly globalized value propositions are placed under a modern non-hierarchical network organization. Each organization has its own vision, coordination, communication, and motivation structure.

Clarifying the concepts of globalization, multinationalization, and semiglobalization, and outlining the vision, the competitive strategy, and the coordination, communication, and motivation structures of the semiglobal corporation, this book appeals to several market segments. First, it is a concise reader for international marketing and management professionals, and international business strategists who must constantly update and upgrade their understanding of the international business environment. Second, it is a good supplement for upper-level international business, international marketing, and international management courses. Third, the book is a good reader for social scientists and the general public who want to keep up with the direction of globalization and its implications for business and everyday life.

Acknowledgments

The author is grateful to Abraham Stefanidis and Maria Kalogeropulou for their assistance with the preparation of the figures, tables, and the index in this book.

Business Strategy in a Semiglobal Economy

1

Introduction: The Rise of the Semiglobal Economy

Strategy assumes its rightful place in the hierarchy of decision making when it's part of the business model: integrated with the realities of the external environment, the financial targets, and the business's operating, people, and organizational activities.[1]

We must continue to pursue multiple strategies and parallel initiatives to ensure that we are offering the right mix of brands and benefits to our customers and the optimal combination of profitability and service for our customers.[2]

In the last quarter of the twentieth century, business strategists advised corporate executives to abandon the traditional hierarchical model of business organization for a modern non-hierarchical model: level corporate hierarchies, narrow product portfolios, and organize production by activity rather than by task. The basic premise for this paradigm shift was a self-evident trend, the turning of the world economy from a multinational market, a collection of separate national and local markets, into a global market, a single integrated market. This book argues that in the middle of the first decade of the twenty-first century, this premise is no longer self-evident. The world economy, or at least parts of it, is not turning into a global but into a semiglobal market, and competing in this market requires a new business model, the semiglobal corporation, which combines the two organizations rather than substitutes the one for the other.

When globalization resumed its course in the mid-1970s, it seemed a universal trend that would eventually turn every industry and every region of the world economy into a single integrated market, where commodities and resources would flow freely across consumer-homogeneous local, national, and international markets, and location would no longer be a source of competitive advantage. From the late 1970s to the mid-1990s, world merchandise exports rose from 11 to 18 percent of world GDP, and service exports from 15 percent to over 22 percent, while sales by foreign affiliates exceeded the world's total exports.[3] Foreign direct investment (FDI) outflow rose by 28.3 percent in the period 1986–90 and by 5.6

percent in the period 1991–93. World cross-border credit to non-banks soared from $766.8 billion in 1984 to $2,502.3 billion in 1994. Globalization accelerated in the early to mid-1990s as the diffusion of information technology and the establishment of North American Free Trade Agreement (NAFTA) and World Trade Organization (WTO) accelerated cross-border trade. Trade flows between Canada and Mexico on the one side and the United States on the other almost tripled, while world capital imports grew at a double-digit rate.

By the middle of the first decade of the new millennium, globalization no longer seems a universal trend, for several reasons. First, economic integration has advanced in different gears across world regions and countries. Economic integration advanced in a high gear in countries like Ireland, Finland, and Switzerland, and in a low gear in countries like Israel, Spain, Portugal, and Greece, while it has remained stuck in neutral in many African and Southeast Asian countries that continue to remain on the sidelines of the global economy.

> The poorest countries (for example, in Africa) have been left out of the process of economic development. Even within developed or rich countries, the long-run evolutions of Great Britain and Argentina remind us that relative or absolute decline is always a possibility and that convergence is never automatic but is associated with the choice and implementation of an adequate strategy, given a changing international regime and a radical change in technological innovation.[4]

In 2005, market-opening reforms were concentrated in twenty-six OECD countries and in twenty-five east and central European countries and former Soviet republics. For the period 1990–2001, intra-trade in merchandise imports accounted for 60 percent of the European Union (15) trade, for 40 percent of NAFTA (3), and for around 22 percent of the Association for Southeast Asian Nations (10). Reflecting such a clustering of trade, most large companies conduct their business in these three areas.[5] In the early years of this century, Singapore's and Hong Kong's merchandise trade (exports plus imports) account has accounted for about 150 percent of GDP compared to Pakistan's 20 percent. As of 2002, close to 60 percent of world trade was concentrated among ten countries; and 33 percent among three countries, the United States, Germany, and Japan.[6] Ten countries received 80 percent of global investment flows, while the majority of cross-border acquisitions occurred in high-income countries, most notably in the United States, Canada, France, and Germany; 84

percent of newly acquired or established U.S. multinational affiliates were located in developed countries.[7]

Second, economic integration has advanced in different gears across industries. Economic integration is shifting to a higher gear in textiles, as a 1974 trade pact expires, eliminating a number of quotas and tariffs that limited the flow of garments from developing to developed countries. Economic integration is also shifting to a higher gear in services that have become the target of a new wave of outsourcing. Globalization remains in low gear in a number of industries that continue to be dominated by "local clusters," geographic concentrations of companies related by common skills, technology, inputs, regulatory frameworks, and culture, like those of Silicon Valley, Napa Valley, Hollywood, and Sanjyo (Niigata, Japan). Commodities and resources cannot flow freely across markets, and location continues to be a source of competitive advantage. "Paradoxically, the enduring competitive advantages in a global economy lie increasingly in local things—knowledge, relationships, and motivations that distant rivals cannot match."[8]

Economic integration has shifted into reverse gear in a third group of industries that have regressed to trade protectionism and government regulation. The steel industry is a case in point. In December 2001, citing a surge in imports in twelve steel products, the United States imposed ad valorem duties ranging from 8 to 40 percent, and tariff-based quotas up to 20 percent. The food industry is another case in point. The EU has banned genetically engineered altered products, a ban that hurts American farmers, while the United States requires producer registration and early import notification, slowing the flow of goods in local markets. Compounding the problem, concern over the spread of terrorism has slowed down the flow of resources and commodities across national borders.[9] Business travelers take longer to obtain visas, slowing down trading in sophisticated equipment, like aerospace products and metal cutting machines, that must be inspected by customers before shipment. Some observers go so far as to declare the end of globalization.[10]

As economic integration shifts to different gears across industries, so do trade flows. The WTO reports that for the period 1990–2001, exports of industries at the center of trade liberalization, like machinery and transportation equipment and office and telecom equipment, have experienced the highest growth, while exports of industries still under protection, like food and industrial supplies, have experienced the slowest

Figure 1.1 **U.S. Trade Flows for Highly Globalized and Highly Localized Industries, 1989–90 and 1999–2000**

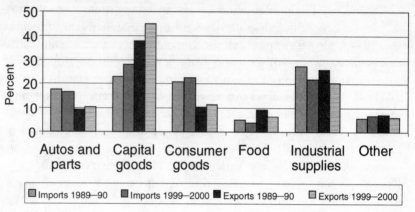

Source: Data were taken from *Survey of Current Business*, various issues.

growth. *The 2001 Economic Report of the President* (USA) finds that capital goods, consumer goods, and auto parts are highly globalized, while industrial supplies and food sectors are less globalized. U.S. capital goods imports, for instance, increased from 23 percent in 1989–90 to 28.2 percent in 1999–2000, while exports increased from 37.8 percent to 44.8 percent. Food imports increased by 5.2 percent in 1989–90 and 3.9 percent in 1999–2000, while exports increased by 9.4 percent in 1989–90 and 6.3 in 1999–2000 (Figure 1.1). Trade flows have shifted to a lower gear in less globalized industries, such as repair and maintenance services, credit origination services, entertainment, and medical care services that are localized. For the period 1990–2002, the share of transportation and travel service exports has declined while the share of other commercial services has increased (see Figure 1.2). Global trade in services has declined by 1.3 percent, while global foreign direct investment dropped by 53 percent. In 2001, global merchandise trade slumped by 43 percent to $6.08 trillion, the first decline since 2001, dragged down by a decline in information technology trade, which accounted for 60 percent of that decline.

Third, international businesses continue to face local consumer diversity. For many products, consumers retain their preferences even within highly integrated regions, such as the European Union, NAFTA, and Asian Pacific Economic Council. The preferences of Greek consumers, for

Figure 1.2 **World Exports of Commercial Services by Category, 1990, 1995, and 2002**

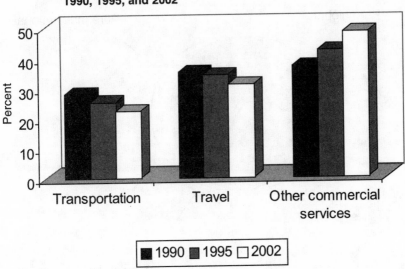

Source: "International Trade Statistics," http://www.wto.org/english/res_e/statis_e/its2003_e/its03_bysector_e.htm, May 26, 2005.

instance, are different from those of other southern Europeans, and most notably from those of northern Europeans; and the preferences of Mexicans are different from those of North Americans. The preferences of Asians differ from those of both Europeans and Americans. For large, multicultural countries like China and India, consumer preferences differ not only from those of developed countries, but from one region to another and from one city to the next.[11] In some cases, local variations in consumer preferences are not pronounced in product selections, but in product configurations that include packaging, delivery, and so on. Consumers in wealthy countries like the United States, northern Europe, and Japan, for instance, buy shampoo in large bottles and sometimes pay with plastic money. In poor countries of Southeast Asia and Latin America, consumers buy shampoo in small quantities and pay in cash.

In short, in the middle of the first decade of the new millennium, globalization is not turning into a universal trend. Economic integration is advancing in different gears across countries and industries, while consumers maintain their preferences even within highly integrated regions. In some industries, economic integration is high, creating "pure"

Figure 1.3 **Pure Global, Pure Multinational, and Semiglobal Markets**

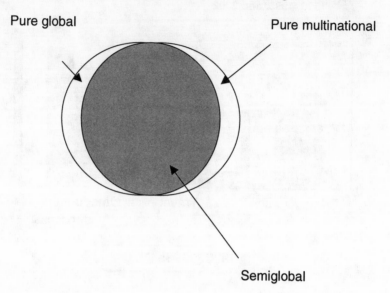

global markets (see Figure 1.3). In other industries, economic integration is low, creating "pure" local markets, while in a third group of industries, no clear winner is emerging. Thus the world economy is increasingly characterized by a semiglobal market, which can be best understood if products crossing national and local markets are viewed as bundles of global and local product characteristics rather than products per se.[12]

Depending on their local-global composition, bundles crossing national and local markets can be classified into three categories: highly globalized bundles, that is, bundles that create value primarily through global characteristics; neutral bundles, that is, bundles that create value through equal contributions of global and local characteristics; and highly localized bundles, that is, bundles that create value primarily through local characteristics (see Figure 1.4). Semiconductors, standard cameras like Canon's AE-1 model, brand name products like Gucci handbags and P&G consumer goods like Ariel detergent, Pamper diapers, and Colgate toothpaste are highly globalized bundles; they create value principally through their global characteristics. Emergency hospitalization services, automobile repair services, laundry services, and so on are highly localized bundles; they create value through local characteristics.

Figure 1.4   **Types of Bundles in a Semiglobal Economy**

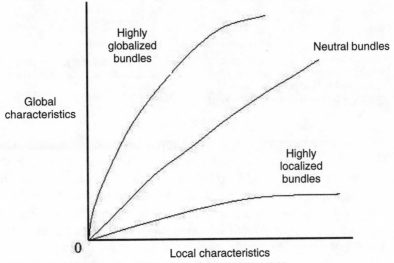

Source: Mourdoukoutas and Mourdoukoutas (2004), p. 527.

In some cases, value propositions offered to customers include just highly globalized or highly globalized bundles. In other cases, they include both highly globalized and highly localized bundles. Automobile offerings, for instance, include highly globalized bundles, such as car engines, and highly localized bundles, such as localized car chassis, repairing, servicing, and financing (see Table 1.1). Cellular phone propositions include highly globalized bundles, such as cellular phones, and highly localized bundles, such as minutes, Wireless Access Protocol (WAP) services, and so on included in localized contracts. IT business solutions include highly globalized bundles of hardware and highly localized bundles of software.

In some cases, value propositions of global and local bundles are offered by joint ventures and strategic alliances. Cellular phone value propositions, for instance, are offered by alliances of cellular phone manufacturers that offer the highly globalizing component, the cellular phone, and cellular phone service providers that offer the highly localize components, minutes, WAP services, and billing. In other cases, highly globalized and highly localized bundles are offered jointly by the same company. Automobile value propositions, for instance, are mostly offered by the same company. Honda's factories provide the highly

Table 1.1

Selected Value Propositions with Both Highly Globalized and Highly Localized Bundles

Value proposition	Highly globalized bundles	Highly localized bundles
Automobiles	Engines, brakes	Financing, repairing, servicing
Cellular phones	Cellular phones	Minutes, messaging, WAP services
IT business solutions	Hardware	Software
Insurance policies	Underwriting	Sales

globalized components of the value proposition, the automobile, while local dealerships provide the highly localized components, sales, financing, repairing, satellite subscription, and so on. This means that automobile companies compete in the globalized and the localized segments of the semiglobal economy at the same time. Information technology companies also compete in both segments of the semiglobal market. IBM competes both in the highly globalized market for hardware bundles, and in the highly localized markets for software. Broadcom Corporation competes in several industry segments with different degrees of globalization/localization, such as integrated circuits and related applications, and system-level and motherboard-level solutions. PMC-Sierra, Inc., competes in several segments of the network equipment market. "Our chips and chipsets can also be divided into the broadly defined functional categories listed below [line interface units, framers and mappers, packet and dell processors, and so on]. As with descriptions of the network, particular categories may overlap and a device may be present in more than one category. In addition, some products, particularly multiple chip sets, integrate different functions and could be classified in one or more categories."[13] Some of these categories are more standardized, and cater to the global market segment, while others are localized, and cater to the local market segment. "Due to the complexity of the telecommunications network, it is not possible to sharply delineate the networking functions or markets served. In addition, many of our products may be used in multiple classes of networking equipment that are deployed across all of the market areas identified below [access, metro, enterprise/storage, and consumer], while some of our other products have highly specialized functions."[14] The products of the power conversion industry are tailored to two different market segments: third party customers (merchants) and those sold within the manufacturer's own company

Table 1.2

Selected Features of Global and Multinational Segments of the Semiglobal Economy

Feature	Global	Multinational
Degree of integration	High	Low
Degree of imitation	High	Low
Pricing power	Low	High
Degree of consumer homogeneity	High	Low

or manufactured by the company itself (captive market). The merchant market is highly competitive, with around 1,000 merchants in 2002.

Each segment of the semiglobal economy displays its own peculiarities and specificity (see Table 1.2). The highly globalized segment displays a high degree of integration of local, domestic, and international markets, rapid technological progress and product obsolescence, a high degree of imitation, and a high degree of consumer homogeneity. The cellphone, the semiconductor, and computer manufacturing industries, for instance, provide highly globalized bundles. Nokia's chipsets, the "brains" of cellular phones, are sold with the same ease in America as in Finland. Intel's microprocessors, the "brains" of PCs, are sold in Finland with the same ease as in America. At the same time, cellular phone chipsets and microprocessors are subject to rapid product changes and obsoleteness and growing imitation by newcomers from Asia and Latin America as well as a quick market saturation, especially for older models.

Highly globalized bundles quickly turn into commodities, that is, standardized products that easily become the target of imitation. This means that international businesses offering global products are at the whim of intense competition that limits their pricing power, and under the constant influx and outflux of challengers that push profits toward the economy average. Industries that earn above-the-economy-average earnings experience entry of new competitors, while industries that earn below-average earnings experience exit of competitors, which creates price and profit gyrations: The entry of new competitors drives prices and profits sharply lower, while the exit of competitors drives prices and profits sharply higher.

The localized or multinational segment displays a low degree of integration and, in some cases, a retreat from competition, slow technological progress and product obsolescence and imitation, and a high degree of consumer heterogeneity. The insurance service and the restaurant service industries, for instance, face a low degree of integration of their world markets and a high degree of variations in consumer preferences from one local market to another. AIG cannot sell insurance policies in Tokyo and Beijing with the same ease as in New York. Its policies must receive clearance from local regulators, and its sales force must apply different sales practices for each market. Likewise, McDonald's restaurants cannot expand with the same ease in Tokyo as in New York. They must also obtain regulatory clearance and adapt their menu and services to local tastes and preferences. Siebel's software cannot be sold with the same ease in Bulgaria and Romania as in the United States without customization to comply with local language, accounting, and legal standards. Wineries and movie studios enjoy the economies of the learning curve and local clusters that give local competitors an advantage over distant competitors. A low degree of integration shelters local competitors from outside competition. This means that local competitors are price makers, that is, the visible hand of management rather than the invisible hand of the market sets prices. Local competitors are further sheltered from the influx and outflux of competitors and the price and profit gyrations associated with them.

The rise of the semiglobal business environment requires the development of a new business model, the semiglobal corporation, which combines and balances the conventional hierarchical model of the multinational corporation with the modern model of the non-hierarchical global corporation rather than substituting the one for the other. This means that the semiglobal corporation is a dual rather than a single business organization, and has a dual competitive strategy, a dual vision, and dual coordination, communication, and motivation structures.

A distinctive characteristic of the semiglobal corporation that sets it apart from the transnational corporation and matrix corporation featured in the international business literature is that it organizes its operations according to the global/local content of its value propositions rather than according to geographical regions, products, or contribution to the parent company's performance: Highly localized value propositions are placed under a multinational organization, a hierarchical organization, while highly globalized propositions are placed under a global organization, a non-hierarchical organization. This means that the success or failure of a semiglobal business strategy depends on how skillfully its management assesses the degree of globalization and localization of its different market segments, and develops the vision, competitive strategy, and coordination, communication, and motivation structures to address the peculiarities and specificity of each market segment.

A number of companies have been organized as semiglobal corporations. Honda Motor Company, for instance, has both a global and a local vision, a global vision when it comes to its highly globalized bundles like car engines, and a local vision when it comes to its highly localized bundles like car servicing, repairing, and financing. The company has further placed its highly globalized bundles, such as automobile and motorcycle engine R&D and production, and purchasing under a global organization, and its highly localized bundles, such as automobile distribution and service, under a local organization. Tetra Pak has placed its highly globalized plastic and paper products under a global organization and its highly localized service and support activities under a multinational organization. E.ON has placed local customized solutions under a multinational organization and its integrated solutions under a global organization. UK-based Global Graphics has placed its highly globalized hardware business under a global organization, and its software business under a multinational organization.[15]

The remainder of this book, a more detailed discussion of the rise of the semiglobal economy and the semiglobal corporation, is in two parts. Part I takes a closer look at the characteristics of the two segments of the semiglobal economy and explores their implications for business strategy. Part II takes a close look at the semiglobal corporation, its vision, its competitive strategy, and its coordination, communication, and motivation structures.

The chapter-by-chapter discussion is as follows. Chapter 2 discusses the characteristics of the highly globalized market segment of the world economy: the elimination of natural and artificial barriers that drive economic integration and the opportunities and the efficiencies they create for capitalist enterprises; the rapid technological obsolescence and imitation; the intensity of competition; and the price and profit fluctuations. Chapter 3 discusses the characteristics of the highly localized segment of the world economy: the high barriers to entry, slow imitation, limited competition, and steady prices and profits. Chapter 4 discusses the dual vision of the semiglobal corporation: a multinational vision for its multinational unit that consists of a portfolio of separate national missions and core values; and a global vision for its global unit, which consists of a universal mission and system of values.

Chapter 5 outlines two sets of strategies for competing in a semiglobal market: managerial strategies, including such things as cost leadership, local differentiation leadership, and mass localization leadership; and entrepreneurial strategies, including corporate spin-offs, strategic acquisitions, corporate venturing, and strategic alliances. Chapter 6 discusses the dual coordination structure of the semiglobal corporation: a conventional parent-subsidiary multinational organization for the highly localized segment, and a modern network-style global organization for the highly localized segment.

Chapter 7 discusses the dual communication structure of the semiglobal corporation, one for its multinational unit and another for its global unit. Multinational-unit communication is mostly intra-organizational communication that relies mostly on closed communication methods and vertical communication channels: closed IT systems and applications, expatriate rotation and transfers and irregular headquarters visits, and executive and technical personnel conferences. Network-unit communication is mostly inter-organizational communication that relies on horizontal communication channels and closed communication methods: open IT systems, horizontal job rotation and transfers, and global conferences and teams. Chapter 8 discusses four different motivation mechanisms—bureaucratic controls, output controls, incentives, and cultural controls—that the semiglobal corporation applies to hold its pieces together and to minimize opportunistic behavior in its multinational and global unit. Chapter 9 concludes the discussion.

Notes

1. Bossidy and Charan (2004), p. 88.
2. W. Wrigley Jr. Company, *2003 Annual Report*, Chicago, IL.
3. OECD (1996).
4. Berger and Dore (1996), p. 58.
5. Gwynne (2003), p. 11.
6. World Bank Report, "Doing Business in 2005."
7. Mataloni (2000), p. 28.
8. Porter (1998).
9. Iritani (2003), p. A1.
10. For some compelling arguments, see Rugman (2001).
11. Jordan (1996).
12. Customers do not desire products per se, but rather the characteristics embedded in them. That is, customers do not simply wish to own, say, cars per se, but the various combinations of characteristics such as horsepower, style, capacity, fuel efficiency, safety, and comfort. Customers' purchase of one model of a particular

home entertainment system versus others' purchase of another model of about the same price demonstrates that the characteristics of the two systems appeal differently to the two groups of customers. In horizontally differentiated markets where products possess characteristics that increase value for some consumers but decrease it for others, companies search for pricing power by exploring alternative combinations of product characteristics. Horizontal differentiation tends to become significant as the number of characteristics embedded within a product increases. In markets characterized by weak horizontal differentiation, products have only a small number of characteristics that actually matter to potential customers. In these markets, products tend to become commodities and companies tend to compete primarily in terms of cost.

13. PMC-Sierra, Inc., *2002 Annual Report*, Santa Clara, CA, p. 5.

14. Ibid., p. 4.

15. *American Printer*, http://Careers.americanprinter.com 2/10/2005.

Part I

The Two Segments of the Semiglobal Economy

Early Globalization, Multinationalization, and Today's Semiglobalization

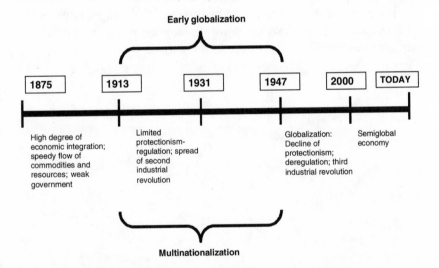

For centuries, the world economy has been caught at the crosscurrents of two opposite trends, localization or multinationalization, the increasing fractionalization and localization of world markets, and globalization, the increasing integration and interdependence of world markets. In the last quarter of the nineteenth century, globalization gained the upper hand (see above). In the first half of the twentieth century, and most notably during the period from 1913 to 1947, multinationalization gained the upper hand. In the second half of the twentieth century, and the last quarter in particular, globalization regained the upper hand. In the middle of the first decade of the new millennium, the world economy continues to be under the crosscurrents of globalization and localization, and in most cases, no clear winner is in sight. This means that the world economy is increasingly characterized by a semiglobal market rather than a purely global or a purely local market.

A hybrid of global and local markets, the semiglobal market consists of a highly globalized and a highly localized segment. The highly globalized segment displays a high degree of economic integration of local and national markets, rapid product obsolescence and imitation, and intense competition. International businesses competing in this sector face an unstable and unpredictable demand for their products and resources; they are price takers, and under the constant threat of entry of new competitors that create wide price and profit fluctuations. The highly localized segment displays a low degree of integration, slow product obsolescence and imitation, and limited competition. International businesses competing in this sector enjoy a steady and predictable demand; they are price makers and under little threat from genuine competitors.

2

The Highly Globalized Segment

The markets for the RF Monolithics Inc.'s products are intensely competitive and are characterized by price erosion, rapid technological change and product obsolescence. In most of the markets for the Company's products, the Company competes with very large, vertically integrated, international companies, including AVX, EPCOS Electronic Parts and Components, Murata Manufacturing Co., and Triquint Semiconductor Inc. that have substantially greater financial, technical, sales, marketing, distribution and other resources, and broader product lines, than the Company. The Company also expects increased competition from existing competitors as well as competition from a number of companies that currently use Surface Acoustic Wave (SAW) expertise largely for internal requirements. In addition, the Company experiences increased competition from companies that offer alternative solutions such as phase locked lop technology, which combines a semiconductor with a traditional crystal. The Company believes competitors may duplicate the Company's products, which would cause additional pressure on selling prices and which could adversely affect market share.[1]

The mobile phone market is very competitive. We face challenges from other established market participants, as well as from new entrants, including those that have traditionally focused on different segments of the consumer electronics industry. The competitive environment is characterized by rapid changes in both technology and markets.[2]

The company's business is extremely competitive, particularly with respect to prices, franchises, and, in certain instances, product availability. The company competes with several other large multi-national, national, and numerous regional and local distributors.[3]

Globalization, the increasing integration and interdependence of national and local markets for certain commodities and resources, is the resumption of an old trend that began around the middle of the nineteenth century and accelerated in the last quarter of the century but eventually stalled because of protectionism, totalitarianism, and war in the first quarter of the twentieth century. This means that today's globalization has a number of common characteristics with that of early globalization: a high degree of integration of local and national markets, rapid technological change and product obsolescence, and a high degree of imitation and intensification of competition, with three major qualifications. First, today's economic integration, imitation, and technological obsoleteness occur at a far faster pace than those of early globalization. Second, today's globalization extends from physical to virtual integration of world markets, lowering national borders and limiting the effectiveness of government regulations that protect local industries. Third, today's economic integration can be better understood if products crossing national boundaries are seen as bundles of global and local product characteristics rather than as products per se.

Today's physical and virtual integration of national and local markets has created truly global products, like PCs, cellular phones, and TVs, invented in one country, designed in another, manufactured in a third, and marketed and distributed in a fourth.

> The shifts in technology, transportation, and communication as well as the rapid elimination of trade barriers and government regulations in a number of industries have also created true global products, i.e., products that are based on ideas developed in one part of the world, turned into innovations in another part of the world, and manufactured in a third part of the world. Personal computers, television sets, and cellular phones are good cases in point. They are invented in the U.S., Europe and Japan and manufactured in Southeast Asia or China by components made from all over the world.[4]

The creation of truly global products has made today's globalization a far more interdependent and less antagonistic system than early globalization.

> The close interdependency and complementarily among national production processes and country-roles is different from that of the earlier globalization where multinational corporations exported final products made by and large in one country. In that case, national production processes were independent and competing with each other and that could explain the eventual rise of regionalism, nationalism, protectionism that put regions and countries in head-to-head competition and antagonism with each other, antagonism that led to the World War I, ending earlier globalization and giving rise to a moribund, a fragmented world market.[5]

The resumption of globalization is both a blessing and a curse for international business. Globalization's blessing is the new efficiencies and opportunities it creates. Businesses can now communicate efficiently and effectively with their partners, suppliers, and customers and manage better their supplies, inventories, and distribution network. Local producers can sell their products in distant world markets with the same ease and speed as in their home country. Sony, for instance, can sell its color TV and game consoles with the same ease in New York as in Tokyo. Likewise, Intel can sell its chipsets with the same ease in Tokyo as in New York. Sony and Intel can further communicate more efficiently and effectively with partners, customers, and employees around the world, thus facilitating the sale of their products to the emerging markets of the former Soviet Republic and China. Globalization's curse is the new risks and uncertainties brought about by the high degree of integration of domestic and local markets, intensification of competition, high degree of imitation, price and profit swings, and business and product destruction.

> Today's globalization is not as rosy and cozy a system as it is often portrayed in popular publications. It is not just about new frontiers and friction-free markets, enhanced business opportunities and soaring financial markets. It is also an obscure system of price and business destruction brought about by the opening of national and local markets to competition, and the spread of information technology that eliminated the information vacuum that often gives an advantage to one firm over another. Globalization is a system of perpetual self-destruction of conventional products, ways of doing business, and competitive strategies and practices—a system of friction between winners and losers.[6]

Corporations offering highly globalized bundles face unstable and unpredictable customer demand and business opportunities and their products quickly become commodities, leaving them little or no pricing power and under constant pressure by new competitors that drive profits toward the economy average. Industries that have above-average earnings in the short term are flooded with new competitors in long term, and prices and earnings decline. Conversely, industries that earn profits below the economy average prompt the exit of competitors. Entry and exit eventually drive profits across industries to the economy average.

The remainder of this chapter, a more detail discussion of the characteristics of globalized industries, is in six sections. The first section discusses the high degree of integration of national and local markets of global industries, the second addresses rapid technological changes, the third section addresses the high degree of imitation, the fourth discusses cosumer homogeneity, the fifth focuses on the intensification of competition, and the sixth section concentrates on price and profit fluctuations.

A High Degree of Integration of Local and National Markets

Economic integration is an important condition for the normal functioning and rapid growth of markets. It eases the flow of economic resources and commodities across markets and fuels efficiencies and new business opportunities. Economic integration is driven by the removal and eventual elimination of natural barriers, such as transportation and communication inefficiencies, and artificial barriers, such as tariffs, quotas, and government regulations that separate national and local markets. America's nineteenth-century economic integration, for instance, was driven by the elimination of natural barriers: the shortening of the distance across local markets through construction of canals and the spread of waterways at the beginning of the century, the development of steamships and the spread of the railroads in the middle of the century, and the spread of telecommunications at the end of the century.

The world's economic integration in the last quarter of the twentieth century was driven by four factors. The first was the collapse of right wing totalitarian regimes around the world and the fading of nationalist sentiments that supported government intervention in the economy. The second was the collapse of capitalism's long-time enemy, communism, which kept a large part of the world off-limits for capitalism and supported union militancy and activist government policies. The collapse of communism and right wing totalitarian regimes further paved the way for market-friendly political regimes, which have proceeded with the privatization of government enterprises and the deregulation of local and national markets. Food services at public facilities, janitorial services, security services, sanitation services, and even jail services are in many states and municipalities contracted out to the private sector. The third factor driving economic integration was the completion of GATT talks and the formation of the World Trade Organization, the proliferation of regional trade partnerships like NAFTA, the extension of the EU, and the strengthening of APEC through the further lifting of trade barriers.[7] The fourth was the spread of information and telecommunications technologies, which has added another piece to the puzzle of a global economy: instant communications that have shortened the distance among national and local markets.[8] For many commodities and resources, especially capital, the world economy has been transformed from a fragmented, multinational market to a global market—a single, integrated market.

Economic integration lowers transaction costs and eases the flow of commodities and resources across regions and industries, creating new business opportunities for local and national industries. America's nineteenth-century economic integration lowered transaction costs across industries and regions. The spread of steam-powered ships, for instance, cut cross-Atlantic shipping costs by 80 percent, a trend that continued throughout the twentieth century and most notably in the second half with the introduction of the big containerized cargo carriers.[9]

> Ocean shipping costs have fallen substantially in the past half of century, perhaps by as much as a factor of four or five. Oil tankers of roughly 10,000 tons displacement have been replaced by supertankers of up to 500,000 tons, with no increase in crew size. Merchant steamers of 5,000 to 8,000 tons have been replaced by containerized cargo carriers displacing 100,000 to 150,000 tons. Loading and off-loading by large crews of longshoremen has been virtually eliminated. Integration with domestic transportation networks of road and rail is speedy, efficient, and less prone to disruption.[10]

Economic integration also allowed for the prompt and timely delivery of commodities and resources, reducing the uncertainty of transactions. In 1800, before the construction of canals in the United States, interregional trade was slow and costly. "The trade between the Northeast and South was a coastwise trade, while that with the West was overland when it involved valuable manufactured goods which could stand the high cost of wagon transportation or by coastwise trade to New Orleans and thence upriver if they were bulky items."[11] It took, for instance, four weeks to move merchandise from Lake Erie to New Orleans, two weeks to Georgia,[12] and one week from Lake Ontario to Virginia. In 1830, after the canal construction, transportation time from Lake Erie to New Orleans was cut to two weeks, and to Georgia to one week, while the time from Lake Ontario to Virginia was cut to three days. Canals lowered transportation costs from twenty cents per ton-mile in 1810 to three cents per ton-mile in 1830.[13]

Lower transportation costs and prompt and timely delivery expanded business opportunities. The building of the Great National Pike, for instance, allowed western farmers to transport sheep and cattle to the big markets of eastern states. The opening of the Erie Canal in 1825 and the completion of the western canals in the 1830s offered farmers the opportunity to ship grain and meat from Ohio and Indiana to New York. For the period 1816–60, tonnage of vessels on the western rivers and lakes soared from a few thousand tons to 400,000 tons. For the period 1835–60, grain shipments from the West to Buffalo reached 3 million barrels.[14]

> The opening of the Erie Canal permitted access to the rich lands of western New York and central Pennsylvania, and large farm units began appearing in those areas. In the South cotton was well entrenched by 1820 and the westward shift of cotton farming was exploding. The new cotton states, with their large plantations, surpassed their Atlantic coast predecessors in the mid-1830s. Large scale farming was a part of the American scene by 1860.[15]

The spread of the railroads expanded trade opportunities between the western and southwestern regions and the eastern region. For the period 1835–60, for instance, flour shipments from those two regions to the eastern region increased from 30 percent to 78 percent, while corn shipments increased from 2 percent to 81 percent.[16] For the period 1815–60, the value of trade between the West and the South recorded in receipts at New Orleans increased from around $10 million to $180 million.[17] Between1860 and 1910, passenger rates fell from 2.8 cents to 1.9 cents per mile, while average tonnage miles declined from 2.2 cents to 0.75 cents.[18] The spread of railroads allowed for the creation of the meatpacking and fruit industries and the rise of large companies like Swift and Company in the 1880s and the United Fruit Company in 1899.

As was the case with early economic integration, today's economic integration is a source of efficiency propelled by declining tariffs and communication costs. Average worldwide tariff rates dropped from around 40 percent in the late 1940s down to around 5 percent by late 1990s. Industrial countries' tariffs on parts and components declined from 5 percent in 1988 to 2.5 by 2000. Leasing costs for phone calls and data transmission from Los Angeles to Bangalore, India, fell from around $60,000 in 2000 to below $10,000 by 2004.[19] Lower tariffs and cheaper communication are speeding up cross-border trade, investments, intra-firm trade and equity and portfolio investment flows, and expanding business opportunities beyond domestic markets:

- World export growth increased from around 14 percent in 1970 to close to 24 percent in 2001.
- World trade increased from about $200 billion in 1960 to about $4 trillion by 1993.[20] U.S. trade increased from $123,182 million in 1977 to $512,626 million in 1994.[21]
- The U.S. direct investment position abroad increased from $207,752 million in 1982 to $711,621 million in 1995. In the same period, direct investment to the United States increased from $124,677 million to $560,088 million. Over the 1993–96 period, net private flows to developing countries averaged $150 billion a year. [22]
- Cross-border mergers & acquisitions (M&A) have soared from close to $81 billion in 1991 to $720 billion in 1999.
- The intra-firm-trade share of U.S. parent companies increased from 32 percent of total exports in 1990 to 36 percent in 1999, while that of Japanese parent companies increased from 16 percent to 31 percent.[23]
- Equity and portfolio investment flows to developing countries rose from less than 1 percent of developing country GDP in 1983–89 to 2–4 percent of GDP in each of the years 1994–96. In the first four months of 1996 alone, international placements of equities reached $15.3 billion, more than double the $6.9 billion for the corresponding period in 1995.[24]

The creation of NAFTA, for instance, allowed Canadian furniture makers, like Shermag and Dutailier International, to expand their presence to the U.S. market. Before NAFTA, nearly all of Shermag's sales were in the local market. After NAFTA, 70 percent of its sales have been in the United States. Since 1994, the company's annual sales quadrupled, reaching $100 million. Dutailier's sales have also soared, from C$20 million prior to 1994 to C$100 million after.[25] The expansion of the EU allowed Italian cloth makers to sell their garments in Paris with the same ease as in Rome, and Greek yogurt and feta-cheese makers to sell their products in France and Germany with the same ease as in the Greek market, while the collapse of communism opened up the markets of Eastern Europe and the former Soviet republics to Western products and competition. The creation of WTO, and the precipitous decline in trade protectionism and regulation, allowed corporations like Souza Cruz, Hutchison Whampoa, Samsung Electronics, Vitro S.A, and Reliance Industries Ltd., from smaller, less developed countries like Brazil, China, South Korea, Spain, Mexico, and India, to reach beyond their home markets. As of 1999, the headquarters of ten multinational corporations were located in China, compared to none in 1962; South Korea was also the headquarters of ten multinational corporations compared to none in 1962; and Spain was the headquarters of four multinational corporations in 1999 compared to none in 1962.[26]

In short, economic integration and the removal of natural and artificial barriers that limited trade across regional national and local boundaries eased the flow of resources and commodities from one market to another, fostering economic efficiency and spurring new business opportunities. Similar effects have been wrought by rapid technological changes.

Rapid Technological Changes and Product Obsoleteness

New technology has always been a source of change for the economy and society. It transforms the production, distribution, and consumption of commodities, making old products, processes, and business models obsolete. The spread of the telegraph in the early 1860s, for instance, replaced the Pony Express riders that delivered mail across the country. The expansion of the railroads in the second half of the nineteenth century changed production and distribution of commodities throughout the United States. Swift's centralized meatpacking system turned traditional slaughterhouses obsolete. The refining of sugar from a new material, sugar beets, made traditional sugarcane refining obsolete. The development of the Bonsack cigarette-rolling system and its deployment by James B. Duke made the hand-rolling process obsolete. The development of solid-state components for TVs made the conventional vacuum tube obsolete. In the 1990s, digital copiers have made analog copiers obsolete, while in the early 2000s liquid crystal displays and plasma TVs are making traditional tube TVs obsolete.

One of the distinctive characteristics of today's technology is the pace at which it spreads in the economy. It took about sixty years for the full diffusion of water-power iron technology, fifty-five years for steam and rail technology, fifty years for electricity, chemicals, and the internal combustion engine, forty years for petrochemicals, electronics, and aviation technologies, but only twelve years for the IT technology (1990–2002). It took less than two decades to transform cellular phones from a luxury to a necessity.

Few products have ever fallen so fast from luxury perk to ubiquitous commodity. When they first hit the market in the early 1980s, cellphones were the province of moguls, who toted around brick-size models or used ones tethered to their cars' armrests. Then technological advances made phones smaller and cheaper to manufacture, and growing national networks and competition among carriers brought prices down.[27]

The quickening of the pace of technological diffusion has shortened product cycles, accelerating product obsoleteness, that is, products are turning economically obsolete well before they turn physically obsolete.

In the early days of industrialization, commodities turned obsolete when they were all worn out and had no more use value for their owners. In today's global economy, commodities often turn obsolete well before they are worn out and even if they have some use value left for their consumers. This means that the economic value of certain commodities is far below their physical value. This is especially the case for high-technology products, which are quickly made obsolete by new, more advanced products.[28]

In the semiconductor industry, for instance, product cycles are as short as six months. "In the semiconductor industry, prices decline rapidly as unit volume grows, further competition develops and production experience is accumulated. The life cycle of our products is very short, often less than a year."[29] In the automobile industry, high performance cars go out of fashion well before they wear out. In the software industry, product obsoleteness is incorporated in the software, that is, software companies set timetables to phase out old software versions and replace them with new ones.

Since software doesn't wear out, software makers set timetables for phasing out programs. Just when big clients work out the kinks in complex software systems, the software companies tell them they need to install new versions. This gives software companies a chance to impose fresh licensing fees and a big chance to sell existing customers new features, usually unavailable for older version.[30]

Another characteristic of today's technology is its effects on business organizations and management practices. Rapid technological changes favor horizontal organizations that combine scale with flexibility, speed, and innovation rather than vertical organizations. "Innovative technologies are providing opportunities for new firms to enter markets on the basis of technical advantages. Such changes are likely to be disruptive to mature organizations. At the same time, economies of scale are likely to affect the size of enterprises, giving advantages to large market-dominant organizations and to first movers."[31]

In short, economic integration speeds up the spread of new technology that quickly turns products and business models obsolete, which constrains the profitable deployment of assets. Economic obsoleteness further requires the quick design and manufacturing of new models, which lead to modularization and a rapid degree of imitation and market saturation.

Rapid Imitation and Market Saturation

Imitation, the replication of a product, a process, or a business model by the competition, is an integral part of global industries. Successful businesses have always become the targets of imitation. In the mid-nineteenth century, American entrepreneurs like Samuel Slater, Francis Lowell, and later on Andrew Carnegie, assimilated a number of European technologies that turned them into formidable competitors in the textile industry. In the 1870s, sugar refineries imitated one another by introducing new plants that lowered refining costs. "In any sort of sudden, massive alteration in the organization of many businesses, the force of example is strong, and the new forms are 'in the air' and faddism."[32]

In the late nineteenth century, Philip Armour quickly replicated Gustavous Swift's meatpacking model, while Italian garment manufacturers borrowed textile manufacturing technologies from England. In the 1920s, European entrepreneurs traveled to America to assimilate its technology, management, and business regulation systems. In the 1950s, Japanese entrepreneurs like Eiji Toyoda and Taiichi Ohno assimilated American management practices. In the 1970s and the 1980s, American companies imitated Japanese quality circles (QC) and total quality management (TQM). Dell's "sell-direct" model was quickly imitated by Compaq Computer and Gateway Computers, and even by fresh produce distributors, like FreshDirect. McDonald's franchise model is imitated by upstarts, Burger King and Wendy's in the United States, Moss Burger in Japan, and Goody's in South Europe. The success of Nokia, Motorola, and Ericsson in the cellphone industry is replicated by Chinese upstarts. "A slew of little known companies are flocking to mobile-phone manufacturing rapidly turning the basic handset into a commodity and threatening to price industry leaders out of the market."[33]

An important difference between today's imitation and that of the past is its speed and magnitude, especially in the semiconductor and electronics industries, where successful products quickly attract the entry of new competitors. Intel's new chips, for instance, are quickly matched and surpassed by competitors AMD and Sun Microsystems. Sony's MP3, CD players, and cellphones are replicated by Korean and Chinese producers who have access to the very same pool of resources as Sony. A factor that speeds up product replication is state-of-the-art technologies that allow competitors to replicate designs. Toys are a case in point. Three-dimensional scanning devices allow competitors to reproduce new toy designs within a few minutes after their release. "The problem has worsened with the development of so-called rapid prototypes, which can take a three-dimensional computer scan of a plastic or wood toy and reproduce a sample within hours."[34]

Another factor that speeds imitation is the increasing standardization and modularization of parts and components used in the production of electronic products that can be easily acquired in world markets.

> With each passing year, Sony's new models of MP3 players, handycams, CD players, and cell phones are reduced more quickly to rank commodities by the industry's overstocked supply chain for key components. The Sony's, Sanyo's, and Samsungs of the world—not to mention Chinese upstarts—all have access to the same huge pool of chips, liquid crystal displays, audio pickups, power supplies, and packaging. To see what impact that has on prices, look no further than the DVD market, where Sony once ruled the roost. Recently, some of the hottest models are Chinese DVD players selling for less than $100. [35]

Chinese companies, for instance, can hire Italian designers, buy state-of-the-art equipment from China, and hire American marketers and so on, competing head to head with their American, European, and Japanese counterparts.[36]

> From China to Eastern Europe to Central America, companies such as Xoceco—with limited technical skills, resources and experience—are reshaping the consumer-electronics business. Instead of spending millions of dollars to design chips and software to power their gadget, they're

simply buying those components from other manufacturers and then heavily undercutting the industry leaders' prices.[37]

Component standardization and modularization has led to the increasing fragmentation of the value chain, precipitating outsourcing and imitation.

> Modularization has a profound impact on industry structure because it enables independent, nonintegrated organizations to sell, buy, and assemble components and subsystems. Whereas in the interdependent world you had to make all of the key elements of the system in order to make any of them, in a modular world you can prosper by outsourcing or by supplying just one element. [38]

A good example of a company that has fallen victim to standardization and modularization led by high-tech leaders Intel and Microsoft is Sun Microsystems. In the early 1990s, the company bundled together its own computer chips and software to develop the powerful servers that powered the Internet revolution of the late 1990s. Yet it was not long before hardware from Intel and software from Microsoft caught up with Sun Microsystems. "The result: The Silicon Valley legend that once boasted of putting the dot in dot-com is staring into an abyss. Sun's quarterly sales have fallen more than 40 percent from their peak, even as other tech companies now report stable or even increased revenue."[39]

> Sun appears to be the latest casualty of the rising tide of tech standardization, led by Intel and Microsoft. Many companies in the history of high-tech —Digital Equipment Corp. and Apple Computer Inc., among others— believed they could resist standard designs and thus ultimately charge a premium for their products. In the end, a lot of these companies were either acquired or hang on in the industry as smaller players.[40]

A high degree of imitation turns products into commodities, "permanent fixtures," attracting new entrants, especially in automobiles and electronics industries: "In industry after industry, bright ideas quickly become permanent fixtures. Today's leading edge is tomorrow's condition of entry. In the car market, anti-lock brakes were heralded as a major step forward. BMW trumpeted its invention. Now, anti-lock brakes are no longer an advantage, and BMW has moved to 'telematics' in joint venture with Motorola."[41]

Compounding the problem of imitation, market saturation, especially in mature countries, leaves little room for growth in highly globalized industries.

In short, rapid imitation and market saturation are an integral part of global industries. Successful products, processes, and business models are quickly replicated by the competition.

Consumer Homogeneity

Global industries trade highly globalized bundles that are normally standardized bundles. This means that customers for these products have no strong preferences regarding which bundles they buy, and therefore, highly globalized bundles can be marketed with the same ease around the world. Cellular phone chip sets are standardized bundles of technological features, and therefore, cellular phone buyers around the globe have no strong preferences as to who makes them, as long as they work. The same is true regarding brand-name products that are broadly recognized around the globe, like Coca-Cola, McDonalds, Gucci handbags, Nike shoes, and so on.

Intense Competition

A high degree of integration, rapid technological change and product obsolescence, easy imitation, and consumer homogeneity turn global industries into open seas where every vessel can sail and spread its net for the same catch. This means that competition for catching and selling fish intensifies among the vessels that sail the ocean first, from new vessels, which arrive to join the party, and from new technologies in catching fish.

The telecom gear sector is a good example of intensification of competition in highly globalized industries. As of 2004, the sector was dominated by thirty-two direct and indirect competitors, including Cisco Systems, Nortel Networks, and Hitachi Technologies (see Table 2.1). Furthermore, the sector has been under competitive pressure from alternative technologies: improved conventional copper wire communications offered by telecom gear makers, fiber optics gear, and wireless communication gear. The semiconductor industry, the computer industry, the appliance industry, and the contract manufacturing industry have all been under pressure from newcomers from less

Table 2.1

Major Competitors in Selected Highly Globalized Industries

Industry	Competitors
Telecommunications equipment	Ciena Corp.; Cisco Systems; Nortel Networks; Hitachi; NEC; Alcatel Alsthom Group; Lucent Technologies; Fujitsu Group; Siemens AG; Huawei Technologies; Corvis Corp.; Tellum Corp.; ADC Telecom; ADRAN, Inc.; Allen Telecom; Broadcom Corp.; Blackbox; DSP Group; Oak Technology; Andrew Corp.; Juniper Networks; Foudry Networks; Scientific-Atlanta; Tellabs, Inc.; Sycamore Networks
Optical fiber	Corning; Furukawa OFS; Fujikura; Sumitomo, Pirelli; Danka; Alcatel; Alcoa Fujikura
Cellular handset makers	Nokia Corp.; Motorola, Inc.; Erickson; Siemens AG; Sony; Kyocera; Ningo Bird Co.; LG Electronics, Inc.; Sewon Telekom Co.; Phillips Electronics NV; Segem SA; TCL Mobile Communications; Legend Group
Flash memory chips	Infenion Technologies AG; Toshiba Corp.; SanDisk Corp.; Eastman Kodak; Samsung; Memorex Products, Inc.; Silicon Storage, Inc.; TDK Corp.; Sony Corp.; SimpleTech, Inc.; Netac Technology Co.; PQI Corp.; Micron Technology Fuji; Feyia Corp.; Crucial Technologies; Matsushita Electric; Hewlett Packard; PNY Technologies
Contract manufacturers	Celestica, Inc.; Solectron Corp.; Jabil Circuit; JDS Uniphase; Sanmina-SCI Corp.; Plexus Corp.; Symbol Technologies; Safeguard Scientific; Plantronics, Inc.; Microtune, Inc.; Flextronics International; Avnet, Inc.

developed areas, including aerospace companies from Brazil, semiconductor companies from Korea, and computer makers from Taiwan and China. "The upstarts range from green entrepreneurs to well-heeled manufacturers that have achieved success in products such as computers or washing machines and are finding it easy to move into other consumer electronics," in the words of Ramstad and Dvorak.[42]

> The new rules of the game are letting unknown companies race into increasingly advanced markets. China's TCL Corp. until this year chiefly purchased phones from Korean manufacturers, relabeled them with its brand and sold them in China. In recent months, Britain's TTPCom Inc. and France's Wavecom, Inc. provided software and chip sets that allowed TCL to create not only its own phones, but ones with built-in cameras, unveiled last month.[43]

In the wireless communication industry, major Western mobile phone makers like Motorola, Nokia, and Siemens AG have been losing market share to Chinese companies like Ningbo Bird Co., TCL Mobile, and China Kejan. In 2002, in the home appliance industry, China's Haier Group controlled 50 percent of the U.S. market for small refrigerators and 60 percent of the market for wine coolers, while Galanz controlled 40 percent of the European microwave market.[44] In the personal computer industry, the Legend Group controls 20 percent of the world market for motherboards. In the Internet gear market, Huawei Technologies competes head-to-head with Cisco Systems, and has captured 3 percent of the market for routers. In the consumer electronics market, Sichuan Changhong Electric controls 10 percent of market for rear-projection TVs.

In short, a high degree of economic integration has turned global industries into open seas, where scores of established competitors are pitted against each other and against newcomers and are facing price and profit gyrations.

Price and Profit Gyrations

The elimination of entry barriers and the intensification of competition have brought global industries close to the ideal of what economists call "perfect competition," which has three important implications for corporate pricing and profitability. First, companies are faced with an unstable and unpredictable product demand, which makes company revenues erratic and unpredictable. Second, prices are set by the "invisible hand" of the markets rather than by the "visible hand" of management. This means that individual firms have no pricing power; they are price takers. Third, global industries face the constant influx and outflux of competitors, which creates capacity shortages and gluts and profit gyrations (see Figure 2.1).[45] Profitable industries attract the entry of new competitors and that drives prices and profits lower, and in some cases turns profits into losses. Conversely, unprofitable industries prompt the exit of inefficient companies, and that drives prices and profits higher. This process perpetuates itself until profits converge to the economy average. "It is part of the definition of industrial competition that every resource in an industry earns as much, but no more than, it would earn in other industries. The self-interest of the owners of productive resources (including, of course, that most important resource, the laborer) leads them to apply their resources where they yield the most, and thus to enter unusually attractive fields and abandon unattractive fields."[46] In

Figure 2.1 **Influx and Outflux of Competitors in Global Industries Create Profit Gyrations**

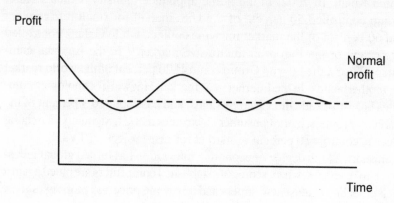

Entry and Exit and Profits

Figure 2.2 **U.S. Local Phone Market Revenue**

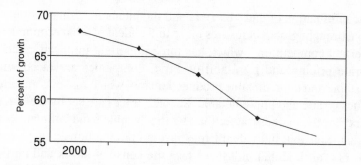

Source: Rosenbush, Crockett, and Haddad (2003).

the U.S. local telephone services industry, for instance, new entrants have gained 16 percent market share, while Baby Bells' revenues have dropped from $68 billion to $58 billion (Figure 2.2).[47]

The influx and outflux of competitors is often exacerbated by demand fluctuations. A precipitous decline in demand, for instance, could accelerate price and profit declines and speed up the exit of inefficient companies from the industry. "Increased competition could result in pricing pressures, decreased gross margins and loss of market share that may materially and adversely affect our business, financial conditions and results of operations."[48] The semiconductor and the electronics industries are two cases in point. A rise in the industry profitability in the early 1990s was followed by an influx of new competitors, driving prices, sales, and profits lower. RF Monolithics' annual sales swung from $55 million in 1998 to $47 million in 2000, and $43 million in 2002. Gross profit margins swung from 39.2 percent in 1998 to 8.5 percent in 2000, to 24.5 percent in 2002. Sony's operating profit margins fell from 4 percent in 1997 to 1 percent by 2002. Teradyne's profits fell between 12 percent and 28 percent. Micron Technology's profits swung from a loss of $234 million in 1998 to $1.5 billion profit in 2000 to a loss of $907 million in 2002 (Figure 2.3). The personal computer industry is a third case in point. In 2001, entry of new competitors and market saturation was followed by a 28 percent decline in the personal computer prices in the United States (Figure 2.4). One of the companies that pulled out of this industry is Arrow Electronics: "[Our] strategy requires us to participate in those markets where our ability to provide products and value-added services differentiates us and generates acceptable financial returns. During 2002, we examined our role in the commodity computer products business and came to the conclusion that, in this market, customers require fewer value-added solutions and base their decisions primarily on price."[49] A number of other companies, including Gateway, suffered heavy losses. Again, the decline in industry prices and profitability prompted the exit of marginal companies from the market.

Price and profits in other global industries display a similar pattern. The fiber optics industry is a fourth case in point. In the late 1990s, when demand was high and profit margins hefty, a number of European and Asian competitors entered the industry. Combined with market saturation, the entry of new competitors was followed by a crash in fiber optics gear prices and a squeeze in profit margins. "Perhaps never before has the efficiency of an industry's technology got so far ahead of demand, creating a glut of capacity that will take years to work off—and crippling dozens of companies in the process."[50] The crash in fiber optics prices caused an outflux of firms from the industry. According to *Telegeography, Inc.* statistics, annual fiber optics prices of 150 megabyte-per-second data in New York declined from around $1.16 million to below $100,000.[51] By the early 2000s, a number of competitors, including Japanese giant Fujitsu, exited the fiber optics market.

Figure 2.3 **Profit Fluctuations in Selected Firms with Exposure to Highly Globalized Markets, 1992–2000/2002**

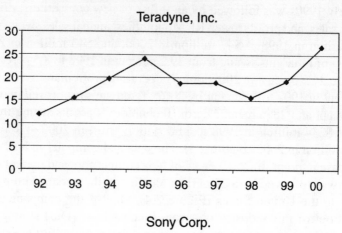

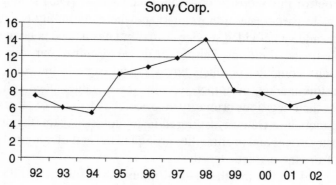

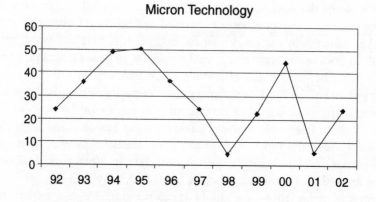

Source: Data taken from *Value Line*, various issues.

Figure 2.4 **Price Changes in Globalized Industries**

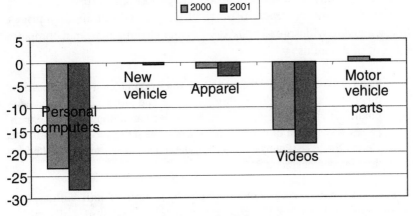

Source: Data taken from Bureau of Labor Statistics, various years.

Declining prices and profitability and the outflux of companies that follow them does not last forever. They eventually reverse course: As companies exit the industry, prices stabilize and eventually firm up, and profit margins follow suit. The dot.com industry is a case in point. Companies that survived the industry meltdown have seen firming prices and profit margins. In the online travel industry, Expedia.com has turned profitable. In computer direct sales, the failure of many start-ups has allowed Dell Computers to stay profitable. In the financial service industry, mortgage brokers like Lending Tree.com have turned profitable. In retailing, the failure of scores of smaller competitors has allowed survivors like Amazon.com, Yahoo, and e-Bay to turn losses into profits.

Today's price and profit swings in highly integrated industries parallel those of early U.S. economic integration that followed the building of canals and the expansion of waterways. "The era of expansion between 1831 and 1839 may be summarized as follows: The initial expansion was set off by the conjunction of rising cotton prices and the structural changes in the three regions brought about by the development of regional interdependence."[52] The growing integration of the country and the expansion of 1831–39 pushed commodity prices, especially cotton prices, higher, attracting new entrants to the industry from Europe. "The improving profitability of cotton and western staples again attracted foreign capital into plantation expansion and *productive* internal improvements. The revival of western regional expansion and cotton trade provided the necessary stimulus for expansion of manufacturing in the East. Both domestic wholesale and export prices rose sharply."[53]

The economic contraction of 1839–43 pushed commodity prices lower, causing widespread bankruptcies and pushing marginal competitors out of the industry.

> The period from the fall of 1839 to 1843 resembles a similar era just ninety years later in that both were severe and prolonged drops in economic activity. There was a precipitous decline in domestic and export prices, a cessation of capital imports, and the return of securities to the United States as Pennsylvania, Maryland and other states defaulted on their interest payments.[54]

Price and profit swings accelerated in the late nineteenth century, that is, the period 1875–1900, often referred to as "early globalization." Emerging high-profit-margin business attracted scores of new competitors, expanding productive capacity and causing price and profit destruction, which was reflected in the performance of the U.S. commodity price index. After rising during the Civil War, U.S. commodity prices fell sharply until the early 1890s. Specifically, the wholesale price index fell from 174 in 1870 to 135 by 1886, and to 82 by 1890. Indicatively, bromine prices plummeted from $4.50 in 1867 to 20 cents by 1884; salt prices dropped from 67 cents per barrel in 1882 to 23 cents by 1905; and gasoline prices, from 25.7 cents in 1871 to 4.9 cents in 1895. Every emerging industry, from nail manufacturing to oil refining, sugar refining, and tobacco, eventually underwent the process of price destruction. The introduction of new technologies and the acceleration of demand were followed by the entry of new competitors and market saturation, which drove prices and profits lower, prompting exit from the industry.

> In many industries, especially new ones or ones that enjoyed some kind of significant improvements in the technology of production, manufacturers initially found themselves in an enviable position. Growth was rapid and profits were good as the producers expanded to meet the demands for the product. Eventually, however, demand leveled off as manufacturers grew to the point where they turned out as much as (and often more than) the market wanted. Then problems set in as firms struggled for a larger share of what suddenly become an increasingly stable or much more slowly growing market. Profits might actually decline, or they might stop growing at the previous high rates. Manufacturers were likely to believe themselves in trouble and to start searching for solutions.[55]

The improvements in profit positions attained through plant expansion and modernization, then, lasted only until the industry caught up and the same old squeeze came back into effect. The industry was locked into a losing situation. New plants and technology could lower costs, but the scramble for market share sufficient to spread high capital costs over enough sales to provide a profit pushed prices ever lower. [56]

The success of the street and interurban lines industry, for instance, attracted scores of small companies. Ohio, for instance, had more than fifty different interurban lines, which expanded industry capacity, eroding fare rates and industry profitability. The early profitability of the sugar industry of the late 1860s drew scores of small sugar refineries. "The attraction of profits brought many new businesses into industry refining. Stability, however, was compromised when the industry capacity outstripped demand. Competing firms were forced to reduce their prices in order to sell enough refined sugar to cover at least the out-of-pocket or variable cost of production."[57] A new method of making nails from wire rather than from metal plates in the late 1880s attracted scores of competitors that boosted the industry's capacity ahead of demand, undermining prices and profits. In the oil drilling industry, the discovery of oil in a number of states prompted the entry of scores of oil drillers into the industry, undermining industry prices and profitability.

In short, global industries are under constant pressures from new competitors that undermine their pricing power and profitability: Industries that earn above-the-economy-average profits attract new competition, which drives prices and profits lower. This means that the survival and prosperity of global competitors hinge on their ability to devise strategies that limit competition and price and profit destruction. One such strategy pursued by the global industries of the late nineteenth century was the formation of informal and formal trade associations and cartels that limited competition and stabilized prices.

During the three decades after 1865, . . . manufacturers in industry after industry found their profits or growth rates unsatisfactory and turned to various forms of cartel-like behavior for an answer. Sometimes that behavior took the form of an informal pool for higher prices, lower production levels, or apportioned markets. Sometimes it manifested itself in a trade association, a somewhat more formal means of cooperation, yet one that still left each firm an independent entity, free in the end to pursue its own course if it chose to do so.[58]

Railroads, for instance, formed regional pools to control railroad traffic and to fix prices. A formal trust formed by early global industries was that of Standard Oil, which came to control 90 percent of the American oil market. The trust further allowed the company to cut transportation and refining costs by obtaining volume discounts from the railroad industry and by closing inefficient refineries. In Europe, the North Atlantic Shipping Conference and the Mediterranean Conference set international shipping rates, while the dynamite cartel divided the world markets between Anglo-German and French producers, an issue to be further addressed in the next chapter.

Another strategy applied by early global industries was the expansion of the scale and the scope of their organization, in two ways: horizontally, by introducing larger scale technologies or by combining their operations with competitors (mergers and acquisitions), and vertically, by expanding upstream and downstream in the product supply chain. Upstream by internalizing a number of activities previously performed by suppliers, and downstream by internalizing activities previously performed by independent distributors, transportation companies, and retailers.

A third strategy was massive advertising campaigns. Mass marketing and advertising allowed salespersons to reach a mass market and tie consumers to their products. As Pine puts it, "The job of these salespersons, as with all mass producers, is not to figure out what the customer wants so much as to sell what the manufacturer has already built."[59] Mass marketing and advertisement in the form of publications and showrooms, for instance, allowed I.M. Singer & Company to rapidly expand the market for sewing machines, Sears Roebuck to become a household name in retailing, General Motors to catch up with Ford, and Coca-Cola to become a world brand name. Mass marketing further shortened the economic life of products and allowed large companies to overcome the saturation and price wars characterizing mature markets. "Price competition has largely receded as a means of attracting the public's custom, and has yielded to new ways of sales promotion: advertising, variation of the products' appearance and packaging, 'planned obsolescence,' model changes, credit schemes, and the like."[60] A fourth strategy was to carve a market niche, as did Buckeye Steel Casting Company. The company managed to escape fierce competition in the cast-iron and steel products industry by developing a new product to join railroad cars.[61]

A fifth strategy was the development of radically new products, new technologies, and new business models, a strategy followed by meatpacker Swift and cigarette maker Duke.

Today's global industries cannot cope with the destructive forces of globalization by forming pools, trusts, and cartels. In most countries around the world, such strategies face a host of antitrust legislations. Instead, today's global industries have pursued a number of managerial strategies that expand the scale and scope of their organization. In retailing, Wal-Mart has thrived by focusing on operational effectiveness, that is, by bringing consumers good-quality products at low cost. In computer retailing, Dell Computers has succeeded through innovation, for example, by applying the just-in-time inventory system to computer production and retailing. In computer hardware manufacturing, manufacturers like Dell and IBM have managed to expand the scale and scope of their operations and cut costs by hiring contract manufacturers like Solectron and Sanmina-SCI. In computer software, Microsoft has prospered through innovative software and marketing strategies that cross the boundary of antitrust law, and by creating "economies of networking" that the competition finds hard to imitate. In the automobile industry, companies have survived by bundling cars together with services, and by forming alliances with suppliers, employers, and competitors to cut costs and to develop new products. In the flash-card memory industry, long-time competitors SanDisk and Toshiba coproduce memory cards to cut costs, an issue to be addressed in subsequent chapters.

To sum up, today's highly globalized market segments share a number of common features with those of early globalization: a high degree of integration, rapid technological obsolescence and imitation, extensive competition, and price and profit gyration. Economic integration eases the flow of resources and commodities from one market to another, fostering economic efficiency and new business opportunities. At the same time, economic integration speeds up the diffusion of new technology and imitation, which quickly turns products and business models obsolete, constraining the profitable deployment of firms' assets. Successful products, processes, and business models are quickly replicated by the competition. The constant pressure from new competitors undermines pricing power and profitability: Industries that earn above-the-economy-average profits attract new competition, which drives prices and profits lower. The survival and prosperity of global competitors hinge on their ability to devise strategies to cope with the destructive forces of globalization, that is, strategies that limit

The Strategy Box
Consumer Electronics: A Highly Globalized Industry

The consumer electronics industry displays all the characteristics of a global industry: a high degree of integration, rapid product obsolescence, a high degree of imitation, intense competition, and price and profit gyrations.

High Degree of Integration. Consumer electronics have been at the top of trade liberalization. With a few exceptions, electronic products are free of tariffs and quotas. They can be sold with the same ease across national and local markets. Cellular phones, personal computers, video recorders, and TVs can be sold with the same ease in London as they can in New York, Tokyo, and Beijing.

Rapid Product Obsolescence. Like fresh fruit and vegetables, electronic products lose value for every day that goes by. Cellular phones, VCRs, MP3 players, and new computers often turn obsolete well before they physically wear out.

High Degree of Imitation. Consumer electronics products are an easy imitation target for two reasons. First, raw materials and components are easy to purchase in global markets. Second, components are highly modularized, and assembly is inexpensive in China and other low-wage Asian countries. This means that established consumer electronics makers are under the constant threat of entry by smaller start-up challengers.

Intense Competition. A highly integrated industry, the electronics industry is constantly under intense direct and indirect competition. Direct competition comes from existing and emerging competitors, mainly electronics companies from China, Taiwan, and South Korea. Indirect competition comes from alternative technologies.

Price and Profit Gyrations. A high degree of integration, rapid technological change, and easy imitation make the consumer electronics industry highly competitive. This means that consumer electronics makers experience considerable price and profit gyrations. Successful products quickly attract imitators, creating excess capacity and supply gluts and price erosion. Sony's success with a number of electronic gadgets in the early 1990s, for instance, attracted the entry of Korean and Chinese manufacturers in the industry, driving prices lower and dragging down Sony's profits. DVD player prices, for instance, dropped from $500 in 1997 to around $70 by 2002. For the period 1992–2003, Sony's operating profit margins fluctuated between 5 percent and 15 percent.

competition and price and profit destruction. One such strategy pursued by global industries of the late nineteenth century was the formation of informal and formal trade associations and cartels that limited competition and stabilized prices. Another strategy was horizontal expansion that allowed companies to cut costs by expanding the scale of their operations, either organically or through mergers and acquisitions, a strategy that in some cases resulted in market concentration and the creation of a multinational market.

Notes

1. RF Monolithics, Inc., *2002 Annual Report*, Dallas, TX, p. 8.
2. Nokia, *2002 Annual Report*, p. 37.
3. Arrow Electronics, Inc., *2002 Annual Report*, Melville, NY, 2003, p. 4.
4. Mourdoukoutas (1999b), p. 21.
5. Ibid.
6. Ibid., p. 20.
7. As of 2000, 137 counties had joined WTO, compared to 23 that joined WTO's predecessor, the General Agreement of Trade and Tariffs (GATT). According to the IMF, 69 economic unions were established in the 1990s, compared to 20 in the 1980s, and none in the decades prior to 1960. And though traditionally regional associations have functioned as a deterrent to globalization, they now accommodate it. In fact, interregional trade has increased substantially in the last twenty years.
8. International phone minutes soared, from a few million in late 1960s to 200 billion by 2002; the cumulative number of countries connected to the Internet ballooned from 3 in 1990 to 220 in 2002, while the cumulative number of Internet hosts soared from 80,000 in 1990 to around 147 million by 2002. For details, see Gabel and Bruner (2003).
9. Musa (2000), p. 10.
10. Ibid., p. 12.
11. North (1996), p. 102.
12. For more details, see Atack and Passell (1994), pp. 145 and 152.
13. Ibid., p. 155.
14. North (1996), pp. 107 and 109.
15. Whitten (1983), p. 90.
16. Atack and Passell (1994), p. 166.
17. North (1996), p. 104.
18. Davis et al. (1972), p. 510.
19. Drucker (2003).
20. IMF, *International Financial Statistics*, various issues.
21. *Survey of Current Business*, February 1997, vol. 77, no. 2.
22. Ibid., July 1996, vol. 76, no. 7.
23. Ibid.
24. Anonymous (1996).
25. Chipello (2003), p. A2.
26. Gabel and Bruner (2003), p. 8.

27. Drucker (2004), p. A1.
28. Mourdoukoutas (1999b), p. 46.
29. Intel, *2002 Annual Report*, Santa Clara, CA, 2003.
30. Delaney and Bank (2004), p. A5.
31. Adams (2004), p. 39.
32. Porter (1992), p. 75.
33. Bolande (2003), p. A6.
34. Fowler (2003), p. B1.
35. "Can Sony Regain the Magic?" *Business Week*, Mar. 11, 2002, pp. 72–76 (cover story).
36. For details, see Hout and Hemerling, (2003), pp. 31–33.
37. Ramstad and Dvorak (2003), p. A1.
38. Christensen (2003), p. 131.
39. Tam (2003), p. A111.
40. Tam (2003), p. A16.
41. Hirsh and Wheeler (1999), p. 3.
42. Ramstad and Dvorak (2003), p. A1.
43. Ibid., p. A14.
44. Zeng and Williamson (2003), p. 92.
45. Normal profit is the opportunity cost of capital committed in a certain line of business, that is, the minimum return to stay in that business.
46. Stigler (1983), p. 10.
47. Rosenbush, Crockett, and Haddad (2003).
48. Broadcom Corporation, *2002 Annual Report*, Irvine, CA, p. 13.
49. Arrow Electronics, Inc., *2002 Annual Report*, Melville, NY, 2003, p. 2.
50. Berman (2002), p. B1.
51. Dreazen (2002), p. B1.
52. North (1996), p. 198.
53. Ibid., p. 201.
54. Ibid., p. 202.
55. Porter (1992), p. 64.
56. Whitten (1983), p. 110.
57. Ibid.
58. Porter (1992), p. 66.
59. Pine (1999), p. 91.
60. Baran and Sweezy (1996), p. 115.
61. Blackford and Kerr (1986), p. 178.

3

The Highly Localized Segment

In the Defense business area, and within the framework of the multi-domestic strategy preferred practice is to set up multi-domain industrial operations in the client countries, teaming as appropriate with local partners, implementing local workshares and meeting direct offset requirements.[1]

Multinationalization, the increasing fragmentation and fractionalization of international, domestic, and local markets, represents the resumption and in some cases the continuation of an old trend that began at the eve of World War I and accelerated toward the end of World War II.[2] Thus today's multinationalization has a number of elements in common with early multinationalization: A low degree of integration of national and local markets, slow technological change and product obsolescence, and slow imitation, all of which, with two qualifications, turned the world market into a collection of separate local and national markets limiting competition. The first qualification is that today's multinationalization is ever harder to sustain. New technologies and new business models constantly undermine and diminish the efficiency and effectiveness of market entry barriers, opening markets to competition. Second, today's multinationalization can be best understood if products crossing national and local markets are viewed as bundles of global and local characteristics rather than as products per se.

Multinationalization is a mixed blessing for business. On the one hand, it limits the ability of local and domestic corporations to compete beyond their home turf. AIG, for instance, cannot sell insurance policies in Tokyo and Beijing with the same ease as in New York. It must receive clearance from local regulators, and its sales force must apply different sales practices. Likewise, McDonald's and Burger King cannot expand their franchises with the same ease in Tokyo as in New York. They need to obtain regulatory clearance and adapt their menu and services to local tastes and preferences. Siebel Systems and Oracle Software cannot sell their software with the same ease in Bulgaria and Romania as in the United States. They need to customize it in compliance with local accounting and legal standards. U.S. pharmaceutical companies like Pfizer and Merck cannot sell their products in Japan with the same ease as on their own home turf. They need to obtain regulatory approval and comply with local labeling and advertising requirements.

On the other hand, multinationalization creates local market sanctuaries that shelter local competitors from outside competition, as was the case for decades in the telecom and transportation industries. "For many industries and corporations, the Old World market regime, that is the multinational market system, provided a cozy environment, a sanctuary. Trade barriers often kept potential foreign competitors off this market, and government regulation kept domestic competitors out of local markets. Protectionism, for instance, kept many foreign competitors off national telecommunication and transportation markets."[3]

Multinational competitors face a steady demand and business opportunities and little threat from new competitors, which implies two things. First, the visible hand of management replaces the invisible hand of markets in coordinating the allocation of resources and in setting commodity and resource prices. Second, multinational competitors face little pressure from the entry of new competitors to the industry, which allows them to maintain profits above the economy average even in the long term.

The remainder of this chapter, a more detailed discussion of the peculiarities and specificity of highly localized industries, is in six sections. The first section discusses the factors that slow the integration of multinational markets: industry protectionism and government regulation, ideology, unionism, and local clusters. The second discusses slow technological change and product obsolescence: Products of highly localized industries maintain their economic value, that is, their economic value stays close to their physical value. The third section addresses the factors that slow imitation in highly localized industries: local regulations, local clusters, and the vertical integration of highly localized industries. The fourth section analyzes consumer heterogeneity; the fifth, the limited competition; and the sixth, steady prices and profits.

Low Degree of Integration

As discussed in Chapter 2, economic integration, the removal of natural and artificial market barriers, is a precondition for the development of the market system, but it is not always easy to achieve. Economic integration and the intensification of competition that follows it create regional and national inequalities and friction between winners and losers that slow down or even reverse economic integration. The world's late-nineteenth-century economic integration, for instance, was followed by the intensification of conflict among nations and social classes that fueled the spread of totalitarianism, trade protectionism, and unionism, not to mention the destruction of the two World Wars. The spread of totalitarianism provided support for communist and fascist regimes, which in their own different and yet common ways limited the functioning of markets and in some cases abolished them altogether: Communism placed the Soviet, the Chinese, and the Central and Eastern European economies under central planning. Fascism placed the German, the Spanish, the Italian, and the Portuguese economies under complete government control. But even in countries like the United States, which escaped totalitarianism, the spread of communist ideas ignited union and government regulations that constrained the flow of commodities and resources within local and national markets.

The rise of unionism and activist political coalitions in the 1920s and 1930s brought many services previously provided by private business under government control. The rise of trade protectionism limited the flow of resources and commodities across national borders. Even before 1914, France and Germany had already raised trade barriers, which made imports prohibitively expensive.[4] For instance, following the 1919 Versailles Treaty, which imposed punitive economic sanctions on Germany, world trade growth stumbled, growing by 0.7 percent during the period 1913–29, and declining by 1.15 percent for the period 1929–38.[5] The decline in U.S. external trade further underscores this trend. Exports dropped from $10,776 million in 1919 to $5,448 million by 1930. U.S. trade took yet another dip after the Trade Act of 1930, the prelude of the infamous Smoot-Hawley tariff, which pushed U.S. tariffs to a rate of 70 percent of imports, about five times higher than in 1913; by 1936 U.S. exports dropped to $3,539 million.

Government protection in the form of import tariffs and quotas provided domestic producers an advantage over foreign producers. In North America, government regulation turned a number of industries into market sanctuaries. AT&T is a case in point. For decades, the company enjoyed a telephone monopoly and steadily growing profits. Nortel Telecom is another case in point. For over a century, it was a subsidiary of Bell Canada, a regulated monopoly, which provided Nortel Networks with a guaranteed market, R&D support, and technical information.[6] In

Asia, government protection and regulation sheltered a number of domestic industries from competition. In Japan, stiff tariffs and strict permit requirements protected the domestic semiconductor industry from foreign competition. The Large Department Store Law sheltered the retailing industry from large domestic and foreign competitors, while financial regulation sheltered banks from both domestic and foreign competition. In Germany, the proliferation of professional guilds, chambers of commerce, cross-equity holdings, and *Interessen-gemeinschaften*, or "communities of interest," constrained the entry of new competitors into established industries.[7]

As was the case with the early economic integration, today's economic integration has created its own regional and national inequalities and winners and losers that have slowed globalization and in some cases reversed it. In the steel industry, the U.S. government has imposed tariffs on foreign steel to protect domestic producers. In the food industry, the EU has imposed a ban on bioengineered products to protect its farmers from imports from large producers, most notably those in the United States. And even some segments of the now deregulated telecom industry continue to remain under government regulation. In local telecom services, for instance, Baby Bells continue to be the gatekeepers of the telecom lines that connect American households.

> Despite passage of the Telecom Act, the telecommunications industry, particularly incumbent local exchange carriers such as our wireline subsidiaries, and advanced services including DSL, continue to be subject to significant regulation. The expected transition from an industry extensively regulated by multiple regulatory bodies to a market driven industry monitored by state and federal agencies has not occurred as anticipated.[8]

In the insurance industry, national and local governments impose their own rules and regulations regarding the underwriting and distribution of insurance products.

> A substantial portion of AIG's General Insurance business and a majority of its life insurance business is carried out in foreign countries. The degree of regulation and supervision in foreign jurisdictions varies from minimal in some to stringent in others. Generally, AIG, as well as the underwriting companies operating in such jurisdictions, must justify local regulatory requirements. Licenses issued by foreign authorities to AIG subsidiaries are subject to modification or revocation by such authorities, and AIU or

other AIG subsidiaries could be prevented from conducting business in certain of the jurisdictions where they currently operate. . . .

In addition to licensing requirements, AIG's foreign operations are also regulated in various jurisdictions with respect to currency, policy language and terms, amount and type of security deposits, amount and type of reserves, amount and type of local investment and the share of profits to be returned to policyholders on participating policies.[9]

Economic integration of international markets is often constrained by local business clusters, local brands, and fragmented distribution systems that provide local competitors an advantage over distant ones.[10] Local clusters, for instance, give Hollywood movie makers an advantage in the U.S. market over foreign movie makers. Local clusters also give an advantage to Napa Valley wine makers and South France wine makers over wine makers elsewhere. Local brands and fragmented distribution systems give Chinese brewing companies an advantage over their American and European counterparts.[11] The same is true for Japan's distribution system, with its many layers of wholesalers and retailers and *keiretsu* groups, which limit access of foreign competitors to local markets.

In short, friction between winners and losers has forestalled and in some cases regressed economic integration, creating a fractured, moribund industry that limits the flow of goods and services across local and national markets, and competition, as does the low degree of technological change.

Low Degree of Technological Change and Product Obsoleteness

The low degree of integration and the lack of new entrants exert little pressure on the industry members to introduce new products and new technologies. Products of highly localized industries preserve their economic value, that is, their economic value remains close to their physical value. The telecom industry is a case in point. Dominated by large companies with plenty of resources and state-of-the-art research labs, the industry is conducive to the development of new technologies. Yet, sheltered from competitors, industry members are not compelled to bring new technologies to the market. "With its revenue secure and growing, and its markets protected from competition, AT&T's combative muscle atrophied. Its profits were capped by federal and state regulators, so the company placed little value on entrepreneurial ventures."[12] Digital line subscriber (DSL) technology is a good illustration of the point. Though the technology was developed in the late 1980s by the Baby Bells, the industry was not in a rush to introduce an alternative, a high-margin technology, high-speed Internet business access. It took a serious challenge by upstarts like Covad Communications to bring DSL to the market ten years after it was developed. Voice over the Internet protocol (VOIP) is another case in point. Though the technology was around since the mid-1990s, Baby Bells were not in the rush to replace their copper wires with it:

> Despite its advantages VOIP can't replace traditional phone systems overnight. For one thing, the big national and regional phone companies have huge amounts of money invested in traditional gear and aren't in a hurry to write that off. They also have long-established relations with customers, many of whom would be reluctant to jump to a technology that isn't fully tested.[13]

And with plenty of resources, the telecom industry has launched a series of campaigns to block the advance of the Internet and other fiber optics technologies developed in its own labs. "Flawlessly executing one of history's consummate campaigns of political lobby-gagging of rivals, AT&T has blocked Internet advance in the U.S., where both the Internet and other fiber optics were invented, largely at Bell Labs."[14]

In short, market fragmentation shelters local competitors from competition, exerting little pressure on industry members to write off their fixed assets and technologies and adopt new ones. The low degree of imitation has similar effects.

Slow Imitation

Imitation has always been an integral part of the business world. Successful technologies and business models have always attracted imitators. Yet the degree of imitation in highly localized industries is quite low for a number of reasons. First, imitation is constrained by local regulations. In the cable services industry, for instance, imitation is constrained by licensing. Successful cable service providers may attract imitators, but not in their own home turf. Time Warner Cable, for instance, can replicate Cablevision's business model and technology in its own domain, New York City, but not in Cablevision's domain, Long Island. Second, imitation is constrained by the presence of local clusters that provide local competitors the advantage of synergies and the learning curve, the experience they have accumulated by serving the local community for years. Clusters, for instance, make it difficult to replicate the success of the movie industry outside Hollywood, the success of the winery industry outside Napa Valley, and the success of the leather industry away from northern Italy. "The manufacturing towns of northern Italy are built on clusters of small, often family-run firms that share information, know-how and business. Como has its silk industry, Lucca its leather goods, Montebelluna its shoes, and Biella its wool, to name a few. In the past, the communal approach was admired for its flexibility and shared economies of scale."[15] Third, imitation is constrained by proprietary and interdependent architectures and vertical integration that give established competitors the scale advantage. Early computer manufacturing is a case in point. Computer hardware makers like IBM performed every supply-chain activity from product invention to innovation and manufacturing inside their own borders. This made computer hardware products too complicated and too integrated and too proprietary for would-be imitators, an issue to be addressed further in subsequent chapters.

Consumer Heterogeneity

For many products, consumers retain their preferences even within highly integrated regions, such as the European Union, NAFTA, and APEC. The preferences of Greek consumers, for instance, are different from those of other southern Europeans, and most notably from those of northern Europeans; and the preferences of Mexicans are different from those of Americans and Canadians. The preferences of Asians differ from those of both Europeans and Americans, even for brand name products, such as cigarettes. As BAT's marketing director, Jimmi Rembiszewski, puts it,

> You will find today that most international brands do have consistent advertising strategies and executions, pack designs and family line. But varying taste tailored to the local acceptance. One could sum it up to say that there are significant global convergence in all optical (habits and practice) brand areas but still strong local resistance to taste or internal convergence.[16]

For large multicultural countries like China and India, consumer preferences differ not only from those of developed countries, but from one region to another and from one city to the next. In some cases, local variation in consumer preferences are not so much in product selections, but in product configurations, which include packaging, delivery, and so on. Consumers in wealthy areas like the United States, northern Europe, and Japan, for instance, buy shampoo in large bottles, and sometimes pay with plastic money.[17] In poor countries of Southeast Asia and Latin America, consumers buy shampoo in small quantities in cash. As Unilever's chairman puts it:

> With new technologies the world is getting smaller, and often we find that consumer needs are, in fact, the same. But sometimes, they are not, and you have to adapt to this.
>
> For example, Unilever produces washing powder. The sole purpose—to clean clothes well and make them smell good—is universal. The differences involve consumer habits. In a rural, developing country, women wash clothes in a river, whereas people in a modern society use a machine. Those differences require different washing powders to do the job. Packaging is also different. For example, in wealthier countries people can afford to buy a month's supply of shampoo. In poor countries, where a whole bottle of shampoo is the equivalent of a week's pay, we offer small sachets of our product at a very low price.[18]

Limited Competition

A low degree of integration and slow technological obsolescence and imitation turn highly localized industries into closed seas, sanctuaries dominated by a few vessels controlling the industry output through explicit and implicit agreements. This was especially the case in the first half of the twentieth century, when antitrust regulation was still in its infancy and industry cartels controlled and regulated markets, especially in Europe. In the first decade of the twentieth century, for instance, German industry was dominated by 385 cartels. A "typical cartel" was the Rhenish-Westphalian Coal Syndicate, which regulated production and prices and appeared in various forms, at one time including as many as ninety companies in its ranks, and commanding control of 50 percent of domestic coal production. In Great Britain, J.C. Coats commanded 95 percent of the British retailing industry sales, Dunlop Rubber Company, 90 percent of the rubber industry sales, and Imperial Chemical Industries, Ltd. the product of mergers among a half dozen of chemical companies, had complete control of the chemical industry. In the 1920s, U.S. industry was dominated by oligopolies created by waves of mergers and acquisitions. "The country experienced its second major merger movement during the 1920s, and oligopoly came to characterize a growing number of American industries. America's system of capitalism, as a result, contained fewer elements of competition than before. In 1909, oligopolistic industries produced 16 percent of America's industrial goods. By 1929, they made 21 percent."[19] Market concentration and control varied across industries. In the chemical industry, DuPont controlled 64.6 percent of all soda blasting powder, 72.5 percent of all dynamite, and 75 percent of all sporting powder.[20] In the oil industry, seven companies— Standard Oil of New Jersey, Royal Dutch Shell, Anglo-Persian, Socony-Vacuum, Gulf, Texas, and Atlantic Refining Company—controlled almost the entire world oil output. In the early 1950s, six firms controlled 68 percent of the Canadian petroleum industry, 93 percent of the refining industry, and 100 percent of the copper, nickel, and iron ore industries.[21] In the farm equipment industry of the mid-1950s, four companies—Allis-Chalmers, Deere, Massey-Harris, and International Harvester—dominated the U.S. market, with International Harvester commanding a 20 percent share. Four companies—Deere, Oliver, Case, and International Harvester—dominated the segment for tractor plows, while a handful of companies dominated most of the other segments (see Table 3.1).

A similar pattern is observed in today's highly localized industries. In the United States, three companies control 26 percent of sales in the pharmaceuticals sector, while in the defense sector five companies control 80 percent of the market. Similarly, three companies control 64 percent of the cable TV market, and four companies control 66 percent of the college textbook industry (see Table 3.2).

Market sanctuaries and industry concentration shelter local competitors from distant challengers, but not from residual and indirect competitors, that is, from residual challengers, genuine competitors, and alternative products and technologies. In the aluminum wire market of the late 1940s and the early 1950s, market barriers sheltered Alcoa from competition from copper wire makers, but not from other manufacturers of aluminum cable. In the American local telephone industry, regulations shelter the industry from direct competition, that is, from new

Table 3.1

Estimated Market Shares (in units) **of International Harvester and Principal Competitors in Selected Farm Implements, 1956**

Implement	Approx. market share (percent)	Principal competitors
Combines	20	Allis-Chalmers, Deere, Massey-Harris
Corn pickers	25–27	Dearborn Motors (Ford), Deere, Allis-Chalmers, Oliver, New Idea
Tractor plows	25	Deere, Oliver, Case
Cultivators	27	Deere, Ford, Case, Allis-Chalmers
Cotton pickers	65	Deere, Rusk, Allis-Chalmers
Mowers	25–30	New Idea, Deere, Case
Farm tractors	28–30	Ford, Deere, Massey-Harris, Allis-Chalmers

Source: A.D.H. Kaplan, Joel B. Dirlan, and R.F. Lanzilloti, *Pricing in Big Business: A Case Approach,* The Brookings Institution, Washington, DC, 1958.

Table 3.2

Market Concentration in Selected Highly Localized Industries, 2003
(percent of U.S. sales)

Industry	Major competitors	Market concentration (%)
Pharmaceuticals	Merck, Pfizer, GlaxoSmithKline	26
Defense contractors	Raytheon, General Dynamics, Boeing, Northrop Grumman, Lockheed Martin	80
Cable TV	Comcast-ATT, Time-Warner, Cox Communications	64
College textbooks	McGraw-Hill, Pearson, Thomson, Houghton Mifflin	66

Source: Author's calculations from various sources.

entrants stringing their own wires to bring telephone services to homes and businesses, but not from residual entrants, leasing the lines of Baby Bells at controlled prices, and reselling them to retail customers; nor from VOIP, cellular phone, and wi-fi providers, like Delta Three, 8x8, TheGlobe, Net2Phone, and Vonage.

The upheaval wrought by the race of both cable companies and telcos to harness the Internet for digital voice communications promises to be monumental. Battle lines are emerging. On the defensive are the Baby Bells, which have long enjoyed dominance in the lucrative local phone service. Rising up to snatch a piece of their prized core market are cable companies and, now, AT&T.[22]

Phone companies around the world are facing a common threat. New voice-over-Internet-protocol (VOIP) technology is allowing cable TV companies to eat into phone companies' bread and butter by rolling out inexpensive voice services, which they can package with existing TV and high-speed Internet services. Desperate to fight back with their own bundles, phone companies are scrambling to find ways of pushing into cable's mainstay: television.[23]

The Bells in particular, face a flood of rivals, ranging from well-capitalized cable outfits to shoe-string-financed start-ups and resuscitated dot-coms once given up for dead. The coming free-for-all will change the face of the U.S. telecom business. This is, in short, a very big deal.[24]

The telecom marketplace is full of disruptive alternatives—so many that customers can turn for satisfaction to almost any price point: broadband by wire or wireless, short or long distance; voice over phone lines or digital cellphone or Internet; television by broadcast or cable or Internet.[25]

In the European telecom industry, BT Group, Cable and Wireless, Vodafone Group, and France Telecom face challengers like Tesco PLC, upstarts like Virgin Group, banks like Lloyds TSB PLC, and utility companies like Centrica PLC—to mention but a few—which sell low-cost telecom services. In the American cable industry, regulations shelter local monopolies from competition from other cable providers, but not from competition from satellite service providers, like Dish and Direct TV, and regular TV programming. In the pharmaceutical industry, patents protect pharmaceutical products from competition from other brand name products, but not from generic products. In the restaurant industry, competition comes in the form of geographical expansion and the development of new concepts that appeal to different market segments.

In short, a low degree of economic integration, slow technological diffusion and product obsolescence, and a low degree of imitation have turned highly localized industries into a closed sea dominated by a few competitors having the market power that lets them enjoy steady prices and profits.

Steady Prices and Profits

The persistence of entry barriers and limited competition bring multinational markets close to the model of imperfect competition and most notably to that of oligopoly. Members of highly localized industries are price makers, that is, the visible hand of management rather than the invisible hand of the market coordinates the production and distribution of resources. "In many sectors of the economy the visible hand of management replaced what Adam Smith referred to as the invisible hand of market forces. The market remained the generate of demand for goods and services, but modern business enterprise took over the functions of coordinating flows of goods through existing process of production and distribution, and of allocating funds and personnel for future production and distribution."[26] This means that management dictates prices to markets, not the other way around. As DuPont's legendary CEO General Henry du Pont put it: "We are every day dictating to our agents as to prices, terms, and conditions to govern them; but we do not allow anybody to dictate to us as to what prices, terms, and conditions we shall dictate. We do our own dictating."[27]

In the first two decades of the twentieth century, price dictating was placed in the hands of the "executive committee," comprised of executives from development engineering, accounting, finance, sales, and so on. "Pricing decisions were made or influenced by executives from production, development engineering, accounting, finance, sales, and public relations divisions. They were usually considered part of the general strategy for achieving a broadly defined goal."[28] By the third decade, price dictating was placed in the hands of professional managers and was made more visible, especially during economic contractions, most notably during the Great Depression, when oligopolistic industries experienced less price pressure than did competitive industries. "The visible hand of management, already significant in the 1880s and 1890s, grew in importance during the 1920s. This practice of administered prices allowed some companies to survive the Great Depression, for prices especially fell less in oligopolistic industries than in ones characterized by competition."[29] By the1950s, pricing was placed in what Galbraith called "technostructure," a group of marketers and engineers who have assumed control of both commodities and resource pricing, bypassing antitrust laws and turning the concept of market coordination into an "illusion."

The mature corporation has taken control of the market—not alone the price, but also what is purchased—to serve not the goal of monopoly but the goals of its planning. Controlled prices are necessary for this planning. And the planning, itself, is inherent in the industrial system. It follows that the antitrust laws, in seeking to preserve the market, are an anachronism in the larger world of industrial planning. They do not preserve the market. They preserve rather the illusion of the market.[30]

As featured in conventional microeconomic textbooks, the visible hand of management follows a number of models in setting prices. One model is the explicit cooperation or cartel that allocates geographical territories among its members and assigns quotas to them (see Table 3.3). The Rhenish-Westphalian Coal Syndicate, for instance, controlled markets by assigning its members production quotas in proportion to their size and production capacity. American and European gunpowder and aluminum producers controlled markets by agreeing to stay away from each others' markets. The North Atlantic Shipping Conference and the Mediterranean Conference fixed shipping rates for these two areas.

Another model is implicit cooperation whereby industry members adhere to the same price, changing prices infrequently, because that is the best solution for everyone.[31] This model was especially popular among manufacturers trying to counter the intensification of competition and the price erosion that followed early globalization. "The search for reliable methods of controlling prices and output and therefore profits continued into the early years of the twentieth century, and it was especially common in new industries and in those that underwent significant technological changes involving high capital investments and high fixed costs."[32]

A third model is the price leadership model, whereby the dominant firm in the industry sets the price and other firms follow suit. The steel industry of the late 1940s appears to be consistent with the price leadership model. Prices posted by market leader U.S. Steel were consistently higher than those of its followers, and based on a steady profit margin. "United States Steel states that it employs a 'stable margin' price policy, that is, in general it aims at maintaining margins despite variations in sales volume. In so doing it uses standard costs computed on the basis of 80 percent of capacity as normal, and including an assignment of overhead burden to every product."[33] In the 1980s, dominant banks such as Manufacturers Hanover (early 1980s), Bankers Trust (mid-1980s), and Chase Manhattan (late 1980s) led the industry in adjusting interest rates.

Table 3.3

Price Making in Highly Localized Industries: Six Models

Model	Description	Examples
Explicit cooperation	Form a trust or a cartel	Rhenish-Westphalian Coal Syndicate
Implicit cooperation	Stick with the prevailing price; avoid price changes that could trigger a response from competitors	Steel and auto industries in 1950s and 1960s
Price leadership	Follow the leader	U.S. steel industry in 1940s; U.S. banking industry in 1980s
Price wars	Cut-throat competition	Tobacco industry in early 1900s
Bundling	Selling a package of products and services at one price	Cable and wireless service providers
Versioning	Selling different product versions to different market segments	Information service providers

A fourth model is the "price wars" model, whereby industry members are engaged in cut-throat competition. Dominant players eliminate opponents by aggressive price cutting. In 1892, for instance, Rockefeller's Standard Oil eliminated opponents in the kerosene market by cutting its price to 7.5 cents per gallon, well below the 25 cents prevailing in the market. The entry of the American Tobacco Company to the British market in the early 1900s was followed by cut-throat competition with its domestic counterpart, Imperial Tobacco Company. The result was a market sharing agreement whereby Imperial Tobacco Company maintained control over the British and Irish markets, American Tobacco Company maintained control over America and its dependencies, and British American Tobacco, a joint venture of the two, maintained control in the rest of the world.[34]

A fifth model is bundling, the "locking in" of customers through high switching costs, loyalty programs, volume discounts, enhanced services, and rewards. Satellite providers, for instance, package news and movie channels with foreign language channels to discourage customers from switching to other satellite providers or to cable service providers. Cable service providers bundle together TV programming with Internet access and local telephone services.

A sixth model is versioning, the churning out of different versions of the products catering to different market segments. This strategy is particularly popular among information technology providers like Yahoo, which sells different versions of its Internet browser to different market segments (casual versus experienced users, business versus retail users, and patient versus impatient users), and Microsoft, which sells different versions of its software to different market segments (household versus business users, professional versus student users, and so forth).

The visible hand of management is not confined to pricing strategies. It also extends to non-price strategies, M&A, and strategic alliances that allow large players to strengthen their market position and compete more efficiently and effectively against other major players. In the software industry, for instance, large players acquire smaller players to amass the critical mass to go head-to-head against larger players.

> Finding enemies and forming alliances against them is an easy concept to apply to any business in any industry. Target your company's number one enemy and then figure out what other companies and organizations also have a reason to identify them as an enemy. The strength of the bond between two or more companies that share a common competitor is second only to the strength of a bond between two or more companies that are making money together.[35]

Oracle Corporation's effort to acquire Peoplesoft in 2004, for instance, is consistent with such a strategy. The acquisition would have eliminated a major player and allowed the company to compete better against the largest business software player, SAP. M&A and strategic alliances further allow corporations to expand their product offerings in each local market, an issue to be further addressed in subsequent chapters.

As oligopolies, highly localized industries enjoy steady demand and revenues. In 2001, a year many global industries experienced substantial price erosion and losses, highly localized industries experienced moderate price gains. U.S. prices for utilities doubled over the previous year, personal care services rose by 3.0 percent, food service by 3.3 percent, motor vehicle maintenance by 4.0 percent, and medical care by 4.8 percent (see Figure 3.1).

Highly localized industries also experience above-the-economy-average profits, even in the long term (Figure 3.2). For the period 1993–2003, the sales of hospital management provider HCA increased steadily year after year, from $20.30 per share to $41.65 per share. Over the

The Strategy Box
The Automobile Repairing and Servicing Industry: A Highly Localized Industry

The automobile repairing and servicing industry displays some of the characteristics of a highly localized industry: A low degree of integration, limited competition, and steady prices.

Low Degree of Integration. Automobile repairing and servicing is primarily a local industry. Servicing and repairing cannot be outsourced to remote locations. They must be performed in the communities in which automobile owners live. This means that the auto servicing and repairing market is a fragmented market.

Limited Competition. A low-integrated industry, the automobile servicing and repairing industry is sheltered from both direct from distant competitors and from indirect competition, from alternative forms of servicing and repairing.

Steady Price and Profits. A low degree of integration and limited competition make the automobile retailing and servicing industry a low-competitive industry. This means that automobile repairing and servicing outlets experience little price and profit gyrations. In 2000 and 2001, a period of rapid price erosion in highly globalized industries, the auto repairing industry experienced moderate price increases (see Figure 3.1).

Figure 3.1   **Price Changes in Localized Industries for 2000–2001**

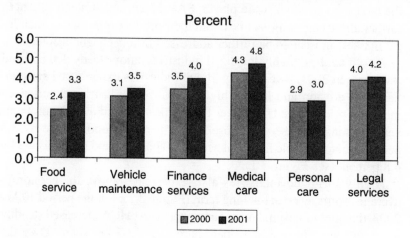

Figure 3.2 **Operating Profit Margin Fluctuations of Selected Firms, 1993–2002/3**

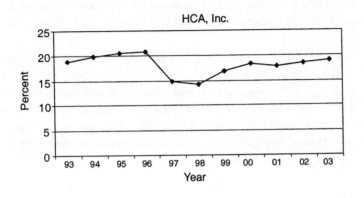

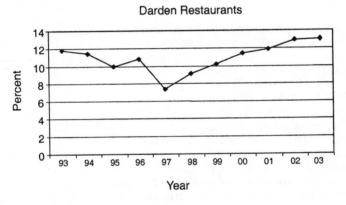

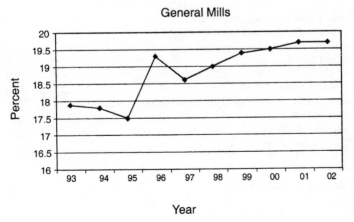

same period, the company's operating profit margins fluctuated between 14.8 percent and 20.8 percent. Darden Restaurants' operating profit margins displayed a similar pattern, fluctuating between 7.4 percent and 13.5 percent; and General Mills' fluctuated between 17.5 percent and 19.8 percent.

To sum up, highly localized industry in the semiglobal economy is characterized by a low degree of economic integration, slow technological change and obsolescence, and a degree of imitation, which create local market sanctuaries, sheltering local competitors from distant competitors. Market sanctuaries in turn allow industry members to set their own prices, applying a number of oligopolistic strategies to be addressed in more detail in subsequent chapters.

Notes

1. Company web page, 10/2/03, Thales Group SA.
2. Early multinationalization can be traced back in fourteenth- and fifteenth-century Europe and continued in the seventeenth- and eighteenth-century colonial economy.
3. Mourdoukoutas (1999b), p. 26.
4. Wilkins (1970), p. 199.
5. Beaud (1983), p. 189.
6. Macdonald (2000).
7. Micklethwait and Wooldridge (2003), p. 91.
8. SBC Communications, *2003 Annual Report*, San Antonio, TX.
9. AIG, *2003 Annual Report*, New York, Form 10-K, p. 12.
10. Local competitors have the advantage of the "learning curve": the experience they have accumulated by serving the local community over time, and the advantage of synergies that come with participation in local clusters.
11. Kahn, Bilenfsky, and Lawton (2004).
12. Crossen and Solomon (2000), p. A1.
13. Grant and Latour (2003), p. A9.
14. Gilder (2004).
15. Rhoads (2003), p. A1.
16. Rembiskzewski, "Think Global—Act Global—Adapt Local," speech at the DSB Dorland annual conference, quoted in Lawrence and Collin (2004).
17. Prahaland (2004).
18. Caminiti (2005), p. 20.
19. Blackford and Kerr (1986), p. 267.
20. Colby (1984), p. 139.
21. Hymer (1976), p. 132.
22. Gabel and Bruner (2003), p. 46.
23. Heinzl (2004).
24. Savitz (2004), p. 19.

25. Donlan (2005), p. 39.
26. Chandler (1977), p. 1.
27. Dale (1960), p. 33.
28. Kaplan, Dirlam, and Lanzillotti (1958), p. 22.
29. Blackford and Kerr (1986), p. 273.
30. Galbraith (1972).
31. When competitors contemplate raising their prices, they must take into consideration how their competitors will respond. If price cuts are expected to be more than matched by the competition, it is not a good idea to pursue this policy. Conversely, if price increases are less than matched by their competitors, it is not a good idea to pursue this policy either. Thus, the best policy is to "stick" with the prevailing prices.
32. Porter (1992), p. 64.
33. Kaplan, Dirlam, and Lanzillotti (1958), p. 22.
34. Hymer (1976), p. 89.
35. Read (2000), p. 49.

Part II

The Portrait of the Semiglobal Corporation

The first part of the book argued that in the middle of the first decade of the new millennium, a number of industries are faced with a semiglobal business environment that consists of a highly globalized and a highly localized segment, each displaying its own characteristics. The highly localized segment is characterized by a high degree of integration of local and national markets; rapid technological advances and product obsolescence, and imitation and saturation; intense competition; and price and profit fluctuation. The highly localized segment is characterized by a low degree of integration of local and national markets; a slow rate of technological advances, product obsolescence, and imitation; limited competition; and steady prices and profits.

The second part of the book profiles a new business model suitable for competing in the semiglobal market, the semiglobal corporation, a hybrid of the conventional multinational corporation and global corporation models, and describes its vision, competitive strategy, coordination mechanisms, communication channels, and motivation systems.

Vision

The semiglobal corporation views the world economy both as a highly globalized market and as a highly localized market: a highly globalized market when it comes to its highly globalized value offerings, and a multinational market when it comes to its highly localized product offerings. This means that the semiglobal corporation must behave both as a responsible global and local citizen at the same time. As a global citizen, it must promote global harmony and eudaimonia, adhering to a universal ethical code. As a local citizen, it must promote local harmony and eudaimonia, adhering to a portfolio of local ethical codes.

Competitive Strategy

To achieve an above-industry-average rate of return, the semiglobal corporation applies a number of managerial and entrepreneurial strategies. Managerial strategies include cost cutting measures to achieve a global cost leadership; the expansion of local bundle characteristics to achieve local differentiation leadership; and a combination of the previous two strategies to achieve both a global cost and a local differentiation leadership. Entrepreneurial strategies include corporate spin-offs, strategic acquisitions, corporate venturing, and strategic alliances.

Coordination

The semiglobal corporation coordinates its operations according to the global/local content of its value propositions. Highly localized value propositions are placed under a conventional hierarchical multinational unit, consisting of a parent unit and a collection of subsidiaries. The parent makes all strategic decisions regarding R&D, financing, marketing, and entry into new markets, while subsidiaries make local personnel and marketing decisions and deal with local community affairs. Parent and subsidiaries are engaged in extensive intra-firm trade; subsidiaries are prohibited from trading with each other and with third parties without the parent's consent.

The highly globalized bundles are placed under a modern non-hierarchical global unit, consisting of a core unit and several peripheral units. The core unit acts as a support office that handles common network matters, drafting a vision and arranging financing, research and development, and product and business branding. Network units handle their own internal business, production schedules, personnel hiring, local marketing, taxation, and local community relations, and are free to trade and cooperate with each other.

Communication

The semiglobal corporation relies on both IT systems and managerial systems to recycle information and knowledge among the members of its organization. Yet each of its two units relies on different channels of transmitting information and knowledge. Multinational-unit communication is mostly intra-organizational communication that relies on closed communication methods and vertical communication channels: closed IT systems and applications, expatriate rotation and transfers and irregular headquarters visits, and executive and technical personnel conferences. Network-unit communication is mostly inter-organization communication, relying on horizontal communication channels and closed communication methods: open IT systems, horizontal job rotation and transfers, and global conferences and teams.

Motivation

The semiglobal corporation relies on a multiple motivation system to hold its pieces together and to address the agency problem faced by both its multinational and its global units. The multinational unit resolves its agency problem in two ways: through corporate centralization that concentrates decision-making power at headquarters, and is supported and reinforced by bureaucratic motivation mechanisms that control the behavior of subsidiaries; or through decentralization that diffuses decision-making authority throughout the organization, and is supported and reinforced by performance motivation mechanisms that control the consequences of subsidiaries' management behavior.

4

Vision

It is our mission to improve the lives of customers and communities where we all live, work and play. We will continue to develop and build products in local markets around the world to create value for all of our customers. Our established directions for the 21st century provide a balance of fun for the customer and responsibility for society and the environment.

Honda's vision, 2004 annual Report 2003

As the world's foremost pharmaceutical company, Pfizer accepts a special responsibility to society as well as to our shareholders. In our view, serving these two constituencies does not present separate challenges. We strive to be part of the solution to the world's health care problems—not only through our core business activities of discovering and developing medicines, but also through social investments, philanthropy programs and ongoing engagement with all those who care about creating a healthier world.[1]

Pfizer's vision

The global corporations must foster relations, not only with their customers and the communities in which they operate, but also with nations and the environment. For this reason, Canon's goal is to contribute to the prosperity of the world and the happiness of humanity, which lead to continuing growth and bring the world closer to achieving Kyosei.

Canon's corporate philosophy, 2003 annual Report

Nokia is a global and multi-cultural company. We seek diversity, because it is an important asset that enables us to achieve extraordinary results.

Nokia Corporation's corporate philosophy

For nearly twenty years Microsoft was a very successful company by almost every standard of business performance. Its software products brought to life almost every PC, its sales and market share soared, delivering hefty returns to its stockholders and most notably to its founders. Furthermore, Microsoft was a major contributor to the United States and the world community, both as a taxpayer and as a socially responsible partner, especially in the poor areas of the world, where Bill Gates's foundation supported a number of social programs to fight diseases and poverty.

In recent years, Microsoft continues to be a successful company, but it has encountered a number of problems with U.S. and overseas regulators, local competitors, and community activists that threaten to derail its early successes. And it is not alone. Dell Computer has encountered its own problems in China, where local upstarts like Lenovo have pushed Dell off the retail market. CitiCorp had its own share of problems with local regulators in Great Britain and Japan, where regulators shut down its corporate investing division. Nike's advertising campaigns have drawn the angry protests of civic groups and governments around the world.

At the core of Microsoft's, Dell's, CitiCorp's, and Nike's problems is the failure of their leadership to articulate a sensible vision that treats the world economy as a hybrid of two market segments, a highly globalized segment and a highly localized segment, rather than a "pure" global market and to address the peculiarities and specificity of each segment.[2] For Microsoft, this failure is most pronounced in countries like South Korea and Thailand, where the company's global strategy of "one size fits all" has backfired, drawing scores of protests by local competitors, governments, and civic groups.[3] "When strategies from a home market are transported abroad without modification, they may underperform or even backfire spectacularly, as happened to Microsoft in Korea. There are national differences in policies, wealth, commercial environment, infrastructure, history, language, and so on."[4]

Articulating a sensible and proactive rather than reactive vision, that is, a *core ideology* and an *envisioned future* for the semiglobal economy, is a tricky, complex, and difficult task.[5] It is tricky because it requires the combination and compromise of the two opposite trends of globalization and localization. It is complex because it requires a good knowledge and understanding of both a universal system of values that shapes the rules of conduct in the global segment of the semiglobal market and a portfolio of local values that shapes the rules of conduct in the multinational segment. It is difficult because image/reputation is a community good that must be shared and treasured by all members of the organization. One mistake by a subsidiary can destroy the image of the entire organization. "It is not only the headquarters that bears the externalities of the actions of one subsidiary but the entire network of subsidiaries. As the actions of subsidiaries are not isolated, they need coordination and integration. Subsidiaries need to conform to the same rules and need to agree on what the rules are in the global area."[6]

The semiglobal corporation must have a dual vision, one for its highly globalized segment and one for its highly localized segment. This means that its management must wear both a global and a local "hat" at the same time, be both a good global citizen, promoting global harmony and eudaimonia and adhering to a universal system of values, and a good local citizen, promoting local harmony and eudaimonia and adhering to the different, local systems of values, which is the subject of this chapter.

A Vision for the Highly Localized Segment

The highly localized or multinational segment of the semiglobal market is a collection of national and local markets separated from each other by trade barriers, government regulations, information inefficiencies, and heterogeneous consumer preferences, a mixed blessing for international business. On the one hand, market barriers limit opportunities beyond the home market while raising the cost of transactions across markets. On the other hand, market barriers create sanctuaries that shelter local business from international competition, limiting the interdependence of local markets with each other and the world economy as a whole. Thus, the welfare of each local market depends more on domestic than global factors: an increase in the welfare of the world economy does not necessarily increase the welfare of every local economy. Market sanctuaries further support and reinforce local culture and value systems; ignoring them can be costly to international business. "Overlooked cultural differences not only discourage product sales but can also stymie productivity within corporations that employ workers in and from different countries."[7]

Competing efficiently and effectively in such a business environment requires much more than corporate philanthropy and local marketing. It requires the adoption of a conventional hierarchical multinational organization unit whereby each national market is a separate entity to be exploited with the establishment of local subsidiaries that operate as local corporations with a local mission adhering to the local rules of business conduct.

Multinational Harmony and Eudaimonia

A collection of independent subsidiaries organized as local corporations, the multinational unit of a semiglobal corporation has the mission of securing free intra-firm trade and capital flows, the protection of local resource and commodity markets from outside competitors, and the expansion to new geographical territories. This means that the multinational unit must envision the world economy both as an open and a closed sea: an open sea when it comes to intra-firm trade and capital flows, the trade and capital flows between the headquarters and subsidiaries, and expansion to new territories; and a closed sea when it comes to the entry of new competitors in individual local markets where the semiglobal corporation has already established a presence.

To preserve both an open and a closed multinational system at the same time, the multinational unit of the semiglobal corporation must behave as a good citizen in every local market in which it conducts business, taking a local approach to harmony and prosperity and adhering to local ethical codes.

> Companies entering or hoping to expand their operations in new markets have found that it is critical to demonstrate how their presence will contribute to the local market. For manufacturing companies, this often means establishing a local plant to train workers in an industry sector and respond to protectionist sentiments. For service companies, such as banks, community outreach programs help establish a favorable local identity. [8]

As Canon's president, Fujio Mitarai, has put it, "We want a company that is welcome and respected in every country. So, in matters where people are concerned, we take a local approach." This means that the multinational unit of the semiglobal corporation must strike a balance between its own interests and the interests of each and every community where it operates. This can be accomplished in a number of ways.

First, the multinational unit can make sure that trade between the parent and its local subsidiaries benefits not just the parent and its home country, but its subsidiaries and their host countries too, through local community reinvestment programs, local philanthropy, and product localization. Honda, for instance, reinvests 80 percent of its U.S. profits back to the United States to demonstrate its commitment to the local community. The company further allocates its manufacturing facilities not on just the basis of logistics and efficiency, but also on their contribution to the welfare of the local communities. It now has over 100 factories in thirty-three countries.

Sony Corporation is a major philanthropist in the communities where it conducts business. "Sony's corporate philanthropy efforts in the U.S. are directed toward contributions to the communities where the company has a significant presence. Programs within Sony Electronics Inc. are coordinated by the Community Affairs Department through the utilization of Community Investment Councils made up of employee volunteers at larger facilities, and Community Involvement Coordinators at smaller sites" (2004 Annual Report, p. 15). Italy's oil giant Eni is a major contributor in Kazakhstan's local economy, building libraries and the prime minister's residence, and providing training to government officials.[9]

In the Middle East, LG Electronics markets Qiblah Indicator phones that allow Muslims to identify Makkah Al Mukkramah, the direction of their prayers. The company further sponsors music festivals in the Middle East and cultural events for Mexican schools. In Thailand, Hitachi Corporation donates books to local libraries, and in Europe it has set up the Hitachi Europe Charitable Trust (HECT) to support local communities, while in San Francisco, company Community Action Committees (CAC) help repair and improve the houses of disabled. In its home base, San Diego, California, QUALCOMM has formed the Institute for Innovation and Educational Success, which supports teachers and students at K-12 schools and universities. Exxon Mobil supports local artifact exhibits of oil-producing countries like Nigeria.

Second, the multinational unit can strike a balance by avoiding predatory policies, which drive local competitors out of business, unleashing local unrest, as has been the case against Microsoft in Asian countries where the company allegedly drives local competitors off the market; and by avoiding hard diplomacy exercised through "managed trade," which intensifies bilateral disputes, fueling trade protectionism.[10]

Third, it can cultivate close ties with local officials, as has been the case with traditional multinational corporations MNCs, which have been setting up foreign affairs agencies at their headquarters, a kind of tiny state department with their own "diplomats," traveling the world and developing close and favorable ties with national and local governments.

> Some companies with large and widespread overseas interests frequently maintain their own edition of a tiny State Department. Their overseas subsidiaries, branches, and representatives report more or less regularly. Their economic departments keep them informed of business and financial

conditions. They have their own resident or traveling diplomats. Emphasis is given to cultivating personal relations with the proper officials in government both in America and aboard and, so far as possible, in developing a favorable state of public relations.[11]

Fourth, the multinational unit can strike a balance between its own interests and the interests of the communities where it operates by launching infrastructure projects that give the semiglobal corporation less of an image of "imperialist despoiler," and more of an image of "imperialist builder," as has been the case with early American and European multinationals that invested in the building of railroads and schools in Africa and Latin America, and the British corporations that helped build Hong Kong's physical and administrative infrastructure.

> More often, though, multinationals were not so much imperialist despoilers as imperialist builders—of institutions, of infrastructure, and confidence. In Africa and Latin America, mining companies found themselves obliged to invest in railways and schools. The princely hongs of Jardine and Swire did as much to create Hong Kong as the British government. Many colonial officers retired to join companies, taking their Kiplingesque ideas about imperial duty with them.[12]

In short, the multinational unit of the semiglobal corporation should envision both an open and a closed world economy: an open economy to accommodate intra-firm trade and financial flows, and a closed economy to protect domestic markets from new competitors. This vision should be carried out with subtle economic diplomacy that gives the multinational unit more of an image of "imperialist builder" rather than "imperialist despoiler," striking a balance between the interests of stakeholders of the semiglobal corporation and the interests of the local communities where it conducts business, and incorporating a portfolio of regional values.

Core Values: A Portfolio of Regional Values

The multinational unit of the semiglobal corporation must adhere to regional and local culture systems as shared by the prevailing philosophical and ethical values. In the United States and Europe, for instance, foreign subsidiaries must pay close attention to Western values of individual liberty, worker participation, human rights, and the Christian values of wealth sharing (see Table 4.1). In Japan, foreign subsidiaries

Table 4.1

A Multicultural Code for the Multinational Market

Region/Country	Core values	Description
Europe	Catholicism/Protestant ethic/Social democracy	Worker participation, human rights, wealth sharing
India	*Dharma*	Fulfillment of inherent duty
Thailand	*Santutthi*	Self-restraint
Middle East	*Zakat*	Duty to assist the poor, respect for authority
United States	Individual liberties/ Protestant ethic, openness	Individual freedom, merit, voluntary contribution to charitable organizations
Japan, Korea, and China	*Kyosei, kankei, guanxi, inmak*	Symbiosis, living and working together for the common good, concern for employees' livelihood, emphasis on mutual obligations

must adhere to *kyosei* (living and working together for the common good) and *kankei* (connections). This means that they must demonstrate concern for their employees' livelihood as expressed in the implicit guarantee for lifetime employment, housing subsidies, and concern over consumers' interests as expressed in implicit product guarantees. In Korea, foreign subsidiaries must adhere to *inmak*, that is, they must develop a social network. In China, foreign subsidiaries must adhere to *guanxi* (system of mutual obligations), and function as "welfare agencies," contributing to the needs of the community, in schools, hospitals, roads, and so on. Thai subsidiaries must adhere to the Buddhist concept of *santutthi* (the importance of self-restraint); Indian subsidiaries must adhere to the Hindu *dharma* (the fulfillment of inherent duty); and subsidiaries in Muslim societies, such as in the Middle East, must adhere to Muslim *zakat* (the duty to help the poor).[13]

Although different local value systems share a number of common values, the ranking of these values varies across countries. Koreans and most Southeast Asians, for instance, rank family cooperation and group harmony at the top of their value list, whereas Americans put equity, freedom, and openness ahead of family and cooperation.

Out of this discussion and reporting process, patterns in similarities and distinctions between the groups could be observed. For example, all Malaysian cultures (Malay, Chinese, and Indian) listed the value of "respect for elders" in 100 percent of the sessions, but [it] was not mentioned once by U.S. participants. Family and maintaining community (and often harmony) were frequently reported by all Malaysian cultures, whereas family was mentioned sporadically by U.S. participants, but never community. The most common distinctive values expressed by U.S. participants were freedom, independence, and self-reliance. The Chinese distinguishing stated values included long-term accumulation of wealth, hard working, filial piety, and food. The ethnic Malays' reported unique values were hospitality, gentility, speaking softly, adherence to religious requirements, and neighborly sharing of food. The Indian groups often referenced the belief of cause and effect, such as Karma as a strong influencing value, and anxiety over what, when, and where to do things based on family expectations, and traditional beliefs.[14]

In short, in conducting business in diverse markets, the multinational unit of the semiglobal corporation must develop a portfolio of local values that reflects the ethical codes of the local societies in which it performs business as part of being a good international diplomat and a good local citizen.

A Vision for the Highly Globalized Segment

The highly globalized segment of the semiglobal market is a single, integrated, open market, which is a mixed blessing for international business. On the one hand, an open market is a source of opportunity and efficiency. Local business can compete on a level field in every market around the world. On the other hand, an open market is a source of compounded risks and uncertainties manifested in price and profit swings caused by rapid technological changes, product obsolescence, and imitation, and by market saturation, all of which increase the interdependence of local markets on each other and the world economy as a whole. Therefore, the welfare of each local market depends more on global than on local factors: fluctuations in global welfare are followed by fluctuations in the welfare of the local economies. An open market also becomes a source of a "demonstration" effect that tends to create homogeneous customer tastes and a "universal" system of values and rights.

Competing efficiently and effectively in such a business environment requires a mission that promotes global harmony and eudaimonia, adhering to a universal code of ethics like Aristotelian ethics.

Global Harmony and Eudaimonia

Globalization has flourished on the premise of an open society, which will remain open as long as corporations grow with—not without—international and local communities, spreading the benefits of globalization broadly among its stakeholders, labor, and the world community. When envisioning its future, the global unit of the semiglobal corporation must see not just profits for its stockholders and hefty bonuses and perks for its managers, but an open society free from the tyranny of the central planners of communist regimes and the statism of fascist regimes. Global harmony and global eudaimonia must become the ultimate goals of the global unit of the semiglobal corporation.

Global Harmony

As discussed in the preceding chapters, today's globalization is not a new trend, but the reemergence of an old trend that can be traced back to the last quarter of the nineteenth century with the expansion of cross-country trade and investments. This trend was forestalled by the spread of national and regional inequalities that fueled the rise of communist and fascist regimes, central planning, regulation, nationalism, trade protectionism, and war, producing a fragmented multinational rather than an integrated global economy.

To avert a similar scenario, international business must address one of the side effects of globalization, the growing inequality among geographical regions and social groups. The global unit of the semiglobal corporation must assume a larger responsibility and contribute resources to strengthen international organizations such as the World Trade Organization, the International Monetary Fund, and the United Nations.

The redistribution of the benefits of globalization and the building of democracies are only the necessary conditions for the openness of the world economy. To be viable, these policies must take a step further toward global eudaimonia.

Global Eudaimonia

Developed by Aristotle, the term eudaimonia means the material and the spiritual prosperity of a community, the ultimate goal, the telos, of society. To enjoy material eudaimonia, communities must reach beyond conventional political democracy and inequality to economic democracy, the opening up of local markets to competition, and the placing of consumers rather than producers and government bureaucrats at the center of the economic universe. This involves the elimination of private and government monopolies and outdated government regulations that constrain consumer choices and raise the cost of living and poverty rates in many parts of the world. According to the 2002 *Index of Economic Freedom* co-published by the Heritage Foundation and the *Wall Street Journal*, countries that are mostly free enjoyed a higher per capita GDP, higher rate of economic growth, longer life expectancy, and low poverty rates. Private and government monopolies and regulations impede entrepreneurship and economic development, sentencing the people of many resource-rich countries to poverty. "The reason the people of Angola, Somalia, Haiti and Ukraine are poor is not because the West does not share its riches. They are poor because their governments pursue destructive economic policies that stifle enterprise."[15]

Opening up local markets to competition requires three things: First, a better understanding of different cultures and problems, and a firm commitment to spreading the benefits of globalization to the poorer regions of the world, as, for example, a number of the world's large corporations, including IBM, Ford Motor Company, Bayer, and Bank Boston have pursued by supporting Brazil's Zero Hunger Program. Ford has further joined forces with local unions to improve adult literacy, to provide cars and auto parts to mechanics schools, and to paint hospitals.[16] Medical device maker Medronics contributes millions of dollars to Patient Link, a program to improve community facilities that promote alternative therapies, such as Parkinson's Action Networks that improves patient understanding of new medical breakthroughs and public policies that may speed up their regulatory approval and affordability. Pfizer Corporation is among the leading contributors to United Way, donating $2 million per working day to provide medicine, medical care, and community service to developing countries like Morocco, Tanzania, and Vietnam. In addition, the Pfizer Share Card initiative assists uninsured individuals with an annual income of $18,000 or less to purchase a thirty-day supply of a medicine for $15. The Sharing the Care program—a partnership with the National Governors Association for Community Health Centers and Connection Care—provides medicines to low-income patients through 380 community centers and physicians networks. The International Trachoma Initiative and the Diflucan

Partnership programs provide antibiotics and HIV/Aids medicines to thirteen developing countries.

Second, freer and open local markets also require policies, such as partnerships with civic organizations, to deter market concentration and the formation of monopolies, which limit economic freedom. Pfizer, for instance, has partnered with Japanese consumer and civic groups to open the Japanese market to foreign medicines, an issue to be further addressed in the next chapter. Third, freer and open local markets also require a good global citizenship that provides for spiritual eudaimonia, the well-being of the world community, which may not be served by market forces alone, which often lead to the depersonalization of social systems and alienation, the root cause of psychological stress that may diminish the spiritual welfare of the world community. The same applies to environmental pollution, global warming, and nuclear proliferation, all sources of anxiety that can only be addressed globally.

One way to accomplish this objective is through comprehensive recycling programs. Apple Computer, for instance, has such a program. In 1999, Apple Computer recycled 87 tons of confidential and white paper, 202 tons of mixed paper, 56.5 tons of cardboard, 1.92 tons of aluminum, 7.6 tons of plastic bottles, and 6,700 cubic ft. of polystyrene. Dell Computer organizes recycling tours around the world to recycle unwanted computer equipment. Contract manufacturers like Sanmina-SCI Corporation, Benchmark Electronics, and Solectron have developed lead-free processes and instituted reduction of hazardous substances (RoHS) programs worldwide.

In short, globalization has been founded on the premise of a free international and local market system that can remain open and free if the benefits of globalization are spread across the nations and social groups involved.

Aristotelian Ethics

Aristotle lived in a much smaller and simpler world than the one we live in today. Yet his philosophical system, the premise that individual virtues should rule and guide human behavior, is not dated and can be applied to today's business organizations. Professor Collins, for instance, claims that Aristotle inspired the development of corporations to serve the needs of individuals and society. Professor Newton further argues that "virtue ethics" are important in ensuring compatibility between the objectives of the members of an organization and those of society. Aristotle's list of virtues builds on the four virtues emphasized by his teacher Plato: wisdom, courage, self-control, and justice (see Tables 4.2 and 4.3).

Wisdom

According to Aristotle, wisdom is "scientific knowledge" and "intuitive intelligence" and the capacity to distinguish between actions that one ought to pursue and those one ought not to pursue as well as one's capacity to judge another person's behavior rightly. Applying this to business, wisdom is the cumulative experience of an enterprise from its inception to the present that helps the enterprise to navigate between extreme actions that may upset its internal or external relations. Understanding the importance of wisdom, every major corporation conducts internal and external training of its employees. Some companies, like the Mitsui Group, keep scripts of company wisdom that advise new generations of employees to practice prudence, frugality, and especially close cooperation.[17]

Management must understand the peculiarities and specificity of the international and local markets and the possibilities and limitations of its own organization. In managing human resources across countries, for instance, management must steer between the individualism of Western societies and the group behavior of Asian societies. Management must also be responsive to needs and aspirations and ethical codes of local communities and make a distinction between policies it ought to pursue and policies it ought not to pursue, steering away from actions that may undermine its external and internal relations. When preparing its menu for the markets of India, Japan, and China, McDonald's, for instance, must take into consideration local tastes and preferences and understand local competition, avoiding extreme policies that may intimidate local competitors. When selling its Bollgard insect-protected cotton seeds around the world, Monsanto must understand how farmers from the United States to India manage their business. "If Monsanto tries to sell a product, such as our Bollgard insect-protected cotton, to all cotton farmers around the world, we will have very spotty success. We have to understand how the cotton farmer in the Mississippi Delta manages the business, and we have to understand how the cotton farmer in India manages the business. Understanding the difference is critical to our success."[18]

Table 4.2

An Aristotelian Ethical Code for Highly Globalized Markets

Code	Description
Wisdom	Management should know the possibilities and limitations of a global organization, steer between the extremes of individualism and group behavior, be sensitive to the peculiarities and specificity of the local community.
Courage	Dare to invent and innovate, pioneer new products and markets, steer between the extremes and vices of excess, cowardice, and recklessness.
Self-control	Avoid greed, arrogance, and self-indulgence; do not make promises you cannot keep.
Justice/ Fairness	Equitable treatment of the members of the organization; share risks and rewards; just treatment of partners and associates, suppliers, and clients, and the general public; spread the wealth among the members of the society.

Table 4.3

Selected Companies with Aristotelian Ethics

Code	Company
Wisdom	Nextbridge, Inc.; Washington Group International; Gaz de France; Seasilver, Inc.; MSJ Group of Companies; Berrett-Koehler; Wisdom Consulting, Inc.; LG Electronics; Hitachi
Courage	TDK Corp.; Matsushita Electric; LG Electronics; Hitachi
Self-control	Mc2 Management Consulting; Andercol SA; Omron Corp.; UTI Group
Justice/Fairness	Darden Restaurants; Matsushita Electric; Sony Corp.; Johnson Controls; Daystar Technologies; Symbiosis Software Development; LG Electronics; N.V. Philips; Toyota Motor Company; Nestle

Wisdom further means global awareness and understanding of diverse standards and regulations of different cultures, and the effect of these factors on cross-border management. American managers, for instance, appreciate straight answers from their employees; otherwise they consider them dishonest. European and Asian managers are appreciative of less-straight answers from their employees; otherwise they consider them rude and aggressive. Corporations should never promise what they cannot deliver, damaging their credibility. The woes of Enron and America on Line discussed below are two cases in point.

Wisdom further means the embracing and discovery and diffusion of new technologies for the development of new products and for the better communication within the company and with the outside world. Yet wisdom alone is never sufficient to navigate the rough oceans of the highly globalized segment of the semiglobal economy; it must be supported and reinforced by courage to make the right decisions when the time is ripe.

Courage

According to Aristotle, "the courageous man is he that endures or fears the right things and for the right purpose and in the right manner and at right time, and who shows confidence in a similar way." By contrast, "he that exceeds in fear is a coward, for he fears the wrong things, and in the wrong manner, and so on with the rest of the list."[19]

Courage in international businesses is the virtue of daring to invent and innovate, abandoning old business and products and pioneering new products and markets, as a Schumpeter-style entrepreneur. As the TDK Corporation motto states:. "Always perform with courage. Performing power is born by confronting contradiction and overcoming it." Courage steers one between the extremes and the vices of excess, cowardice, and recklessness. In designing its strategy, for instance, the management of the semiglobal corporation must be daring and yet cautious. Just assuming new challenges indiscriminately, rushing into new markets without calculating the risks and the rewards, could prove reckless. Contemplating for too long venturing into a new market, on the other hand, could prove cowardly. The management of the semiglobal corporation must also dare to assume responsibility for choices that might have adverse effects on the international or local community and try to remedy them. Courage also means assuming responsibility for reckless behavior that can shatter the image of the corporation. As Keidanren, the Japanese Federation of Economic Organizations, urged its members after a host of corporate scandals were made public in 1997, "Companies must strive to meet a higher standard of ethics and to abide by the principle of self-responsibility," a principle that is closely related to the virtue of self-control.

Self-control

Caught in a euphoria brought about by opportunity and greed, corporations like individuals often lose sight of their limits and possibilities; they lose control of their destiny and become arrogant, insensitive, and self-indulgent, spoiling their relations with the community. As Plato put it, self-control is about knowing "one's self," the possibilities and the limits of human capabilities, how far people can reach without risking failure, spoiling relations with others. Aristotle's message is clear and loud: "The man who runs away from everything in fear and never endures anything becomes a coward; the man who fears nothing whatsoever but encounters everything becomes rash."[20]

Knowing "one's self," exercising self-restraint, is a difficult task, especially if the "one" is an institution, a large corporation with an international presence. How can one put limits on such an organization? How can one keep the management of such an organization from becoming self-indulgent, arrogant, and insensitive to the needs of the global and local community?

For some corporations this is an impossible task. Take the case of Enron, MCI Worldcom, and Global Crossing, for instance. All these companies failed to recognize their own limitations, and instead of steering away from excess and from unrealistic goals, they ended up in bankruptcy. In 1996, in an attempt to expand the number of subscribers to its services too quickly, the management of America on Line introduced a flat monthly rate for unlimited use. What the management failed to provide, however, was the capacity that would allow all these users to sign on at the same time. The result was scores of customer protests. AT&T became too aggressive with acquisitions, buying up companies that did not fit well with its core business, for example NCR, which was acquired in the early 1990s. The company also became self-indulgent and complacent about its dominance in long-distance service and underestimated the competition, which gradually chipped away at its market share. Ford and Volkswagen merged their Latin American operations, only to end in a bitter and costly divorce a decade later. In a yet a third case, Tyco pushed its way too quickly into Europe, with serious consequences for its bottom line. But one does not have to limit oneself to the United States to find examples of companies that lost control of their destinies. A number of South Korean and Japanese companies rushed to buy assets in the United States and drove up prices in the late 1980s, only to find themselves with big losses by the mid-1990s. Matsushita's acquisition of MCA and its divestiture a few years later at a fraction of the acquired price is just one of the many cases that demonstrate how loss of self-control can shatter corporate images, hurt bottom lines, and erode competitive positions.

Justice

Justice is the highest virtue in the interaction of a member with the other members of a group, whether that group is a corporation or society as a whole. As Aristotle summarized it in a proverb: "In justice are all virtues found." Justice also relates to fairness, the equitable treatment of the members of a corporation by management as well as the just treatment of partners, clients, suppliers, and the general public. What this means for the global unit of the semiglobal corporation is that it should treat each and every group, each and every member, as an equal partner, an entrepreneur who shares the risks and the rewards of the partnership. This principle must be reflected in all aspects of the global unit's organization, decision-making structure, employee recruitment, compensation, promotion practices, and working conditions. Fairness further means sensitivity to the cultural mosaic of its labor force and clientele, avoiding practices and actions that may insult or humiliate its labor force or insult its consumers. In August 1996, for instance, a Vietnamese court found a manager at a South Korean owned factory, a Nike subcontractor, guilty of humiliating workers.[21] Almost a year later, and while the dispute between labor and management in the company's Vietnamese factories continued, Nike came up with an "Allah" shoe model that the Muslim community found insulting. In 2004, Nike continued its provocative advertisements by featuring an American athlete killing a dragon, China's symbol of power.

Fairness must also provide the basis for the spreading of the gains of globalization, filling the vacuum caused by the weakening of local and national governments. It must contribute to the provision of funds for the creation of a safety net for small corporations and individuals who cannot keep up with the intensification of competition and the demands of new technology.

To sum up, faced with a dual world market economy, the semiglobal corporation must devise a dual vision, one for its highly globalized segment and another for its highly localized segment. This means that the semiglobal corporation must be both a good local and global citizen at the same time.

Good local citizenship means different things to different societies. In most European countries, good local citizenship means spreading the benefits of economic growth to all members of society. It further means respect for workers' rights and, in some cases, mandatory inclusion of labor in business decision making. In China, good citizenship means that companies are expected to contribute to society by building and supporting schools, hospitals, and so on. In Japan, good citizenship means concern for the employees' livelihood as expressed in the implicit guarantee of lifetime employment, housing subsidies, and concern over consumers' interests as expressed in implicit product guarantees. In America, good citizenship means contributing to philanthropy.

Good global citizenship means adhering to a set of universal values like those discussed by Aristotle—courage, self-control, wisdom, and justice—and taking a step further toward global eudaimonia, the material and the spiritual well-being of a community, the ultimate goal or the telos of society. To reach material and spiritual eudaimonia, many communities need to take a step beyond conventional democracy and inequality and advance toward an economic democracy that opens up markets to competition and puts consumers rather than producers and governments behind the steering wheel of the economy. Semiglobal corporations must work closely with governments to deter market concentration and the formation of monopolies, provide a safety net for those left behind in the race of capitalism, and address additional side effects of globalization: psychological stress, environmental pollution, and nuclear proliferation. In addition, a clear and sound vision provides the foundation for the competitive strategy of the semiglobal corporation, an issue to be addressed in the next chapter.

Notes

1. Pfizer, *2002 Annual Report*, New York, 2003, p. 18.
2. Corporate vision first became a popular business issue in the 1970s and the 1980s, as corporations grew larger and more diverse in terms of employment, management, ownership, and customer base, and came to rely more on a sound vision to hold their pieces together and reach their business goals, and less on close monitoring and control. A sound vision is of particular importance for international businesses that serve distant overseas markets with diverse social institutions, policies, and cultures that make close monitoring and control of each market an impossible

task. A sound vision strengthens relations among company employees, contributing to knowledge sharing and to contextual and organizational learning.

3. Microsoft's missteps in Southeast Asia were acknowledged by the company's senior officials at the International Geographical Union Congress held in Glasgow in August 2004. For details, see Amer (2004).

4. Wilkin (2004), p. 45.

5. Core ideology is a set of eternal values that justify the very existence of the corporation, create a common conscience among its members, and rule its relations with consumers, suppliers, and the community. Envisioned future is a set of far reaching objectives that define the mission, the telos, the ultimate goal of the corporation in the Aristotelian philosophy, and the Ithaca, the ultimate destination of a long voyage in Homerian and Cavafian poetry. For more details, see Lipton (1996), p. 66; Neff (1995), p. 15; and Mourdoukoutas (1999a).

Collins and Porras (1996, p. 65) emphasize that the core values and the envisioned future or mission of the corporation should not be confused with business strategies and practices that may change according to circumstances.

6. Pestre (2004), p. 5.

7. Amer (2004), p. 45.

8. Aboulafia-D'Jaen (1998), p. 22.

9. Kahn (2005), p. A6.

10. The U.S. Commerce Department's "advocacy center" has managed to win several deals for American MNCs: a $2.6 billion energy contract for General Electric in Indonesia; a $1.6 billion contract for McDonnell Douglas in China; a $1.4 billion contract for Raytheon in Brazil; a $65 million contract for General Railway Signal in Taiwan; and a $5.5 million contract for Teradyne in South Korea. The Japanese Ministry of Trade and Industry (MITI) founded the Japan External Trade Organization (JETRO); the Export Council and Trade Council Classified by Overseas Commodities; export finance (Export Advance Bill System, Foreign Exchange Fund Loan System, Export-Import Bank); export insurance system; export promotion taxation systems; inspection systems of export goods; improvement of the design of goods and the prevention of imitation; maintenance of order in foreign trade by the Export and Import Trading Law.

11. Berle (1954), p. 135.

12. Micklethwait and Wooldridge (2003), pp. 167–68.

13. Donaldson (1996), p. 188.

14. Doorly (2003), p. 53.

15. Ibid.

16. Smith (2003), p. C3.

17. Koren (1990).

18. Caminiti (2005), p. 21.

19. Aristotle *The Nichomachean Ethics*, Clarendon Press, p. 67.

20. Ibid., p. 35.

21. *Far Eastern Economic Review* 159(34), Aug. 22, 1996.

5

Competitive Strategy

Whatever the initial motivation for its investment in new operating units, the modern industrial enterprise has rarely continued to grow or maintain its competitive position over an extended period of time *unless the addition of new units (and to a lesser extent the elimination of old ones) has actually permitted its managerial hierarchy to reduce costs, to improve existing products and processes and to develop new ones, and to allocate resources to meet the challenges and opportunities of ever-changing technologies and markets.*[1]

To us, global means serving our customers in a streamlined, integrated and coordinated fashion. Our approach enables us to execute with greater precision, economic leverage and flexibility to provide customized supply-chain solutions that deliver the greatest value to customers.[2]

Rapid technological advances characterize the computing and tele-communications industries, and our ability to compete depends on our ability to improve our products and processes faster than our competitors, anticipate changing customer requirements, and develop and launch new products to meet changing requirements, while reducing costs at the same time.[3]

- In 2004, General Motors reorganized itself from a multinational holding company of four regional companies to a global company managed by one executive overseeing all major functions including product design and engineering. The move is expected to cut product design and manufacturing costs by raising the global content of its value propositions to customers.[4]
- Daimler Chrysler is working with Mitsubishi and Hyundai to develop the first family of "world engines" to power as many as one million small vehicles. Inspired by Henry Ford's fundamental premise that less expensive vehicles attract more customers, they seek to reduce costs by exploiting economies of scale. The Daimler-Chrysler-Mitsubishi engine follows a similar effort by Ford Motor Co. and Mazda Motor Corp. to develop an engine for their cars as well as for cars produced by Volvo. Separately, Daimler Chrysler, Mitsubishi, Hyundai, Ford, and Mazda bundle their cars together with multiple services for local markets such as towing

and maintenance, interest financing, theft insurance, security systems, global positioning systems, and satellite radio subscriptions.
* Cable service providers like Long Island–based Cable Vision are expanding bundle offerings to include high-speed Internet connections and local telephone services. Traditional telecom providers like SBC Communications are teaming up with satellite providers to expand their local product offerings to include high-speed Internet connections and satellite TV services.

These examples highlight a number of managerial and entrepreneurial strategies international businesses apply to address the peculiarities and specificity of the semiglobal market, and to achieve an above-industry-average rate of return for their stockholders. To address the intensification of competition and price erosion that undermines profitability in highly globalized segments, international businesses apply a host of managerial strategies that improve the efficiency and effectiveness of their value propositions: they narrow their product portfolio, introduce new technologies and state-of-the-art logistics, merge their operations with those of competitors, outsource non-core activities to third parties, and form alliances with competitors.

To address market barriers and consumer diversity in their highly localized market segments, international businesses differentiate value propositions, tailoring them to local consumer preferences. In some cases, product differentiation is marginal, adding just a few new features to existing products. In other cases, product differentiation is massive, adding different features for different customer markets. To deal with market saturation in both segments of the world economy, especially in the highly globalized segment, international businesses follow a host of entrepreneurial strategies: corporate spin-offs, strategic acquisitions, corporate venturing, and strategic alliances that allow them to discover and exploit new business opportunities.

This chapter, a more detail discussion of the competitive strategies of the semiglobal corporation and their limitations, is in two sections. The first section discusses managerial strategies, that is, strategies that improve operational effectiveness: global cost leadership strategies, local differentiation leadership strategies, and mass localization leadership strategies. The second section discusses entrepreneurial strategies, that is, strategies that expand business opportunities: corporate spin-offs, strategic acquisitions, corporate venturing, and strategic alliances.

Figure 5.1 **The Semiglobal Corporation Managerial Strategies Grid**

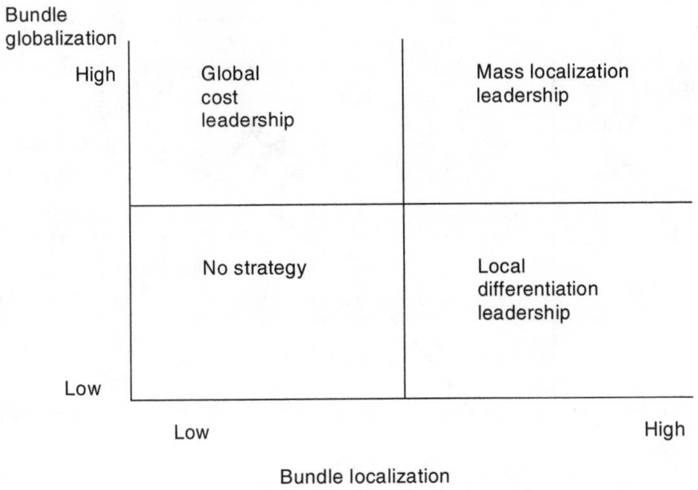

Managerial Strategies

Management is one of the major functions of every business enterprise. Successful managerial strategies allow companies to achieve superior performance, that is, an above-industry-average rate of return.

Managerial strategies for the semiglobal economy can be best understood and explored if products crossing national and local markets are seen as bundles of global and local product characteristics rather than products per se, as discussed briefly in Chapter 1. Within this framework, semiglobal corporations can achieve an above-industry-average rate of return with three generic strategies: raising the global content of bundle offerings to achieve global cost leadership; raising the local bundle content to achieve local differentiation leadership; and combining the previous two strategies to achieve mass localization, that is, both a global cost and a local differentiation leadership (see Figure 5.1).[5]

Global Cost Leadership

Global cost leadership is about raising the global content of value propositions to achieve an above-industry-average rate of returns (see Figure 5.2). This means a greater homogeneity and standardization of value propositions and a greater emphasis on cost competition over product

Figure 5.2   **Global Cost Leadership: Raising the Global/Local Characteristics Mix of Bundle Offerings**

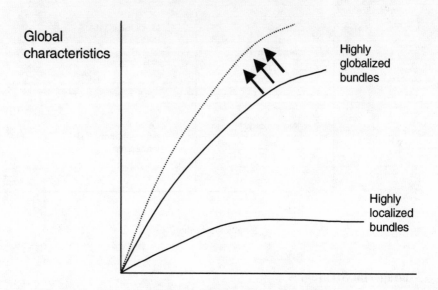

competition, which can be accomplished through a number of conventional and modern ways: efficient use of labor and capital, use of state-of-the-art logistics and outsourcing of non-core activities.

Efficient Use of Labor

Depending on management's objectives, "efficient use" of labor can be defined in a number of ways. Traditionally, it meant producing the maximum output per unit of labor input. More recently, efficient use of labor means delivering the maximum customer value with every labor unit. In the short run, this can be accomplished in four ways. First, it can be accomplished by adjusting labor input to changing output (in the first case) and demand conditions (in the second case). Labor, for instance, must be adjusted over the business cycle in line with bundle demand fluctuations: expanded during cyclical upturns and contracted during economic downturns. In the aftermath of the burst of the high-tech bubble in the early 2000s, many corporations applied layoffs to cut costs. Contract manufacturer Solectron, for instance, eliminated 12,000 positions or 16 percent of its labor force, Tellabs laid off 3,450 or 38 percent of its labor force, and Corning cut 10,000 positions or 25 percent of its labor force.

Second, more efficient use of labor can be accomplished by swapping high-paid with low-paid workers, a popular strategy in the service sector where workers cannot be easily replaced by technology or outsourcing. "The approach, which is perfectly legal, doesn't eliminate the position but rather the high-paid person in it. The technique is especially attractive to service business such as retail. Like so many companies today, they face massive pressure to cut their labor costs. But unlike manufacturers, they have jobs that can't easily be automated or shipped overseas."[6]

Third, efficient use of labor can be promoted by routinely weeding out unproductive workers. "Weeding out the weakest links is common in many companies. Giants such as General Electric and Cisco Systems routinely rank employees at least once a year to identify chronic underperformers. Some companies promptly fire the 5 percent to 10 percent lowest performers, while others give those employees special training or mentoring programs before dropping the ax."[7]

Fourth, labor efficiency can be increased by subcontracting or outsourcing labor-intensive operations to low-cost countries, like China and Vietnam, an issue to be further addressed below.

Adjusting labor to market conditions is not always easy, however, especially in countries with stringent labor regulations or a strong tradition of long-term employment. In Europe, for instance, unions oppose layoffs of their members, especially high-paid senior workers. In Japan, large corporations have a tradition of not laying off regular workers, but containing labor costs by freezing hiring or by cutting bonuses or even basic salaries. Labor adjustment policies demoralize the labor force and become the target of imitation by the competition, quickly eliminating competitive advantages.

Efficient Use of Capital

The term "efficient use of capital" means deriving the most output or the most customer value per unit of input—in this case, capital—depending on the management objectives adopted, which can be accomplished through economies of scale, the cost savings associated with a larger production: the larger the production of a product, the lower its average cost, and the higher the profit margins.

International businesses can achieve economies of scale in a number of ways. First, they can do so through the introduction of new technologies. Intel, for instance, has for years managed to cut the costs of its microprocessors by shifting production to larger manufacturing facilities."In 2003, the company shifted production from 200 mm (8-inch) wafer manufacturing facilities to 300 mm (12-inch) wafers, churning out more than twice as many equivalent chips per wafer as 200 mm wafers."[8] Corning has managed to cut its flat panel production costs by the introduction of large generation substrates that allow the manufacturing of more and larger panels from each substrate.[9] The introduction of new technology has allowed Sharp, the leading manufacturer of flat panel TVs, to enjoy higher productivity and higher profit margins. For the period 1999–2004, Sharp enjoyed close to a 5 percent profit margin, twice that of Sony and about three times that of Matsushita.[10] In 2005, Hitachi introduced a new storage disk that allowed desktop PCs to store a trillion bytes, twice as much as current models, cutting storage costs in half. The introduction of two new technologies, Platinum Multicast and FLO (Forward Link Only), by QUALCOMM allowed the company to cut the cost of multimedia content delivery over cellular devices.[11]

Introducing new technology to boost productivity and to cut the cost of value propositions is not a new strategy. In the late nineteenth century, Andrew Carnegie improved efficiency by mass-producing steel, cutting production costs and lowering prices. In the automobile industry early in the twentieth century, Henry Ford improved efficiency by mass-producing, mass distributing, and mass advertising the Model T car, cutting car prices from $850 in 1908 to $360 by 1916.

> Ford's success was not just about building cars more swiftly, but also about bringing both mass production and mass distribution under the roof of a single organization. An "integrated" industrial firm could find economies of scale in everything from purchasing to advertising—and thus pump an endless supply of cigarettes, matches, breakfast cereals, film, cameras, canned milk, and soup around the country. The key was to own as much of the process as possible. Ford even owned the land on which grazed the sheep that produced the wool that went into his seat covers.[12]

Mass production of kerosene allowed Standard Oil Corporation to cut kerosene production costs from 2.5 cents in 1879 to 0.4 cents by 1885. Mass production allowed German chemical producers BASF, Bayer, and Hoechst to cut the price of Alizarin from DM200 per kilogram in 1878 to DM9 by 1886, underselling foreign competitors. In the retail industry late in the twentieth century, Wal-Mart founder Sam Walton improved efficiency with large retail outlets and volume sales, which again translated into lower costs and lower prices for consumers.

Second, the semiglobal corporation can achieve economies of scale through M&A. In the energy sector, Calpine's $576 billion acquisition of SkyGen Energy LLC and Panda Energy International in 2000 boosted the company's capacity by 60 percent by the year 2004. Devon Energy Corporation's $3.4 billion acquisition of Anderson Exploration, Inc., turned Devon to the largest oil and gas producer in North America. In the steel industry, Nucor's stream of acquisitions in the late 1990s and the early 2000s gave the company a cost edge against its competitors.[13] In the computer hardware sector, the merger of Compaq with Hewlett-Packard allowed the two companies to eliminate a number of product duplications, including the HP Jornada and Omnibook and Compaq's Itanium-based servers, saving the new company $0.9 billion in sales costs, $1.6 billion in operating expenses, and $0.5 billion in R&D costs.[14] In forklift manufacturing, Toyota's acquisition of BT Industries allowed the company to cut the distribution and sales costs of its forklift trucks.

Pursuing economies of scale through M&A is not a new strategy either. In the late-nineteenth-century oil industry, Standard Oil expanded the scale of its operations by acquiring competitors or driving them out of business, as did American Tobacco, United Fruit, U.S. Steel, International Harvester, and GE. In the first quarter of the twentieth century, William C. Durrant expanded the product offerings of GM by merging twenty-five smaller automobile companies, including Buick, with Oldsmobile and Cadillac to create a larger company. Swift's expansion to meat distribution allowed the company to set its prices seventy-five cents per hundredweight below the competition.

> The combination of high-volume production with innovations in distribution translated into a significant cost advantage. Swift was able to set a price up to seventy-five cents per hundred pounds cheaper than his competitors who still relied upon the shipment of live cattle. As his methods took hold and demand increased rapidly, he established additional packing plants in Kansas City, Omaha, and other locations.[15]

Third, international businesses can achieve economies of scale through alliances and joint partnerships, where two or more companies, often former competitors, pull their resources together to mass produce a product while maintaining their independence. Automobile maker Daimler Chrysler, for instance, has teamed up with Mitsubishi and Hyundai to develop the first family of world engines to power as many as one million small vehicles. Ford Motor Company has teamed up with Mazda Motor Corp. to develop an engine for their cars as well as cars produced by Volvo. The alliance between Renault and Nissan saved the two companies $3.3 billion in the areas of purchasing and product development. The External Equipment Provider alliance allowed member companies like Dow Corning, Nordson Company, and DEK to improve productivity and cut costs by standardizing their materials, equipment, and procurement. The coproduction alliance between flash memory chipmakers SanDisk, Toshiba, and Hitachi allowed the three companies to cut costs for digital camera chips. The FreeMove, an alliance among major European mobile service providers Orange, Telefonica, T Mobile, and TIM, allowed these companies to expand the scale of their operations, reaching 170 million customers. Fourth, international business can achieve economies of scale by forming consortia that allow global units to gather a critical mass to enter overseas markets. For instance, New Zealand's EE Group, a consortium of thirty firms, got a project to build 40,000 apartments in Turkey.[16]

In short, international businesses can achieve efficient use of their capital through economies of scale, which can be accomplished with the introduction of new technology, M&A, strategic alliances, and business consortia. However, each of these methods has its own limitations, especially M&A. First, M&A often becomes synonymous with downsizing, which demoralizes the remaining labor force, eroding the company's long-term competitiveness. Second, M&A often becomes a source of cultural clashes, especially among established corporations with well-defined cultures and relations. "A merger can be like a death. Everything you're worked for, every relationship you're forged— they are suddenly null and void."[17] Third, the larger size that comes with mergers is often followed by diseconomies rather than economies of scale, as was the case with RJ Nabisco in the 1970s and the 1980s. Fourth, M&As have a strong demonstration effect. A merger of two companies is often followed by the merger of two other companies, and so on, until either a price war or government regulation of the industry becomes imminent, eliminating or even reversing any early scale gains.

State-of-the-Art Logistics and Managerial Practices

Logistics are mathematical and statistical models that allow companies to gather and process information, cut inventory cost, employee training costs, product design and development costs, and procurement and office management costs, as well as improve delivery schedules. The just-in-time inventory system, for instance, allows companies to cut costs by eliminating warehousing, loading and unloading costs, and accounting overhead costs. In the automobile industry, just-in-time allowed Japanese companies to gain a competitive edge over their Western counterparts. Toyota's just-in-time system allows the company to cater its products to consumer preferences: make what customers want, and deliver it where and when they need it. "Toyota starting thinking in terms of pulling inventory based on immediate customer demand, rather than using a push system that anticipates customer demand. In the *Toyota Way,* 'pull' means the ideal state of just-in-time manufacturing: giving the customer (which may be the next in the production process) what he or she wants, when he or she wants it, and in the amount he or she wants."[18] Software from Verity K2 Enterprise allows companies to create teams of experts by tracking search patterns and "host links." "Matchmaking" software ActiveNet allows large corporations like Northrop Grumman, GlaxoSmithKline, and Morgan Stanley to better utilize their vast labor force by identifying groups with synergistic expertise. "The program comps through thousands of employee profiles and millions of internal documents—from e-mails to PowerPoint slides—and suggests synergistic matchups between workers, based on what software's algorithms perceive as someone's interests and expertise."[19]

In the computer industry, sound logistics allowed Dell Computer to cut inventory time from forty-five days to twenty-six to thirty hours and to distribute a fifty-two-week forecast for its suppliers. Software from Unispace, Inc., has allowed HP to save $1 million in one year by replacing a manual customer and supplier monitoring system with an automatic centralized system. In the banking industry, online transaction systems cut buyers' and sellers' settlement time by 50 to 60 percent. Logistics systems from Sun Microsystems and Infosys allow banks to cut costs and improve product quality by reducing customer waiting time by up to 89 percent and by shortening teller reconciliation by an average of 90 percent. In the beverage industry, Coca-Cola's online teenager panel allowed the company to cut product-development research by 50 percent. In the food industry, Kraft Foods' electronic survey systems cut research time by 30 percent and research costs by 25 percent.[20] In networking, Internet-based applications such as e-sales and e-learning save Cisco Systems 40 to 60 percent compared to traditional instructor-based costs. In the brokerage business, the Internet allows companies to cut substantially the cost of communicating with their clients. Between 1999 and 2004, Vanguard experienced a 50 percent decline in customer phone calls, with 80 percent of customers communicating with the company via the web.[21]

In the electronics component distribution industry, logistics allowed Arrow Electronics to cut the number of its warehouses. In the brewery industry, BudNet, a sophisticated software program, allows beer giant Anheuser Busch to closely monitor sales and competitors' marketing campaigns more efficiently and effectively. "Anheuser uses data to constantly change marketing strategies to design promotions to suit the ethnic makeup of its markets and as early warning radar that detects where rivals might have an edge."[22] In retailing, Wal-Mart relies on sophisticated inventory and purchasing management systems to cut its retailing costs below those of its competitors. "Wal-Mart uses its mountain of data to push for greater efficiency at all levels of the store, where products are stocked based on expected demand, to the back, where details about a manufacturer's punctuality, for example, are recorded for future use. The purpose is to protect Wal-Mart from a retailer's twin nightmare: too much inventories, or not enough."[23] In the online retailing industry, logistics allowed Amazon Corporation to become "the biggest bookstore on earth," and Ebay the largest auctioneer on earth. In the appliance industry, online auctions allow companies like Whirlpool to save millions of dollars on resource supplies. In the automobile industry, mySAP SRM software has helped the company reduce expenditures by 15 percent a month. PeopleSofts's and Siebel's Enterprise Software automation allows companies to optimize the procurement and staffing of external resources in the organization, while the Peoplesoft's Human Resource Management System allows organizations to effectively manage their human resources: recruitment and hiring, compensation, retirement, and compliance with local regulations. Kronos's Workforce Central suite allows companies to manage their payroll and labor management applications and to optimize critical employee-related processes.

Logistics cut costs in another, indirect way, by allowing companies to reorganize their production, reducing the number of parts that go into each product and grouping products. "Substantial cost savings have resulted from reducing the number of parts in each model and from using original approaches to modular assembly for some items, such as instrument panels. Modularization simplifies assembly, as well as lowering costs. We are also trimming costs by grouping our passenger car models in platform families while contributing to increase our model variations."[24]

In short, logistics allow companies to cut inventory, product design, and development costs, but logistics have their own their limitations. First, some logistics can work only if accompanied by the right management practices that are often hard to implement. Second, some logistics work if certain macroeconomic conditions are in effect. Just-in-time, for instance, works well under steady or declining resource prices, but not under rising resource prices. Third, logistics strategies can be easily imitated by the competition. Successful logistics hardware and software can be easily purchased in the market. This means that logistics alone is not a source of sustainable competitive advantage; the erosion of the competitive advantage of the Japanese semiconductor and computer industries in the 1990s attests to this. Japanese companies that based their strategies on standard logistics and management practices eventually lost their competitive edge to their American and European counterparts.

Outsourcing

Outsourcing is the transfer to third parties of a number of value chain activities that used to be performed in-house. IBM hired two subcontractors, Sanmina and Solectron, to handle its PC assembly operations for $3.8 billion. Sanmina and Solectron further agreed to buy or lease IBM's affected assembly plants and equipment in Mexico and Scotland. Telefon AB L.M. Ericsson outsourced its handset manufacturing to Singapore-based Flextronics International, Ltd. Du Pont outsourced its IT department to Computer Science and Andersen Consulting for $5 billion. Computer Science and Andersen Consulting took on 1,200 of Du Pont's employees that worked in that department. Merrill Lynch outsourced its domestic networking infrastructure to AT&T Solutions.

Outsourcing is the acceleration and broadening of an old trend—subcontracting—and has passed through three stages. In the first stage, outsourcing was synonymous with subcontracting, the hiring of third parties by large manufacturing corporations for the purpose of cost cutting (Table 5.1). In the automobile industry, Japanese automakers have

Table 5.1

Stages of Subcontracting and Outsourcing: Activities and Purpose

Stage	Activities	Purpose
First	Manufacturing	Cost cutting
Second	Non-core activities	Cost cutting\Organizational flexibility
Third	Non-core activities	Functional flexibility/Innovation

been routinely subcontracting component production, under long-term buyer-supplier agreements, often backed by cross-equity holdings, known as buyer-supplier *keiretsu*. Toyota, for instance, has been buying components from a number of subcontractors, including Aichi Steel Works, Nippondenso, and Kanto Autoworks. In the electronics industry, American and European electronics makers shifted the production of components and assembling to low-cost Asian and Latin American countries.

In the second stage, outsourcing expanded beyond subcontracting of parts and components to non-core activities, such as security, cleaning and catering, and photocopying, for the purpose of eliminating duplication, cutting costs, and increasing organizational flexibility. Outsourcing of this sort is carried out through partnerships and alliances between original equipment manufacturers (OEMs) and contract manufacturers. Juniper Networks' relations with subcontractors, for instance, extend to a number of activities that stretch from prototyping to manufacturing: material procurement, assembly, test, control, and shipment. Such relations allow the company to save on working capital, to quickly adjust its inputs and outputs to changes in market conditions, to reduce delivery and shipment time, and to reduce warehousing costs.[25]

Outsourcing is of particular importance in the semiconductor industry, where OEMs save on fixed and operating costs associated with the ownership of fabrication facilities. "By subcontracting our manufacturing requirements, we are able to focus our resources on design and test applications where we believe we have greater competitive advantages. This strategy also eliminates the high cost of owning and operating a semiconductor wafer fabrication facility."[26] OEMs can further benefit from outsourcing from the economies of scale arising from pooling together small production bundles into a single large batch, and from process expertise, as well as access to capital and to expensive technology.

In the third stage, subcontracting and outsourcing extended to other activities, like product design, distribution, and after-sales service, for the purpose of functional flexibility and innovation. In the semiconductor industry, for instance, outsourcing allows companies to concentrate their efforts in developing, designing, and testing new products. "By using independent foundries to fabricate our wafers, we are better able to concentrate our resources on designing, development and testing of new products. In addition, we avoid much of the fixed capital and operating costs associated with owning and operating fabrication or chip assembly facilities."[27] In some cases, companies outsource the development of their products to third parties altogether. Insurance companies like Europe's Allianz outsource software development to India's Wipro and Infosys Technologies. The world's largest elevator company, Otis, for instance, outsourced to India's Wipro Technologies the development and deployment of an e*Service portal that allowed Otis's customers to place review service calls on a 24-hour basis, and to access elevator performance and maintenance records. The portal also offers customers the ability to go over financial forms, orders, and invoices in their own language (twenty-seven languages). Allianz used Wipro for rapid development and deployment of software that extended its host application.

Outright outsourcing is not a universal trend, however. Some companies, like Samsung Electronics, "make" most of their products in-house (see Figure 5.3). Other companies, like Tellabs and Monolythic Systems, "buy" almost all their manufacturing products in the market, that is, hire third parties to manufacture their products. A third group of companies, like Texas Instruments, choose a middle solution, manufacturing some of their products internally and others externally. Specifically, Texas Instruments manufactures most of its analog products internally while it outsources most of its digital products.

> Staying ahead of the curve requires significant capital expenditures for new manufacturing capabilities. Texas Instrument's (TI's) strategy is to build up internal capacity to a point that supports a level of market demand that TI believes is sustainable. When demand periodically moves above this level, the company supplements its in-house capacity with production from external foundries. Over time, this strategy should reduce the amount of capital expenditures required to meet demand and the resulting depreciation. It also should keep TI's internal manufacturing assets more fully utilized, resulting in better return on these assets.[28]

The ratio of insource/outsource depends on the speed at which different activities evolve. Activities that evolve quickly should be outsourced,

Figure 5.3 **Insourcing/Outsourcing Choices for Select Corporations**

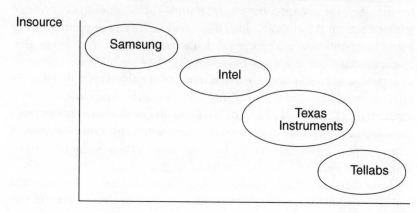

while activities that evolve slowly should be performed inside the organization. Digital production techniques that evolve quickly should be outsourced, while analog production techniques that evolve slowly should be insourced.

In short, outsourcing allows companies to focus on their core competences and to cut costs, but it has its own limitations and "unintended consequences," which if not addressed, can turn it into a bad business strategy. Outsourcing is easy to be replicated, and therefore, it is not a source of sustainable competitive advantage. Outsourcing provides certain competitive advantages to early-movers—that is, to companies that adopt it first—but it is not proprietary. It cannot be patented, preventing others from adopting it. If outsourcing hardware manufacturing provides IBM a cost advantage, it also does so for its competitors, such as HP, Dell Computers, and Sun Microsystems, that will follow suit. If outsourcing call centers cuts costs for American Express, it also does so for its credit card competitors. This means that outsourcing works only as long as some industry members have not yet adopted it. Once this happens, outsourcing is no longer a source of competitive advantage.

Outsourcing leads to the fragmentation and disintegration of the product supply chain, inviting new competitors into the industry and undermining pricing power and profitability. Outsourcing of manufacturing, for instance, is feasible only if it can be separated from other supply chain activities: product development, branding, marketing, distribution, and after-sales services. The supply chain turns from a single integrated process performed within the boundaries of traditional corporations to a fragmented and disintegrated process, a collection of separate and disjointed activities, performed across several independent subcontractors. And although such a fragmentation and disintegration of the value chain offers corporations a number of well-publicized advantages, it has an unintended consequence: it makes entry of new competitors to the industry easier, intensifying competition, shortening product cycles, and squeezing return on invested capital.

To understand how this works, let us imagine a perfectly fragmented and disintegrated TV supply chain: every activity from the new TV concept development, to design, manufacturing, marketing, and so on can be performed by independent subcontractors. This means that any company that has no capability to make and sell TVs can enter the TV industry, as long as it comes up with sufficient capital to pay subcontractors to handle the different value chain activities. The problem, though, is that once the product hits the market, nothing prevents another company from doing exactly the same thing, and then another, and another, until the TV industry becomes crowded with companies pitting against each other in a cut-throat competition that eliminates industry profitability. What seemed to be a good strategy for each company in the beginning turned into a bad strategy for everyone at the end. By carrying outsourcing to the extreme, industry members open the door wide to competition, reversing whatever outsourcing's early positive effects may have been, and then some.

But what if outsourcing is not carried that far? What if companies outsource only their "non-core activities," and retain their "core activities" —the things they can do best—in-house? Certainly this strategy cuts costs and improves product quality, but it has another unintended consequence: it nurtures corporate complacency. By focusing on things that they can do best, company managers become complacent about their achievements and think that what is the best product for their customers today will be the best product tomorrow. Corporate complacency, in turn, leads to corporate blindness, the failure of management to see that its markets have reached saturation or are undermined by alternative products.

Outsourcing's unintended consequences for companies and industries that adopt it extend to the relations of these companies with one of their partners—labor. If each and every activity of the product supply chain is gradually farmed out, what binds labor with management and stockholders? If company engineers and marketers who develop new product ideas can sense that their jobs will eventually be farmed out, why should they be loyal to the company? Would it not be better to part from the company and pursue their own product supply chain by farming out the development, the manufacturing, and so on to outsourcing companies themselves?

Outsourcing also undermines relations with a third company partner—the domestic and local community. By shifting production and jobs overseas, outsourcing has a devastating impact on both parties, which often unleashes tidal ideological and political waves that may reverse all the gains from outsourcing, and then some. Let us not forget that people who live in these communities are not just workers, they are customers and citizens too. As customers, they may end up boycotting the products of corporations shifting production from one location to another just for the sake of profits. As citizens, people may end up supporting legislation that increases the cost of doing business in their community.

In short, what seems to be trendy in business strategy is not always a good strategy. If carried to an extreme, outsourcing turns corporations into opportunistic institutions, without a vision and on a collision course with its most valuable partners: labor, customers, and the community.

To sum up, cost-cutting strategies allow international business to achieve an above-average rate of return, but they are only temporary, that is, they do not yield sustainable competitive advantages. According to a Mercer Management Consulting study, of 116 companies that drastically cut costs in the 1990–91 recession, only 29 percent succeeded in improving their performance in the 1994–99 expansion, compared with their peers.[29] This means that international business must consider alternative strategies, like local differentiation, as sources of sustainable competitive advantage.

Local Differentiation Leadership

Local differentiation leadership involves raising the local characteristics content of bundle offerings to attain an above-industry-average rate of return (see Figure 5.4). In Europe, personal products makers like Procter and Gamble raise the local content of their brand name products, turning them into local brands: "Now P&G operates a unique strategy for each country. Its toothpaste brand Crest remains Blend-a-Med in Germany and AZ in

Figure 5.4 **Localization Differentiation Leadership: Raising the Local/ Global Characteristics Mix of Bundle Offerings**

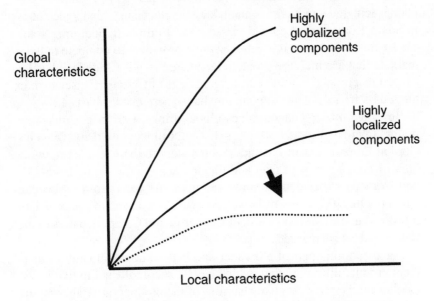

Italy. And a more local approach with Pampers is paying off in Germany, where P&G claims to be one of the few consumer goods companies growing in what is considered Europe's toughest market."[30]

Chemical companies routinely raise the local content of their product offerings by adding local characteristics such as services and customer support to their global products. Dow Chemical bundles its products with a comprehensive service plan that provides its customers a prompt response to any problems with its products. Automobile makers churn out different bundles of standardized car features with localized car features. Honda, for instance, has developed a number of automobile models tailored to different local markets around the world.

Cellular phone providers routinely bundle the global product, the cellular phone, together with local service contracts that include "anytime minutes," "night and weekend minutes," "additional minutes," "long distance minutes," and "roaming." Nokia differentiates cell phones and other wireless communication products along two dimensions: first, a functional category: voice, entertainment, imaging, media, and business applications; and second, a style category: premium, fashion, classic, active, expression, and basic. Its business organizer, for instance, is a premium business application, while its PDA is a classic imaging product. The company further follows other cell phone makers like Motorola and Erickson and their strategic partners by bundling cell phones with local message content, karaoke music in China, video clips in South Korea, and recorded messages in Europe. In addition, Nokia works closely with local wireless service providers to compete in local markets that are highly regulated. Software provider Autodesk has localized its products for the emerging markets of China and elsewhere in the Asia-Pacific, where the company has experienced robust sales.[31]

Beverage maker Diageo mixes global drinks with local drinks and liquors to create product offerings that cater to local markets. Diageo's Gordon Edge, a mix of gin and lemon, caters to the UK market, while Safari Luna, a mixed of fruit and liquor, caters to the Netherlands. Allied Domecq's Presidente brandy and cola mix caters to the Mexican market, while TG, a mix of Scotch and guanana, caters to the Brazilian market. Campari's Mixx, a mix of grapefruit and Campari, caters to the Italian and Swiss markets.

Localization is part of a broader and better known strategy of marginal product differentiation, which can be accomplished in two ways: by altering the physical characteristics of the product or by altering the ways the product is delivered to customers, allowing international businesses to expand their market penetration in local established markets and to exploit market niches: "There are always ways to differentiate, through both how to add value and how to deliver it. Value is created in commodity products through improving the consistency of the offering, making it more convenient or aggressively customizing it to the customer's operation. This value can be delivered either through the product itself or through service enhancement."[32]

Intel, for instance, differentiates its products by speed, media, and customization in developing "platforms" of multiple chips catering to four market segments: home computers, computers and servers, mobile gadgets and cellular phones, and network infrastructure devices.[33] Estee Lauder's product divisions differentiate their products for different market segments. Estee Lauder targets the working woman. Clinique targets women in their twenties, while Jane targets teenagers. Applied Materials differentiates the technical characteristics of its products and services to address customers' productivity, cost, and return-on-investment needs. Texas Instruments customizes its analog signal products for different market segments, such as wireless, automotive, hard-disk drives, and printers. The company also customizes its digital signal processing products for several markets, including digital cameras, digital audio players, and multimedia storage disk drives. In the early 2000s, GE added more that a dozen new capabilities expected to contribute close to 90 percent of the company's 2005 earnings.[34]

Marginal product differentiation and localization is not a new competitive strategy. In 1930s, automobile companies like GM differentiated their products by income, developing a broad line of automobile products catering to different market segments, for "every purpose and every purse": Cadillac for the upper class, Oldsmobile and Buick for the middle class, and Chevrolet for the lower class. In the 1960s and the 1970s, Japanese corporations expanded their presence in world markets by changing their attributes. Japanese automobile makers like Toyota and Honda, for instance, manage to gain substantial market share in the U.S. market by introducing smaller, more efficient and more maneuverable cars with front-wheel drive. Japanese radio receiver makers like Sony managed to capture most of the U.S. market by miniaturizing radio receivers, while plain paper copy makers made their headway in the U.S. market by introducing simple, liquid toner copiers.

Local differentiation can be accomplished both internally and externally. In the consumer electronics sector, Sony relies on its own resources and expertise to differentiate its products. For the period 1950–2001, Sony Corporation successfully developed twenty-seven innovative products, including the first tape recorder, transistor radio, VCR, "Triniton" color TV, digital audio tape (DAT), and digital video camcorder. Nokia has also relied on its own resources to churn out new products. "While many Asian rivals buy cheap off-the-shelf electronics, Nokia has the guts of its handsets custom-made to its own designs. Nokia also complicated its task by doubling its product portfolio in just over a year, developing camera-phones and handsets with full-alphabetical keyboards, rather than just churning out tens of millions of near-identical phones. Nokia now makes about 40 different models."[35] Korean conglomerates like Samsung Electronics produce internally almost every component going into their products. In the pharmaceuticals industry, Johnson and Johnson relies both on its own resources and on outside resources. The company's acquisition of McNeil Laboratories added a number of over-the-counter drugs popular in the U.S. market, including Tylenol. The acquisition of LifeScan, Inc., added glucose monitors, and the acquisition of

Neutrogena added a number of beauty aids, while the acquisition of DePuy added a number of orthopedic products. In the soft drink industry, Coca-Cola relies on its own resources for carbonated drinks, but on outside resources for non-carbonated drinks. For this purpose, the company has formed alliances and joint ventures with consumer staples companies like Nestle to provide non-carbonated drinks like iced coffee and iced tea. PepsiCo's acquisition of alternative drinks maker South Beach Beverage Co. and Quaker Oats, the owner of Gatorade, the leading sports drink, expanded the company's drink portfolio to competing products.

In the electronic banking industry, companies rely on alliances to differentiate their products. The strategic alliance among Spain's Banco Popular, IBM, and German financial service company Allianz is a fourth case in point. The three companies agreed to create an Internet portal and to launch a business-to-business (B2B) partnership. Allianz and Banco Popular invested one billion pesetas ($5.66 million) as seed capital for the portal. IBM provided the technology for the portal and the B2B project. In the food industry, JM Smuckers expanded its U.S. product portfolio by acquiring peanut butter product maker JIF. In the networking industry, Cisco Systems and Nortel Networks relied on a stream of mergers and acquisitions. In the 1990s, Cisco acquired about seventy companies, while Nortel Networks acquired ten companies, including IP network maker Bay Networks, Internet protocol services provider Shasta, and enterprise network maker Peripheronics.[36]

Successful bundle localization expands the revenues of semiglobal corporations in two ways. First, it promotes the exploitation of local market niches that have been neglected as too small and too expensive to be worth the effort. Hewlett Packard, for instance, has managed to expand its presence to the Indian digital photography market by replacing the electric battery charger with a solar battery charger and by leasing rather than selling its digital cameras to local professional photographers. Shampoo makers have also managed to expand their presence in India and other poor countries by packaging their products in small, affordable packages. Product differentiation allowed SanDisk to raise its revenues by 85 percent and to improve its profit margins. Second, successful localization lowers the elasticity of bundle offerings, and therefore raises the pricing power of semiglobal corporations. The more localized the bundle, the lower its price elasticity and the higher the pricing power of the provider. Conversely, the more globalized the bundle is, the higher its elasticity and the lower the pricing power of the

Figure 5.5   **Localization Intensity and Pricing Power**

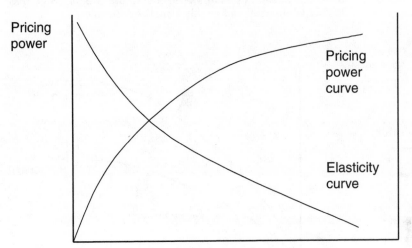

Pricing
power

Pricing
power
curve

Elasticity
curve

Degree of localization

Source: Adapted from Mourdoukoutas and Mourdoukoutas (2004), p. 528.

provider. Figure 5.5 shows the relationship between the degree of localization and the pricing power of a bundle. The degree of localization is measured by the value of the bundle attributed to local characteristics, whereas pricing power is the inverse of the bundle price elasticity.

In short, bundle localization is the raising of localization intensity of bundle offerings to achieve an above-average rate of return in local markets by expanding corporate revenues. However, bundle localization has its own constraints and limitations. First, it becomes an easy target of imitation. Marginal localization that modifies an existing product just to keep up with the competition without adding true value to it is not sustainable. Diageo's strategy of global and local product mixes does not require symmetrical commitments by local partners and has already been matched by Allied Domecq and Campari's mixed drinks. Second, consumers are not always willing to pay premium prices for added product features. Kraft's Ooey Gooey Warm 'N Chewy Chips Ahoy!, an extension of the company's Nabisco Chips Ahoy! product portfolio, is a case in point. Consumers found the $2.99 price too expensive and the product flopped, costing the company $5.5 million.[37] Third, by focusing on marginal product alterations, companies lose sight of emerging trends in their industries. Kraft's obsession with marginal differentiation of its

Figure 5.6 **Mass-Localization Leadership: Raising the Global Content of Highly Globalized and Highly Localized Bundles**

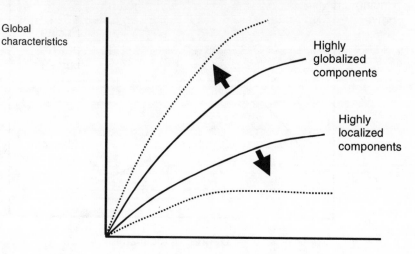

existing products, the Oreos and Oscar Mayer brands, for instance, contributing to the company's missing on the emerging trends in the supermarket industry. "The brands in Kraft's stable—including Jell-O, Oreos, Tang, Oscar Mayer, Maxwell House, Velveeta, Kraft Macaroni & Cheese, Lifesavers, Kool-Aid—are big sellers to be sure. But by endlessly embellishing them, Kraft has largely missed out on several important trends in supermarket food, including soy, cereal bars and organic ingredients, to name a few."[38]

Mass Localization Leadership

Mass localization leadership is the altering of both the global and the local value proposition: raising the global content of highly globalized bundles and the local content of highly localized bundles (see Figure 5.6). Citibank's expansion of its electronic payment system, for instance, allowed the company to cut the cost of its bundle offerings while expanding its presence into new markets. PepsiCo's expansion into alternative drinks allowed the company to both cut costs and tap into new markets. Cablevision's broadband package allowed the company to differentiate its offerings both in terms of cost and of local characteristics, reaching a larger market penetration. QUALCOMM's expansion into high-resolution/low-power-consumption display technologies allowed the company to expand its product portfolio while cutting the cost of each product at the same time.

Mass localization is part of a broader strategy, mass customization, which can be accomplished in three ways. First, it can be achieved through the Internet, intranets, and customer relationship management (CRM) software, which allow companies to frequently interact with customers and tailor their products to the individual needs of each customer. "Using integrated systems, designers of the production process are no longer limited to, say, setting up the computer driven machinery to create one identical window, telephone, or stereo system after another. Now the process can be designed so that it can change the product each time it creates one."[39] Procter and Gamble's web subsidiary Reflect.com allows its beauty product customers to "voice their specific beauty needs and desires with a precision that has never been available before," that is, to interact directly with beauty experts and research scientists, creating products that cater to their specific needs. General Motors' web business unit, eGM, allows the company to connect online with dealers, and to tailor its new car models to consumer needs. Merrill Lynch's web services allow the company to integrate product and market information and to design portfolios catered to individual customer needs. In the banking industry, Citibank leveraged its banking capabilities to expand to electronic payments, a market catering to business clients. Its CitiConnect payment processing system allows customers using electronic exchanges offered by application providers like Commerce One to complete transactions online. Zions Bancorp's offering of electronic document transferring, assign signatures, and process security allowed the company to expand its presence to the business client market.[40] The Internet allowed Ryder System, Inc., to coordinate picking, parking, and shipping, attracting new customers like Northrop Grumman in the defense industry.[41]

Second, mass customization can be accomplished through computer aided design (CAD) and flexible manufacturing (FM). Software from Design Power Corporation, for instance, allows automobile makers to custom design automobiles, while flexible manufacturing allows custom manufacturing them. Third, mass customization can be achieved through strategic alliances that allow companies to expand both the scale and the scope of their operations. In 2002, for instance, two major competitors in wireless communications, Cingular Wireless (a joint venture between BellSouth and SBC Communications, Inc.) and AT&T Wireless, entered an agreement to build out a GSM/GPRS/Enhanced Data Rates for Global Evolution (EDGE) network along America's highways for the purpose of reducing incollect roaming expenses paid to other carriers when customers travel from one state to another. This joint venture follows an agreement between the two companies to swap licenses and operations in a number of states. Specifically, Cingular transferred to AT&T Wireless its license and operations in Alabama, Hawaii, Idaho, Oklahoma, Mississippi, and Washington. At the same time, Cingular received AT&T's licenses in Alabama, Arkansas, Georgia, Kentucky, Louisiana, Mississippi, Tennessee, and Texas. Cingular has also entered agreements with other competitors, like VoiceStream Wireless (now T-Mobil), to exchange spectrum. Localization through alliances is of particular importance in Asia. Local partners have a better knowledge of the peculiarities and specificity of their own markets.

In short, to compete efficiently and effectively in a semiglobal economy, international businesses are becoming more like local service providers by executing two distinct strategies: a global cost leadership strategy and a local product differentiation strategy. To achieve global cost leadership, manufacturers must cooperate with their competitors to reach economies of scale and reduce costs. To achieve local product differentiation, manufacturers must compete with their global partners by cooperating with local service providers to differentiate their offerings through the bundling of global product and service characteristics with local product and service characteristics to create unique product packages for each local market, especially in highly the saturated markets of developed countries. Each of the three strategies has its own limitations, which makes it unsustainable in the long run. This means that managerial strategies are a necessary but not a sufficient source of sustainable competitive advantages, and must be supplemented by entrepreneurial strategies.

Entrepreneurial Strategies

Entrepreneurship, the discovery and exploitation of new business opportunities, is the "other function" of every business enterprise, and the ultimate source of competitive advantage, especially in the highly globalized segment of the semiglobal economy. In contrast to other functions of a business enterprise, entrepreneurship cannot be performed simply by hiring entrepreneurs, but must be nurtured within two sets of institutions that release the individual and collective ingenuity and creativity of corporations. First are institutions that lower internal corporate boundaries, allowing for efficient communication among the members of the organization, such as re-engineering, Quality Circles (QC), and Total Quality Management (TQM), and align the interests of labor and management with those of stockholders, such as employee stock ownership plans (ESOP) and stock options, to be further discussed in Chapters 7 and 8. Second are institutions that lower external corporate boundaries, corporate spin-offs, strategic acquisitions, corporate venturing, and strategic alliances.

Corporate Spin-offs

Corporate spin-offs are detachments of corporate divisions that result in distinct and separate organizations. Spin-offs nurture entrepreneurship in a number of different ways. First, they allow large corporations, often diverse conglomerates, to reduce their size and to narrow their focus on their core business. Ford's spin-off of its consumer finance unit, for instance, reduced the company's size and narrowed its product portfolio to its core business, automobile design and manufacturing. 3Com's spin-off of its Palm Computing division narrowed the company's focus on networking, where the company could compete more efficiently and effectively against Cisco Systems and Nortel Networks. Lucent Technologies' spin-off its PBX Systimax Structure and cabling and data business accelerated the company's transition from a traditional equipment maker to an Internet equipment maker. Alcatel's spinning-off its magazines and vineyards divisions narrowed the company's focus on its high-technology products.

Second, spin-offs are an efficient and effective vehicle for transferring resources from declining to expanding businesses. GE's flurry of acquisitions and spin-offs and product swaps, for instance, allowed the company to diversify its operations into service industries. Over Jack Welch's twenty-year tenure, GE spun-off 113 divisions.

Third, spin-offs allow large companies to exploit disruptive innovations, that is, innovations that undermine core business, and to overcome the innovator's dilemma. Quantum's spin-off of the Plus Development division is a case in point. In 1984, as competitive pressure on Quantum's 5.25-inch drives mounted, the company spun-off an engineering group working on a thin 3.5-inch drive for the IBM XT- and AT-class desk computers. Established as an 80-percent-owned subsidiary under the name Plus Development Corporation and housed in its own separate affiliates, the spin-off quickly completed and launched the new product. By 1987, as the 3.5-inch drives had almost replaced the 5.25 inch drives, Quantum acquired the remaining 20 percent.[42]

Fourth, corporate spin-offs allow corporations to expand their market presence in new industries. Fujitsu's spin-off of its Internet business search engine in the later part of 2000, under the name Accela Technology Corporation, enlisted 300 clients, including its long-time competitor NEC. Bayer's spin-off of its film division, AGFA, allowed the company to better market its products and work together with Bayer's traditional competitor, Henkel.[43]

In short, corporate spin-offs allow large, established corporations to nurture entrepreneurship beyond their corporate boundaries in four different ways: by reducing corporate size, narrowing corporate focus, restructuring product portfolio from declining to expanding industries, and helping overcome the innovator's dilemma. However, spin-offs are subject to a number of limitations. First, spin-offs often outgrow the parent company, so it becomes increasingly difficult for the parent company to monitor their performance. Second, spin-offs are at the whim of equity markets, their numbers expanding and contracting along with equity values. Third, spin-offs undermine the parent's profitability. Fourth, what appear to be separate businesses may not always end being that way. Media companies, for instance, thought that the Internet was a separate business, when in fact it was a different form of content distribution.

Strategic Acquisitions

Strategic acquisitions are the acquisitions of smaller corporations, often start-ups, by larger corporations, paid for by cash or equity. Such acquisitions nurture entrepreneurship in a number of ways. First, strategic acquisitions allow large corporations to accelerate their entry to emerging markets that often undermine their core business, that is, to overcome the "innovator's dilemma." Cisco Systems' strategic acquisitions allowed the company to expand its portfolio of products, achieving economies of scale and scope at the same time. Novellus Systems' acquisition of GaSonics International Corporation allowed it to expand its presence to the wafer surface preparation business, while the acquisition of German lapping and polishing equipment maker Peter Wolters allowed the company to expand beyond semiconductor manufacturing. Coca-Cola's acquisition of Russian juice-maker Multon allowed the company to expand its presence into the country's emerging market for soft drinks. Telefonica's acquisition of a 51 percent stake in Cesky Telecom gave the Spanish telecommunications company access to the Czech Republic market.

Second, strategic acquisitions allow large corporations to leverage their technological capabilities to reach a larger market. Tyco International's acquisition of Siemens Electromechanical's components unit, for instance, a perfect fit for Tyco Electronics, allowed the company to leverage its customer base and expand its earnings. Symbol Technologies' acquisition of Telxon Corporation allowed the company to expand its presence into the handheld computer market. Adobe Systems' acquisition of Macromedia, Inc., allowed the company to distribute its software to a broad range of PCs, cell phones, and handheld devices.[44] Third, strategic acquisitions allow large corporations to quickly acquire human resource talent, especially in periods of a severe shortage of highly skilled labor. Pfizer's acquisition of Meridica allowed the company to expand its presence in the pharmacology technologies sector, while its acquisition of the La Jolla research center in California allowed the company to expand its research capabilities in human-centered sciences. QUALCOMM's acquisition of semiconductor design company Spike Technologies, with a design center in Bangalore, India, allowed the company to expand its engineering design base.

In short, strategic acquisitions allow large corporations to expand capacity, accelerate entry to emerging markets, leverage technological capabilities to reach a larger market, and acquire human talent, but they have their own limitations: new acquisitions become increasingly difficult to integrate into the company's organization, they dilute stockholder value, and they are at the whim of market forces. First, as the number of acquisitions grows, it becomes increasingly difficult to integrate the newly acquired firms into the parent's organization and align them to its vision. Second, as many acquisitions are paid with the issuing of new company stock, they dilute stockholders' equity. And third, they are at the whim of markets. They work well in a bull market, but they come to a halt in a down market. Lucent's decision to shut down Israeli-based Chromatis Network, a unit that Lucent had purchased for $4.5 billion two years earlier in a stock swap, is a case in point. The company's products failed to stand up to Lucent's expectations, that is, to win a sufficient number of new customers.

Corporate Venturing

Corporate venturing, the forging of close relations between large corporations and start-ups, takes three forms: (1) the acquisition of equity stakes, as is often the case in the pharmaceutical industry, where large, established corporations invest in biotechnology start-ups in exchange for rights to new drugs; (2) the establishment of a separate venture capital fund or an incubator; and (3) the formation of an alliance with a venture capital firm.

Corporate venturing nurtures entrepreneurship in a number of different ways. First, it allows large companies to diversify to new markets. Exxon's investments in start-ups have allowed the company to diversify its business away from petroleum products. Second, it allows large companies to accelerate the development of new business or the investment in emerging markets. Wal-Mart, for instance, has used a corporate venture partnership to accelerate the development of its Internet business, Walmart.com. Nokia's venture investing has allowed the company to diversify into the emerging Internet communications, home communications, and mobile display appliances markets. The acquisition of a 25 percent stake by the corporate venturing branch of the Greek ice cream company Delta in start-up specialty ice cream maker and retailer Dodoni allowed Delta to expand its product portfolio and get access to Dodoni's retail outlets. Third, corporate venturing is a vehicle of promoting technology to start-ups. Cisco and Intel, for instance, acquired equity stakes in start-ups that are their customers.

In short, corporate venturing takes three forms, a direct equity stake, a separate venture capital fund, and an alliance with a venture capital firm. Corporate venturing allows established companies to diversify their operations, acquire new technologies, and accelerate entry to new markets.

Strategic Alliances

Strategic alliances are entrepreneurial webs or networks of traditional corporations with their suppliers, customers, competitors, and the glo-

Table 5.2

Selected Co-competition Agreements

Companies	Purpose of cooperation
SanDisk-Matsushita-Toshiba	Secure digital cards
Toyota-GM	Environmental technology
Mazda-Ford	Fuel-cell technology
Honda-Isuzu-GM-Renault	Diesel engine
Renault-Nissan	Diesel engine
Toyota-BMW	Diesel engine
Ford-GM	Six-speed transmission

bal and local community. In some cases, alliance networks extend even among former competitors, such as SanDisk with Matsushita and Toshiba, Toyota with GM, and Mazda with Ford (see Table 5.2). SanDisk Corporation, for instance, has teamed up with competitors Matsushita and Toshiba to form the Secure Digital Association, or SD Association, for the joint development and promotion of a secure digital card. The three companies will separately market and sell flash memory products developed by their joint venture FlashVision. SanDisk has also entered into cross-licensing agreements with several of its competitors including Intel, Matsushita Electric, Samsung, Sharp, and Sony. Toyota Motor Company has entered an alliance with GM to develop environmentally safe technologies, while Mazda and Ford have entered an alliance to develop fuel-cell technologies.

Strategic alliances nurture entrepreneurship in large corporations in a number of different ways. First, they allow management to outsource its non-core operations and to better manage inventories, speeding product development at the same time. Cisco's strategic alliances with contract equipment manufacturers allowed the company to work closely with customers for the design and development of new products, passing on manufacturing to contract manufacturers. The strategic alliance between Lucent Technologies and electronic-component distributor Arrow Electronics provided Lucent Technologies with a number of services: component programming, inventory management, flat panel display, and connector and cable assembly system integration.

Second, strategic alliances allow the semiglobal corporation to enter new markets. American and European companies form alliances to enter the Japanese market while Japanese and U.S. companies form alliances to enter the European markets. A partnership between American-based electronic component distributor Arrow Electronics and Japan-based electronic component and chain supply service provider Marubun, for instance, allows the two companies to better serve Japanese companies that have established facilities in North America. The strategic alliance between Xillinx and IBM allowed the two companies to combine several key technologies, such as PowerPC processors, which allowed the two companies to expand their presence in the communications, storage, and consumer applications markets. The strategic alliance between the Greek ice cream company Delta with two multinational companies, Danone and Arla Foods, allowed the company to expand into the butter and cheese market, while the strategic alliance between Delta and Chipita Eastern Europe allowed Delta to expand its presence in Eastern Europe.

Third, strategic alliances allow large corporations to collaborate in the development of complex products that require extensive technical knowledge scattered both inside and outside corporate boundaries, in marketing departments, distribution centers, private and public databases, and private and public research departments.

> In an industry as complex as chipmaking, collaboration is critical. Working closely with customers, we're creating the vital chipmaking process that will enable tomorrow's faster, more powerful electronic products. Our unique Mayday Technology Center is focused on this teamwork philosophy. Set up to stimulate a fab environment, it's a place where customers come to test and refine advanced process technologies—well before these systems arrive at the fab. The upshot? Getting new chips to the market faster![45]

> Collaboration enables firms specializing in fundamentally different technologies to combine this expertise to create totally new products and processes. The partners' considerable costs and risks of developing new technologies can also be shared. Collaboration is a non-binding way to test the possibilities of diversifying into a new field, and may enable the realization of other strategic aims, including entry into foreign markets, and surmounting regulatory and licensing barriers. Alliances may also be a precursor to the establishment of industry-wide standards.[46]

Automobile companies, for instance, form technical alliances with several parts and components suppliers to design, develop, and manufacture new automobiles.[47] Computer and telecommunications companies form alliances to develop new products such as cellular phones and network equipment, and Internet retailers form alliances with distributors and marketers. The alliance between Lockheed Management Data & Systems and several other high technology companies is a case in point. Specifically, to develop a mapping system prototype, Lockheed Management & Data Systems, the business unit of Lockheed Martin Corporation, formed an alliance with several companies—including Marion Composites, GTE Government Systems Corporations, Codar Technology, MTI Technology Corporation, CalComp Technology, and Tangent Imaging Systems—that will develop parts of the product.[48] The alliance between Xilinx Corporation and Conexant Corporation allowed the Xilinx product to link together multiple high-speed systems, dramatically improving integration and system performance. An alliance between IBM and Storage Tek allowed the two companies to develop and market high-end devices. The alliance between Seven Up and Dr. Pepper allowed the two companies to promote their brand product portfolio efficiently and effectively. The alliance between AT&T and Hewlett-Packard allowed the two companies to develop a communication network for the home shopping market. Texas Instruments has teamed up with Samsung Electronics, LG Electronics, and Toshiba for the development of complex products, such as DLP (digital light processing) products used in the development of high-definition TVs. Sun Microsystems' alliance with Advanced Micro Devices allowed the company to offer two products, one for the upper-end market and another for the low-end market.

Fourth, strategic alliances allow companies to achieve the critical mass and market power to control the value chain, as has been the case with telecom providers like Vodafone.

> For years, service operators and phone manufacturers coexisted peacefully, bonded by a mutual dependency. Companies such as Vodafone didn't want to miss out on hot new phones and phone makers relied on service providers' huge orders. But as the cellphone market slowed, their goals diverged. Now Vodafone wants to control the look and feel of a cellphone rather than leave those choices to phone makers. Its profit growth is likely to come from selling add-on services and the most effective way to market them is to embed Vodafone's software inside customer's phones.[49]

Fifth, strategic alliances with competitors and the community are of particular importance for entering and competing in highly competitive markets like the Japanese market, and in emerging markets where government continues to hold a good grip over the economy, like the Chinese market. Exxon's partnership with Fujian Petrochemical allowed the company to expand its presence in China. By joining forces with trade associations and chambers of commerce, and government agencies to open and exploit overseas markets, "trade associations lobbied politicians vigorously for business interests. A few, most notably the National Association of Manufacturers, worked with officials of the federal government to expand markets for American products overseas."[50]

To sum up, the semiglobal corporation can compete with two sets of strategies, managerial strategies and entrepreneurial strategies. Managerial strategies are classified in three categories: cost leadership strategies, which involve efficient use of labor, capital, state-of-the art logistics, and outsourcing; local differentiation leadership strategies; and mass localization leadership strategies. Entrepreneurial strategies include corporate spin-offs, strategic acquisitions, corporate venturing, and strategic alliances. Entrepreneurial strategies allow companies to integrate market and technical information for the discovery and exploitation of new business opportunities, partnering with customers and employees, and partnering with suppliers, competitors, and the community. In contrast to routine managerial strategies, entrepreneurial strategies are based on collaborations and strategic alliances among companies that are hard to imitate, and, therefore, are sustainable. The difficulty in imitating these bundles is not so much in the technological sophistication of the bundle, but in the underlying complex relationships that develop and deliver it. Relationships create social capital, which unlike financial capital cannot be borrowed in international markets. As Victor Fung, chairman of Li & Fung, puts it, "Someone might steal our database, but when they call up a supplier, they do not have the long relationship with the supplier that Li & Fung has. It makes a difference to suppliers when they know that you are dedicated to the business, that you've been honoring your commitments for 90 years."[51] Collaboration requires efficient and effective coordination, communication, and motivation structures.

Notes

1. Chandler (1990), p. 17.
2. *2001 Annual Report*, Milpitas, CA, p. 9.
3. *2003 Annual Report*, Intel Corporation, Santa Clara, CA, p. 11.
4. Hawkins and Lublin (2005).
5. This framework was adapted from Michael Porter's generic strategy framework.
6. Tejada and McWilliams (2003).
7. Cross (2001).
8. Intel, *2003 Annual Report*, Santa Clara, CA, p. 8.
9. Corning, *2004 Annual Report* and 2005 proxy statement, p. 60.
10. Einborn and Rocks (2004), p. 56.
11. QUALCOMM, *2004 Annual Report*, San Diego, CA, p. 4.
12. Micklethwait and Wooldridge (2003), p. 65.
13. Foust (2005), p. 70.
14. Caulfield (2003), p. 54.
15. Pusateri (1984), p. 194.
16. Jayne and Baker (2002), p. 22.
17. Welch and Welch (2005), p. 218.
18. Liker (2004), p. 105.
19. Kaihla (2004), p. 52.
20. Keenan (2001).
21. McDonald (2004).
22. Kelleher (2004), p. 48.
23. Hays (2004), p. BU9.
24. Toyota, *1998 Annual Report*, Toyota City, Japan, 1999, p. 8.
25. Juniper Networks, *2002 Annual Report*, Sunnyvale, CA.
26. Broadcom Corporation, *2002 Annual Report*, Irvine, CA, 2003, p. 12.
27. PMC-Sierra, Inc., *2002 Annual Report*, Santa Clara CA, 2003, p. 7.
28. Texas Instruments, *2003 Annual Report*, Dallas, TX, p. 4.
29. Reported in Hamel and Schonfeld (2003), p. 64.
30. Mazur (2004).
31. Ante (2005), p. 72.
32. Hill, McGrath, and Dayal (1998), p. 5.
33. Clark (2003), pp. A1, A2.
34. GE, *2004 Annual Report*, p. 4.
35. Pringle (2003), p. A7.
36. Heinzl (2004), p. 2.
37. Ellison (2003), p. B1.
38. Ibid., pp. B1, B6.
39. *The Interactive Market: B to B Strategies for Delivering Just-in-Time, Mass-Customized Products*, New York: McGraw-Hill, 2001, p. 108.
40. Coleman (2004), p. A7.
41. Keenan and Mullaney (2001), p. 27.
42. For a detailed discussion, see Christensen and Raynor (2003) pp. 104–5.
43. Ewing (1999).
44. Berman and Bank (2005), p. A3.

45. Applied Materials, *2003 Annual Report*, Santa Clara, CA, Feb. 2004.

46. Davis (1997), p. 391.

47. The alliance between Mazda and Ford and between GM and Isuzu are two cases in point.

48. Lockheed Martin Corporation Press Release, June 25, 1997.

49. Pringle (2004), p. A1.

50. Blackford and Kerr (1986), p. 186.

51. Magretta (2002), p. 1.

6

Coordination

I declared war on geographic fiefdoms. I decided we would organize the
company around global industry teams.[1]

Honda Motor Company coordinates its activities in two ways: by geographic region, and by business function and product group. Honda's
geographic organization consists of the headquarters and six major regional subsidiaries that handle its operations in Japan; North America;
Latin America; Europe, the Middle East, the Near East, and Africa; China;
and Asia (other than Japan and China) and Oceania. The headquarters
are run by the executive council and the president and CEO, while the
subsidiaries are run by executive regional committees and regional officers. Honda's business and product organization consists of the headquarters and several divisions: corporate planning, quality innovation, R&D,
engineering, IT, purchasing, business support, business management, mo-
torcycles, automobiles, power products, and parts (see Figure 6.1).

Honda's dual coordination structure typifies a hybrid model of international business organization, the semiglobal corporation, which organizes its operations according to the global-local content of its bundle
offerings. "Honda's organization reflects its fundamental corporate phi-
losophies. Each regional operation carries out its businesses so as to
quickly and efficiently respond to customers needs around the world,
while each business operation makes arrangements for each product,
establishing a system of high effectiveness and efficiency."[2] Highly localized offerings are placed under a localized or multinational unit, a
hierarchical organization that consists of the parent corporation and a
collection of subsidiaries, normally one for each major regional or national market managed by regional executive councils. The parent company drafts the unit vision and makes most decisions regarding marketing
and manufacturing, alliances with third parties, entry to new markets,
and so on. Parent and subsidiaries are engaged in extensive intra-firm
trade, where subsidiaries are buying final products and consulting services from the parent, and selling raw materials for intermediary products. Highly globalized offerings are placed under a global unit, a

Figure 6.1 **Honda: A Typical Semiglobal Corporation**

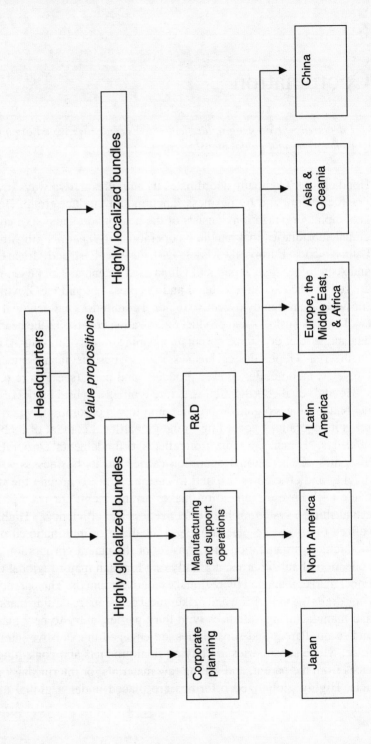

non-hierarchical network-like organization consisting of the support office and several independent entities. The support office manages the common affairs of the network, the drafting of the unit vision, the arranging of financing, and the coordination of research and development projects. The network units manage their own affairs, production schedules, hiring of personnel, local marketing and distribution, taxation, and local community relations.

The multinational and the global units of the semiglobal corporation are not new international business organizations. Multinational organizations can be traced back to the conventional model of the multinational organization adopted by most international businesses in the first three decades of the twentieth century in response to increasing fragmentation of international markets brought about by the proliferation of trade barriers, government regulations, and diverse product standards and taxation systems that made international investing a more economic and more rational alternative to exporting. Global organizations can be traced to the conventional model of the global corporation adopted by most international businesses in the last quarter of the twentieth century in response to the growing integration and interdependence of world markets.

This chapter, a detailed discussion of the dual coordination structure of the semiglobal corporation, is in two sections. The first section discusses the multinational unit, and the second section discusses the global unit.

The Multinational Unit: Headquarters Versus Subsidiaries

The multinational unit of the semiglobal corporation is a geographically based hierarchical organization that treats the world economy as a collection of separate markets. The multinational unit consists of the parent company or headquarters at the top of the hierarchy, normally located in a developed country, and several wholly or majority-owned subsidiaries at the bottom of the hierarchy, usually one for each major regional market (see Figure 6.2). Each region has its own manufacturing, marketing, and accounting unit. Honda's multinational unit, for instance, consists of the Tokyo headquarters and six regional divisions, one for each major world region. Royal Vopak's multinational organization consists of the Rotterdam, Netherlands, headquarters and five major subsidiaries, one for Asia, one for Latin America, one each for North

Figure 6.2 **The Coordination Structure of the Multinational Unit: Headquarters Versus Subsidiaries**

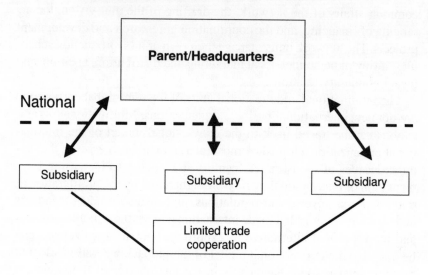

America, one each for Europe and Africa, and one for the Middle East. E.ON Corporation's multinational organization consists of separate subsidiaries for fragmented markets, like that of China. Parent subsidiary organizations can be best understood as a pyramid system, a principal-agent relationship, whereby the parent corporation is the "principal," occupying the top of the pyramid (headquarters), and the subsidiaries are the "agents," occupying the bottom of the pyramid.[3] Decision-making authority within this organization can be allocated in two ways: through corporate centralization, which allocates most of the decision-making authority to the top of the hierarchy, the headquarters; or through corporate decentralization, which allocates most of the decision-making authority to the bottom of the hierarchy, the subsidiaries.[4] Corporate centralization is associated with formal relationships, control mechanisms, and standardized corporate procedures that define and divide the tasks to be performed by each member of the organization. Here, the chain-of-command decisions are made and transmitted throughout the hierarchy. Corporate decentralization is associated with informal relationships, control mechanisms, and standardized corporate procedures that define and divide the tasks to be performed by subsidiaries.

Corporate centralization and decentralization have their own advantages and disadvantages. One of the advantages is the firm grip and control of the entire organization by the headquarters, the internalization and protection of proprietary technology and corporate secrets, and the close monitoring of financial flows. Another advantage of corporate centralization is the economies of scale arising from a large organization. A third advantage is the better integration of the organization's activities and a unified corporate strategy. One of the disadvantages of corporate centralization is bureaucracy and the lack of flexibility in dealing with changing market conditions and new technologies. Therefore, centralization is the most appropriate system in coordinating a small number of subsidiaries located close to headquarters in a stable market environment. One of the advantages of corporate decentralization is that it provides the organization the much needed flexibility to deal with rapidly changing market conditions, but it is often chaotic and inadequate for protecting proprietary technology and corporate secrets and monitoring financial flows. Therefore, decentralization is the most appropriate system for coordinating a large number of subsidiaries in unstable market environments.

The parent-subsidiary organization is not a new model of international business organization. The first multinational organizations can be traced to the rise of the fourteenth- and fifteenth-century European market at the end of Medieval Age, and the rise of the Medici Bank (Italy), and the Fugger and the Hochstetter families (Germany), which expanded their presence throughout Europe; the proliferation of commendas, partnerships between financiers and merchants for the exploitation of overseas markets; and the development of the legal foundation for the creation of "artificial persons." Multinational business organizations can also be traced to the seventeenth- and eighteenth-century multinational economy and the setting up of colonial trade outposts as well as the rise of the English East India Co. (1600), the Dutch East India Co. (1602), the Hudson Bay Co. (1670), the Levant Co., and the Company of Adventures of London, and its Spanish, Russian, and Italian "analogues."

> The true ancestors of the modern multinational companies, however, are not the churches, colleges and universities, guilds, or other Roman, medieval, or post-medieval examples of the capacity of the law to create

"artificial persons," but the great trade companies—the East India Company, the Hudson Bay Company, La Compagnie des Indes, The Company of Adventures of London Trading into Africa, and their Spanish, Russian, Italian, and German analogues.[5]

Today's multinational organizations can be traced to the multinational market of the first three decades of the twentieth century created by the proliferation of nation-states, trade barriers, government regulations, and diverse product standards and taxation systems that made overseas direct investments a more economic and more rational alternative to exports.[6]

> The birth of the new countries has meant an increasing variety of tariffs, company laws and taxation, which means that it is administratively easier and economically more rational for companies to operate within the areas of their markets. Also, with the growing sophistication of products and the development of consumer tastes, has come the need for local packaging and labeling services and the provision of stocks and spare parts.[7]

> The modern theory of FDI suggests that the MNE [multinational enterprise] develops in response to imperfections in the goods or factor markets. Then the country specific advantage of a nation—which leads to trade—is replaced by a firm specific advantage internal to an MNE—which leads to FDI.[8]

European trade barriers, for instance, made manufacturing in Europe more attractive for American machinery manufacturers than exporting from home. Government regulations, especially the growing government control of local chemical and basic materials industries of developing countries, made local manufacturing almost mandatory for American and European chemical and basic materials industries. The proliferation of diverse product standards made it more efficient and effective for American and European consumer companies to manufacture products locally rather than import them from home, creating a geographically dispersed organization.

> What has been characterized as the second industrial revolution occurred in the United States in the late 19th century with the birth of the national corporation. This led to the development of geographically dispersed corporations, large-scale financing and big vertically-integrated organizations. By the early 20th century American firms were making direct

investments abroad. Farm equipment, printing presses, sewing machines, and revolvers, were being manufactured in England by American firms. European firms followed suit and began to manufacture their products in non-colonial areas of the world. The era of multinational operations had now begun.[9]

Direct investments by all firms all over the world rose from $15 billion in 1915 to $26 billion by 1940 to $66 billion by 1960 and to $5.98 trillion by 2000. U.S. foreign direct investment increased from $7 billion in 1914 to $17 billion by 1929 to $32 billion by 1960.[10] Over the same period, portfolio investments increased from just below $1 billion to $7.2 billion.[11] The number of product lines of U.S. subsidiaries manufactured overseas increased from 294 in 1955 to 674 in 1965, and 1,633 in 1975, while the number of product lines of European subsidiaries manufactured overseas increased from 120, to 374, and to 803 respectively.[12]

In most cases, direct investment followed the parent-subsidiary model whereby parents set up overseas subsidiaries, normally one for each major regional or national market. In 1911, Standard Oil had subsidiaries in Canada, Central America, South America, and Europe. In the 1920s, Siemens had subsidiaries in the United States, Canada, China, Japan, and Australia, as well as in every European country and almost every Latin American country. In the 1930s, GM had subsidiaries in Germany, the UK, Denmark, Brazil, Egypt, South Africa, Japan, and Australia, and by the early 1950s it had set up factories in Spain, Ireland, and Brazil. In 1939, U.S. banks had forty-seven subsidiaries in Latin America, sixteen in Europe, and eighteen in Asia.[13] In the 1960s, Clark Equipment operated four regional subsidiaries: Clark Europe, Clark Argentina, Clark Brazil, and Clark Australia. First National City Bank also set up four regional subsidiaries: Asia-Pacific, Western Hemisphere, Europe-Africa-Middle East, and the United States. IBM World Trade Corporation (IBMWTC) had regional offices in Europe, Canada, South America, and the Caribbean. The number of parent corporations soared from 3,077 in 1914 to 39,463 by 1994 and 63,459 by 2000, while the number of subsidiaries reached 689,520 by 2000.[14]

Decision-making authority in these early multinational organizations was highly centralized, as was the case with the predecessor of the multinational corporation, the late-nineteenth-century multidivisional-departmentalized corporation. Geographic regions and countries were placed under the international division, side by side with domestic divisions, with the responsibility for coordinating international sales and establishing and operating overseas subsidiaries.

> U.S. enterprises commonly accompanied developments of this sort with the creation at headquarters of an international division, more or less equal in status with other divisions of the enterprise. The international division was generally charged with establishing and operating the overseas producing subsidiaries of the enterprise and keeping an eye on exports to foreign markets. The usual assumption was that foreign business, wherever it took place, had some common elements, thereby justifying its own corps of specialists.[15]

Subsidiaries resembled the parent company, functioning as "implementers" rather than "contributors"; they just produced or sold the parent's products. The international division ran subsidiaries directly through "executive committees." Decision-making authority was transmitted from the company president to the international division director (normally a VP), and on to the managing director and to subsidiary directors (line officers), as was the case with domestic divisions.

> The organization charts of international firms are deceptively similar to those of one-country companies. They all follow a remarkably standardized pattern of line and staff organization. In this pattern, the orders and power are, of course, transmitted through the line officers, while staff officers may advise at various levels. Organizational authority descends directly from the president to the sales organization and the plant management, or, in the international firm, to executives in Australia or Venezuela.[16]

Corporate centralization was exemplified in the late-nineteenth- and twentieth-century DuPont Corporation, organized as a Delaware holding company of two subsidiaries, E.I. du Pont Nemours Company of New Jersey, in control of powder and dynamite operations, and E.I. du Pont de Nemours of Delaware, in control of smokeless powder operations. The company was divided into three divisions: manufacturing, sales, and marketing. Each division in turn included two separate departments. The manufacturing division included three departments: smokeless powder, black powder, and dynamite. Marketing and sales were also organized and controlled by committees. Every activity from manufacturing, to product design, engineering, maintenance, and marketing, was placed under the control of the Wilmington headquarters.

Before its reorganization in 1935, Westinghouse Electric Corporation had a similar coordination structure, with most of the decision-making authority concentrated at the top, the "headquarters group." "Before the reorganization, all major decision making—and much that was minor—as well as all basic financial and cost knowledge were concentrated in a small group of top executives. Most important of this 'headquarters group' were the chairman of the board, who was also the chief executive; the president, or second in command; and four vice presidents, in charge of manufacturing, engineering, and finance."[17]

Corporate centralization was reinforced by the vertical integration of the value chain; almost every value chain activity, from product design to manufacturing and marketing, was performed in-house. Unilever, for instance, owned tea plantations in Kenya, Tanzania, and India, and palm oil plantations in Congo and Ghana, and distribution networks. Carnegie Steel performed almost the entire steel-making process in-house, from iron ore and coal mining, to pig iron smelting, to transportation and retail sales. Coal producer Frick Coke Company acquired a fleet of Great Lakes ore ships and developed its own railroad system to transport its raw materials and products. Meatpacking leader Swift owned refrigeration warehouses and retail outlets, Standard Oil owned its own oil fields, transportation, and distribution lines, and retailing outlets, and United Fruit had its own wholesale distribution system throughout the United States, which included refrigeration and cooling systems. American Tobacco Company had its own warehouses, and building and curing facilities. Clark Equipment Company owned factories that churned out material and components to be used in the production of its trucks and construction machinery, and IBM performed most value chain activities in-house, from R&D to manufacturing, and even distribution and retailing.

> Historically, during its Closed Innovation period, IBM deployed all its technologies exclusively within its own systems and services. If you wished to buy a chip from IBM, you could only buy the chip inside an IBM component. That IBM component, in turn, was sold exclusively as part of an IBM subsystem, which was only available as part of an IBM system. The business model deployed all of IBM's innovations through IBM's own systems, which were sold only through IBM's own distribution, and serviced, supported, and financed by IBM—exclusively.[18]

Vertical integration extended into two directions—upstream in the value chain toward the supply and the transportation of materials and components, and downstream in the value chain toward the distribution, transportation, and retailing of final products—and was often preceded by horizontal mergers and acquisitions, resulting in large, multifunctional corporations.

> Corporations which employed mass-production techniques soon found it necessary to extend their operations beyond the single function of production by a forward integration toward the purchaser of the firm's goods or a backward integration toward the basic materials which would eventually make up the finished product. In some instances, vertical integration was preceded by horizontal combination. Two or more firms which produced similar products joined into one new and larger organization. Through this process of extension, those industries which formed the core of national economy emerged into the modern multifunction business enterprises.[19]

Vertical integration has a number of advantages and disadvantages. One advantage is the "smooth" operation of the organization, that is, the flow of resources across divisions and the separation of ownership from management. "Such hierarchies appeared to be essential to the smooth working of corporations, as a way to exploit scale economies and facilitate the flow of materials in production and marketing, as a means of transferring resources among divisions when a firm operated as an internal capital market, and as a device to formalize the separation of ownership and control."[20]

Another advantage of vertical integration is economies of scale associated with a large production size, and the economies of scope associated with a broad product portfolio offered within the same organization, both translating to lower costs. As mentioned in Chapter 5, Swift's expansion to meat distribution, for instance, allowed the company to set its prices seventy-five cents per hundredweight below the competition.[21] Also as mentioned in Chapter 5, Ford's expansion into the production of components brought mass production and mass distribution "under the roof" of a single organization to achieve economies of scale in almost every value chain activity from purchasing to advertising.[22]

A third advantage of hierarchical organizations was the creation of barriers to entry by challengers. The more integrated the value chain, the larger the investment required to enter the industry. A fourth advantage of vertical integration was the close guarding of company secrets, especially R&D, the source of new products. "Companies that compete with proprietary, interdependent architectures *must* be integrated: They must control the design and manufacture of *every* critical component of the system in order to make *any* peace of the system."[23] Companies must rely on their own divisions to make products rather than on outside suppliers.

> The logic underlying this approach to innovation was one of closed, centralized, internal R&D. At its root, the logic implies a need for deep vertical integration. In other words, in order to do anything, one must do everything internally, from tools to materials, to product design and manufacturing, to sales, service, and support. Outside the fortified central R&D castles, the knowledge landscape was assumed to be rather barren. Consequently, the firm should rely on itself—and not feeble outside suppliers—for its critical technologies.[24]

These advantages of the MNC must be weighted against a number of disadvantages. One of the disadvantages of vertical integration is the overlapping of activities. Hierarchies create activity overlaps and inefficiencies. Ford's car design is a case in point. The company's design function is allocated to several groups that work separately and independently from each other, which has created "internal fiefs" and expensive vehicle design overlaps. "Ford's culture has shown considerable resistance to change despite the company's deepening crisis. It has tried and failed more than once in the past decade to regain the knack for low-cost, high-quality engineering and manufacturing that propelled founder Henry Ford from garage mechanic to billionaire a century ago."[25] Another disadvantage is corporate bureaucracy and organizational inertia, which lead to market detachment and the galvanization of customer needs around low-cost standardized products. A third disadvantage, as discussed in Chapter 5, is corporate complacency, the bias toward thinking that what is the best product for customers today will be the best product tomorrow.

In short, in their early days, multinational corporations were highly centralized hierarchical organizations, a microcosm of the central planning model installed in the Soviet Union at the end of the second decade of the twentieth century. Most of the decision-making authority was allocated at the top, to the company president and the vice president of the international division and its functional staff, and transmitted to regional and national subsidiaries. Multinational corporations were highly integrated institutions, performing most of the value chain activities in-house, which eventually led to problems with coordination, communication, and control, especially as multinationals stretched their operations across several locations distant from the headquarters. "More time was required to communicate decisions to all concerned, to receive reports from the multiple production and sales units, and to handle the increasingly interrelated and growing span of control."[26] Communication between headquarters and subsidiaries became increasingly difficult across distant markets with diverse languages and cultures. "Even with such substantial information, executives of headquarters may find it difficult to evaluate appropriately and balance critical environmental variables in their decision making."[27] Centralization turned into a costly bureaucratic system. "Centralization is costly to operate. As the overseas organization grows in size and complexity, managers at the center are swamped with requests for information, guidance, and support decisions. To respond appropriately, they feel they need to reinforce their resources, capabilities, and knowledge base, thereby increasing the size and bureaucracy of the decision-making unit."[28]

To overcome communication and coordination problems, multinational corporations abandoned corporate centralization and the international division in favor of corporate decentralization, shifting some decision-making authority to subsidiaries. In some cases, the transition from centralization to decentralization was confined to local issues, such as the hiring and training of local personnel, local marketing and distribution, and the handling of local regulation. In other cases, decentralization was extended into local strategic issues, turning subsidiaries into autonomous "profit centers."

> The international division is most commonly organized along geographic lines, with regional managers having responsibility for specific areas. The geographic pattern of organization offers a definite allocation of line authority in a company that is widely dispersed around the world and has limited product lines. It enables management to coordinate its activities, product lines, and staff services in a given area and country and to adjust to environmental parameters. It permits decentralization of authority to regional and country affiliates, which can be profit centers.[29]

Corporate decentralization of this sort has been exemplified in American companies since early 1930s, when firms such as GM, DuPont, GE, and Westinghouse Electric turned subsidiaries into independent profit centers that could pursue their own strategy. Westinghouse Electric, for instance, was organized in six product divisions, four major companies, and one international company. Each product division and the international company were run as separate businesses, although the headquarters still had the ultimate say in strategic matters.

> In the decentralization, the many different plant operations were grouped together, on the basis of like products, into six major product divisions, four major companies, and one international company, all reporting to an executive vice-president. The management of such a division and separate company was given greater responsibility and authority and could run his unit partly as though it were a separate business subject only to the overriding policies and controls of headquarters.[30]

GM was organized in five product divisions, each one serving a separate market, and bought supplies from its auto component divisions through buyer-seller agreements.

Corporate decentralization continued in the postwar period, and is still with us today, with subsidiaries assuming different roles, depending on their core competencies, resource capabilities, and proximity to consumer markets. Subsidiaries located in labor-endowed Asian countries, for instance, assumed the role of manufacturers, while subsidiaries located in large American and European consumer markets assumed the role of marketer.

> As expected, our results show that a subsidiary has different characteristics and strategic roles in each location. For example, a subsidiary is relatively more responsible for low cost manufacturing in Asia, one in Western Europe for marketing activity, and one in North America for innovative activity. These results show that Japanese MNCs tend to divide value-added activities, and allocate each activity primarily to each location.[31]

Honda's Thai subsidiary, for instance, manufactures the Fit Aria model for export to Japan, while the UK subsidiary manufactures the CR-V model for export to North America.[32] Heineken's Greek subsidiary, for instance, produces beer for export to fifteen countries, most notably to the Balkan region, where Greece has developed close economic ties.

Corporate decentralization did not free subsidiaries from the control of headquarters, which continued to own and control the organization's resources and to make all strategic decisions on new technologies and product development, advertising, purchasing and procurement, and expansion to new markets. It just replaced central planning with corporate colonialism, whereby the headquarters played the role of metropolis and the subsidiaries played the role of colonies, while corporate "bibles" played the role of Navigation Acts, outlining the rules that govern the relations between the headquarters and subsidiaries, as well as the relations among subsidiaries and with third parties in such areas as procurement, product standards, marketing, and so on. "Closely defined rules were set in the 'Ford Bible,' the company manual containing precise instructions on company procedures on accounting sales, production and purchasing. These instructions, based on U.S. experience, dictated standards, such as which side of the car the steering wheel should be on, some times at odds with European conditions."[33]

The Ford "bible" defined the relationship of the headquarters with its subsidiaries, accounting and purchasing procedures, and product standards. Similar arrangements characterized Johnson and Johnson, Procter & Gamble, and Coca-Cola. The practice continued after World War II, and is common today, as headquarters continue to make all important decisions on new technology and management skills for new product development.

> The U.S. multinationals in the period after World War II were generally much more integrated and centralized, and all technology and products stemmed from the home country. The greatest strength of these firms was their ability to internalize the transfer of technology and of management skills across national boundaries. The subsidiaries did enjoy a high level of autonomy, but their competitive advantage derived mainly from transfers of technology, know-how, and brand equity from the center.[34]

Pfizer's "bible," for instance, contains a detailed list of the parent's expectations of its subsidiaries, leadership incentives, coaching, employee performance measures, employee development, and so on.

Though less formal, close headquarters control of subsidiaries was also evident in Japanese multinational corporations, as exemplified by Matsushita Corporation. "Matsushita concentrated assets and expertise at the corporate center, and even its largest and most sophisticated subsidiaries, such as the U.S. company, were more tightly linked to and more highly dependent on the center than subsidiaries in any of the European or American companies in our sample."[35]

Figure 6.3 **Intra-Firm Trade in Services, 1997–2003** (in billions of dollars)

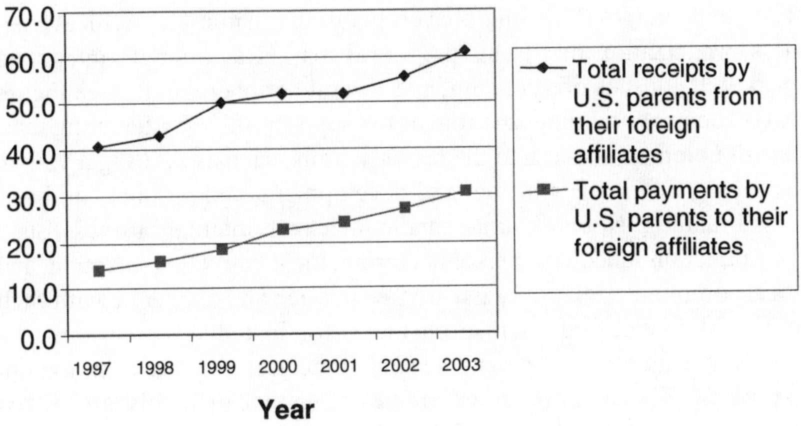

Source: Data from Borga and Mann (2004), p. 31.

As was the case with conventional colonialism, parents and their subsidiaries are engaged in extensive intra-company trade for the benefit of the parent company: Subsidiaries purchase final products developed and manufactured by the parent, at prices that favor the parent. During the period 1997–2003, for instance, payments for services rendered by U.S. affiliates to their parents ranged between $40 to $60 billion annually, while payments for services by the U.S. parents to their affiliates ranged between $15 and $30 billion annually (see Figure 6.3).

In short, the multinational unit of the semiglobal corporation is a decentralized hierarchical organization consisting of the parent and its subsidiaries. In the early days, large corporations adopted a highly centralized hierarchical coordination structure to organize their international divisions, whereby most of the decisions were made at the headquarters. But as they grew in size and diversity, they adopted a less centralized model, a model of corporate colonialism. In this model, the parent makes all the strategic decisions regarding new product development, marketing and manufacturing, alliances with third parties, entry to new markets, transfer pricing, and so on. Subsidiaries make all the decisions regarding local regulations, hiring local staff, and the monitoring of day-to-day operations.

The Global Unit

The global unit of the semiglobal corporation is a non-hierarchical business organization that treats the world market as a single integrated market. It consists of a core unit and several peripheral units (see Figure 6.4). The core unit plays the role of the support office by handling matters of common concern to the network units, such as drafting a vision, arranging financing, research and development, and product and business branding. Network units handle their own internal business, such as production schedules, personnel hiring, local marketing, taxation, and local community relations, and are free to trade and cooperate with each other. McDonald's franchise business, for instance, consists of the company's support office and several franchises scattered throughout the world. The support center handles a number of highly globalized issues, while each network unit handles its own local issues.

Network relations can be best understood as occurring within a multi-agent organization whereby each agent commits resources to the goals of the organization, while maintaining its autonomy. The level of commitment varies according to the number of the tasks to be performed, the number of participating agents, and the allocation of tasks to each agent.[36] FreeMove, a strategic alliance established by a number of major European telecom providers including Orange, Telefonica, T Mobile, and TIM, is organized as a non-contractual network that consists of two levels: an inter-company office staffed by working teams and managers from each of the four companies; and four network units, the companies themselves. This network organization allows members to cooperate on issues of common concern, like service standards and compatibility, procurement, and new product development, while they maintain their independence, competing with each other in local markets. Sony's highly globalized electronics business is organized as a two-level network, a global hub at the core of the network, and five product-group units at the periphery of the network (see Figure 6.5). The global hub's function is to "strategically" integrate the company's resources and explore alternative uses for them. To strengthen cooperation among units and flexibility in dealing with changing market conditions, Sony has created a "management platform," which allows the different group units to cooperate on matters of common concern.

Global organizations can be traced back to the last quarter of the nineteenth century, an era of early globalization and the overseas expansion

Figure 6.4 **The Coordination Structure of the Global Support Unit: Support Offices Versus Network Units**

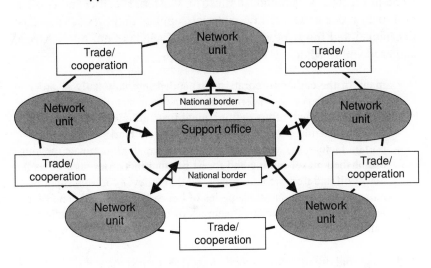

Figure 6.5 **Sony Corporation's Electronic Unit: A Global Organization**

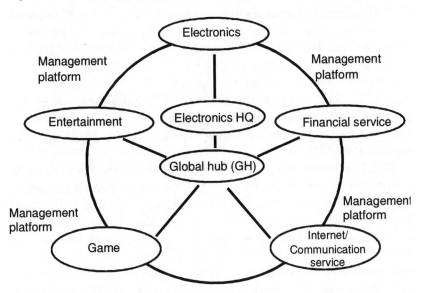

Source: Sony press release, April 2002.

of large manufacturing corporations like DuPont, American Edison, General Electric, Westinghouse Electric, Western Electric, and Otis Elevator. In order to secure raw material supplies and product markets, like nickel and forest product supplies in Canada, palm oil in Africa, and crude oil in Middle East,

> many of the earlier corporations expanded internationally in order to secure supplies of raw materials, one of the main historical driving forces behind the growth of the multinational firm, although the spreading of risk, tax considerations and the capture of new markets, were also important factors. In Canada, international companies dominate the long-established nickel-mining and forest product industries, as well as the newer oil and iron ore enterprises, while Unilever controls supplies of palm oil in Africa, Nestle supplies of cocoa beans in Africa and Latin America, the oil companies' sources of crude oil in the Middle East, and so on.[37]

Today's global organizations can be traced to the last quarter of the twentieth century, to the resumption of globalization and the "liberation" of subsidiaries from the tyranny of the headquarters, to the rise of matrix organizations, a hybrid of functional and multidivisional coordination structures, the leveling of corporate hierarchies, narrowing the size and diversification of product portfolios, and the focus on "core" products to be promoted regionally or globally rather than locally. By the 1960s, MNCs shifted to a "parallel" network. "By the 1960s a new international order had begun to take shape in the chemical industry, along lines markedly different from the system that had prevailed up to World War II. In place of the global network of technical agreements and joint ventures, and the intricacies of business diplomacy, the new structure was characterized by parallel networks of branch plants and sales organizations."[38]

AT&T divided itself into three independent companies, sold its credit card business, and formed alliances to focus on its core telephone services. Pepsi Corporation spun off its restaurant businesses to its stockholders, focusing its strategy on its core soft drink business. America on Line swapped assets with WorldCom, so it could better focus on its core Internet service businesses. Westinghouse Electric sold off most of its traditional manufacturing facilities and went on an acquisition spree of radio stations and TV programmers to focus on its core business, broadcasting. Matsushita Electric Industrial Co. is decentralizing its opera-

Figure 6.6   **The Global Unit: A Collection of Overlapping Networks**

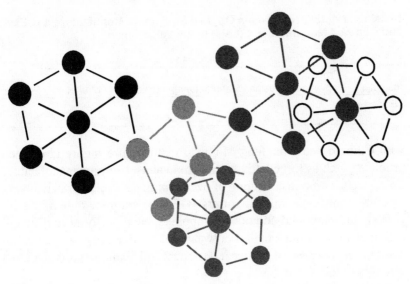

tion, turning divisions into separate entities that cooperate and compete with each other at the same time. TDK Corporation adopted a network of four separate regional headquarters to handle all its major products. Chipmakers like Toshiba and Fujitsu are forming strategic alliances for the development of systems chips, while Hitachi and Mitsubishi Electric are integrating their operations in the development of the next generation of microprocessors.[39] In the 1980s, Matsushita Electric launched an extensive decentralization program that transferred personnel, technology, and resource decisions from the headquarters to overseas subsidiaries. For the period 1980–88, Matsushita increased the number of its overseas manufacturing companies from forty-nine to sixty, and the number of overseas trading companies from twenty-nine to forty-one.[40]

In short, the global unit of the semiglobal corporation is a non-hierarchical multi-agent network of independent entities that compete and cooperate with each other. In some cases, global units become parts of a collection of actual or virtual overlapping networks in the form of contractual and non-contractual strategic alliances and joint ventures that extend over several industries and countries at the same time (see Figure 6.6). Honda's global unit, for instance, is part of a collection of overlapping networks among parts suppliers and other automobile companies that extends over several countries. The company has an alliance

Table 6.1

Division of Activities between Original Equipment Manufacturers (OEMs) and Contract Manufacturers (CMs) in the Value Chain

			Chain Stage			
Institution	Product innovation	Design	Manufacturing	Branding	Marketing	Service
OEMs	X			X		
CMs		X	X		X	X

with China-based Dongfeng Motor to manufacture highly globalized products, such as forged drivetrain components. Contract manufacturer Solectron is part of a collection of overlapping networks formed among original equipment manufacturers (OEMs), contract manufacturers (CMs), and parts and component suppliers, each performing different activities in the value chain. Footwear makers like Nike are part of an overlapping network of footwear designers and manufacturers scattered throughout the world.

The global unit of a semiglobal corporation, a provider of highly globalized bundles that can be easily transferred across national and local boundaries, is a horizontally integrated company. This means that it produces most of the value chain activities outside its corporate boundaries. This is especially the case in the consumer electronics industry, where the rise of overlapping networks has shifted the focus of the division of labor and competition from the corporate level to the value chain level (Table 6.1). Traditional corporations are mutating and permutating into similar entities, confining themselves to their core value chain activities, outsourcing non-core activities to partners and affiliates: suppliers to make parts and components, manufacturers and assemblers to put the product together, and distributors and retailers to bring the product to customers. CMs focus on their own core competencies, that is, design, distribution, and after-sales services, while OEMs focus on their own competencies, that is, product development, branding, and marketing. Telecom equipment makers like Tellabs, for instance, perform product design and branding in-house, outsourcing component production, and product manufacturing, distribution, and after-sales service to contract manufacturers. Computer chip makers like Monolithic Systems and PMC-Sierra are engaged in the design and branding of new chips, also leaving the rest of the activities to contract manufacturers. Nike, Disney, and Cisco Systems focus on product divisions and marketing, outsourcing manufacturing to Asian factories.

> In industries where value has migrated from physical things to intangibles, manufacturing—once a core activity—may have become peripheral. Many companies no longer make the products that bear their name. Nike is a marketing company, not a maker of sneakers. Disney makes Mickey Mouse, but lets efficient Asian manufacturers make tee shirts with Mickey on them. Cisco Systems makes new technology, that is, it generates ideas, even though those ideas are embodied in physical products like routers and switches for the Internet.[41]

In other words, network units of the semiglobal corporation become nodes in overlapping networks. The same company can be both at the core of one network and the periphery of another. IBM, for instance, is at the core of hardware design networks, but at the periphery of contract manufacturing networks. The expansion of subcontracting and outsourcing created a new division of labor between OEMs and CMs. OEMs handle activities that are within their core capabilities, that is, product innovation, branding, and marketing; CMs handle activities that are within their own core capabilities, that is, product design, manufacturing, and service.

In short, the global unit is a horizontal international business organization that consists of the support office and several peripheral units competing and cooperating with each other. In some cases the global unit is a collection of overlapping networks that extend over several industries and countries and are run by a two-level management structure.

Two-Level Management

Networks can be seen as multi-agent organizations coordinated by two-level management. One level is at the core of the network, at the support offices (first-level management) that function like an interior and an exterior department of a central government in handling common network affairs, that is, affairs that arise among network members and matters that arise between the corporation and third parties: drafting of a vision, obtaining financing, and research and development coordination. The other is at each network unit (second-level management) and functions like local administrations in handling its own internal affairs, production schedules, hiring of personnel, local marketing and distribution, taxation, and local community relations.

Two-level management allows global corporations to combine the advantages and disadvantages of centralization and decentralization: they can be centralized enough to reap the benefits of economies of scale and scope, the advantages associated with a large organization; and decentralized enough to reap the benefits of economies of scope, the competitive advantages associated with small production batches that cater products to local and regional markets.

First-Level Management: The Support Office

The support office designs the vision, the strategy, the communication, and the incentive structures of the organization. Support offices may be located in one country/region or in several countries/regions, one for each line of business. Sony Corporation, for instance, has made Japan the headquarters for its hardware products and the United States the headquarters for its software products. TDK and Canon have created three regional headquarters, one for Japan and Asia, one for Europe, and another for the Americas. Specifically, the support office:

- Develops the vision of the organization, that is, the rules of conducting business among network members and between network members and third parties (e.g., developing and implementing policies for treating employees around the world), and the mission that aligns the interests of each network with those of the entire organization, nurturing a common culture and a community of faith and social responsibility.
- Sets the network agenda, and negotiates joint ventures and alliances with third parties.
- Sets up the network communication structure that allows the sharing of information and core competencies among network members and between network members and the support office. Communication channels can be made up of hardware technologies, such as Internet, intranet, groupware, and videoconferencing and software technologies, to assist in managing such things as job rotation and labor transfers, global teams, and global conferences.
- Sets up the network motivation structure, a mechanism that ensures that individual units will pursue and execute the agenda of the network. Support office incentives include network unit bonuses, stock options, and activities that cultivate a community of faith.

Support offices also provide a number of services that may benefit the entire organization, such as the arrangement of common sources of financing, the coordination of R&D activities, and the negotiation of partnership agreements with third parties.

Second-Level Management: Individual Networks

Individual network units are responsible for their own operations and cooperation with other network units in pursuit of the goals set by the support office. Specifically, network units:

- set their own goals in line with those set by the support office;
- allocate authority among their members;
- devise a communication structure that allows their members to interact efficiently and effectively with management;
- devise incentives that align the interests of each member with those of the network and the entire organization.

To sum up, the semiglobal corporation is a hybrid organization that consists of two units, a multinational unit, to handle its highly localized bundle offerings, and a global unit, to handle its highly globalized offerings. The multinational unit is a hierarchical business organization that treats world markets as a collection of separate national and local markets. It consists of a home (parent) company and several subsidiaries, normally one for each major national market. The parent company makes all strategic decisions regarding financing, marketing, production, distribution, new product development, mergers and acquisitions, alliances with other companies, and expansion to new markets. The subsidiaries handle overseas business and are restricted from trading directly and cooperating with each other and with third parties. The global unit of the semiglobal corporation is a non-hierarchical organization consisting of a core unit and several peripheral units. The core unit plays the role of a support office that handles matters of common concern for the network units, such as drafting a vision, arranging financing, research and development, and product and business branding. Network units handle their own internal business, such as production schedules, personnel hiring, local marketing, taxation, and local community relations, and are free to trade and cooperate with each other. In some cases, entrepreneurial networks extend beyond company boundaries, turning the global unit into a collection of overlapping networks extending across several industries and countries. Pulling together this network requires an efficient and effective communication structure.

Notes

1. Gerstner (2002), p. 86.
2. File:/G\Publications\Honda Worldwide Corporate Governance.htm 24/11/2004.
3. Demange (2004), p. 755.
4. Corporate centralization and decentralization in international business litera-ture are often referred as ethnocentric and polycentric organizations, respectively.
5. Rostow and Ball (1975), p. 18.
6. Indeed, a National Foreign Trade Council survey, for instance, confirms that bypassing tariff and import barriers and local regulations, reducing transportation costs, and better access to local materials are the primary factors that tipped the balance between exports and direct investments. For further discussion, see *The Impact of U.S. Foreign Direct Investment on Employment and Trade*, New York: National Foreign Trade Council, Inc., 1971. Also, see Phatak (1974), p. 9.
7. Parkinson (1974), p. 118.
8. Rugman, (1981), p. 39.
9. Phatak (1974), pp. 15, 16.
10. Gabel and Bruner (2003), pp. 28–29.
11. Hymer (1976), p. 3.
12. Vernon (1977), p. 64.
13. Beaud (1983), p. 154.
14. Gabel and Bruner (2003), p. 31. These statistics should be interpreted with caution. Especially in the last quarter of the twentieth century, some of the corpora-tions classified as "multinational" were "global corporations," an issue to be further addressed in Chapter 7.
15. Vernon (1977), pp. 125–26.
16. Martyn (1964), p. 131.
17. Dale (1960), p. 145.
18. Chesbrough (2003), p. 107.
19. Pusateri (1984), p. 192.
20. Meyer and Gustafson (1988), p. 8.
21. Pusateri (1984), p. 194.
22. Micklethwait and Wooldridge (2003), p. 65.
23. Chistensen and Raynor (2003), p. 129.
24. Chesbrough (2003), p. 29.
25. Shirouzu (2003), pp. A1, A13.
26. Dale (1960), p. 146.
27. Dymsza (1972), p. 15.
28. Bartlett and Ghoshal (1989), p. 159.
29. Dymsza (1972), p. 23.
30. Dale (1960), p. 147.
31. Isobe and Montgomery (1998).

32. www.world.honda.com/profile/production, 2/19/2005.
33. Leontiades (1985), p. 28.
34. Aharoni (1996), p. 12.
35. Bartlett and Ghoshal (1989), p. 159.
36. So and Durfee (1996). Also see Lemaitre and Excelente (1998).
37. Parkinson (1974), pp. 117–18.
38. Taylor and Sudnik (1984), p. 195.
39. Naito (2002).
40. Bartlett and Ghoshal (1995) p. 66.
41. Magretta (2002), p. 107.

7

Communication

- At Nokia Corporation, *Nokia People*, a company-published magazine, provides its 53,650 employees information about the company's achievements, competitive strengths, corporate values and culture, management style, and community initiatives, in four languages: Finnish, English, German, and Chinese; while Nokia News Service, an Intranet-delivered news service, provides employees business and local news. "Its broad range of communications activities, channels and media strive to help employees manage and use corporate information they receive in their work and organizational relationships and in doing so, be fully engaged in the delivery of the company's strategy and the Nokia Way."

- At Honda, 250 closed-circuit TVs installed in cafeterias broadcast global and local news, company sales updates, and technological developments. The company has also installed terminals at plant locations where associates can tap into intranets for workplace-related information, and meetings and roundtable discussions allow associates to grasp company policies and to address issues of quality and cost improvements.

- At Nissan, global teams handle product planning and related strategies, such as power trains, vehicle engineering, and purchasing, while geographic teams handle local marketing and sales strategies.

- At the U.S. fiber optics maker Corning, Inc., scientists and engineers are engaged in product development, moving "downstream" from research to development, and "upstream" from product development to research, eliminating the layers of bureaucracy that separated researchers from key decision makers.

- At E.ON Academy, company managers receive training on cross-cultural issues that fosters the creation of "economies of collaboration" across the group's companies, and between the company and its customers and suppliers.

146

These examples highlight some of the methods and channels of communication international businesses apply to disseminate and recycle information and knowledge throughout the organization and simultaneously to address the demands of globalization and localization for efficient and effective communication: IT systems and applications, such as closed TV circuits, the Internet and intranets, and management information systems, such as global and geographic teams; job rotation; and corporate academies and universities.

Each method and channel of communication has its own advantages and disadvantages that makes it more or less suitable for different organizations or organizational units. Some IT systems, like intranets, are closed systems and therefore more suitable for hierarchical organizations like the multinational unit of the semiglobal corporation, while other systems, like the Internet and the Electronic Data InterchangeDI, are open systems, and therefore more suitable for non-hierarchical organizations like the global unit of the semiglobal corporation. Some management practices, like geographic teams, are highly localized, and therefore they are more suitable for handling highly localized activities like sales and marketing, while other management practices, like global teams, are more integrated and more suitable to highly globalized activities like purchasing and procurement. Some communication channels are vertical, providing top management with firm control of its different units, and therefore are more suitable for the multinational unit of the semiglobal corporation. Other communication channels are horizontal, providing management with flexibility, and therefore are more suitable for the global unit of the semiglobal corporation that is faced with rapidly changing market conditions.

The remainder of this chapter, a detailed discussion of the methods and channels of communication of the semiglobal corporation, is in three sections: the first section discusses generic communication methods and channels, the second discusses the communication structure of the multinational unit of the semiglobal corporation, and the third analyzes the communication structure of the global unit of the semiglobal corporation.

Communication Methods and Channels

In its generic form, organizational communication is external and internal. External communication is about the dissemination and recycling of information and knowledge between the company and its customers, suppliers, partners, and the community. Internal communication is about the dissemination and recycling of information and knowledge throughout the organization.

Information and knowledge can be classified in two categories: *explicit* or codified, and *tacit* or implicit. Explicit information and knowledge, such as sales reports, part and component characteristics, production schedules, and industry trends, can be documented in hard form (hard manuals, journals, books and magazines) and in soft form (floppy disks, hard disks, and "visual manuals"). Explicit knowledge can be retrieved and electronically transferred through IT systems and applications through vertical and horizontal communication channels (see Table 7.1).

Tacit information and knowledge, such as contextual knowledge, the knowledge of the different tasks required to complete a business process, and organizational knowledge, the knowledge of the organization business and operations, cannot be documented and stored in hard and soft form. It must be learned through management systems that accommodate actual interaction among the members of the organization. "Tacit knowledge is subconsciously understood and applied, difficult to articulate, developed from direct experience and action, and usually shared through highly interactive conversation, story-telling and shared experience."[1]

The lines between explicit and tacit knowledge are not clearly drawn, however. Accumulated explicit knowledge can be turned into tacit knowledge through information management systems, such as job rotation and transfers, working teams, and the like. Conversely, accumulated tacit knowledge can be codified and eventually stored in "virtual manuals" through IT systems and applications. Buckman Laboratories' standard operating procedure committee, for instance, turns its brainstorming proceedings into digital documents that can be accessed by company employees. Toyota has developed "visual manuals" that combine text and animation to train employees in a number of different skills concerning a broad range of automobile assembly processes.

> Drawing upon the experience of its experts, Toyota selected and organized the best practices for each skill. Toyota applied digital technology to compile these methods into "visual manuals," keeping text to a minimum, while using photos along with short animation and video clips to facilitate rapid comprehension. Slow-motion videos enable trainees to grasp skills that tend to be demonstrated too rapidly by seasoned human experts. Such skills can be as basic as the knack of rolling a bolt from a palm to fingertips. In all, GPC has about 2,000 visual manuals in stock, covering a vast repertoire of automotive assembly processes. [2]

Table 7.1

Selected Communication Methods in Semiglobal Corporations

Method	Description
IT systems and applications	
Internet	An open network that allows the members of the organization to communicate with each other and with third parties
Intranets	Web-based networks that allow organization members to share information and knowledge
Extranets	Allow access of third parties to the company's databases, product prices, shipment times and rates, delivery schedules, and so forth
e-mail	Instant exchange of messages and documents both within and without the organization
EDI	A standardized protocol that links computers of companies and their suppliers, customers, and distributors
Groupware	Applications software that allows instant exchange of messages, document exchanges, on-line chatting, and real-time document sharing that accommodate the formation and functioning of groups and teams
Videoconferences	Virtual meetings within and without the organization
CRM	Software that monitors customer purchasing patterns and sales-force performance
Closed TV channels	Disseminate information within the organization
Online magazines and newsletters	Disseminate information and knowledge throughout the organization
Information management systems	
Job rotation and transfers	The assignment of different jobs to different departments and divisions that allows organization members to develop contextual and organizational knowledge
Working teams	Groups of organization members that handle a single or a number of organization functions
Global and regional conferences	Forums that disseminate information and knowledge among geographically dispersed organization units
Company universities and academies	
	Disseminate knowledge to the members of the organization, partners, and customers
Channels of communication	
Vertical	Communication flows downstream and upstream in the organizational hierarchy
Horizontal	Communication flows across the same layer of hierarchy

Caterpillar has developed an equipment training simulator for off-highway truck operations that teaches equipment operators how to handle different environmental conditions.

In international business, explicit knowledge tends to be more geographically dispersed, while tacit tends to be more localized.

> The nature of the knowledge itself has bearing on how it is managed. Thus, the norm is for codified knowledge that is relatively easy to transmit to be geographically dispersed, whereas highly tacit knowledge tends to remain localized. However, in some cases, highly tacit knowledge is sourced from foreign subsidiaries, and this tends to be driven either by particularly strong and unique local competencies or by particularly strong company-specific networking capabilities.[3]

This means that explicit knowledge can be best diffused through a centralized communication structure, while tacit knowledge can be best diffused through a decentralized communication structure.

IT Systems and Applications

Information technology systems and applications have always been the centerpieces of codified corporate communication. From the Morse telegraph to Graham's telephone, the Internet, intranets, groupware, and videoconferences, IT systems and applications have revolutionized the way businesses communicate with their members and their customers and suppliers. The telegraph, for instance, allowed late-nineteenth-century American corporations to communicate with their agents and subsidiaries throughout the country, and the telephone allowed twentieth-century multinational corporations to communicate with their subsidiaries and clients throughout the world. In the last decade of the twentieth century, customer relationships management (CRM) applications software, the Internet, intranets, and extranets, allow the members of large organizations to cyber-communicate efficiently and effectively with each other and with customers by capturing, refining, searching, and transmitting information and knowledge, while groupware and teleconferencing accommodate the formation and functioning of teams and groups.[4] In retailing, the Internet and CRM software allow consumer electronics manufacturers like Samsung Electronics to deploy "detailers" to gather and process information about stock levels, competitors' pricing, and customer purchasing patterns.[5]

To boost retail sales further, Samsung uses third-party "detailers" who visit stores like Best Buy and Circuit City that carry Samsung products. Detailers monitor stock levels, display conformance, and competitors' products and pricing. They can quickly identify compliance problems with retail promotions, spot any quality issues, and improve product displays. The detailers transmit the information gathered daily via the Internet to Samsung's customer relationship management (CRM) system, which allows the manufacturer to address any problems quickly. That information goes to Samsung's product development, sales, and marketing communications professionals.[6]

Enterprise resource systems (ERPs) allow large corporations to pull together their different departments and divisions within the same hardware system, eliminating the distance between headquarters and subsidiaries. In the chemical industry, Global Enterprise Transportation from G-Log has allowed DuPont to establish a centralized logistics and data warehouse database and to manage efficiently and effectively its global and regional shipments, improving customer service.[7] Alcatel's OmniPCX Enterprise fosters communication among global teams. China-based teams, for instance, can communicate instantly with European and American teams around the clock. The PowWow from Tribal Voice allows companies to exchange text and speech and utilize voice and instant messaging internally, irrespective of their location around the world, at no cost. The system further accommodates online internal staff meetings that allow employees to gather internal and external data and provide advice to each other as well as to customers and suppliers.[8] Toyota's V-Com system allows the company to diffuse automobile model changes simultaneously throughout its factories. Teleconferencing equipment enables companies to efficiently and effectively conduct voice, video, and data conferences by connecting multiple participants around the globe. Sony's videoconferencing system allows companies to book rooms, coordinate diaries, and conduct virtual conferences that accommodate the diffusion and recycling of tacit information and knowledge among remote participants. So-called push and pull and trouble ticketing systems allow cellular phone companies to monitor their networks efficiently and effectively.

In short, IT systems and applications allow companies to disseminate and recycle codified information and knowledge efficiently and effectively to their members, partners, customers, and suppliers, as is the case with information management systems.

Information Management Systems

Information management systems are organizational arrangements that allow employees of large companies to develop both contextual and organizational knowledge that helps the organization cut costs, improve product quality and customer service, and develop new products. They include job rotation, labor transfers, working teams, global and regional conferences, corporate universities and academies, and vertical and horizontal communication channels.

Job Rotation and Labor Transfers

Traditionally, the term "job rotation" refers to regular assignment and reassignment of organization members to different job tasks from one department to another within the same division. The term "job transfers" refers to the regular and irregular shifts of labor from one division to another. In a fruit juice factory, for instance, job rotation and organization member transfers can take the form of regular shifting of production workers to the packaging and sales divisions, and the transfer of their colleagues in those divisions to the production division. Microsoft engineers and marketers move from one division to another, as dictated by Microsoft's needs and their own career objectives. "The company's organizational structure is a shifting collection of teams, grouped into products, managed in divisions that correspond to Microsoft's major product lines. Developers and marketing specialists have remarkable freedom to plot their own carriers, joining and leaving teams as Microsoft's priorities and their own interests change."[9]

Job rotation eliminates monotonous tasks and allows employees to develop "contextual knowledge," that is, knowledge of the entire production process rather than a single task—the skills that will enable employees to choose the task in which they can contribute the most in the company.[10] Labor transfers allow labor and management to develop "organizational knowledge," that is, knowledge of the entire organization and its objectives, functions, and operations.

In international business, job rotation and labor transfers can take two forms: vertical, across positions in different hierarchies, like expatriate assignments from headquarters to subsidiaries; and horizontal rotation and transfers across positions in the same hierarchy, like expatriate assignments across subsidiaries, and the assignment of executives and specialists to business partners. Transfers of corporate executives from one subsidiary to another, for instance, allow them to develop a better understanding of how the company is organized, preparing them for managerial positions, an issue to be further addressed below.

Working Teams

Working teams are at the core of internal corporate communication, especially when it comes to the development and recycling of organizational knowledge in a rapidly changing market environment and the delivery of organizational synergies.

> Team working is a central part of any learning organization in that membership of team is an excellent way for knowledge to be both shared and created within the firm. Teambuilding is a key method combining not only the existing knowledge of a group, but also its abilities to create new knowledge. Team working involves effective working inside the organization, while the associated idea of networking refers to teambuilding that takes place throughout the domain of an organization's environment. Organizations benefit from effective teambuilding because it can deliver organizational synergy.[11]

Working teams can be classified in four categories: single-function teams formed within the same division across different locations; multi-function teams formed across different divisions and departments; single-company teams formed within the same or different divisions within the same company; and multi-company teams formed across companies (see Table 7.2). A good example of cross-functional teams are Nissan's Value-Up Program teams from different departments, which are created for the purpose of producing quantifiable, measurable results through the use of tools. In the early 2000s, Nissan had 300 such teams pulling together experts from different business divisions for the purpose of developing the company's business and cutting costs and coming up with breakthrough ideas. "Many different professionals within the company, representing various business sections and geographical regions, are brought together to solve problems by focusing on specific issues, introduce new ways of thinking—and to rethink current business processes."[12] Another good example of cross-function teams are Caterpillar's global teams, which handle all stages of product development, from design to marketing and support.[13]

Table 7.2

Types of Teams in the Semiglobal Corporation

Type of team	Structure	Purpose
Single-function	Formed within the same division across different locations	Bring together company-wide expertise in that area
Multi-function	Formed across divisions and departments	Bring together expertise across different departments
Single-company	Formed within the same division or across divisions of the same company	Bring together company-wide expertise in different areas
Multi-company	Formed across companies	Bring together experts from different companies for the development of complex products

Cross-functional teams are particularly important for new product development, which requires multiple sources of market and technical information.

> Successful new products don't, for example, emerge out of a process in which marketing sends a set of specifications to R&D, which sends blueprints and designs to manufacturing. But joint opportunity analysis, in which functional and divisional people share ideas and discuss alternative solutions and approaches, leverages the different strengths of each party. Powerful internal connections make communication clear, coordination strong, and communication high.[14]

Cross-function teams are credited with the successful development and launch of new automobile models like the Maxima, the Ultima, and the Quest, and for Microsoft's first version of Windows NT, which was the product of a team of 250 developers who wrote 6 million codes and successfully marketed the product to computer manufacturers.

In international business, working teams take two forms, geographic and global. Geographic teams focus on localization issues, while global teams focus on global/scale issues. Nissan's geographic teams focus on marketing and sales issues, while its global teams focus on technology and procurement, an issue to be addressed below.

Global and Regional Conferences

Traditionally, scientists and professional convened in global and regional conferences to exchange ideas and research findings, and to strengthen personal ties and professional cooperation. Today, corporate executives from different levels of management and different corporate units around the globe also convene in global and regional conferences to exchange ideas about manufacturing, procurement, distribution, marketing, and new product development. Some Japanese companies, for instance, hold annual conferences for their middle and upper management from all over the world. Matsushita Electric Corporation holds an annual meeting of 7,000 managers to discuss the directions for the year.[15] Seagram Corporation holds biannual regional conferences among middle and upper management to discuss the company's vision. In some industries, like pharmaceuticals and medical devices, companies invite clients to conferences to get feedback on the effectiveness of certain products. In other industries, such as software development, companies invite computer programmers and salespeople to get feedback on existing products and to gain support for the development of new ones.

Corporate Universities and Academies

Corporate universities and academies are part of company efforts to disseminate and recycle knowledge produced both within and without the company through training courses and seminars. E.ON's academy, for instance, provides its senior management cross-cultural training in a number of different locations: London, Munich, and Washington, D.C. "Global organizations are complex arrangements of businesses, product groups, functions, and geographies. The same is true for E.ON. As our group expands internationally, E.ON managers are increasingly asked to work in multi-cultural, multi-business teams, and swiftly transfer best practices across organizational boundaries."[16] Motorola University provides customized courses in quality management, and in foreign languages and cultures. "You can count on Motorola University instructors to incorporate a related activity or application into each hour of the Six Sigma training programs, and to provide examples that are relevant for your organization."[17] QUALCOMM's CDMA University trains 3G wireless operators and infrastructure manufacturers in the design and operations of CDMA-based networks.[18] Toyota's Global Production Center provides training in the use of V-Comm in digital engineering, global pilot production, and project preparation. Heineken University allows employees from different subsidiaries to exchange information and knowledge about new product development.

Communication Channels

Communication channels are transmission mechanisms that carry messages between senders and receivers, and can take two forms: vertical channels, which carry messages upstream and downstream across recipients and receivers in different organizational hierarchies; and horizontal channels, which carry information across the same hierarchy levels or across different organizations. Downstream and upstream communication is mostly formal, taking the form of new product descriptions, job descriptions, visions, technologies, and sales goals, flowing downstream, and sales reports and new product and technical inquiries, flowing upstream. Horizontal communication is mostly informal personal communication, running back and forth across different members at the same level of hierarchy or across agents from different organizations.

In short, international business can disseminate information and knowledge through IT systems and application and management systems. Messages can flow vertically and horizontally. Each method and channel of communication has its own advantages and disadvantages that make them more or less suitable for different organizations or organizational units. Some IT systems, like intranets, are closed and therefore more suitable for hierarchical organizations like the multinational unit of the semiglobal corporation, while other systems, like the intranet and the EDI are open, and therefore more suitable for nonhierarchical organizations like the global unit of the semiglobal corporation (Table 7.3). Vertical channels provide top management with firm control of its different units, and therefore are more suitable for the multinational unit of the semiglobal corporation. Horizontal channels provide management with flexibility, and therefore are more suitable for the global unit of the semiglobal corporation that is faced with rapidly changing market conditions.

The Multinational Unit: Closed and Vertical Communication

Multinational communication is mostly intra-organization communication that can be best understood within the "principal-agent model" explained in Chapter 6, whereby the headquarters is the principal at the top of the hierarchy and the subsidiaries are the agents at the bottom of the hierarchy.

Table 7.3

Communication Methods in the Semiglobal Corporation

Communication methods and channels	Multinational unit	Global unit
Closed IT systems	**	*
Open IT systems	*	**
Job rotation and transfers		
Vertical	**	*
Horizontal	*	**
Working teams		
Regional	**	*
Global	*	**
Business conferences		
Regional	**	*
Global	*	**

Note: * = Least frequent; ** = Most frequent.

Communication within this organization can be centralized or decentralized. Centralized communication is mostly closed communication flowing vertically in the organization, back and forth between headquarters and subsidiaries, downstream, from headquarters to subsidiaries, and upstream, from subsidiaries to headquarters. In such a system, no communication across subsidiaries is allowed. Downstream information in the form of viewpoints, instructions, and technological and managerial know-how allows headquarters to communicate the company vision, business goals, practices, and policies to subsidiaries in line with the company's strategies and policies. Upstream information in the form of sales and profit reports, budgetary requests, and technical inquiries allows subsidiaries to update headquarters on local issues and problems. Decentralized communication is also closed communication, flowing back and forth between headquarters and subsidiaries, but some communication across subsidiaries is allowed.

Communication centralization and decentralization have their own advantages and disadvantages. Centralized communication provides the headquarters with better control over the flow of information throughout the organization, but it is subject to intentional or unintentional distortion throughout the hierarchy, which may slow decision making and even lead to wrong decisions. The degree of communication centralization depends on five factors: (1) the value of the subsidiary's knowledge stock: the greater the subsidiary's knowledge stock, the closer the attention to be paid by the headquarters; (2) the nature of the knowledge

stock: subsidiaries with unique knowledge will be more closely monitored; (3) the degree of vertical integration of parent-subsidiary transmission channels: the more vertically integrated the transmission
channels, the higher the knowledge outflow from the subsidiary to the
parents; (4) the motivational disposition of headquarters and subsidiary
executives, that is, the willingness to transmit or to block knowledge;
and (5) the ability of each unit to absorb and process knowledge.[19]

Centralized and decentralized communication is accommodated by a
number of different methods. First, there are closed IT systems and applications, such as intranets and extranets, which limit access to corporate information and knowledge to the members of the organization and
selectively to customers, suppliers, and partners. IBM's intranet system
and directory allow employees to share information with each other and
to communicate with customers, suppliers, and collaborators. Johnson
and Johnson's intranet system allows its researchers to share documents
instantly and to work jointly on certain projects such as disease mapping. Ford's intranets and groupware allow its engineers to use virtual
work spaces to design cars. Teleconferencing equipment enables companies to efficiently and effectively conduct voice-, video-, and data-
conferences by connecting multiple participants around the globe. TDK
uses intranets to disseminate the results of internal specialist surveys of
human errors, and Buckman Laboratories' corporate intranet, K'Netix,
allows employees to mine market and technical data. Pfizer's intranet
allows employees from different subsidiaries within the same geographic
region to share information about the company and its products. Greek
subsidiary employees, for instance, have access to the EuCan-AfMe
(Europe, Canada, Africa, Middle East) intranet, which provides employees information on new product development, company business initiatives, regional and local conferences, and so on. Unilever's Plumtree
portal integrates the company's 700 intranet sites, providing employees
from around the world a "single window on their work."

Microsoft's ToolBox website allows company employees to exchange
ideas about new programs with other employees, bypassing their managers. Vignette V6 Content Collaboration Server allows companies to
exchange customized information content with employees, suppliers,
distributors, customers, and partners in multiple formats. Enterprise software from SAP and SAR 3 and JP1 hardware from Hitachi allow Mitsui
USA to accommodate efficient and effective job scheduling among the
six Mitsui subsidiaries in the United States, Mexico, Canada, and the

parent's Japan headquarters. SAP software also allows Heineken N.V.'s headquarters to communicate with its subsidiaries and to coordinate sales with production and distribution.

Second, communication can be accommodated through vertical expatriate rotation and transfers, downstream from headquarters to subsidiaries, and upstream from subsidiaries to headquarters; and horizontally, from one subsidiary to another. Such communication allows the members of an enterprise to develop two types of knowledge: contextual knowledge, that is, knowledge of the entire production process, and organizational knowledge, knowledge of the entire organization. Expatriate assignments accommodate the transfer and assimilation of technical and managerial skills and expertise from the headquarters to subsidiaries, and align the cultures of headquarters and subsidiaries, making it easier to decode messages flowing back and forth between headquarters and subsidiaries, an issue to be further addressed in the next chapter.

Third, communication can take place through executive and technical personnel conferences and meetings where members from different divisions in the headquarters meet with subsidiary executives to address matters of company-wide planning, product development and manufacturing, engineering, marketing, finance, and so on. Sometimes executive conferences are held near R&D or manufacturing facilities, where subsidiary executives can get a better idea about business operations.

> The corporate group also arranges conferences attended by executives of the various operations units. For example, there is an annual world-wide product planning conference. Occasionally there are also world-wide conferences for engineering, manufacturing, marketing, finance, personnel and industrial relations, and public relations. Corporate executives make frequent trips to the operations units and, to a limited extent, are transferred from operations units to the parent company and from the parent company to the operations units.[20]

Other times, technical personnel meetings take the form of informal online forums and chatting. Buckman Laboratories' (BL) online Tech Forums, for instance, allow organization members to share technical and market information that is codified, stored, and retrieved as needed. "Knowledge management roles at BL are explicitly defined and assigned. They are of two classes, those that facilitate the direct and emergent exchange of knowledge through the forum, and those that support refining and achieving the record of those exchanges for future use."[21] Another online company forum allows employees from different sites around the world to post questions on the web and to receive answers within minutes from different employees or management.[22] At Novartis, online brainstorming brings together expertise from different disciplines and operations. "Internal connections at Novartis were also crucial at each stage of the process. In drug development these dense networks allow the frequent brainstorming sessions and included members from distinct scientific disciplines, such as chemistry and biology. Manufacturing success was built on healthy internal connections between members of the global development team in Switzerland and the manufacturing team in Ireland." [23]

Fourth, regular and irregular headquarters and subsidiary executive visits and exchanges also promote communication. Matsushita subsidiary managers visit headquarters two or three times a year, giving the headquarters the opportunity to inform subsidiary managers about new product developments. NEC executives made 10,000 overseas trips just within a year.[24] Clark Equipment executives meet monthly to review business operations and adjust product and marketing schedules to prevailing market conditions. Monthly executive meetings "bridge" the semiannual planning sessions, where the operations group gets the opportunity to compare and contrast actual compared to planned performance and to develop a more realistic plan.

> To assure this interchange, corporate and line management meet monthly to review on [a] 30-day basis the results of the previous month and the expectations for the next. Frequent short-term corrections are made; production schedules may be raised, lowered or revised according to the latest marketing information. These meetings, by taking stock of the business each and every month, provide an automatic discipline against sliding —by not allowing unfavorable situations or trends to continue unnoticed and uncorrected. Similar sessions are held monthly within the operating organizations.

> These monthly sessions bridge what Clark considers to be our two most important planning sessions of the year—the semi-annual Planning meetings, held in December and again in July. At these sessions, each operating group makes a formal presentation on its past performance versus plan expectations for the forthcoming 6- and 12-month periods. The key managers from both the operations and corporate level take part, so that

there is staff to staff, as well as manager to manager involvement. Although the presentations may be formal, the discussion is not. There is give and take at all levels. The object is not to win or lose an argument, but to produce the best information and the most realistic plan. [25]

Fifth, communication takes place among geographical teams mostly developed within each subsidiary to handle local marketing and sales issues in each of the geographical regions where the company conducts its core business. Nissan's geographical teams, for instance, handle local marketing and sales issues. "The primary concept behind it is cross-functionality, bringing together employees across corporate and physical borders so that creative thinking—and even healthy conflict—can be brought to bear on the challenges for Nissan as it continues to grow and change."[26] Heineken N.V.'s subsidiaries have developed local cross-functional "project teams," and Pfizer has developed both regional and global cross-functional teams.

In short, multinational unit communication is mostly intra-organizational communication that can be centralized, flowing vertically, downstream and upstream, between headquarters and subsidiaries or decentralized, and also can permit some horizontal flows across subsidiaries. Centralized and decentralized communication is accommodated mostly by closed IT systems and applications, expatriate rotation and transfers, executive and technical personnel conferences and meetings, and geographic teams developed within subsidiaries.

The Global Unit: Open and Horizontal Communication

Global unit communication is mostly inter-organizational communication that can be best understood within the multi-agent model of manufacturer-supplier and manufacturer-customer alliances and joint ventures introduced in Chapter 6. Communication within this organization is open and horizontal, flowing back and forth across the agents involved and accommodated by a number of open communication methods.

First, there are open IT systems and applications, such as the Internet and EDI, which allow for efficient and effective communication among different agents involved in the network. Open IT systems, for instance, allow for close collaboration between original equipment manufacturers (OEMs) and contract manufacturers, creating an efficient supply chain. "Creating a more efficient and effective supply chain requires deeper, more collaborative relationships with our OEM customers and with our supply chain partners, vendors and suppliers. This new era of synchronous collaboration demands real-time information exchange, close interaction of people and processes, and the ability to share and move parts and products seamlessly around the world."[27] Cognizant Technology Solutions Corporation's software brings together management teams located at remote customer sites and offshore development centers.[28] Lucent's website, lucent.com, provides a comprehensive customer training program on installing, operating, and repairing its equipment. IFX Online provides Internet services that allow franchises to communicate online with franchisers and other franchises, filing sales and royalty reports and sharing experience tips.[29]

Second, open and horizontal communication can be promoted through job rotation and transfers, which spread tacit knowledge both inside the organization and outside the organization, to customers and partners. To foster closer communication and cooperation with customers, Broadcom assigns sales managers to major clients to discuss product design prototypes, speeding the development of new products. The company also provides customers advance information on most reference platform designs. "We believe this enables our customers to achieve easier and faster transitions from the initial prototype designs through final production releases. We believe these reference platforms also significantly enhance our customer's confidence that our products will meet their market requirements and product introduction schedules."[30] Toyota assigns technical consultants to its suppliers to transfer knowledge of Toyota's new technologies, new products, and new management practices.

Third, horizontal communication can be achieved through global conferences that spread both codified and tacit knowledge. A good example of a global conference is Honda's *Jikon* annual meeting whereby the company shares information with suppliers about strategic issues, such as globalization, new product development, introduction of new technologies, tapping into new markets, and cost savings and quality improvements.

> Honda tells the suppliers what kinds of new products it intends to introduce and what types of markets it plans to cultivate in the coming years. The company then discusses the suppliers' strategic direction in terms of technology, globalization, major investments (such as capital goods and

plan expansion), and ideas about new products. The meetings also cover improvements that could be necessary in the quality, cost, and delivery of the vendor's product.[31]

Fourth, global teams can promote communication by allowing the global unit of the semiglobal corporation to bring together market and technology expertise from different countries and cultures around the world and to give management a better picture of the international customer.

> Global teams address certain problems and affect the bottom line in ways that are fundamentally different from the ways individuals approach the same situation. They maximize expertise from a variety of people, provide companies a more accurate picture of international customers' needs, and profit by the synergy necessary to unify the varying perspectives of different cultures and different business functions.[32]

In some cases, global teams are cross-functional, spreading over several divisions. Global teams are often supported and reinforced by local customer account teams, providing a link between local customers and global business managers: "Global business managers coordinate activities across divisions to effectively satisfy our customer's requirements and have direct access to our senior management to quickly address customer concerns. Local customer account teams further support the global teams and are linked by a comprehensive communications and information management infrastructure."[33]

The U.S. heavy-equipment-maker Caterpillar, for instance, has created global teams that are cross-functional. They handle product design, marketing, product support, technical service, and accounting. High-technology companies, such as Intel, IBM, and Hewlett Packard, have created similar teams. French chemical giant Rhone Poulenc has also set up global research teams for the development of new products and processes, and so have European and Japanese automakers and pharmaceutical companies.[34]

Global teams are inevitably confronted with cultural barriers that impair their function and diminish their effectiveness. When it comes to product development, for instance, American and British global teams tend to be more pragmatic and concerned about the ways consumers will value a new product while the French are concerned more about abstract issues and less with practical matters, such as the marketability of new products.[35] Another cultural barrier confronting global teams is the attitudes that the stronger team members have toward the weak members. In the United States, for instance, the stronger members see the weaker members as a burden on team performance, while in Japan, the stronger members see the weaker members as a challenge they must reckon with. Along the same lines, Japanese and European team members tend to be more concerned about fairness and equity, while American team leaders tend to emphasize performance and merit.

To sum up, the semiglobal corporation deploys a dual communication structure, one for its multinational unit and another for its global unit. The multinational unit communication is mostly intra-organizational communication that relies on closed communication methods and vertical communication channels: closed IT systems and applications, expatriate rotation and transfers and irregular headquarter visits, and executive and technical personnel conferences. Network unit communication is mostly inter-organization communication that relies on horizontal communication channels and closed communication methods: open IT systems, horizontal job rotation and transfers, and global conferences and teams.

Notes

1. Zack (1999), p. 46.
2. Toyota, *2003 Annual Report*, Toyota City, Nagoya, Japan, p. 10.
3. Ram and Pietro (2004), p. 3.
4. Zack (1999), p. 50.
5. O'Connor (2004).
6. Ibid., p. 46.
7. www.logisticsonline.com, 2/10/2005.
8. Davy (1998).
9. Bick (1999), p. 49.
10. Iwami (1992).
11. O'Keeffe (2003), p. 240.
12. Nissan, *Annual Report 2003*, Tokyo, Japan, p. 11.
13. Mullich (1997).
14. Shapiro (1988), p. 122.
15. Kono (1985).
16. E.ON Academy GmbH2002.
17. www.Motorola.com.
18. QUALCOM, *2005 Annual Report*, San Diego, CA, p. 23.
19. Gupta and Govindarajan (2000).
20. Prasad and Shetty (1976), p. 17.
21. Zack (1999), p. 51.
22. Elliot (1998).

23. Cross, Liedtka, and Weiss (2005), p. 126.
24. Bartlett and Ghoshal (1989), p. 160.
25. Davis (1997), p. 33.
26. Nissan, *Annual Report 2003*, Tokyo, Japan, p. 10.
27. Solectron, *2001 Annual Report*, Milpitas, CA, p. 7.
28. Cognizant Technology Solutions Corporation profile, Finance.yahoo.com.
2/14/2005.
29. Bennett (2005), p. D7.
30. Broadcom Corporation, *2002 Annual Report*, Irvine, CA, p. 14.
31. Liker and Choi (2004), p. 112.
32. Solomon (1995), p. 50.
33. Sanmina-SCI, *2004 Annual Report*, San Jose, CA, p. 6.
34. Mullich (1997).
35. Neff (1995).

8

Motivation

QUALCOMM's compensation and benefits philosophy and programs significantly contribute to creating and sustaining a competitive advantage in the labor market that translates to leadership and innovation in our addressed business markets. The company's unique mix of compensation, benefits, equity participation and workplace environment characterized by integrity, innovation, collaboration and inclusion, leads QUALCOMM to a distinctive position as an employer.[1]

We believe that Agere Systems employees should act in the interests of Agere Systems stockholders and the best way to encourage them to do that is through an equity stake in the company. We do this in a number of ways. Stock option grants have been made to most employees. In addition, we have an employee stock purchase plan that enables employees to purchase Agere Systems stock at a discount through payroll deductions and 401(k) plans under which U.S. employees can invest in Agere Systems common stock. Our goal is to have market competitive stock programs that encourage each employee to act like an owner of the business.[2]

The adage that "you get what you measure" is in a sense true at Toyota as well. Toyota long ago realized that the key to organizational learning is to align [the] objectives of all of its employees toward common goals. The underlying value system of Toyota's culture does that to a great degree. But to get everyone involved in continuous improvement in a way that adds up to corporate improvements requires aligned goals and objectives and constant measurement of progress towards those objectives.[3]

QUALCOMM's, Agere System's, and Toyota's employee compensation approach typifies four motivation mechanisms businesses apply to align the behavior, interests, goals, and attitudes of individual members with those of the organization: bureaucratic mechanisms that seek to align the behavior of individual members with those of the organization; performance mechanisms that seek to align individual with organization goals, such as costs, quality, customer service, and rate of return on invested capital (ROI's); incentive mechanisms that seek to align the interests of individual members with those of the organization, such as bonus, stock options, and restricted stock; and cultural mechanisms that seek to align member attitudes to those of the organization.

Each motivation mechanism has its own advantages and disadvantages that make it more or less suitable for different organizations, and most notably for the semiglobal corporation. Bureaucratic and performance mechanisms, for instance, provide top management with better control of the organization, and therefore are more suitable for hierarchical organizations like the multinational unit of the semiglobal corporation. Incentives and cultural mechanisms give the members of the organization more autonomy, and therefore are more suitable for non-hierarchical, multi-agent organizations that compete in highly globalized markets.

This chapter, a detailed discussion of the motivation mechanisms of the semiglobal corporation, is in three sections. The first section discusses the four generic motivation mechanisms, the second section discusses the motivation structure of the multinational unit of the semiglobal corporation, and the third section discusses the motivation structure of the global unit.

Motivation Mechanisms

In everyday life, motivation is what makes people do things: go to school, pursue a career, join a political party or a sports club, attend Sunday mass, donate funds and goods to charities, engage in disputes, and break the law. In business organizations, motivation is a set of mechanisms that align the members' behavior, goals, interests, and attitudes with those of the entire organization: bureaucratic controls, performance controls, incentives, and cultural controls.

Bureaucratic controls are mechanisms that seek to align the *behavior* of organization members with that of the organization through standardized and formalized rules and procedures that define the acceptable and non-acceptable norms of member behavior and the tasks to be performed (see Table 8.1). In some cases, bureaucratic controls are written in individual or collective bargaining agreements and company handbooks, while in other cases they are unwritten rules, just a matter of company traditions and routine practices, monitored by scores of upper, middle, and lower management.

Bureaucratic controls can be traced back to the last quarter of the nineteenth century and are exemplified in the multidivisional corporation where they were exercised by layers of upper, middle, and lower management. Upper management divided up the work to be performed into separate tasks, while middle and lower management made sure that such tasks were implemented. Carnegie Steel, for instance, was managed by layers of management to direct the efforts of mill and furnace workers, salespersons, and marketing specialists. "Carnegie's employees were organized in layer upon layer of managers, from foremen to direct his gangs of workers, to mill and furnace managers, to money managers, salesmen, marketing specialists, and two dozen partners with equity in his firm."[4]

Bureaucratic control was improved and even perfected by Henry Ford and his chief production engineer, Frederick Taylor, in the Ford Motor Company assembly lines, and supported and reinforced by the separation of ownership from control and by improved accounting systems, which placed management in the hands of professional managers.

> These managers were new figures in an agrarian society: people who didn't own the organizations they worked for but nevertheless devoted their entire careers to them. They had a high sense of their calling (some even looked down on the mere amateurs who founded the companies). And they pioneered many of the tools of the modern corporation.[5]

> The evolution of managerial hierarchies and monitoring procedures followed many paths from the railway era onwards, but two key ingredients permitting the efficient operation of ever larger bureaucracies were increasing managerial professionalism and improved cost accounting, as well as other forms of statistical monitoring, within firms.[6]

Performance controls or "management by objective" are mechanisms that seek to align the *goals* of organization members with those of the organization through a number of indicators, such as sales, value added, profits, market shares, and equity appreciation, that measure the consequences of the behavior of organization members on organizational performance rather the behavior per se. Performance indicators are part of detailed corporate budgeting and planning that set annual, tri-annual, and even five-year business targets, and allocate resources accordingly, and monitor actual performance against planned performance.

Performance controls were exemplified in Sloan's GM, organized in

Table 8.1

Types of Motivation in International Business

Types of motivation	Description
Bureaucratic	Seeks to align the behavior of organization members with those of the organization through long-standing standardized and formalized company practices, written or unwritten rules that explicitly outline the expectations of the organization from its members.
Output	Seeks to align the goals of organization members with those of the organization through a number of performance yardsticks, such as sales, profits, and market shares that measure the performance of individual members or groups vis-à-vis the organization expectations.
Incentives	Seeks to align the interests of organization members with those of the organization through rewards and sanctions that indirectly control the behavior of the members of the organization.
Cultural	Seeks to align the attitudes of the organization members with those of the organization through a sound vision that emphasizes the social function of the organization.

Source: For details, see Harzing and Sorge (2003), p. 203.

separate divisions—profit centers, with their own cost and revenue targets set by headquarters. Division managers who met or exceeded their targets were eventually promoted to larger divisions, and eventually joined the headquarters, while those who failed to do so were demoted, and eventually dismissed. Performance controls were advanced in Sears, Roebuck and Company, and perfected in Jack Welch's GE, where the organization was divided in several units, profit centers that had their own procurement and business strategy.

Incentives are rewards and sanctions designed to align the *interests* of organization members—most notably stockholders—with those of the organization. They allow company stakeholders—managers, employees, and stockholders—to share the risks and the rewards of their partnership: they convince workers and managers to think like stockholders and be responsive to competition and consumer demands. As IBM's former CEO Louis Gerstner explained when his company introduced an incentive-based compensation system:

I wanted IBMers to think and act like long-term shareholders—to feel the pressure from the marketplace to deploy assets and forge strategies that create competitive advantage. The market, over time, represents a brutally honest evaluator of relative performance, and what I needed was a strong incentive for IBMers to look at their company from the outside in. In the past, IBM was both the employer and the scorekeeper in the game. I needed my new colleagues to accept the fact that external forces—the stock market, competition, the changing demands of customers—had to drive our agenda, not the wishes and whims of our team.[7]

One of the most broadly applied incentives, for instance, is a bonus that ties organization members' compensation to certain operation results. Other incentives are Employee Stock Ownership Plans (ESOPs) and stock options that tie organization members' compensation to that of the equity performance. In this sense, incentives indirectly control the behavior of the members of the organization, creating a type of partnership capitalism.

Cultural motivation systems seek to align member attitudes and beliefs with those of the organization through a sound vision that specifies the mission of the organization and the core values that define the relations among the members of the organization. Cultural mechanisms emphasize the social function of the firm, trying to cultivate trust among the agents involved and reducing the need for monitoring.

Different motivation mechanisms are not independent of each other. Bureaucratic mechanisms define the acceptable and non-acceptable forms of behavior for reaching performance targets and compliance with local laws and ethical standards. Performance control mechanisms provide measurable evidence of the efficiency and effectiveness of bureaucratic controls, while incentives and cultural controls support and reinforce performance control mechanisms; and all four mechanisms rely on corporate planning and budgeting to set, monitor, and evaluate targets. This means that they must be used jointly rather than independently, especially in large and diverse international business organizations. Yet each motivation mechanism has its own advantages and disadvantages that make it more or less suitable for each segment. Bureaucratic mechanisms give headquarters better control over subsidiaries, but impair its flexibility in dealing with rapidly changing market conditions. Bureaucratic controls also impair creativity and the ability of management to develop or introduce new technologies. Therefore, bureaucratic mechanisms are more suitable for organizations that face standardized tasks

Table 8.2

Types of Motivation in the Semiglobal Corporation

Types of motivation	Multinational unit	Global unit
Bureaucratic	**	*
Performance	**	*
Incentives	*	**
Cultural	*	**

Note: * = Least suitable; ** = Most suitable.

and stable local markets, like the multinational unit of the semiglobal corporation (see Table 8.2). Incentives and cultural motivation systems give headquarters less control over subsidiaries but foster flexibility and creativity, and therefore are more suitable for the global unit that is faced with rapidly changing market conditions and price and profit swings.

The Multinational Unit: Bureaucratic and Output Controls

As discussed in the previous chapters, parent subsidiary organizations are "principal-agent" organizations facing the "agency problem," that is, the alignment of behavior, goals, interests, and attitudes of subsidiaries ("agents") behind those of the headquarters ("principal"). The parent-subsidiary agency problem is magnified by international market information inefficiencies and asymmetries: Subsidiary managers, for instance, have better information on their own market than do distant headquarters, and, therefore, may not behave as expected by the headquarters: "In managing culturally distant subsidiaries, agency costs are greater because of the information asymmetry problem, whereby information available on-site may not be available to a parent company."[8] This means that multinational organizations assume a higher degree of risks and uncertainties than do single-nation organizations, which requires a higher level of control to ensure that their behavior is consistent with the organization goals.

Accordingly, parent corporations often find that by investing in companies that are operating in different environments they increase the level of uncertainty or risk of return on their investments. Thus, corporate headquarters' control of subunit behavior and performance becomes a central

Table 8.3

Multinational Unit Coordination and Motivation

	Coordination	
Motivation mechanism	Centralization	Decentralization
Bureaucratic	**	*
Performance	*	**

Note: * = Least frequent; ** = Most frequent.

integrating function in MNCs. Indeed, headquarters must attempt to increase control over foreign subsidiaries in order to reduce the uncertainty of their investment, since such control ensures that the behaviors originating in separate parts of the organization are compatible and support common goals.[9]

Information asymmetries and compounded risks and uncertainties put headquarters in a delicate situation: while they cannot decide on matters about which they have incomplete knowledge, they cannot relinquish decision making to subsidiaries either, because the interests of subsidiaries may not coincide with those of headquarters and the entire organization.

The parent-subsidiary-agency problem can be addressed in two ways: through corporate centralization, which concentrates decision-making power at headquarters, and through decentralization, which diffuses decision-making authority throughout the organization. Corporate centralization can be supported and reinforced by bureaucratic motivation mechanisms that control the behavior of subsidiaries, while corporate decentralization can be supported and reinforced by performance motivation mechanisms that control the consequences of subsidiaries' management behavior (see Table 8.3).

Bureaucratic control can be exercised in three ways. First, it can be exercised through executive committees that run subsidiaries directly from the headquarters, as was the case with highly centralized American multinationals at the turn of the twentieth century as discussed in Chapter 6. Second, it can be exercised through standardization, which turns subsidiaries into headquarters replicas that operate in the same way as the parent; and through formalization, the use of written or unwritten rules and procedures that define and divide tasks to be performed by subsidiaries. American multinationals, for instance, rely mostly on written rules and procedures, as exemplified in the "Procter and Gamble way": "While subsidiary managers were free to modify the company's products to respond to local preferences, they were required—by standard policies and even organization structures—to follow the well-developed 'Procter way' of marketing."[10] Rules are contained in corporate "bibles" that provide a detail description of labor and management responsibilities. Japanese and European multinationals rely mostly on unwritten rules and longstanding traditions and practices.

Third, bureaucratic control can be exercised through expatriate assignments that ensure the understanding and the implementation of parent policies by subsidiaries, especially the understanding and implementation of strategic functions of the organization, such as marketing. Marketing expatriates have a good knowledge of both the local markets and the organization's global systems and provide the market intelligence and personal insight for developing direct ties between parents and subsidiaries.

> Those marketing managers that have social knowledge of the country/market and at the same time have an understanding of the global systems function of the organization, manage coordination among foreign operating units and provide an efficient type of control for the parent organization. These individuals play a central role in implementing and maintaining corporate injunctive norms (i.e. norms of efficient and effective response, those being either prescriptive or proscriptive) by providing the market intelligence, personal insights critical for success in many foreign markets, and personal contacts, which are the foundations for relationships.[11]

Nurtured in the headquarters' culture, expatriates contribute to the implementation of parent policies indirectly, as carriers of the headquarters culture to subsidiaries: They contribute to the alignment of subsidiary values and attitudes with those of the headquarters.

> Underlying MNCs' use of staffing control is the assumption that managers whose nationality is the same as that of the MNC headquarters will hold very similar goals to those of the corporate level. Thus, staffing control is viewed as a type of cultural control because it results in a greater sharing of values and goals between MNCs leaders and the top managers of their foreign subsidiaries. Because of this congruence, subsidiary managers are expected to be more likely to act in accordance with headquarters' interests than are foreign managers.[12]

The cultural role of expatriates is more pronounced in "ethnocentric" organizations, that is, organizations that try to replicate the home organization structure and culture in their overseas subsidiaries, and less emphasized in polycentric and geocentric organizations.

> In an international organization, the managing and staffing approach strongly affects the type of employee the company prefers. In a company with an ethnocentric approach, parent country nationals usually staff important positions at headquarters and subsidiaries. With a polycentric approach, host country nationals generally work in foreign subsidiaries while parent country nationals manage headquarters positions. An organization with a geocentric approach chooses the most suitable person for a position, regardless of type.[13]

Even within ethnocentric organizations, the role of expatriates varies across subsidiaries, depending on the size, age, type of industry, and strategic importance of each subsidiary. Larger and older subsidiaries are expected to have a smaller percentage of expatriates in their labor force than are smaller subsidiaries. Expatriates may have a larger presence in the auto industry and a smaller presence in the food industry.

> The fact that larger subsidiaries have a smaller proportion of expatriates in their workforce can be seen as an artifact of this measure: the percentage of expatriates will naturally be smaller in larger subsidiaries, even though the absolute level is larger. The managing director is more likely to be a parent country national in the automobile industry and more likely to be a host country national in the food and beverages industry. Finally, subsidiaries of larger multinationals are more likely to have a large number of expatriates in top-5 positions. However, since all of these universalistic factors influence only one measure of the same concept and all of them influence a different measure, we can safely conclude that overall the country-of-origin affect is much stronger. There is one other universal contingency though that does have an impact on both the percentage of expatriates in the total workforce and the nationality of the managing director: subsidiary age. The older the subsidiary, the lower the expatriate presence, which reflects the tendency of multinationals to use expatriates to set up new subsidiaries.[14]

In short, bureaucratic controls are exercised through executive committees, organization rules and procedures, and expatriate assignments that seek to align the behavior of subsidiaries with those of the headquarters. But they do not always work, especially in large, decentralized multinational organizations, where they have either been substituted or supplemented by performance controls that align the goals of subsidiaries with those of the headquarters (as has been the case with Toyota's North America Parts Operations [NAPO] subsidiary Stretch Goals program), or supplemented by localized targets and initiatives that create a sense of ownership among local members.

> NAPO's expanded organization had become difficult to motivate and manage. Stretch Goals addressed this situation by allowing leadership to centrally manage the program, yet locally motivate associates. It is difficult to make a large organization function effectively as a unit without instituting complicated hierarchies, rules, and regulations. However, localizing targets and initiatives increased the sense of ownership. As groups started celebrating their first successes, the program spread like virus from person to person, creating positive momentum. The Stretch Goals message was able to penetrate and motivate even the smallest work group, while enabling the entire organization to act as one.[15]

Toyota's 2000 three-year cost cutting goals for NAPO included a 50 percent reduction in inventory costs, a 25 percent reduction in freight rates, a 50 percent reduction in package expenses, and a 25 percent increase in space utilization. The customer quality service improvements goal included a 50 percent reduction in errors, a 50 percent reduction in lead time, and a 50 percent reduction in back orders.[16]

Operating plans are usually overly optimistic, underestimating the conflict within the subsidiary divisions and functional groups.

> Trying to optimize the entire supply chain through initiatives dictated by headquarters is overly optimistic. It underestimates the conflicts that naturally exist in the supply chain. A better approach is to recognize that tensions exist between functional groups with unique goals—and to capitalize on them. Stretch Goals takes advantage of this tension by setting aggressive targets, placed in conflict with one another, in order to define and drive the relationships between groups.[17]

Performance-control mechanisms are supported and reinforced by corporate planning and budgeting that monitors and evaluates actual targets vis-à-vis policy targets. Performance controls were popular among American multinationals in the 1950s and 1960s, as exemplified by pre-Gerstner IBM, when the headquarters-based Management Review Committee drafted the company objectives and policies that formed the basis for the seven-year "Strategic Plan Guidance" for its World Trade Corporation (WTC). Each area converted headquarters guidelines into a strategic plan that was approved by headquarters and turned into an operation plan that included the company product portfolio for the next seven years, and the personnel, marketing, finance, and administrative policies to support it.

> Once the WTC "Strategic Plan" was approved by corporate headquarters, it was used as the starting point the following year by WTC headquarters of an "Operating Plan Guidance." This document contained specific operating guidelines in quantitative and qualitative terms for present and planned products for the coming years. The areas and countries then converted this guidance into detailed area and country "Operating Plans" which were in turn assessed and approved by WTC headquarters before aggregation to the "WTC Operating Plan" and submission to corporate headquarters for final approval.[18]

Pfizer's annual performance planning begins in December when the parent company sets the subsidiary management targets, continues in January when subsidiary management sets its own targets for employees, continues into March when employee development programs are developed, and into July when the first six-month targets are evaluated and revised, and then ends in November with the evaluation and grading of actual performance vis-à-vis targets.

In recent years, performance controls are accommodated by enterprise network software (ERPs) that allows headquarters to closely monitor the costs and revenues of each subsidiary vis-à-vis targets. Wal-Mart's ERP, for instance, can monitor online the performance of each store around the globe. Heineken N.V.'s SAP software allows the company to monitor online sales and production targets.

In short, the multinational unit of the semiglobal corporation can address the agency problem in two ways, through corporate centralization and decentralization. Corporate centralization and decentralization are supported by bureaucratic and performance motivation mechanisms that seek to control the behavior of subsidiaries and to align their goals with those of the headquarters.

Network Unit Motivation: Incentives

As discussed in Chapter 6, network organizations can be best understood within a model of a non-hierarchical multi-principal organization that takes a number of different shapes and forms: joint ventures and strategic alliances whereby each agent commits resources toward the organization's goals while maintaining its independence; virtual overlapping networks of original equipment manufacturers (OEMs) and contract manufacturers (CMs); overseas franchise agreements; and long-term buyer-seller agreements.

Multi-agent organizations are faced with their own agency problem, particularly the opportunistic behavior of one or more agents. In technology-based strategic alliances and joint ventures, for instance, some agents may take advantage of other agents by failing to contribute the promised resources or by walking away from the network with corporate secrets of other agents or by exploiting the bargaining power they enjoy. In buyer-seller agreements, large buyers can take advantage of their market position to squeeze suppliers in the value chain, as has been the case with Vodafone and cellular phone manufacturers, Wal-Mart, and so on. Conversely, large suppliers may squeeze small buyers in case of resource shortage, as has been the case with Apple's iPod components in the late 2004s.

Opportunistic behavior in network organizations can be best addressed through a two-level management structure: one at the core of the network, at the support offices that function like an interior and an exterior department of a central government that handles common network affairs, that is, affairs that arise among network members and matters that arise between the corporation and third parties, drafting of a vision, obtaining financing, and research and development coordination; and the other at each network unit that functions as local administrations, handling their own internal affairs, production schedules, hiring of personnel, local marketing and distribution, taxation, and local community relations.

Two-level management is supported by a two-level incentive motivation system that seeks to align the interests of network units with those of the support center, and cultural control mechanisms that align the interests and attitudes of network members with those of the organization.

First-Level Management Incentives: Aligning the Interests of Individual Network Units with Those of the Corporation

Support offices rely primarily on incentives to align the interests of the management of each network with those of the entire corporation.

First-level management incentives must foster both competition and cooperation among network members; they include bonuses and profit sharing, stock options, and restricted stock.

Cash Bonuses and Profit Sharing

Cash bonuses are monthly, quarterly, or yearly sums paid to executive and key employees attaining or exceeding certain sales, profit, and service quality targets, as well as product development and delivery goals. Applied Materials, for instance, pays a cash bonus to executives who meet certain annual revenue and net income growth targets. GE ties bonuses to sales growth, customer satisfaction, and new ideas.[19] Nextel Communications pays a cash bonus to executives who achieve certain service quality, cash-flow, and financial targets; optimize technology utilization standards; and enhance strategic relations. SPX Corporation rewards division managers according to their contribution to the company's incremental value added. IBM pays research unit managers performance-based cash bonuses based on the sales of the business divisions that commercialize the research of those units. Home Depot pays store managers bonuses based on store profitability. Major insurance, brokerage firms, and banks pay their own bonuses to district and division managers who meet or exceed sales targets. The spread of incentive plans varies from industry to industry. In traditional industries, incentive plans are concentrated among top executives. In high technology industries, incentive plans are spread among all employees.[20]

Cash bonuses and profit sharing schemes often provide a substantial boost to the base salaries of employees, and management in particular. The employees of French cosmetics company L'Oreal, for instance, receive 16 percent of their compensation in the form of profit sharing. In 2003, the company paid $43 million in bonuses as part of its Worldwide Profit Sharing Plan. In 2004, Nucor Corporation's president received $2,682,000 in bonuses, almost four times more than his annual base salary of $690,000. Dow Chemical's president received $2,262,500 in bonuses, almost three times his annual $712,500 base salary; IBM's president received $5,175,000 in bonuses, almost three times his $1,660,000 base salary; and Oracle Corporation's CEO received a bonus of $3,179,000, almost five times his annual salary of $675,000.[21]

In some cases, the size of cash bonuses is a function of three factors:

- an effective profit threshold, that is, the profit level that will trigger the bonus compensation;
- target performance, that is, the performance at which the target award will be earned;
- the maximum performance, at which the maximum award will be earned.

For 2001, Symbol Technologies' bonus threshold was set at 85 percent of the corporation's 2001 business plan target. Target performance was set at 100 percent of the 2001 business plan, and maximum performance was set at 115 percent of the 2001 business plan. Nextel Communications pays eligible employees 0.55 days' pay for every two percentage points of corporate pretax revenue gains, or a total payment based on 4 percent of net income, whichever is greater. For the year 2000, cash bonuses amounted to 29.5 days per employee. Intel Corporation's cash bonus accounted for 4 percent of its net annual income or 29.5 days per employee. Veritas Software's executive bonuses are tied to the company's net income per share as specified in the operating plan: if net income per share exceeds 90 percent of the plan, executives receive 50 percent of the excess profit as a bonus. If net income is 110 percent of the plan target, executives receive 150 percent of the excess profit as a bonus. The maximum bonus is set at 250 percent of the profit in excess of the plan target. McData Corporation's bonus is calculated as a percentage of the base salary compensation and ranges from 25 percent to 35 percent for executive officers, depending on the company's quarterly and annual performance; 30 percent of the executive bonus is tied to quarterly profits, and 70 percent is tied to the annual profits. Texas Instrument's 2005 profit sharing plan pays a 2 percent bonus to eligible employees provided that a 10 percent operating margin is reached.

In other cases, bonuses are determined by the business unit performance and the overall organization performance. Genentech's bonus is determined by four factors: corporate and financial performance (earnings per share, meeting specific productivity and budgeting goals); commercial performance (sales and profit margin growth); R&D performance; and employee-development performance. Agere Systems' and Lucent Communications' bonuses are determined by two factors: the performance of the company or of the relevant business unit, and individual and organizational performance, a formula that fosters competition and cooperation among different network units.

> Our compensation program reinforces the company's business and financial objectives. Employee compensation will vary based on company and individual performance. When the company performs well based on financial and non-financial measures, employees will receive greater incentive compensation. When the business does not meet objectives or is facing financial challenges, incentive awards will be reduced. An employee's individual compensation will also vary based on the person's performance, the contribution and overall value to the business.[22]

> We believe that an employee's compensation should be tied not just to how the individual employee performs, but also to how well both the employee's team and the company perform against both financial and non-financial goals and objectives. When the company's performance is better than the objectives set for the performance period, employees should be paid more, and when the company's performance does not meet one or more of the key objectives, any incentive award payment is at the committee's discretion.[23]

Cash bonuses and other short-term profit sharing plans based on quarterly or annual performance are subject to three major limitations, however. First, employees and managers may become too preoccupied with short-term goals that determine bonus size, such as monthly, quarterly, or yearly profits and sales, at the expense of long-term goals, such as market shares and new product development. Second, employees and managers may quit after the bonus is paid, and end up working for the competition that may offer a more attractive compensation package. Third, employees and managers may be unwilling to cooperate with one another if such cooperation hurts their short-term performance and the size of their bonus. The drawbacks of cash bonuses are largely absent from ESOPs, stock options, and restricted stock.

ESOPs

ESOPs are accumulations of equity shares by company-established trusts on behalf of employees. Accumulated shares can be newly issued shares, shares purchased with funds contributed by employees, or shares purchased by company-borrowed funds. According to the National Center for Employee Ownership (NCEO), in the United States there are 11,500 ESOPs covering 8.5 million employees. The number of companies offering ESOPs has soared from a few hundred in the early 1970s to 10,000 in 2000. In the United States, for instance, companies have two types of ESOPs, qualified, and non-qualified. Qualified ESOPs allow employees to use pre-tax dollars to purchase equity in a company-set savings plan. Companies often match these contributions with their own equity or cash.[24] Non-qualified ESOPs allow employees to use after-tax payroll dollars to purchase company shares at a discount from their market value. Intel Corporation, for instance, has both tax-qualified and non-qualified ESOPs. Its retirement ESOPs are defined contribution plans for the purpose of accumulating retirement funds for employees and managers, and allow the company to make contributions to these funds. The company contribution is discretionary and varies with its performance. As of December 31, 2003, EMC Corporation had authorized the issue of up to 21.9 million shares of common stock to its full-time employees, who can have up to 10 percent of their salaries withheld for the purchase of such shares. The price is set at 85 percent of the fair market price on the day of the subscription.

Stock Options

Employee stock options were initially introduced in the 1940s as a reward to top executives. In the 1980s, stock options spread to almost every category of employees, from executives to hourly employees. NCEO estimates that as of 2001, 10 million employees received stock options. In the electronics industry, eligibility varies from close to 100 percent of top executives to around 75 percent of senior managers and international employees. Likewise the value of the option compensation varies from around $500,000 for top executives to a few thousand dollars for sales and hourly employees.

Some executives receive stock options that can amount to multiples of their annual salary, even in case of a small appreciation of the stock. Corning's 2004 option package plan included 105,000 shares exercised at $10.40 (stock traded at $11.30); 105,000 shares exercised at $12.79; and 239,000 shares exercised at $12.70. Intel CEO's 2000 option package could be worth $7,696,100, almost thirteen times his then current annual salary, provided that the company's stock appreciated by

5 percent over the vested period. The 2000 package for Nextel Communications' CEO was worth $5,915,234, almost twelve times his base salary. EMC Corporation, for instance, grants stock options to employees who "have a significant impact upon the Company's business and earnings." (EMC Corporation, 2004 Annual Report, p. 6) The 2004 Applied Materials' executive stock option plan granted options according to three criteria: the executive's responsibility level, individual performance, and independent equity compensation survey data.[25] The Texas Instruments' Employee Stock Purchase Plan provides for options to be offered semiannually to all eligible employees in amounts based on a percentage of the employees' compensation. The option price per share may not be more than 85 percent of the fair market value on the date of the grant. In 2004, the plan granted 700,000 shares (with an exercise price of $32.39) to the president and the CEO, 2.39 percent of the total shares granted to employees that year. The Symbol Technologies' stock options plan allows corporate executives to buy the company's stock at a predetermined price over a vested period of ten years. The 2001 option package of Oracle Corporation's CEO Larry Elison was worth $706 million, and the 1998 package for Disney's CEO Michael Eisner was worth $570 million.

Employee stock options are not confined in the United States; they extend to several countries, particularly in Europe.[26] In Germany, under value-oriented schemes, large companies like Daimler Benz AG and SGL Carbon AG offer three programs: fixed options, variable options, and stock appreciation rights. Fixed options entitle employees to purchase the stock of their company at a fixed price over a fixed period. In 1996, Daimler Benz AG issued convertible bonds that allowed employees to take advantage of long-term appreciation in the company stock. Variable options allow employees to purchase the stock of their company at a variable price and over a variable period. In 1997, for instance, Henkel KGaA gave its employees the right to receive a bonus of up to 15 percent of their basic earnings for a three-year period, provided that the Henkel share price rises over the said period more than the DAX index.[27] Stock appreciation rights (SARs) entitle employees to receive a cash payment, which amounts to the difference between the market price and the SAR exercise price. In 1996, Carbon AG granted 840,500 SARs to seventy members of its management, exercisable over a five-year period.[28]

In short, stock options are an effective vehicle of turning the members of an organization from wage earners into partial owners of a corporation, sharing the risks and the rewards of the partnership with common shareholders. Stock options eliminate the need for close supervision and monitoring and minimize the risk of opportunistic behavior that threatens the cohesion of network corporations. But they have a major drawback, namely, current and future equity and earnings dilution. According to a Bear, Stearns & Co. study, in 1998 stock options had a 92 percent dilution effect on Cedant Corporation's profits, a 65 percent dilution effect on Network Appliance's profits, and a 44 percent effect on Peoplesoft's profits.[29] Stock options have become the subject of legal disputes between employers and employees.[30] One area of dispute is over the time the options are exercised. Another area of dispute is over termination just before the options become vested or quitting just after the option becomes vested. Employees terminated shortly before they are about to receive big options gains sue their former employers. Conversely, employers sue their former employees who quit shortly after their options contracts become vested. Another area of dispute is the fate of options contracts when the company is acquired or sold shortly before options become vested, a problem that does not arise with restricted stock.

Restricted Stock

Restricted stock is stock issued to employees that can be sold only after a certain term, provided that two conditions are met, such as, that the employee does not leave the company before the term is over, and that the employee meets certain financial goals. Microsoft's restricted stock program, for instance, is tied to the company's performance. For managers, the amount of grants varies by their length of tenure with the company. GE's restricted stock units (RSUs) program grants company shares to 600 leaders of the company, including top executives.

Restricted stock has a number of advantages and disadvantages. First, restricted stock has more intrinsic value. Second, unless the company fails, restricted stock still has some value. And third, option grants are a better reward if the stock decreases in value. "Companies may decide that restricted stock better aligns employees and outside shareholders and that it benefits employees even if the stock's price declines over the life of the grant, unlike options, which can expire worthless. Restricted stock could become a poster child for an era of diminished stock-market expectations."[31]

In short, first-level incentives seek to align the interests of network management with those of the entire organization. To be sufficient, first-level management incentives must be supplemented by second-level management incentives.

Second-Level Management Incentives: Aligning the Interests of Individual Network Unit Members

As part of a network and yet autonomous entities, network units must design their own incentives so as to motivate their own members to pursue the objectives of both the unit and the objectives of the entire corporation. Incentives are of particular importance for network units that are too large to monitor and measure the performance of each member. In this sense, second-level management incentives are designed by the management of network units to motivate their members to work together in pursuing certain objectives, such as sales or profit targets, new product development, and so on. Network unit incentives may be classified as team incentives, promoting the formation and the effective functioning of teams, and individual incentives, promoting individual effort and creativity. Team and individual incentives may include monetary rewards, such as bonuses, and non-monetary rewards, such as private and public praise by management, outstanding achievement plaques, and lunches with the unit president.

Team Incentives

With the production of many commodities requiring contextual knowledge, that is, knowledge of the entire production process rather than single tasks, team effort has increasingly replaced individual effort. Yet convincing people to work together is not easy especially in Western societies accustomed to rewarding individual initiative rather than group conformity. In such societies, team incentives serve as the glue that holds its members together in pursuing certain goals set by management.

To be effective, team incentives should be assigned to the entire group rather than individual members so every member has a stake in the outcome of the team effort. Mini-mill steelmaker Nucor is a case in point. Each group of workers receives a basic salary and a bonus that is based on the rate by which the group exceeds production targets.[32] If the group, for instance, exceeds production targets by 50 percent, every member receives a 50 percent raise.

Connecting rewards and sanctions to the entire group's performance rather than to individual members' performance in turn creates a powerful incentive for peer pressure, for example, group members who are on time discipline the members who are not on time. Peer pressure further reduces close team supervision and monitoring and the costs associated with it. Peer pressure, moreover, puts workers into a less defensive position than does management pressure, reducing labor-management disputes.

Team incentives are not always formal and monetary, but can be informal and non-monetary, in the form of, for example, praise from management, lunch or breakfast with top management, a photo in the company newspaper, a recognition plaque, or nomination for a club membership, all of which inject and reinforce self-confidence. "Take every opportunity to inject self-confidence into those who have earned it. Use ample praise, the more specific the better."[33] Insurance companies, for instance, reward top-performing agents with membership in million dollar clubs. Food companies reward sales managers with free food, and airline companies reward employees with free tickets. Manufacturing companies like Nucor and Toyota publicly recognize employees with zero workplace absences.

Team incentives may be negative, in the form of sanctions. Team members who fail to cooperate with other members and deliver on their assignments may be sanctioned by the other members and the company. Microsoft, for instance, fires the worst team performers, whereas Cisco Systems and GE regularly rank employees, laying off non-performers. Nucor's workers who are late for a shift lose a day's bonus and those who miss a shift lose a week's bonus.

As is the case with network unit incentives, team incentives promote cooperation between teams within and across network units. This can be accomplished with network-wide bonuses and profit sharing, stock options, and activities that cultivate a community of faith within each network unit. Team incentives must be further supplemented by individual incentives that reinforce team incentives and cultivate individual creativity at the same time.

Individual Incentives

In his less known contribution to the understanding of human behavior, *Moral Sentiments*, Adam Smith, the author of *The Wealth of Nations*, outlines a number of motives guiding individual behavior, ranging from the pursuit of monetary rewards, such as wages and bonuses, to non-monetary rewards, such as the pursuit of power associated with promotion, the satisfaction from reaching certain goals and career advancement, and the visibility and public recognition that often come with them.

Adam Smith's pioneering work on moral sentiments has attracted scores of followers among academicians, business executives, and management consultants searching for the proper rewards to align the interests of individual employees with those of their team or the entire corporation. Northrop Grumman's individual incentive system, for instance, rewards individuals from each group who receive outstanding annual reviews. Northrop Grumman also has a Timely Appreciation Plan that includes outstanding employee awards, employee suggestion awards, customer service awards, and sales awards. Microsoft has sabbatical leaves and paid vacations to exotic resorts for employees who meet strict deadlines for software development. Nike promotes employees who discover new products into managers who oversee the development, production, and marketing of these products. L'Oreal pays up to 2.5 weeks' extra compensation for individual employees who achieve the company's targets. Formal rewards include field trips, as well as educational and personal growth and stock ownership plans. Major retailers, for instance, give their employees the right to buy company stock below the market price.

The relative importance of each of these incentives may vary from individual to individual, depending upon age, education, and work attitudes. Younger employees, for instance, are more motivated by promotion and visibility, while older employees are more motivated by recognition, power, and respect. More educated employees are more concerned about career advancement, while less educated employees are more concerned about monetary rewards. Workaholics may derive satisfaction from work itself rather than monetary rewards.

In short, incentives play an ever more important role in deterring opportunistic behavior and in aligning network member interests with those of the organization. Incentives eliminate the need for close supervision and monitoring and minimize the risk of opportunistic behavior that undermines the cohesion of network corporations, like global corporations. An aggressive stock option plan can eventually turn the global unit of the semiglobal corporation into a holding company where the network units are its owners. Yet incentives may not always be sufficient to motivate all members of a large and diverse corporation, especially those who do not work for monetary rewards alone. They must be supplemented by cultural controls that cultivate a community of faith.

Network Unit Motivation: Cultural Controls

Culture, a system of values, attitudes, and beliefs people hold to be true, has always been an important motivating factor in every organization. It is the "glue" that holds institutions together and provides support for one norm of behavior over another and one policy over another.

In business organizations, culture is the basis for developing and nurturing a "community of fate" among the agents involved in the network. A community of faith can be achieved in three ways (see Table 8.4). The first is through a sound vision that defines the social function of the firm, the contribution of the enterprise to the society at large, and a set of values that define the rules of conduct of the enterprise. This means that network management must balance individual excellence with community dedication, as was the case with Athenian leaders in ancient Greece. "The greatest Athenian leaders delicately balanced their individual vision and personal excellence with dedication to community orientation and collaboration. Leaders who failed to maintain the right balance could quickly lose their capacity to lead, and might find themselves dismissed."[34]

Network management must also respect the different cultures and attitudes among its members. Take the difference in attitudes toward teams in the United States and Japan, for instance. Whereas in Japan weak team members become a challenge for management and coworkers, who assist them to catch up with stronger members, in the United States weak members become the targets of management and coworkers and eventually are expelled from the team and the organization.[35] The same is true with corporate alliances with suppliers, where Japanese manufacturing companies help weaker suppliers to catch up with stronger suppliers. In some cases, Japanese automakers assist their American suppliers to become competitive even if those suppliers sell parts to competing automakers.[36]

Second, a community of faith can also be engendered though participatory management, that is, bottom-up decision making, as was the case in Athenian *politeia*, which was the product of sound citizenship rather than sound leadership. "Unlike most modern organization designs, the Athenian *politeia* did not start with a strategy, then devise a structure,

Table 8.4

Activities That Cultivate a Community of Common Faith

Factor	Description
Vision	A mission and a set of core values that define the social character of the network. Balance individual excellence with community dedication.
Participatory management	Bottom-up decision making. Empower the different network units to participate in decision making.
Improvement in working conditions	Make the working environment safe and pleasant.

and finally plug people into the framework. It began with the people themselves, and let values and structure and design emerge through the aligning practices of citizenship. The result was sustained, dynamic performance."[37] Participatory management empowers the members of the organization to express their opinions and concerns about issues in the workplace, and even if they are not satisfied with certain decisions, it makes it less likely that they will oppose them. In companies like Toyota, participatory management also means the utmost concern for the community, for the customer who buys the cars that come off the assembly line, and the empowerment of workers to halt production lines for troubleshooting. "Toyota team members treat the next person on the production line as their customer and will not pass a defective part onto the customer. If a team member finds a problem with a part or the automobile, the team member stops the line and corrects the problem before the vehicle goes any farther down the line."[38]

Third, a community of faith is promoted through a strong emphasis on improving working conditions, making the work environment free of pollution and other health hazards, and pleasant: for example, reducing the burden of heavy work, creating a dustproof working environment, cutting down on noise, and making the workplace safer.[39] Fourth, a community of faith is encouraged by helping employees fulfill their family responsibilities and develop their careers. "We must be mindful of ways to help our employees fulfill their family responsibilities. Employees must feel free to make suggestions and complaints. There must be equal opportunity for employment, development and advancement for those qualified."[40]

In short, each unit of the semiglobal corporation is faced with the "agency problem." The multinational unit is faced with the opportunistic behavior of subsidiaries, as magnified by geographic and cultural distance and information inefficiencies. The network unit is faced with the opportunistic behavior of one or more agents that may try to take advantage of the network.

The multinational unit agency problem can be resolved either though corporate centralization, which concentrates decision-making power at headquarters, or through decentralization, which diffuses decision-making authority throughout the organization. Corporate centralization is supported and reinforced by bureaucratic motivation mechanisms that control the behavior of subsidiaries, whereas corporate decentralization is supported and reinforced by performance motivation mechanisms that control the consequences of subsidiaries' management behavior.

The global unit agency problem can be resolved through a two-level management structure: one at the core of the network, at the support offices, and the other at each network unit. Each level is supported by an incentive motivation mechanism that seeks to align the interests of network units with those of the support center, and a cultural control mechanism that aligns the interests and attitudes of network members with those of the organization.

Notes

1. QUALCOMM, *2005 Annual Report*, San Diego, CA, p. 22.
2. Agere Systems, *2004 Annual Report*, on Form 10-K, p. 48.
3. Liker (2004), pp. 261–62.
4. Micklethwait and Wooldridge (2003), pp. 64–65.
5. Ibid., p. 60.
6. Schmitz (1993), p. 68.
7. Gerstner (2002), p. 96.
8. Gong (2003), p. 728.
9. For details, see Chang and Taylor (1999), p. 542; and Harzing and Sorge (2003), p. 206.
10. Bartlett and Ghoshal (1989), p. 162.
11. Harvey and Novicevic (2002), p. 528.
12. Chang and Taylor (1999), p. 544.
13. Treven (2001), p. 181.
14. Harzing and Sorge (2003), p. 198.
15. Oxnard (2004), p. 33.
16. Ibid., p. 31.
17. Ibid., p. 32.
18. Davis (1979), p. 54.
19. Palmeri and Byrnes (2005).
20. For a detail discussion, see Blasi, Kruse, and Bernstein (2003).

21. "CEO Compensation Survey 2004," *Wall Street Journal*, Apr. 11, 2005, pp. R7–R10.

22. Agere Systems, *2004 Annual Report*, on Form 10-K, p. 48.

23. Lucent Technologies, *2004 Annual Report*, Murray Hill, N.J., p.37.

24. Qualified ESOPs are subject to a number of constraints and limitations. They are limited to the employees of the company (sec. 423 of the IRS code). First, stock purchases must be approved by the board of the company within twelve months before they are purchased. Second, any employee who owns more than 5 percent of the company may not participate. Third, all eligible employees must be allowed to participate. Fourth, the purchase plan may not be less than 85 percent of the stock's fair purchase price. Fifth, the maximum offering period cannot exceed twenty-seven months. Finally, an employee may not purchase more than $25,000 of stock.

25. Applied Materials, *2004 Annual Report,* Santa Clara, CA.

26. Bernhardt (1999).

27. Ibid., p.125.

28. Ibid., p. 126.

29. Cohn (1999), p. 44.

30. Jacobs (2001).

31. Bary (2003), p. 21.

32. Ghemawat (1995).

33. Welch and Welch (2005), p. 66.

34. Ibid., p. 27.

35. Besser (1995).

36. Scheffler (1997).

37. Brook and Ober (2003), p. 14.

38. www.toyotageorgetown.com/qualdex.asp, 2/16/2005.

39. Ogasawara and Ueda (1996).

40. Johnson & Johnson Credo, www.jnj.com/our_credo/index.htm, 3/23/2005.

9

The Future of the Semiglobal Corporation

Strategy means making clear cut choices about how to compete. You cannot be everything to everybody, no matter what the size of your business or how deep its pockets.[1]

This book began with the premise that in the middle of the first decade of the new millennium the world economy became caught in the cross-currents of two opposite trends, globalization and localization, that shape a multiple world business environment.

Economic integration has advanced in different stages across geographic regions and countries. In some regions, economic integration is in high gear (e.g., northern Europe and NAFTA), in others regions, it has advanced in low gear (e.g., southern Europe), while in a third group of regions, it has been stuck in neutral or even has gone into reverse gear (e.g., Africa).

Economic integration has also advanced in different gears across industries. In some industries, globalization has prevailed, yielding a "pure" global market, a perfectly integrated world market environment. In other industries, localization has prevailed, yielding a "pure" local market, a perfectly segmented world market environment. In a third group of industries, neither globalization nor localization prevails, yielding a "hybrid," a semiglobal market.

The two segments of the semiglobal economy should not be seen as separate and isolated from each other, but integrated with each other, which can be best understood if products crossing national and local markets are viewed as value propositions that include both highly globalized bundles that deliver value primarily though global characteristics, such as automobile engines and cellular phones, and highly localized bundles that deliver value primarily though local characteristics, such as automobile repairing, servicing, and financing. This means that semiglobal markets are made up of two integral segments, a highly globalized and a highly localized segment.

In some cases, semiglobal value propositions are offered by joint ventures and strategic alliances of two or more companies. Cellular phone value propositions, for instance, are offered jointly by alliances of cellular phone manufacturers that provide the highly globalized component of the proposition, the cellular phone, and cellular service providers that provide the highly localized component like minutes, messaging, and billing. In other cases, highly globalized and highly localized bundles are offered jointly by the same company. Automobile value propositions, for instance, which include highly globalized bundles like engines and highly localized bundles like automobile financing and repairing, are offered by automobile companies. This means that automobile companies compete simultaneously in the globalized and the localized segments of the semiglobal economy. Information technology companies also compete in both segments of the semiglobal market. IBM competes both in the highly globalized market for hardware bundles, and in the highly localized markets for software. Broadcom Corporation competes in several industry segments with different degrees of globalization/ localization: integrated circuits and related applications, and system-level and motherboard-level solutions. PMC-Sierra, Inc., competes in several segments of the network equipment market. Some of these categories are more standardized, catering to the global market segment, while others are localized, catering to the local market segment.

Each segment of the semiglobal market environment has its own distinct characteristics. The highly globalized segment is characterized by a high degree of cross-border economic integration, rapid technological progress and product obsolescence, and a high degree of imitation, which expose local competitors to local and international competition and to market saturation. Highly globalized bundles quickly turn into commodities, and highly globalized industries face the constant influx and outflux of competitors that push profitability rates ever closer to the economy average. Industries that earn above-the-economy-average earnings attract new competitors, while industries that earn below-average earnings prompt the exit of competitors that feed into price and profit fluctuations: the entry of new competitors puts downward pressure on prices and profits, while the exit of competitors drives up prices and profits. This means that the survival and profitability of global competitors depends on their ability to devise strategies to address the destructive forces of globalization, that is, strategies that limit competition and price and profit destruction.

The highly localized or multinational segment is characterized by a low degree of cross-border economic integration, limited competition, and slow technological progress and product obsolescence and imitation, which insulate local competitors from outside competition, strengthening pricing power and profitability. Highly localized segments enjoy steady and above-economy-average profitability both in the short term and long term.

The rise of the semiglobal economy has challenged the conventional international business strategy wisdom on several grounds. First, it has challenged the "one strategy fits all" proposition that advocated the application of the same strategy in every national and local market. Second, it has challenged the "think global, act local" proposition that advocates the localization of products through localized marketing campaigns, close relations with government bureaucrats, and generous local philanthropy. Third, it has challenged the proposition that non-horizontal network-like business organizations are better suited to competing in international markets than conventional hierarchical organizations.

Addressing these challenges requires the development of a new business strategy model, the semiglobal corporation, a hybrid of the conventional hierarchical model of the multinational corporation and the modern model of the non-hierarchical global corporation. The semiglobal corporation is a dual rather than a single business organization, with a dual competitive strategy, a dual vision, and dual coordination, communication, and motivation structures.

Vision

The semiglobal corporation views the world economy both as a highly integrated or globalized market and as a low integrated or localized market: a highly integrated market for its highly globalized value offerings, and a lowly integrated market for its highly localized product offerings. This means that the semiglobal corporation must act as both a responsible global and local citizen at the same time. As a responsible global citizen, it must promote global harmony and eudaimonia, adhering to Aristotle's code of ethics, courage, self-control, wisdom, and fairness, and reaching for the global eudaimonia, the material and the spiritual well-being of a community, the ultimate goal, the telos, of society. The semiglobal corporation must work closely with governments to deter market concentration and the formation of monopolies, provide a "safety net" for those left behind the rough race for globalization, and address the "side effects" of globalization: psychological stress, environmental pollution, and nuclear proliferation.

As a responsible local citizen, the semiglobal corporation must promote local harmony and eudaimonia, which means different things in different societies. In most European countries, good local citizenship is synonymous with the diffusion of the gains of economic growth and international trade to all members of society, respect for workers' rights and, in some cases, mandatory labor participation in corporate boards and decision making. In China, good citizenship is synonymous to mandatory corporate welfare: the contribution to society by building and supporting schools, hospitals, universities, and so on. In Japan, good citizenship is synonymous with concern for employee welfare as expressed in the institutions of lifetime employment, enterprise unionism, and seniority wages. In America, good citizenship is synonymous with corporate responsibility and philanthropy. A clear and sound vision provides the basis for an efficient and effective competitive strategy.

Competitive Strategy

To achieve an above-industry-average rate of return, the semiglobal corporation applies a number of managerial and entrepreneurial strategies that address the peculiarities and specificity of the highly globalized and highly localized segments of the semiglobal economy. Managerial strategies allow the semiglobal corporation to better utilize its resources in delivering customer value, through cost cutting, marginal localization, and mass customization of its value propositions. Entrepreneurial strategies allow the semiglobal corporation to integrate market and technical information for the discovery and exploitation of new business opportunities through corporate spin-offs, strategic acquisitions, corporate venturing, and strategic alliances partnering with customers and employees, and partnering with suppliers, competitors, and the community. Entrepreneurial strategies are based on collaborative relationships that create social capital, which cannot be acquired in international markets. Collaboration requires efficient and effective coordination, communication, and motivation structures.

Coordination

The semiglobal corporation coordinates its operations through two units, a multinational unit that coordinates the highly localized bundles of value propositions, and a global unit that coordinates the highly globalized bundles. The multinational unit is a hierarchical business organization that consists of the parent company and several subsidiaries, normally one for each major national market. The parent company handles all strategic decisions on financing, marketing, production, distribution, new product development, mergers and acquisitions, alliances with other companies, and entry to new markets. The subsidiaries handle overseas business and are constrained from trading directly and cooperating with each other and with third parties without the prior consent of the parent. The global unit is a non-hierarchical business organization that treats the world market as a single integrated market. It consists of a core unit and several peripheral units. The core unit plays the role of the support office by handling matters of common concern for the network units, such as drafting a vision, arranging financing, research and development, and product and business branding. Network units handle their own internal business, such as production schedules, personnel hiring, local marketing, taxation, and local community relations, and are free to trade and cooperate with each other.

Communication

The semiglobal corporation applies both IT systems and managerial systems to recycle information and knowledge among the members of its organization. Yet each of its two units applies different channels of transmitting information and knowledge. Multinational unit communication is primarily intra-organizational communication that relies mostly on closed communication methods and vertical communication channels: closed IT systems and applications, expatriate rotation and transfers and irregular headquarters visits, and executive and technical personnel conferences. Network unit communication is primarily inter-organization communication that utilizes horizontal communication channels and closed communication methods: open IT systems, horizontal job rotation and transfers, and global conferences and teams.

Motivation

Each unit of the semiglobal corporation is faced with the "agency problem." The multinational unit is faced with the opportunistic behavior of subsidiaries, as magnified by geographic and cultural distance, and information inefficiencies. The network unit is faced with the opportunistic behavior of one or more agents that may cheat on other network members.

Opportunistic behavior in multinational organizations can be resolved though corporate centralization that concentrates decision-making power at headquarters, and corporate decentralization that spreads decision-making authority throughout the organization. Corporate centralization is supplemented by bureaucratic motivation mechanisms that control the behavior of subsidiaries, whereas corporate decentralization is supplemented by performance motivation mechanisms that control the consequences of subsidiary management actions rather than the actions themselves.

Opportunistic behavior in network organizations can be resolved through a two-level management structure: one at the core of the network, at the support offices, and the other at each network unit. Each level is supported by an incentive motivation system that seeks to align the interests of network units with those of the support center, and a cultural control mechanism that aligns the interests and attitudes of network members with those of the organization.

In short, globalization and internationalization are not necessarily interchangeable trends. They can coexist, each affecting different segments of the world economy. This means that international strategy cannot be carved in stone like ancient Greek texts that survived for centuries. Business strategists must constantly

- assess the forces of globalization and localization and the way they shape the international business environment;
- redesign their strategies to address the change in balance between the forces of globalization and localization;
- develop value propositions that contain the right mix of highly globalized and highly localized bundles;
- develop dual organizations that place highly localized bundles under a hierarchical, multinational organization, and highly globalized bundles under a non-hierarchical global organization;
- address the mutations and permutations of the value chain, mapping their core strategies of the future and adjusting their strategies accordingly.

Note

1. Welch and Welch (2005), p. 6.

Bibliography

Abo, T. 1995. "Cross-border Aspects of Foreign Subsidiary Management." *Management International Review* 35(1), special issue.

Aboulafia-D'Jaen, D. 1998. "Find the Common Thread in Global Communication." *Communication World* 15(9), Oct.–Nov.

Abrinck, J., Hanery, J., Kletter, D., and Nelson, G. 2000. "Adventures in Corporate Venturing." *Strategy and Business* 22 (1), pp. 119–28.

Adams, F.G. 2004. *The E-Business Revolution and the New Economy.* Mason, OH: South-Western.

Aharoni, Y., 1996. "The Organization of Global Service," *International Studies of Management and Organization*, (26) 2, p. 12.

Amer, S. 2004. "Different Strokes." *Successful Meetings* 53(11), pp. 44–51.

Ante, S.E. 2005. "Autodesk: A Software Vet's Growth Spurt." *Business Week*, Apr. 4, p. 50.

Atack, J., and Passell, P. 1994. *A New Economic View of American History.* New York: W.W. Norton.

Backman, R. 2004. "H-P Outsourcing: Beyond China." *Wall Street Journal*, Feb. 23.

Ball, D. 2003. "Liquor Makers Go Local." *Wall Street Journal*, Feb. 13, p. B3.

Banoo, S., and Caroline, R. 2000. "Competitive Strategy Is about Being Different." *Business Times* (Kuala Lumpur), Mar. 1.

Baran, P., and Sweezy, P., 1996. Monopoly Capital, New York: Modern reader Paperbacks.

Bartlett, C., and Ghoshal, S. 1989. *Managing Across Borders.* Boston: Harvard Business School Press.

———. 1995. *Transnational Management: Text, Cases, and Reading in Cross Border Management.* Boston: Irwin McGraw-Hill.

———. 2003. "What Is a Global Manager?" *Harvard Business Review*, Aug., pp. 101–7.

Bary, A. 2003. "Echo in the Valley: Microsoft's Move on Employee Options Puts Heat on Other Outfits to Do Likewise." *Barron's*, July 14.

Beaud, M., 1983. *A History of Capitalism: 1500–1980*, Monthly Review Press, New York.

Begley, T., and Boyed, D. 2003. "The Need for a Corporate Global Mind-Set." *MIT Sloan Management Review*, Winter, pp. 25–38.

Belderbos, R., and Heijltjes, M. 2005. "The Determinants of Expatriate Staffing by Japanese Multinationals in Asia: Control, Learning and Vertical Business Groups." *Journal of International Business Studies* 1(14), pp. 1–14.

Belson, K. 2004. "As Newcomers Swarm, Sony Girds for a Fight." *New York Times*, Feb. 8.

Bennett, J. 2005. "A Franchiser's Path to International Success Is Often Paved with Pitfalls." *Wall Street Journal*, Apr. 7, p. A7.

Berger L.P., and Huntington, P.S. 2002. *Many Globalizations*. New York: Oxford University Press.

Berger, S., and Dore, R. (eds.). 1996. *National Diversity and Global Capitalism*. Ithaca, NY: Cornell University Press.

Berle, A.A., Jr. 1954. *The 20th Century Capitalist Revolution*. New York: Harcourt, Brace.

Berman, D., and Bank, D. 2005. "Adobe Plans to Acquire Macromedia." *Wall Street Journal*, Apr. 18.

Berman, K.D. 2002. "Innovation Outpaced the Marketplace." *Wall Street Journal*, Sept. 26, pp. B1, B8.

Bernhardt, S. 1999, "The Supply of Non-Cash Remuneration: Employer Responses." Tasmanian State Convention, Taxation Institute of Australia, October, pp. 153–59.

Besanko, D., Dranove, D., and Shanley, M. 2000. *Economics of Strategy*. 2nd ed. New York: John Wiley & Sons.

Besser, T., 1995. "Rewards and Organizational Goal Achievement: A Case Study of Toyota Manufacturing Company," *Journal of Management Science*, 32(3) May.

Best, M. 1990. *The New Competition*. Cambridge, MA: Harvard University Press.

Bick, J. 1999. *The Microsoft Edge*. New York: Pocket Books.

Blackford, G.M., and Kerr, K.A. 1986. *Business Enterprise in American History*. Boston, Houghton Mifflin.

Blasi, J., Kruse, D., and Bernstein, A. 2003. *In the Company of Owners*. New York: Basic Books.

Blumberg, F.D. 1998. "Strategic Assessment of Outsourcing and Downsizing in the Service Market." *Managing Service Quality* 8(1), pp. 5–18.

Bolande, H.A. 2003. "China's Handset Makers Look to Go Global." *Wall Street Journal*, Jan. 30.

Borga, M., and Mann, M. 2004. "U.S. International Services: Cross-Border Trade in 2003 and Sales Through Affiliates in 2002." *Survey of Current Business*, Oct., pp. 25–28.

Bossidy, L., and Charan, R. 2004. *Confronting Reality: Doing What Matters to Get Things Right*. New York: Crown Press.

Bourdreau, M.C., Loch, D.K., and Straub, D. 1998. "Going Global: Using Information Technology to Advance the Competitiveness of the Virtual Transnational Organization." *Academy of Management Executive* 12(4), Nov., pp. 120–28.

Brook, M., and Ober J. 2003. "Beyond Empowerment: Building a Company of Citizens," *Harvard Business Review*, July–August.

Brooks, B. 2001. "Adding Value to a Product Is Necessary." *Business Journal*, Nov. 24, p. 1.

Buckley, P., and Hashai, N. 2004. "A Global System View of Firm Boundaries." *Journal of International Business Studies* 35, pp. 33–45.

Caminiti, S. 2005. "The Global Company: A CEO Discussion." *New York Stock Exchange Magazine*, Jan.–Feb., pp. 18–23.

Caulfield, B. 2003. "Saving $3 Billion the HP Way." *Business 2.0*, May, pp. 52–54.

Caves, R. 1992. *American Industry: Structure, Conduct, Performance*. Englewood Cliffs, NJ: Prentice-Hall.

Chan, M., and Chung, W. 2002. "A Framework to Develop an Enterprise Information Portal for Content Manufacturing." *International Journal of Production Economics* 75, pp. 113–26.

Chandler, A., Jr. 1977. *The Visible Hand: The Managerial Revolution in American Business*. Cambridge, MA: Belknap Press of Harvard University Press.

———. 1990. *Scale and Scope: The Dynamics of Industrial Capitalism*. Cambridge, MA: Belknap Press of Harvard University Press.

Chang, E., and Taylor, M. 1999. "Control in Multinational Corporations (MNCs): The Case of Korean Manufacturing Subsidiaries." *Journal of Management*, 25(4), July–Aug., pp. 542–65.

Chaserant, C. 2001. "Cooperation Contracts between Embed Firms." *Journal of Management and Governance*, Sept.–Oct. 2001.

Chesbrough, H. 2003. *Open Innovation: The New Imperative for Creating and Profiting from Technology*. Boston: Harvard Business School Press.

Chipello, C. 2003. "Success of Canadian Exporters Raises Questions on NAFTA Benefits." *Wall Street Journal*, Feb. 24, p. A5.

Choudhury, S. 2003. *Organization 21C*. New York: Financial Times/Prentice Hall.

Christensen, C. 2003. *The Innovator's Dilemma*. New York: Harper Business.

Christensen, C., and Raynor, M. 2003. *The Innovator's Solution*. Cambridge, MA: Harvard Business School Press.

Clark, D. 2003. "Change of Place: Big Bet Behind Intel Comeback: In Chips, Speed Isn't Everything." *Wall Street Journal*, Nov. 18, pp. A1, A2.

Clarke, C., and Douglas, L. 1998. "Conflict Resolution for Contrasting Cultures." *Training & Development* 52(2), Feb., pp. 20–34.

Cohn, L. 1999. "The Hidden Cost of Stock Options," *Business Week*, Dec. 6.

Colby, G. 1984. *Du Pont Dynasty: Behind the Nylon Curtain*. Secaucus, NJ: Lylle Stuart.

Collins, D. L. 1987. "Aristotle and Business," *Journal of Business Ethics*, Vol. 6, Sept.–Oct., pp. 567–572.

Collins, J., and Porras, J. 1996. "Building Your Company's Vision," *Harvard Business Review*, Sept.–Oct., pp. 65–77.

Coleman, C. 2004. "Zions Bancorp Looks to E-Signature Business for Profits." *Wall Street Journal*, Oct. 2, p. A7.

Cross, K. 2001. "The Weakest Links." *Business 2.0*, June 26, pp. 36–37.

Cross, R., Liedtka, J., and Weiss, L. 2005. "A Practical Guide to Social Networks." *Harvard Business Review* 83(3), pp. 350–8.

Crossen C., and Solomon, D. 2000. "AT&T takes on a humbler role." *Wall Street Journal*, p. A12.

Dale, E. 1960. *The Great Organizers*. New York: McGraw-Hill.

Davis, L. 1997. "Cross-Border Buyer-Supplier Development Collaborations." In *The Nature of the International Firm*, eds. Ingmar Bjorkman and Mass Forsgren. Copenhagen: Handelshojskolens Forlag.

Davis, L. et al. 1972. *American Economic Growth: An Economist's History of the United States*. New York: Harper & Row.

Davis, S. 1979. *Managing and Organizing Multinational Corporations*. New York: Pergamon.

Davy, J. 1998. "Online at the Office: Virtual Communities Go to Work." *Managing Office Technology* 9(2), July–Aug., pp. 9–11.

Delaney, J.K., and Bank, D. 2004. "Out with the New: Large Software Customers Refuse to Get with the Program." *Wall Street Journal*, Jan. 2, p. A7.

Demange, G. 2004. "On Group Stability in Hierarchies and Networks." *Journal of Political Economy* 112 (4), Aug., pp.754–778.

Dixit, K.A., and Nalebuff, J.B. 1991. *Thinking Strategically: The Competitive Edge in Business, Politics, and Everyday Life.* New York: W.W. Norton.

Donaldson, T., 1996. "Values in Tension: Ethics Away from Home," *Harvard Business Review,* September–October.

Donlan, T. 2005. "Creative Disruption: Don't Ignore These Cheaper Mousetraps." *Barron's,* Mar. 14.

Doorly, R. 2003. "Four Cultures, One Company: Achieving Corporate Excellence through Working Cultural Complexity." *Organization Development Journal* 21(2), pp. 52–64 (part II).

Douglass, P.E. 1971. *The Coming of Age of American Business: Three Centuries of Enterprise, 1600–1900.* Chapel Hill, NC: University of North Carolina Press.

Dreazen, J.Y. 2002. "Behind the Fiber Glut." *Wall Street Journal,* Sept. 26, pp. B1, B8.

Drucker, J. 2003. "Big-Name Mergers Won't Ease Crowding in Cellphone Industry." *Wall Street Journal,* Feb. 13, pp. A1, A5.

———. 2004. "Global Talk Gets Cheaper: Outsourcing Abroad Becomes Even More Attractive as Cost of Fiber-Optic Links Drops." *Wall Street Journal,* Mar. 11, pp. B1–B2.

Dymsza, A.W. 1972. *Multinational Business Strategy.* New York: Mc-Graw-Hill.

Einborn, B., and Rocks, D. 2004. "How Sharp Stays on the Cutting Edge." *Business Week,* Oct. 18, p. 36.

Eisenhardt, K. 1989."Agency Theory: An Assessment and Review." *Academy of Management Review* 14(1), pp. 57–74.

Elashamawi, F. 2001. *Competing Globally: Mastering Multicultural Management and Negotiations.* Boston: Butterworth and Heinemann.

Elliot, C. 1998. "Buckman Laboratories: In the Know." *Internet Week.com,* August 31. www.knowledgebusiness.com/knowledgebusiness.

Ellison, Sarah. 2003. "Food Marketers Are Torn Between Consumers' Two Different Mind-sets," *Wall Street Journal,* May 2, p. B1.

Engardio, P., Berstein, A., and Kripalani, M. 2003. "Is Your Job Next?" *Business Week,* Feb. 3, pp. 50–55.

Ewing, J. 1999. "Enough Euro Spin-offs to Make You Dizzy." *Business Week* (Int'l edition), May 10, pp. 1–2.

Foust, D. 2005. "Nucor: Soaring on Wings of Steel." *Business Week,* Apr. 4.

Fowler, G. 2003. "Copies 'R' Us." *Wall Street Journal,* Jan. 31, p. B1.

Frey, D. 2003. "How to Use the Power of Packaging to Double Your Sales." www.score.org/workshops/double-sales.html, 1/15/2003.

Gabel, M., and Bruner, H. 2003. *Global Inc.: An Atlas of the Multinational Corporation.* New York: The New Press.

Galbraith, K. 1972. *The New Industrial State.* New York: Penguin.

Geng, L. 2004. "The Use of Expatriate Managers in International Joint Ventures." *Journal of Comparative International Management* 7(1), June, pp. 325–365.

Gerstner, L. 2002. *Who Says Elephants Can't Dance? Inside IBM's Historic Turnaround.* New York: Harper Business.

Ghemawat, P., 1995. "Competitive Advantage and Internal Organization: Nucor Revised," *Journal of Economics & Management,* 3 (4).

———. 2003. "Semiglobalization and International Business Strategy." *Journal of International Business Studies* 34(2), Mar., pp. 138–52.

Ghoshal, S., and Gratton, L. 2002. "Integrating the Enterprise." *MIT Sloan Management Review*, Fall, pp. 31–43.

Ghoshal, S., and Bartlett C. 1996. "Rebuilding Behavioral Context: A Blueprint for Corporate Renewal." *MIT Sloan Management Review* 37, Winter, pp. 23–36.

Gilder, G. 2004. "Stop the Broadbandits." *Wall Street Journal*, Mar. 4, p. A5.

Gong, Y. 2003. "Subsidiary Staffing in Multinational Enterprises: Agency, Resources, and Performance." *Academy of Management Journal* 46(6), Dec., pp. 728–39.

Grant, P., and Latour, A. 2003. "Circuit Breaker: Battered Telecoms Face New Challenge: Internet Calling." *Wall Street Journal*, Oct. 9, pp. A1, A9.

Gupta, A., and Govindarajan, V. 2000. "Knowledge Flows within Multinational Corporations." *Strategic Management Journal* 21, pp. 473–96.

Guth, R. 2003. "Midlife Correction: Inside Microsoft, Financial Managers Win New Clout." *Wall Street Journal*, July 23, pp. A1, A6.

Guth, A.R., and Clark, D. 2004. "Peace Program: Behind the Settlement Talks— New Power of Tech Customers." *Wall Street Journal*, Apr. 5, A1, A3.

Gwynne, P. 2003. "The Myth of Globalization." *MIT Sloan School of Management Review*, Winter, p. 11.

Habharwal, N. 2002. "Service Bundle: Residential Gateways." *www.Hometeam.com/beta/007service.shtml*, 12/31/2002.

Hamel, G., and Schonfeld, E. 2003. "Why It's Time to Take a Risk." *Business 2.0*, 4(3):.62–68.

Harvey, M., and Novicevic, M. 2002. "Selecting Marketing Managers to Effectively Control Global Channels of Distribution." *International Marketing Review* 19(4/5), pp. 525–75.

Harzing, A. 1999. *Managing the Multinationals: An International Study of Control Mechanisms*. Cheltenham, UK: Edward Elgar.

———. 2000. "Of Bears, Bubble-Bees and Spiders: The Role of Foreign Expatriates in Controlling Foreign Subsidiaries." *Journal of World Business* 36(4), pp. 366–79.

Harzing, A., and Sorge, A. 2003. "The Relative Impact of Country of Origin and Universal Contingencies on Internationalization Strategies and Corporate Control in Multinational Enterprises." *Organizational Studies* 24(2), Feb., pp. 187–205.

Hawkins, L., Jr., and Lublin, J. 2005. "Emergency Repairman." *Wall Street Journal*, Apr. 6, p. B1.

Hays, C. 2004. "What They Know about You." *New York Times*, Nov. 14, pp. BU1, BU9.

Heinzl, M. 2004. "Battling the Cable Guy." *Wall Street Journal*, Apr. 29, p. B1.

Heskett, J., Sasser, E., Jr., and Schlesinger. 2003. *The Value Profit Chain: Treat Employees Like Customers, and Customers Like Employees*. New York: Free Press.

Hill, S., McGrath, J., and Dayal, S. 1998. "How to Brand Sand." *Business and Strategy*, second quarter, pp. 22–34.

Hirsh, E., and Wheeler, S. 1999. "Channel Champions: The Rise and Fall of Product-Based Differentiation." *Business and Strategy*, fourth quarter, pp. 43–50.

Hout, T., and Hemerling, J. 2003. "China's Next Great Thing." *Fast Company*, Mar. p. 12.

Howe, R. 1995. "At Starbucks, the Future Is in Plastic." *Business 2.0*, Aug., pp. 56–62.

Hunter, D., Bailey, A., and Taylor, B. 1995. *The Art of Facilitation.* Cambridge, MA: Fisher Books.

Hymer, H.S. 1976. *The International Operations of National Firms: A Study of Direct Foreign Investment.* Cambridge, MA: MIT Press.

Hymowitz, C. 2005. "When Meeting Targets Becomes the Strategy, CEO Is on Wrong Path." *Wall Street Journal*, Mar. 8, p. B1.

The Interactive Market: B to B Strategies for Delivering Just-in-Time, Mass-Customized Products, New York: McGraw-Hill, 2001, p. 108.

Iritani, E. 2003. "U.S. Firms Feel the Pinch of Tighter Border Security; Visitors and Shipments Are Blocked by Red Tape." *Los Angeles Times*, Feb. 18.

Isobe, T., and Montgomery, D. 1998. *Strategic Roles and Performance of Japanese Subsidiaries.* Research Paper 1507, Stanford Graduate School of Business, July 21.

Iwami, M., 1992. "What Is 'Japanese Style Management'?" *Management Japan*, (21)1.

Jacobs, M.A. 2001. "The Legal Option." *Wall Street Journal*, Apr. 12, p. R9.

Jayne, V., and Baker, G. 2002. "Building Critical Mass." *NZ Business* 16(9), pp. 40–43.

Jordan, M., 1996. "Marketing Gurus Say: In India, Think Cheap, Lose the Cold Cereal." *The Wall Street Journal*, Oct. 11, p. A3.

———. 2003. "Good Reason for Smiles." *Wall Street Journal*, July 23, p. B1.

Kahn, G. 2005. "Italy's Eni Challenges 'Big Oil,' Scoring Deals on New Frontier." *Wall Street Journal*, Jan. 18, p. A6.

Kahn, G., Bilenfsky, D., and Lawton, C. 2004. "Another Round: Burned Once, Brewers Return to China—With Pint-Size Goals." *Wall Street Journal*, Mar. 10, pp. A1, A8.

Kaihla, P. 2004. "The Matchmaking Machine." *Business 2.0*, Jan.–Feb., p. 25.

Kalawa, A. 2004. "Outsourcing Is Not the Enemy." *Wall Street Journal*, Feb. 2, pp. A1, A3.

Kanri, H. 2001. "Policy Management in Japanese-Owned UK Subsidiaries." *Journal of Management Studies* 38(5), pp. 651–74.

Kanter, R. 2003. "Thriving Locally in the Global Economy." *Harvard Business Review*, Aug., pp. 119–27.

Kaplan, A.D.H., Dirlam, J.B., and Lanzillotti, R.F. 1958. *Pricing in Big Business: A Case Study.* Washington, D.C.: Brookings Institution.

Kash, R. 2001. *The New Law of Demand and Supply.* New York: Currency Doubleday.

Keenan, F. 2001. "Friendly Spies on the Net." *Business Week*, July 9, p. 28.

Keenan, F., and Mullaney, T.J. 2001. "Let's Get Back to Basics, Folks!" *Business Week*, Oct. 29, p. 48.

Kelia, B., Nordtvedt, R. and Perez, L. 2002. "International Business Strategies, Decision-Making Theories, and Leadership Styles: An Integrated Network." *Competitiveness Review* 12, Winter–Spring, pp. 38–53.

Kelleher, K. 2004. "66,207,896 Bottles of Beer on the Wall," *Business 2.0*, Jan.–Feb., pp. 22–23.

Kendal, R., and O'Donnell, S., 1996. "Foreign Subsidiary Strategy: An Agency Theory Prospect." *Academy of Management Journal* 39(3), June, pp. 81–93.

Ketler, K., and Walstrom, J. 1993. "The Outsourcing Decision." *International Journal of Information Management* 13, pp. 449–59.

Kim, S., and Hart, J. 2002. "The Global Political Economy of Wintelism: A New Mode of Power and Governance in the Global Computer Industry." In *Information Technologies and Global Politics*, eds. J.N. Rosenau and J.P. Singh. Albany: NY: SUNY Press.

Kim, S., and Shin, E.H. 2002. "A Longitudinal Analysis of Globalization and Regionalization in International Trade: A Social Network Approach." *Social Forces* 81(2), Dec., pp. 445–70.

Kono, T., 1985. *Strategy and Structure of the Japanese Enterprise*. New York: M.E. Sharpe.

Koren, L., 1990. *Success Stories: How Eleven of Japan's Most Interesting Businesses Came to Be*. Chronicle Books, San Francisco.

Landers, P. 2002. "Good Medicine: Westerners Profit as Japan Opens Its Drug Market." *Wall Street Journal*, Dec. 2, p. A1.

Larkin, T.J., and Larkin, S. 1994. *Communicating Change: How to Win Employee Support for New Business Directions*. New York: McGraw-Hill.

Latour, A., and Drucker, J. 2005. "SBC and AT&T Are Holding Talks on an Acquisition." *Wall Street Journal*, Jan. 27, p. A1.

Lawrence, S., and Collin, J. 2004. "Competing with Kreteks: Transnational Tobacco Companies, Globalization, and Indonesia." *Tobacco Control* 13, pp. 96–103.

Lemaitre, C., and Excelente, C. 1998. "Multi-Agent Network for Cooperative Work." *Expert Systems with Applications: An International Journal* 14, pp. 117–27.

Leontiades, J.C. 1985. *Multinational Corporate Strategy: Planning for World Markets*. Lexington, MA: Lexington Books.

Liker, J. 2004. *The Toyota Way*. New York: McGraw-Hill.

Liker, J.K., and Choi, T.Y. 2004. "Building Deep Supplier Relationships." *Harvard Business Review* 82(12), Dec.

Lipton, M., Summer, 1996. "Demystifying the Development of an Organizational Vision," *Sloan Management Review*.

Luo, Y. 1995. "Market-Seeking MNEs in Emerging Markets: How Parent-Subsidiary Links Shape Overseas Success." *Journal of International Business Studies* 34(3), pp. 290–309.

McDonald, D. 2004. "Customer, Support Thyself." *Business 2.0*, Apr.

Macdonald, L. 2000. *How Innovation and Vision Created a Giant: Nortel Networks*. New York: John Wiley & Sons.

Magretta, J. 2002. "Fast, Global, and Entrepreneurial: Supply Chain Management Hong Kong Style." Interview. *Harvard Business Review* 76(5), Sept.–Oct., pp. 102–113.

Martyn, H. 1964. *International Business Principles*. New York: Free Press.

Marwick, A. 2001. "Knowledge Management Technologies." *IBM Systems Journal* 40(4).

Mataloni, R.J., Jr. 2000. "U.S. Multinational Companies." *Survey of Current Business*, July, pp. 26–38.

Mataloni, R.J., and Yorgason, D.R. 2002. "Operations of U.S. Multinational Companies: Preliminary Results from the 1999 Benchmark Survey." *Survey of Current Business*, Mar. Washington, D.C.: U.S. Department of Commerce, pp. 16–26.

Mazur, L. 2004. "Globalization Is Still Tethered to Local Variations." *Marketing*, Jan. 22, p. 18.

Meyer, J.R., and Gustafson, J.M. eds., 1988. *The U.S. Business Corporation: An Institution in Transition.* Cambridge, MA: Harper and Row, Ballinger.

Micklethwait, J., and Wooldridge, A. 2003. *The Company: A Short History of a Revolutionary Idea.* New York: Modern Library.

Migliorato, P. 2004. "Toyota Retools Japan." *Business 2.0,* Aug., pp. 39–43.

Morley, M. 2002. *How to Manage Your Global Reputation: A Guide to the Dynamics of International Public Relations.* New York: Palgrave.

Mossberg, W. 2003. "Beautiful But Too Big? New Apple Power Book Boasts 17-Inch Screen." *Wall Street Journal,* Apr. 3.

Mourdoukoutas, P. 1999a. *Collective Entrepreneurship in a Globalizing Economy.* Westport, CT: Quorum Books.

———. 1999b. *The Global Corporation: The Decolonization of International Business.* Westport, CT: Quorum Books.

Mourdoukoutas, P., and Mourdoukoutas, P. 2004. "Bundling in a Semiglobal Economy." *European Business Review* 16(5), p. 527.

Mourdoukoutas, P., and Papadimitriou, S. 2002. *Nurturing Entrepreneurship in a Globalizing Economy: Institutions and Policies.* Westport, CT: Quorum Books.

Mullich, J. 1997. "Intranet strikes a Chord," *PC Week,* Oct. 27.

Musa, M. 2000. "Factors Driving Global Economic Integration." htpp://www,imf.org/external/speeches/2000, 4/1/2000.

Naito, M.2002. "Chipmakers Seek Synergy in Union," June 24, *Nikkei Weekly.*

Neff, J. P. 1995. "Cross-cultural Research Teams in a Global Enterprise," *Research Technology Management,* May–June.

Nohria, N., and Ghoshal, S. 1994. "Differentiated Fit and Shared Values: Alternatives for Managing Headquarters-Subsidiary Relations." *Strategic Management Journal* 15, pp. 491–502.

Nonaka, I., and Takeuchi, H. 1995. *The Knowledge Creating Company.* New York: Oxford University Press.

North, D. 1996. *The Economic Growth of the United States.* New York: W.W. Norton.

O'Connor, R. 2004. "Secrets of the Masters." *Supply Chain Management Review* 8(1), Jan.–Feb., pp. 42–50.

OECD, 1996. *New Dimensions of Market Access in a Globalising Economy,* Paris.

Ogasawara, K., and Ueda, H., 1996. "The Changing Nature of Japanese Production Systems in the 1990s and Issues for Labor Studies." *Asia Pacific Review,* 2(4): pp. 44–59.

O'Keeffe, J. 2003. "Preparing Expatriate Managers of Multinational Organizations for the Cultural and Learning Imperatives of Their Job in Dynamic Knowledge-Based Environments." *Journal of European Industrial Training* 27 (5), pp. 233–55.

Overell, S. 2003. "Big Headache for Maker of Longer-Life Products." *Financial Times,* Nov. 24, p. 4.

Oxnard, T. 2004. "Stretch! How Toyota Reaches For Big Goals." *Supply Chain Management Review* 8(2), Mar., pp. 28–36.

Palmeri, C., and Byrnes, N. 2005. "The Immelt Revolution." *Business Week,* Mar. 28, pp. 64–68.

Parkinson, C.N. 1974. *Big Business.* Boston: Little, Brown.

Patton, J. 1997. "Sidestepping Obsoleteness." *Industry Week* 246(12), Nov. 3.

Perking, A., and Perking, M. 1999. *The Internet Bubble.* New York: Harper Business.

Pestre, F. July 2004. "The Implementation of Ethical Policy in Multinational Corporations." Paper 337, University of Paris.

Phatak, A. 1974. *Managing Multinational Corporations*. New York: Praeger.

Pine, B.J., II. 1999. *Mass Customization: The New Frontier in Business Competition*. Boston: Harvard Business School Press.

Piore, M., and Sabel, C. 1984. *The Second Industrial Divide: Possibilities for Prosperity*. New York: Basic Books.

Polanyi, M. 1996. *The Tacit Dimension*. London: Routledge & Kegan Paul.

Porter, G. 1992. *The Rise of Big Business*. 2nd ed. Arlington Heights, IL: Harlan Davidson.

Porter, M. 1986. *Competition in Global Industries*. Boston: Harvard Business School Press.

———. 1998. "Clusters and the New Economics of Competition." *Harvard Business Review*, Nov.–Dec., 1998, pp. 77–90.

Prahaland, C.K. 2004. *The Fortune at the Bottom of the Pyramid*. Philadelphia: Wharton School Publishing.

Prasad, S.B., and Shetty, Y.K. 1976. *An Introduction to Multinational Management*. Englewood Cliffs, NJ: Prentice-Hall.

Pringle, D. 2003. "How Nokia Thrives by Breaking the Rules." *Wall Street Journal*, Jan. 3, p. A5.

———. 2004. "Cell Division: After Long Peace, Wireless Operator Stirs up Industry." *Wall Street Journal*, Nov. 12, pp. A1, A9.

Pusateri, C.J. 1984. *A History of American Business*. Arlington Heights, IL: Harlan Davidson.

Ram, M., and Pietro, N. 2004. "Is Knowledge Power? Knowledge Flows, Subsidiary Power and Rent-seeking within MNCs." *Journal of International Business Studies* 35(5), Sept., pp. 385–406.

Ramstad, E., and Dvorak, P. 2003. "Off-the-Shelf Parts Create New Order in TVs, Electronics." *Wall Street Journal*, Dec. 16, pp. A1, A14.

Rao, R.A., Bergen, E.M., and Davis, S. 2000. "How to Fight a Price War." *Harvard Business Review*, Mar.–Apr., pp. 107–16.

Read, S. 2000. *The Oracle Edge*. Holbrook, MA: Adams Media Corporation.

Reed, E.S. 2003. "Technology Companies Take Hope in Charity." *New York Times*, Mar. 23.

Reingold, J. 1998. "And Now, Extreme Recruiting." *Business Week*, Oct. 19.

Rhoads, C. 2003. "Into the Fray: Threat from China Starts to Unravel Italy's Cloth Trade." *Wall Street Journal*, Dec. 17, pp. A1, A10.

Rosenbush, S., Crockett, R.O., and Haddad, C. 2003. "What Hath the FCC Wrought?" *Business Week*, Mar. 10, p. 51.

Rostow, E.V., and Ball, G.W. 1975. "Stages of Growth." In *Global Companies: The Political Economy of Global Business*, ed. George W. Ball, p. 18. Englewood Cliffs, NJ: Prentice-Hall.

Rugman, A. 1981. *Inside the Multinationals*. New York: Columbia University Press.

———. 2001. *The End of Globalization*. New York: AMACOM.

Savary, J. 1984. *French Multinationals*. New York: St. Martin's Press.

Savitz, E.J. 2004. "Talk Gets Cheap." *Barron's*, May 24. p. 8.

Scheffler, R. 1997. "Mazda's Synergy Strategy." *Japan Quarterly*, Apr.–June.

Schmitz, J.C. 1993. *The Growth of Big Business in the United States and Western Europe, 1950–1939.* Cambridge, MA: Cambridge University Press.

Segil, L., Goldsmith, M., and Belasco, J. 2003. *Partnering: The New Face of Leadership.* New York: AMACOM.

Shapiro, B. 1988. "What the Hell Is 'Market Oriented'?" *Harvard Business Review,* Nov.–Dec.

Shapiro, C., and Varian, R.H. 1999. *Information Rules: A Strategic Guide to the Network Economy.* Boston: Harvard Business School Press.

Shirouzu, N. 2003. "Ford's New Development Plan: Stop Reinventing Its Wheels." *Wall Street Journal,* Apr. 16.

Skapinker, M. 2003. "Contracted Out Services May Carry a High Price." *Financial Times,* Nov. 24, special report, p. 2.

Smith, T. 2003. "A Philanthropy Rush in Corporate Brazil." *New York Times,* Mar. 30, p. 3.5.

So, Y., and Durfee, E. 1996. "Designing Tree: Structured Organizations for Computational Agents." *Computational and Mathematical Theory,* Fall, pp. 219–46.

Solomon, M.C. 1995. "Global Teams: the Ultimate Collaboration," *Personnel Journal* 74(9), Sept., pp. 49–54.

Stigler, G. 1983. *The Organization of Industry.* Chicago: University of Chicago Press.

Sumi, T., and Tsuruoka, M. 2002. "Ramp New Enterprise Information Systems in a Merger & Acquisition Environment: A Case Study." *Journal of Engineering and Technology Management* 19, pp. 93–104.

Svensson, G. 2001. "'Globalization' of Business Activities: A 'Global Strategy Approach.'" *Management Decision* 39(1), pp. 6–18.

Tam, Pui Wing. 2003. "'Day Zero' Fear Could Boost Windows Rivals." *Wall Street Journal,* October 28, p. B1.

Tayles, M., and Drury, C. 2001. "Moving from Make/Buy to Strategic Sourcing." *Long Range Planning* 34, pp. 605–22.

Taylor, G., and Sudnik, P. 1984. *Dupont and the International Chemical Industry.* Boston: Twayne.

Tejada, C., and McWilliams, G. 2003. "Circuit City Salesmen Zapped on 'Bloody Wednesday.'" *Wall Street Journal,* June 11, p. A1.

Thurm, S. 2004. "Tough Shift: Lesson in India—Not Every Job Translates Overseas." *Wall Street Journal,* Mar. 3, pp. A1, A10.

Treven, S. 2001. "Human Resource Management in International Organizations." *Management* 6(1–2), pp. 177–89.

Udo, G. 2000. "Using Analytic Hierarchy Process to Analyze the Information Technology Outsourcing Design." *Industrial Management & Data Systems* 100(9), pp. 421–29.

Varian, R.H., and Shapiro, C. 1999. *Information Rules: A Strategic Guide to the Network Economy.* Boston: Harvard University Press.

Vernon, R. 1977. *Sovereignty at Bay,* New York: Basic Books.

Wasti, N., and Liker, K.J. 1997. "Risky Business or Competitive Power? Supplier Involvement in Japanese Product Design." *Journal of Production, Innovation, and Management* 14, pp. 337–55.

Welch, J., and Welch, S. 2005. *Winning.* New York: Harvard Business School Press.

Whitten, O.D. 1983. *The Emergence of Giant Enterprise, 1860–1914.* Quorum: Westport, CT.

Wilkin, S. 2004. "Global Differences: Succeeding in Korea Requires Cultivating a Taste for Kimchi." *Barron's*, Sept. 20, p. 45.

Wilkins, M. 1970. *The Emergence of Multinational Enterprise.* Cambridge, MA, Harvard University Press.

Willcocks, L.P. Lacity, M.C., and Kern, T. 2000. "Risk Mitigation in IT Outsourcing Strategy Revised." *Journal of Strategic Information Systems* 8, pp. 285–314.

Williamson, O.E. 1985. *The Economic Institutions of Capitalism: Firms, Markets, Relational Contracting.* New York: Free Press.

Williamson, O.E. 1985. "Opportunism and Its Critics." *Managerial and Decision Economics* 14, pp. 97–107.

World Bank Report. "Doing Business 2005: Poor Nations Struggle To Reduce Red Tape For Business, Miss Large Growth Opportunities." World Bank, Washington, DC.

Wright, C. 2000. "Making a Bundle with Bundling." *Rating Matters* 2, Nov. 21, p. 1.

Yang, C., and Huang, J.B. 2000. "A Decision Model for IS Outsourcing." *International Journal of Market Information* 20, pp. 225–39.

Yang, S., and Grant, P. 2003. "Bell Tolls: How Phone Firms Lost to Cable in Consumer Broadband Market." *Wall Street Journal*, Mar. 13, p. A1.

Young, D. 1998. "Team Heat." *CIO*, Sept. 1, pp. 1–9.

Zack, M. 1999. "Managing Codified Knowledge." *Sloan Management Review* 40(4), Summer, pp. 45–48.

Zahra, S. 2004. "A Theory of International New Ventures: A Decade of Research." *Journal of International Business Studies*, Dec. 23, pp. 1–9. Online edition.

Zeng, M., and Williamson, P. 2003. "The Hidden Dragons." *Harvard Business Review* 81(10), Oct. 23, pp. 88–96.

Zushi, R., Tan, L.W, Allampalli, G.D., and Gibbons, P. 1999. "Singapore Venture Capitalists (VCs) Investment Evaluation Criteria: A Re-Examination." *Small Business Economics* 13, pp. 9–26.

Index

About the Author

Panos Mourdoukoutas (Ph.D., SUNY Stony Brook) began his career at the State University of Pennsylvania and then taught at Long Island University in New York and Economic University of Athens. Professor Mourdoukoutas has represented Greece in the United Nations, traveled extensively throughout the world, and lectured at a number of universities, including Nagoya University, Kobe University, Tokyo Science University, Keimung University, Saint Gallen University, Duisburg University, and Beijing Academy of Social Science. He is the author of several papers presented at academic and business conferences and articles published in professional journals and magazines, including *Barron's* and *Edge Singapore*. He has also published several books, including *The Global Corporation: The Decolonization of International Businesses*; *China Against Herself: Imitation or Innovation in International Businesses*; *The Rise and Fall of Abacus Banking in Japan and China*; *Banking Risk Management in a Globalizing Economy*; *Strategy ADP: How to Compete in the Japanese Market*; *Collective Entrepreneurship in a Globalizing Economy*; *Nurturing Entrepreneurship: Institutions and Policies*; *Japan's Emerging New Economy: Opportunities and Strategy for World Business*; and *When Greece Turned into Little Japan*. In 2001, he received the Literati Club's Highly Commended author award.

THE RETURNED

Thank you and Best Wishes
Jack Devine

THE RETURNED

Jack Devine

Copyright © 2010 by Jack Devine.

Library of Congress Control Number: 2010917439
ISBN: Hardcover   978-1-4568-2193-7
               Softcover   978-1-4568-2192-0
               Ebook   978-1-4568-2194-4

All rights reserved. No part of this book may be reproduced or transmitted in any
form or by any means, electronic or mechanical, including photocopying, recording,
or by any information storage and retrieval system, without permission in writing
from the copyright owner.

This is a work of fiction. Names, characters, places and incidents either are the product
of the author's imagination or are used fictitiously, and any resemblance to any actual
persons, living or dead, events, or locales is entirely coincidental.

This book was printed in the United States of America.

To order additional copies of this book, contact:
Xlibris Corporation
1-888-795-4274
www.Xlibris.com
Orders@Xlibris.com
88377

CONTENTS

ACKNOWLEDGMENTS

Betsy (Graves) Barthlow, for her inspiration. Betsy was a dear friend and companion for twenty years and was the real inspiration behind Jack Devine's book. Betsy was a graduate of the College of William & Mary in Williamsburg, Virginia, and it was there in colonial Williamsburg where Jack Devine, while sitting in a tavern one evening and enjoying his libation, got the inspiration to write *The Returned*.

Joyce Giusti for her encouragement. Joyce is the wife of a fellow golf professional in Halifax, Massachusetts, and kept Jack motivated until he finished his book.

Jim O'Sullivan, for all his editing and overall assistance. Although not a formal editor, Jim has helped Jack with the editing, marketing, and publishing of *The Returned*.

The students and faculty of The Graphics Communications Department at The South Shore Vocational High School in Norwell, Massachusetts, for their creative and artistic skills in designing and creating the book's cover. Study the cover carefully for it depicts the essence of the story in *The Returned*.

CHAPTER ONE

The Stickup

It was a cold and wintry day in Boston, Massachusetts. The year was 1984. Three boys in their late teens and early twenties were standing on a street corner beside Murphy's Variety Store, waiting for Mr. Murphy to stop talking to Mrs. Johansen. A few minutes after she left, the three boys—Joe Davis; Jim Washington, an Afro American; and Dave Baker—walked into the store and looked around. Dave pulled out a gun and said, "This is a stickup. All your money and you will not get hurt." Before anybody could think, Mr. Murphy pulled out a shotgun from under the counter and said, "I have had it with you, punk bastards," and let go with both barrels, not hitting anyone but shattering the plate glass window in front of the store.

Police were nearby talking when they heard the shots. They started toward the store just as the boys ran out. One policeman saw them and said, "Halt!" Not even looking around, they ran down the street toward the warehouses on the wharf with the police in hot pursuit. Finding a door open in one of the warehouses, the boys ran in and hid behind some boxes. The police chased the boys down an alley to the wharf but could not find them. One policeman looking around said, "They could be anywhere in these damn buildings." "Yeah," said the other policeman. "We will look for them, and if we can't find them, we will look again in the morning. If we still can't find them, we will see the owner of the store and get a description."

Meanwhile, in the warehouse the boys got into the boxes to keep warm since it was cold, and then they decided to spend the night. Waking up the next morning the three were puzzled to find it was warm and humid, seeing that the forecast had been for cold and snow. Joe said to Dave, "Go and see if the coast is clear." Dave went outside, and looking around he could not believe his eyes. He came back into the room and said, "You are not going to believe this, but there are no tall buildings and no cars, only horses and carriages; and the people that I see are dressed funny." Joe said, "What the hell are you talking about?" Dave said, "If you don't believe me, come out here and take a look!"

The three walked outside, looked around, and started to stroll up the street. Jim said, "This is really weird. I have never seen anything like this." "This has to be a play, a movie, a circus, or something like that," said Dave. As they walked farther up the street, they heard a shout, "Halt in the name of the king!" The three turned around and were looking at three British soldiers. Dave, reaching for his gun, found that he had left it back in the warehouse. Dave said, "Halt in the name of who?" The soldiers looked at the boys and said, "Look at what we have here." One soldier said, "These youngsters are dressed sort of funny." The other soldier said, "Let's take the three of them to the captain."

The captain William Smyth was a burly man of about six feet. He was sitting behind a desk. One of the soldiers said to the captain, "We found these three sneaking around by the warehouses, and we think we have spies here." Smyth said, "Well now, what do you have to say for yourselves?" Joe said, "Look, I am a little pissed off here. I don't know what the hell is going on. You must be having a play here or something. In any case you have a lot of bad actors. Let's stop this bullshit right now and get us the fuck out of here!"

Captain Smyth said, "Take them to the stockade." One of the soldiers prodded them with his rifle, and the three were transferred in a cart to a makeshift jail out of town. Joe said, "By tomorrow we will wake up and find out this is a bad dream." "You are right," said Jim, and they went to sleep.

The next morning, when the three awoke to find that nothing had changed, a guard came in with breakfast. Dave asked the guard, "What day is it?" The guard replied, "April 6, 1775." "You have to be kidding!" said Dave. "No, I am not," said the guard, "and I think the three of you were in on that tea party in Boston." "You have to be kidding!" replied Dave. "No, I am not," replied the guard who turned around and left. Joe said to Dave, "What the hell are they talking about? What damn party?" "I don't know," said Dave. "This bullshit that is going on here I think they are carrying it a little too far. We have to figure out just what the hell is going on."

Then a voice came from outside the cell and said, "All hell is breaking loose! Some British troops were sent to the Lexington and Concord area to arrest some people named John Hancock and Samuel Adams. Some local militia who call themselves the Minutemen ambushed the British in a big battle. I say to hell with these British sons of bitches. I saw them arrest you boys; and when everybody was milling around, I stole a key, and I am letting you out." "Thanks," said Dave. "What is your name?" "Just call me Torn." "Thanks," said Jim, and with that the three escaped.

Once Dave asked "What is this about ambush and shots?" Torn said, "I think we are going to have ourselves a war." Torn left quickly, and the three headed for a wooded area. Dave suggested that they split up and that they meet back at the harbor at a later time when everything had cooled down. The three then split and went their different ways.

Jim headed south, and in about an hour he came to another wooded area. After about a week of getting food and drink any way he could, he came upon another black man. Jim said, "Hi, where are you going?" The man said, "I am going to fight with General Washington. Any man that was a slave will be set free if we fight against the British." He showed Jim a sign that read, "To all brave, healthy, and able-bodied and well-disposed young men in this neighborhood who have any inclination to join the troops now raising under General Washington for the defense of the—" Jim did not finish reading but looked up and asked the other black man, "What is your name?" "My name is Sam Samuel Dinger; they just call me Dinger for short."

Jim asked, "What the hell kind of a name is Dinger?" The man answered rather harshly, "IT IS MY NAME, SIR, AND I HAVE ALWAYS BEEN CALLED THAT." "I am sorry, Dinger. I didn't mean anything by that. Are you going to fight?" "Yes, sir, for General Washington. I will be free and will not have to go back to the boss I left. I will be a slave no more." By now Jim was beginning to wonder when this nightmare would end. Jim said to Dinger, "Good luck and I hope you find what you are looking for." Then he said good-bye and went on his way.

In about thirty minutes he came upon a farm and saw some workers out in the field. They talked for a while, and a man said "They had one hell of a fight at Breed's Hill, and a black man was a hero." Jim said, "Thank you very much," and continued down the road, still trying to figure out how he had gotten here and what the hell was going on. Posing as a runaway slave, he was receiving meals at farmhouses of sympathizers. About three days later he came upon a settlement with some stores and places to eat.

Walking down a dusty street, he heard a call, "Mr. Jim." Turning around, he saw Dinger. Jim said to Dinger, "How did you get here?" Dinger replied, "Colonel Christopher Green is looking for recruits to join him in Rhode Island. He promises that if you pass muster, you will be immediately discharged from the service of your master or mistress and be absolutely free." Jim, who had not much schooling remembered, some things about the Revolutionary War from when he could stay awake in school. This was crazy because he already knew the outcome. He thought, "I must be in the twilight zone or something, which I would like to get the hell out of and get back to the home I know and get out of this crazy thing."

Jim said to Dinger, "Where are you headed?" "Down to the compound to pick up some food, a rifle, and ammunition at the store." Walking down a dusty street, they came to the store with four horses tied to a hitching post out front. When they walked into the store, Jim asked Dinger, "How much for these weapons?" Dinger replied, "Don't worry, I have enough. We will have to be prepared just in case." "Just in case of what?" asked Jim. "Indians," replied Dinger. "Indians," said Jim, "what the hell do you mean Indians!" "When we hit the woods, there will be a lot of them," said Dinger, "and most of them will be fighting for the British, and they are ruthless. They kill men, women, and children."

Looking around, Jim saw a newspaper called the *New York Mercury* dated April 10, 1775. It read that the welfare of the colonies on this continent "was in jeopardy." While he read, the article wrote of atrocities and quoted letters from the front about trouble from the Native Americans (Indians). Jim was now thinking, "What am I into? What the hell is going on? One day I am running from the police, and the next day people are talking about Indians." Now Jim was saying to himself, "I read about all this bull in school, and the worst thing is I know how this is going to turn out. If I say anything, everybody is going to think I am crazy."

After they finished getting their supplies, Jim said, "Where are we going now, Dinger?" Dinger replied, "We are—or at least I am—going to fight the damn British." "All right," said Jim, "I will tag along, but I don't know about any fighting."

They spent the next week fishing with a tree limb and string. Dinger shot a deer; and they had to cut the deer, gut it and cook it over an open campfire. Jim was now really talking to himself, "I thought it was tough trying to rob people without getting shot, but this is the worst I have ever been through!"

Dinger and Jim came upon a little farm owned by a black man and his family. Jim knocked on the door, and the wife answered, "Can I help you?" Jim, surprised, said, "My friend and me wondered if you had anything to eat." The husband said, "Come on in." Then he asked, "Where you from?" "Around the Boston area," Jim answered. After they had something to eat, the man said "You fellows have been walking all of this time?" "Yes," said Dinger. "Well, maybe I can help you. I have a cousin down the road that needs some goods. I have a horse and wagon, and you people can help. Take the wagon with the goods; that would help a lot. But watch out. There are people looking for runaway slaves that might shoot you and take the goods." "Don't worry," said Dinger, "we are armed." Jim was thinking to himself, "Runaway slaves? What the hell is he talking about?"

"Well," said Dinger, "this will be a break. At least we won't be walking for now. I was beginning to get tired." "Yeah," said Jim, "I was too." After they dropped the wagon off at the cousin's house, they started walking in the woods again. "I have never walked so damn much in all my life!" said Jim. After walking, resting, and sleeping in the woods, they came upon another farm. Looking around, it seemed as if nobody was there. "That's funny," said Dinger. "What?" said Jim. "There is nobody here on a farm like this?" "Yeah," said Dinger. Jim said under his breath, "I wonder what is going on. Something does not feel right." They began to look around again, Dinger looking in one direction and Jim in another. All of a sudden Jim said, "Oh shit, son of a bitch!" He called to Dinger, and Dinger came over and gasped. What they saw was a whole family—husband, wife, and children—murdered, scalped, torn to pieces, and left to be devoured by wild beasts.

Jim became sick at the sight and began to throw up. Dinger said, "It was the Indians." "And I hope they are gone. The fucking Indians," said Jim. "If I had them and their families here, I would shoot the bastards—the whole bunch of them." Dinger said, "Let's move on. There is nothing we can do here." Jim said, "I thought I saw it all, but I never saw nothing like that." As the evening got on, Jim and Dinger decided to rest for the night. It was getting about sunset when all of a sudden they heard a noise. Looking around, they saw a pig. Dinger took his rifle and shot it. The pig went down. "Well," said Dinger, "it looks like we have food for the night." Jim was thinking, "Damn it, here we go again, butchering another animal, first a deer and now a pig. Why couldn't they just have a good steakhouse!" Dinger took care of the pig while Jim tried not to watch. They cooked it, and Jim thought "I guess when you're hungry, you'll eat anything!" Then they went to sleep.

It was midmorning when they woke up. "Wow, you talking about being tired," Jim said. The morning was misty; the forest was deep and dense as they came to a river and proceeded along the river's edge. Dinger said, "Quiet, stay down." "What?" said Jim. "Look," said Dinger, "an Indian. I don't think he sees us." Just then Jim grabbed a rifle and fired. The Indian went down, and they went over to check out the body. Jim started hitting the Indian, who was lying mortally injured on the ground. Jim said to the injured Indian, "You rotten bastard, this is for the family I saw a little while back." He took the butt end of the rifle and hit the Indian, repeatedly killing him. Then he took his knife and tried to scalp him. Dinger said, "What are you doing? We have to get out of here. There might be more of them. He must be a scout. I don't think there would just be one of them; there must be more. Let's get out of here just in case."

Still in a mad state, Jim said, "Bullshit! I wanted justice for that family back there." Dinger said, "You were a little crazy back there." Jim said, "I know I lost it, and I don't know why. I think seeing that family just got to me." They continued down along the riverside. It was now getting late. The sun was going down, and the sunset was beautiful behind the trees and reflecting off the flowing river. As they settled down for the night, Jim was thinking, "I wish I knew what was going on. I guess I woke up, and I am in hell."

Meanwhile back up the river the band of Indians found their comrade dead and his head cut as if he was about to be scalped. The Indians numbered about fifteen, and the leader said, "We will find the ones who did this and kill them." One of the Indians said, "It looks like they went down the river." So the Indians got on their horses and started down the side of the river in search of Jim and Dinger.

CHAPTER TWO

The Teacher

A short while later, as Jim and Dinger were sleeping, a dark shadow came upon them. Awakened by the movement, Jim saw a tall man standing over him dressed in black with his rifle trained upon him. Jim asked, "Who the hell are you?" "Jed Thompson" was his reply. "And what are you doing here standing over me with a gun?" "I rode hard and took a shortcut to tell you that you have some Indians following you," said Thompson. "From what I can see, their intentions are not good. They found their dead companion, and they intend to do the same to you."

(Now Jed Thompson was a man that once had his family killed by some Indians, and he had no love for them.) Thompson said, "We will have to backtrack and steal some of their horses." By this time Dinger was awake. "What the hell is he talking about?" "I don't know how to ride a horse," said Jim. "You had better," said Thompson. Jim said to himself, "Shit, I don't know how this is going to work out." They backtracked for about a day before they came upon the Indians. Two were guarding the horses, and the rest were sleeping. As Jim was watching their horses, Thompson came up silently behind one of the guards and slit his throat. Dinger stabbed the other guard, and Thompson, keeping the horses quiet, led them back into the woods.

Dinger could ride; Jim could not. Thompson then scattered the horses, and the three took off into the woods with Jim riding on the back of Dinger's horse. When the Indians woke up to find their guards dead, they were kept busy chasing their horses. Thompson, Jim, and Dinger rode for about an hour then decided to rest. Jim asked Thompson, "Why are you dressed in black all the time?" Thompson replied, "It makes it harder for me to be seen at night." Jim said, "What do you have in that sack you carry?" Thompson threw the sack at Jim. When Jim opened the sack to find it full of Indian scalps, all he could do was stare at Thompson. Jim then said, "What is a white man doing with us two blacks?" "Saving your lives," said Thompson. "What do you do?" asked Dinger. Thompson replied, "I was a schoolteacher and a pretty good one too. I came home one day and found my family butchered, and then all I wanted to do was to kill all those red bastards."

Jim was thinking, "It's bad enough I kill an Indian and have a band of them chasing us when this crazy bastard goes back and kills two more and steals their horses to boot. Before this is over, this son of a bitch will have Sitting Bull on our ass." The next day they decided to continue riding south toward Rhode Island and Colonel Green. After about an hour, they came to a little village with something like a country store. Jim said, "This is not like driving a Ford." "A what?" said Dinger. "Never mind," said Jim. There was a tavern, and the three were hungry. Thompson had some rope, so he tied the horses to a tree on the outskirts of town, and then they walked down the center of the street toward the tavern.

The townspeople were looking with curiosity at the white man dressed all in black and the two black men especially the tall man in black. As they walked into the tavern, the room was not well lit, but candles were burning on all the tables. The waiter came over to the table, looking at the, black men. Thompson said, "Never mind looking at us. Get us a pitcher of ale." "I am sorry," said the waiter. "I will get your ale." Jim said to Thompson, "What is our plan?" Thompson replied, "I do not like the damn British or the damn Indians. I would like to kill both of those groups, so I plan to meet with up with the new Americans and fight with them." Jim looked at Dinger, and Dinger said, "I will join Mr. Thompson and fight for my freedom." Jim said, "I think you are both crazy," while saying to himself, "If they knew how this was going to turn out, they would give it up right now."

The waiter came over with the ale, and while they were drinking, three locals came over to the table and said to Thompson, "What are you doing with these black slaves?" One of the men started at Dinger with a hunting knife. Thompson said, "I would not do that if I were you." The other man said, "What are you going to do about it?" From underneath Thompson's coat came a long-barreled pistol. Thompson then asked, "How long would one or all of you like to live?" "You can't get all of us," the man said. "Maybe not," replied Thompson, "but I could get you first, and my two friends can take care of the rest of you." The three backed up and then headed out the door. Jim said, "Let's get out of here."

Thompson said, "Sit down and finish your ale." Jim was now thinking, "This man is crazy; he has a death wish. He must think he is Wyatt Earp." They finished their ale and got up.

When they went outside, the townspeople watched the three as they walked toward their horses just outside of town with Jim looking behind him all the way. When they got to their horses, Jim still rode on the back of Dinger's horse, and they headed south again. In about an hour, they were back beside the river. Thompson said, "This is a good place to bed down for the night." Thompson had his bedding, but Jim and Dinger slept on the ground. Before he went to sleep, Jim was thinking, "This damn thing is getting ridiculous. I wish I was the hell out of this mess and could find my way back to the waterfront in Boston. If I could have everything like it was before, I might give up robbing because I would not want to go through this again." Then he fell asleep.

About two thirty in the morning a bad thunderstorm came down the river with heavy rain falling. The heavy rain caused flooding, and the horses broke loose. Thompson woke everybody up and said, "Let's get the hell out of here." The water by now was rushing over the banks. As they ran, the wind was howling, and trees were falling. With the heavy wind and driving rain, it looked like all hell was breaking loose. The three ran for cover. They came upon some rocks with a ledge and stayed there until the storm was over. Dinger said, "I wonder what happened to the horses." Thompson said, "They scattered. I guess they went back to where they came from." They stayed by the ledge for the night.

The next morning Jim said, "Where the hell are we going to get horses? Right now we cannot afford horses." Then Thompson said, "If we cannot afford the horses, then we will have to get them some other way." "What other way?" said Jim. Thompson said, "We will have to steal them." Jim and Dinger looked at each other, and Jim said, "They hang horse thieves, don't they?" Thompson said, "Do you have another way to get them?" "Some teacher," muttered Jim. "What did you say?" said Thompson. "Nothing," said Jim. "I was talking to myself." "Oh," said Thompson. Dinger said, "I will be right back. I am going to look around and try to find out where we are at." Jim thought to himself, "Where we are at? That's good because with what I am going through, I don't know where the hell I am 'at' in this whole damn situation. I still don't know where the hell I am or what is going on."

Jim said to Thompson, "What is Dinger looking for?" Thompson replied, "I don't know. Maybe he's looking for Indians, robbers, or the British." Dinger then came back and said, "There is nobody around." Jim said, "Should we move on?" "No," said Thompson, "we will be all right here for tonight. We can move on tomorrow." The three stayed for the night with nothing happening, and the next morning they started through the woods. All of a sudden Thompson said, "Hold on just a second." "What is the matter?" said Dinger. "Something is not right," replied Thompson. "Let's head for the underbrush." They hid in heavy bushes, and looking around, they saw a band of about fifteen Indians on horseback riding mostly two abreast.

"Wow, we were lucky." "How did you know they were there Jed?" asked Jim. "I just knew," said Jed. "Man, you are good," said Jim. As the Indians passed, they never knew they were being watched. Twenty minutes passed before Jed went out to look around, and they were all gone. "It's all right now," said Jed. As they moved out and headed down a dirt road, they saw a rider coming their way on horseback. It was a black man. "Hi," said Dinger, "where are you headed?" The man replied, "I am going to the Rhode Island and join a group being formed by Christopher Greene. And where are you from?" Dinger answered, "I am from New Hampshire. I was a slave to a General Sullivan. When the British landed, he said that he would free anyone of his slaves prepared to fight for liberty. I said to the general, 'It would be of great satisfaction to me to know that I was fighting for my liberty, sir.' The general thought that this was a reasonable request and set me free."

Jed said, "You sound like an educated man." "Yes, sir, even though I was a slave, the general treated me well. I understand that in the South, it's against the law to educate any slaves." Jim was thinking about this damn thing. "This conversation is getting out of hand." If he had it to do over again, he would forget about robbing people and stay in school. Maybe he wouldn't be in this purgatory if he had. Somehow he had to get back to the harbor and back to that damn warehouse. Jed asked, "Where about are you heading?" "Down to a place called Newport," said the man. Jed said "Gentlemen, I think it has been a long day, and we all should find shelter for the night."

Both Dinger and the other man went to sleep, but Jim and Jed stayed awake. Jed said to Jim, "I don't quite figure you out." "Why?" replied Jim.

"Oh, I don't know," said Jed. "You sort of act funny like you know what is going to happen," Jim said "Yeah, I sort of do know what is going to happen." "What do you mean?" said Jed. "Oh, never mind," said Jim. "I could not explain, and you probably would not understand or believe me if I told you. But I will tell you one thing. If people think this war or whatever the hell we are in will be the end of slavery, they are dead wrong. Dinger and Calvin may be, but their grandchildren won't," Jim said. "You are pretty sure of that are you?" "Yes, I am," replied Jim.

The next morning, when they started out, Jim said, "Where are we headed?" Dinger replied, "As I said before, I am heading to fight with the Rhode Island regiment so I can finally be free." Jim said, "So you can be free? What the hell are you talking about? At this point how can you be more free than you already are? You have no master, you have nobody pushing you, and you can do anything you want. I don't know what the hell you are talking about. Fight for freedom? If you knew what was going to happen, you would know it was all bullshit." Dinger said, "What are you talking about?" Jim, cooling down, said, "Dinger, look, this slavery thing will get no better for a long while; and what you call freedom, you will not see in your lifetime." "What are you talking about?" said Calvin. Jim took a deep breath and said, "Never mind."

Jed then said to everybody, "Boys, it has been a pleasure being with you, but right now I am leaving." Dinger said, "Thank you for your help, sir," Jed replied, "It has been a long time since I have been called sir." Jim said, "Why are you leaving?" "Well," replied Jed, "for years since my family was killed, I have done nothing but hate the Indians and the British. I have to get away and think about things. I was thinking last night with all the killing I have done, I have accomplished nothing. I may go back to teaching when I figure things out, but I was glad to be here where I could help you boys." As Jed packed, he said, "I hope I run into you fellows sometime. Good luck to all of you." And with that, he rode away.

Jim turned and said to Dinger, "He was good, but I will tell you one thing. I am glad I did not have him as a teacher. In my time in my school, he would have been a bastard." Dinger said, "What do you mean in your time?" Looking away, Jim said, "Never mind." The three black men headed toward Rhode Island. Dinger asked the newcomer, "What is your name?" "Calvin," he replied. Jim said, "Yeah, he gave me his name when things were happening, and I forgot to tell you, Dinger." Calvin said to Dinger, "I am heading for Rhode Island too. May I join you?" Dinger said yes. Dinger then turned to Jim and said, "Is that okay with you, Jim?" Jim replied, "Okay, but I am trying to tell you what the hell is going to happen, and you dummies are not listening to me." Calvin said, "There is a colonel Middleton that is the head of the Rhode Island brigade and of all the black soldiers. If we volunteer with him, we will be paid the wages of a regular soldier." "Well," Jim said, "I have to pick up some money somewhere."

CHAPTER THREE

Newport-Groton War

After three days they came to Rhode Island and found the Rhode Island regiment. After the three arrived at camp, the captain summoned them and said, "Our intelligence informs us that we have trouble coming our way. There is a large British army that has teamed up with German troops. Now, gentlemen, these Germans were hired by the British because they are expert riflemen and veteran bayonet fighters. They are tough and among the most feared of all the troops." Jim muttered to himself, "Damn it, this is just great. Now I am going to be in a battle with Germans. Shit, man, this is really hell. First it was the police, then the British, then the Indians, and now it's the goddamn Germans. This is crazy! Please somebody just get me the hell out of this!"

The Germans (Hessians) wore thick uniforms, tall leather hats, and wore their hair in tarred pigtails. They were known to battle to the finish. The Americans were waiting. The time was now getting near, and the atmosphere was getting tense. A lookout said, "I can see them coming. They are about fifteen minutes or so away." The sergeant passed out the rifles and long bayonets. The British and the Germans commenced a full attack. The Germans were shooting, and the Americans stood up and started firing. The British and the Germans were driven back. In awhile they began another attack. This time the Germans were hooting and hollering in German, and nobody could understand them. Jim saw two Germans coming up from behind. He shot one through the head, and before the second one could act, Dinger shot him, killing him at once.

The British and the German troops retreated. This day the battle was won by the Americans. Jim was on a high. "Would you believe it, Dinger, with my first shot I took out that German son of a bitch!" Dinger sort of smiled. The day after the battle the German colonel asked for a transfer to New York because he dared not lead his regiment again lest his men shoot him for having caused them so much loss. Colonel Green summoned his men together and introduced General Sullivan who said, "Gentlemen, I am very proud of you. Today you won a good battle." General Sullivan said in his report on the Battle of Newport that the black regiment was entitled to a proper share of the honors. Jim said, "I hope that also means money."

The British were heading toward the American lines along the Groton River in Connecticut. Colonel Green yelled, "IS EVERBODY WITH ME?" "Yes," replied the regiment in unison. "I am going," said Dinger. "Are you with me?" "Yeah, I guess so," said Jim now thinking, "This is it. If I get out of this one alive, I am going to try to get the hell out of here and somehow find my way back to Boston." Meanwhile Colonel Middleton, head of the brigade, returned to Boston, and Colonel Green headed for the Groton River.

It was warm day in May, and Colonel Green established a position along the Groton River. After a few hours the British launched a full attack. It got bloody. Jim, just ducking a sword that was aimed at his head while he was falling, shot and killed his attacker. "Damn," said Jim. It got worse. The British swords, bayonets, knives, and rifles drove back the rebel defenders and the Rhode Islanders. All hell was breaking loose. Colonel Green refused to retreat. The British were now on the battleground in full force. The colonel was cut down, and his faithful guard of blacks went to his rescue. Dinger grabbed a sword and headed for Colonel Green. Jim said, "Where the hell are you going?" Dinger said, "I have to do this." "Come back you dumb bastard; you don't have to do this," said Jim as British soldiers came for them.

Jim headed for the river and dove in. He remembered what he saw on a TV movie once. There was a bamboo shoot, which he broke off. He submerged underwater, breathing through the shoot. One soldier said, "I thought I saw one of those rebel sons of bitches come this way." Looking around, they could not see anything. Jim was not far away but underwater where they could not see him. After Jim came out of the water soaking wet, he looked around and could not believe his eyes. There were bodies everywhere. He went over to one group; and he saw that everyone was dead—Colonel Christopher Green, the black guards—and he even saw Calvin. Then he found Dinger dead with a bayonet through him. Jim started to cry, saying, "I did not have a chance to say good-bye. I hope somewhere you found your freedom."

By now the British had gone back across the river. Jim could not help anyone because everybody was dead. He headed back to the marsh, and he was alone again. He wanted to get back to Boston. After three days of heading back north through swamp and marshland trying not to be seen by the British, he finally found some dry land where he could rest. Sitting down he began to think about how he gotten to this spot. "This is like an old TV show *The Twilight Zone*. I know I needed the money. I wish I was never in that robbery. I wish now I had stayed in school. I am being punished by somebody that I know. But I would like to go back. Maybe if I get to Boston and find that warehouse, I can meet my friends and somehow go back to where we came from."

All of a sudden he heard some people coming up the road. "Damn, I wonder if this is the British or the Indians." Ducking behind some bushes and looking to see who it was, he saw some men dressed like Americans. Taking a chance, he stepped out to meet them. The leader look astonished to see a black man in their way. He walked up to Jim and said, "Where are you going, and who are you?" Jim replied, "I am trying to get back to Boston, and I just fought with the Rhode Island at Groton. We lost most everybody." The leader said, "You look like you were in one hell of a fight." "Yes," replied Jim. "If there were any survivors, I was separated from them." The leader said, "Just call me Nat. You are welcome to come with us. That Rhode Island group was one hell of a fighting force. We have some food we will share with you."

After settling in for the night, Jim started to wonder what had happened to his other partners and Dave. "Damn, I wish I had gone a different way. I am living a bad dream, and it is something like that Christmas story—that Scrooge story with the ghost of the past and all that. Damn, I can't wait to get back to Boston."

Two days later they finally were back in Boston. Jim said, "Thank you very much for letting me tag along." He ran into a company of black soldiers and joined in with them as they marched through the city streets at a smart step. They halted in front of the mansion on Beacon Street of the white Patriot leader John Hancock. Hancock came out to salute the veterans, and he presented them with a silk flag for their company the Bucks of America. The flag bore the picture of a pine tree, the symbol of American liberty, with a running buck deer, the emblem of the company. It bore a scroll with the initials of John Hancock and George Washington. The flag was accepted by the company's black commander colonel Middleton. John Hancock offered it as a tribute to their courage in battle. Everybody then marched into town where they were entertained with food and drink. Jim mingled in with the crowd. Talking with a man, Jim asked, "Who was that man that gave Colonel Middleton that flag?" The man replied, "That was John Hancock." "Oh, the insurance man," said Jim. The stranger looked at Jim sort of funny and said, "No, he is the president of the Continental Congress." "Oh," said Jim.

One soldier came up to Jim and said, "We are having a time at Boston Common. Colonel Middleton is about ready to retire." "Okay," said Jim. On the way to the common, the soldier said, "Did you know that Colonel Middleton is an accomplished violinist and horse breaker?" "No," said Jim, "but that is one hell of a combination." Jim was thinking that Boston Common was at least a familiar place and maybe he could find his way back from there.

When they got to the common, the black brigade and their friends were having a celebration on the same green lawns that were used for slave trading in the north. There was a gang of white boys from Boston, and they were looking for a fight. They started toward the common, and the women and children began to run away from them down Belknap Street. The white boys enjoyed their fright. The sounds of battle approached. Clubs, knives, and brickbats were flying in all directions. Jim grabbed a rifle that had been left on the ground by one of the bucks. "Son of a bitch. Here we go again with all hell breaking loose!" Hundreds of people, white and black, began pouring into the streets. Colonel Middleton urged his party to turn and resist to the last. His voice could be heard above everybody. He raised and leveled his musket and said, "I will kill the first white man that comes into my range." His party, shamed by his reproaches and fired by his example, rallied muskets, and rifles began to fire wildly.

Then there was hand-to-hand combat. Jim felt a sharp pain in his back and fell to the ground. He was bleeding from being stabbed in the back. In the confusion two rebels said, "Let's see if we can get this man to the doctors." Somehow in the crowd they grabbed Jim and got him away from the area. Each one took an arm, and they brought him to a doctor that they knew. When they got to the house and started to bang on the door, the doctor looked from behind the shades and then answered the door. "Bring him in," said the doctor, "and put him on the bed." He called his wife and said, "Bring some boiling water and bandages. This does not look good. I don't think he is going to make it." Semiconscious Jim was thinking, "Where is Dave?

(Some information was taken from black heroes of the American Revolution.)

Chapter Four

Joe's Adventure

The three boys had split up in the woods. Dave headed east toward Boston, and Jim headed south toward Rhode Island, leaving Joe alone in the woods. He waited for nightfall. When the night finally came, it was warm and muggy. The moon was very bright, and the sky was starry. Joe had to stay low because the moon was so bright, and by now the British were back and milling around. Joe thought he would be seen, so crouching low in the brush, he started to move out. He saw two British soldiers talking just as he stepped on some brush. These two soldiers were closer than he thought. One soldier said, "Did you hear that?" "Hear what?" said the other soldier. "Thought I heard something, some animal, a fox or something," replied the other soldier. The two then carried on with what they were talking about.

Heading away from the harbor toward Roxbury Flats, which was dry at low tide, he was in the common heading toward a place called Fox Hill. Now Fox Hill was where the British shuttled their boats from Boston to Charlestown. After about two hours of walking through thick brush, it was pitch-black, and Joe decided to rest. After resting about three hours, Joe could not sleep. By this time everybody but a few guards were asleep, so Joe continued to head south toward Fox Hill. It was now about two thirty in the morning. As he came close to the flats a little before the hill, he came upon a young man working on something.

"Hi," said Joe. The person turned around, startled. "Who are you?" "My name is Joe Davis. What's yours?" said Joe. "Davis is it?" replied the man. "Well, Davis, you're damn lucky I did not blow your head off!" The man came up with a long-barreled pistol. "Damn!" said Joe "What the hell are you doing?" "What am I doing? What the hell do you mean what am I doing? Why did you sneak up on me this time of night?" "Look," said Joe, "I did not sneak. I have been trying to find Fox Hill almost all night and ended up here." "Well, I thought you were the British, an Indian, a highwayman, or something. My name is Todd Barrett. Where did you come from?" said Todd. "I came in from the Boston waterfront." "The Boston waterfront?" replied Todd. "Yeah," said Joe, "it would be kind of hard to explain. Might I ask what you are doing here this time of morning?" Todd replied, "I am going to head up toward the millpond where I have a boat I can take to Charlestown."

"Look," said Joe, "can I tag along with you for?" "Sure," said Todd. "By the way," said Joe, "I noticed you have a gun and a rifle. Where did you get those?" "My family are British sympathizers," replied Todd, "and they let those damn British take over our farm and use it as headquarters. I hate the British, so late last night I took off with some guns and ammunition just in case I get caught by the damn British." The two headed toward Picae Street to the intersection of Hollis Street and then to the common where they tried to get to Beacon Hill to see if they could get to millpond where Todd had his boat without being detected by the British. By now Todd and Joe had moved up Common Street to Long Acre then to Tremont Street. At Queen Street they headed to millpond, continuing quietly and undercover because by now they were right in the British stronghold.

"We will have to get to my boat before dawn because the British will be taking their boats to Charlestown," said Todd. "What the hell you mean take a boat? Why don't they just take the bridge?" asked Joe. "What bridge?" asked Todd. "There is no bridge to Charlestown; there never was a bridge to Charlestown, and they have to take a boat from Revere. That is why I have my boat at millpond. If we leave before dawn, we will be all right." The two arrived at millpond just before dawn. Todd began to look for the boat, which he had hidden in the brush under the branches and shrub. "I found it," said Todd. "You had me worried there for a moment," said Joe. "It's getting close to dawn, so let's get going," Todd said. "This is great because the water is quiet."

The two boys got into the boat and headed for open water, hoping that when the British started taking their boats across, they would not be noticed and they would be in the flow. Joe asked Todd why they would not be noticed by the British. Todd replied, "Because a lot of the time there are Tories out here rowing or fishing," Joe said "Tories! What the hell are Tories?" "They are Loyalists who are on the British side," said Todd. "You mean citizens of Boston are fighting with the damn British?" asked Joe. "Yes," said Todd, "most of what you call citizens are from England and don't want to go against the king even though the bastard is overtaxing everybody on tea and everything else."

Then they got into the boat and started rowing for Charlestown. Looking west, you could see Barton's Point; and looking east, you could see Copp's Hill and Hudson's Point. They rowed for quite a long time and finally ended up on the west bank of Charlestown. When they stepped onshore, Todd said, "Help me drag the boat over here so we can cover it. We may need it again." They pulled the boat out of sight, covered it, and then pondered their next move. As they moved along, Todd said, "You know, Joe, I have some rations. Why don't we rest and see what is going on?" "Good idea," replied Joe.

The two found a marsh trail and started to make their way west. The marsh grass was fairly tall, and the two moved easily through it. All of a sudden Todd said to Joe, "Hold it. I hear something; somebody is coming toward us." "Damn it," said Joe, "what are we going to do?" "Hold on, don't worry." said Todd. "If he's British, we will have to kill him." "Shit," Joe said to himself, "in all my days of robbing people, I never shot anyone." "Lay low," said Todd with his gun trained on the oncoming person. As the person moved closer, they could see he was not a British soldier, but he could be one of the Tories. Just then Todd jumped out of the brush to the surprise of the man. "Who the hell are you?" asked the man. "Are you a British sympathizer?" asked Todd. The man answered, "What the hell kind of a question is that with you holding a gun on me?" Joe sort of smiled at that answer. The man said, "Of course, I am not a British soldier. I don't have anything to do with those bastards."

Lowering his gun Todd asked, "What is your name?" "My name is Bryan Smith." "Well, Bryan, where you headed?" "I am going to Charlestown," he said. Todd asked, "What are you going to do in Charlestown?" "I work in a tavern. I am not with the British, but I do serve them." Bryan then asked, "What kind of clothes are you wearing?" Joe replied, "What do you mean? These are blue jeans and a sweatshirt." Todd said, "I was going to say something to you about that. You are dressed sort of funny. I am surprised that the British didn't pick up on that by now." Bryan then asked, "What are you people doing here anyway, jumping out of the marsh grass with pistols?" Todd said, "We thought you might be a British soldier." "Well, I am not; and besides, supposing I was one and had three others with me, what would you do then?"

"Good point," said Joe. "By the way," asked Todd, "where are you from?" "Let's say I am from up country. My family is in the shipping business." "What do they ship?" asked Todd. Bryan replied "They ship corn, cattle, horses, fish, and wood mainly to the West Indies." "Sounds like money," said Joe. "Yes, and they don't want to upset the British," replied Bryan. "I think something is going to happen." "What do you mean?" asked Joe. "Well," Bryan said, "I think the British are gearing up for a fight." "How would you like to join us?" asked Todd. "To do what?" asked Bryan. "To fight the British," said Todd. "I don't know about that," said Bryan." I don't like the bastards, but fighting with the rebels I don't know about that." "Look," said Todd, "I know this is tough, but all the regular people are fighting for freedom from the damn British and their damn king." "I know," said Bryan, "but I work around them, and if I start that stuff, I could get killed." "I know you are right," said Todd.

"You know, Joe," said Bryan "there is a loudmouth where I work, and he is about your size, and I think you need a change of clothes. In about an hour or so he will be as drunk as could be. It will be fun when he wakes up and finds himself in—what did you say? Blue jeans and a sweatshirt?"

Joe by now was thinking and wondering, "Just what the hell is going on? It seems like a bad dream!" and hoping he was going to wake up soon. Coming to the outskirts of Charlestown and to the tavern where Bryan worked, Bryan said, "Why don't you wait around for a while?" "Why?" asked Joe. "Well, I was thinking I am sick of this place, and I might just join you." "Okay," said Todd, "but we will not wait all night." "You know," said Joe, "this whole thing is unbelievable." "Why is that?" asked Todd. "If I told you, you would not believe me anyway." "Why?" asked Todd. Joe said, "Never mind. Maybe later."

In about forty five minutes out came Bryan, acting drunk with his arm around another man who was also drunk. "What the hell is he doing?" asked Todd. "I have no idea," replied Joe. Bryan and the other man started toward a wood pile. As the man was about to sit, Bryan took a two-by-four log and hit the man over the head. Joe said, "What the hell is he doing?" "I don't know," said Todd, "but let's find out." As they approached the two men, Bryan was now looking sober and said, "Let's take off his clothes and make the exchange." "Did you kill him?" asked Joe. "I don't think so. He is bleeding a little but not bad. I quit the job, so let's hurry in case somebody misses him and comes out to find him." After they made the exchange, Joe said, "Bryan, you were right; this is a perfect fit." "So," said Bryan, "let's get out of here."

By this time it was close to Pope's Day. Pope's Day was a spin-off of Guy Fawkes Day, and the celebration soon crossed the Atlantic to New England where it became known as Pope's Day, and it resembled Halloween. Each town built a large float called a pope's carriage on which were comic figures of a pope, a devil, and any currently unpopular political figures. In the evening the float was illuminated by paper lanterns, and there were dancers and fiddlers on its platform. It was dragged through the streets under the command of a captain and was followed by a procession of boys and young men beating drums, ringing bells, and blowing whistles. As it came to the wealthier houses, it stopped for an early version of trick-or-treat. The increasingly rowdy celebration ended with a bonfire in which the various figures were burned along with fences and washtubs stolen on the way.

The three were now in Boston, and it looked like a celebration was about to start. This day was going to be different. There were two pope's carriages in town, one belonging to the North End Gang and the other belonging to the South End Gang. As the three headed into Boston, they ended up right in the middle of the Pope's Day celebration. "Damn," said Joe, "look at those floats. Now that is something with the fireworks and the two floats facing each other." Joe then asked, "Now what happens?" Bryan said, "I don't know, but I will tell you something. I have a bad feeling about this one." "Why is that?" Todd asked Bryan. "There should only be one float, not two." All of a sudden a battle broke out between the North End Gang and the South End Gang. Shooting and knife fights started. "What the hell is going on here?" Joe asked. Todd said, "It looks like we have ourselves a brawl." Three men started toward the boys. "Son of a bitch," said Joe. Just then Todd raised his pistol and shot one of the oncomers. One of the men fell. "Is he dead?" asked Joe. "I don't know, but let's get the hell out of here," said Todd.

The two men scattered after the one who was shot went down. In the savage street battle, which continued for twenty-four hours, many were injured, and a few were killed. To the dismay of respectable citizens and contrary to all law, Boston was in the hands of the mob. The three boys took off down a side street for safety. "Damn, what the hell started that?" said Joe. "Even in my day I have never seen anything like that." "What do you mean in your day?" asked Todd. "Never mind," replied Joe.

Bryan said, "There is a man named Samuel Adams, and from what I hear, he had the idea of reconciling the two gangs and directing this mob to political ends." Joe asked "What's this Adams like?" Bryan replied, "He is a middle-aged man. I have seen him a couple of times. His hair is sparse and gray, his clothes are seedy, and he looks like the failure that most people say he is. He failed at working for his father, he failed at working for himself, and he even failed in supporting his family. When he somehow managed to get himself elected as tax collector, Adams nearly went to jail for his carelessness in handling the public funds. The only thing he really cares about is politics, and from what I hear, he shows real talent for it. And before most of the colonists had given the idea a thought, Adams was considering methods of bringing about a complete separation of the new America from the old mother country.

"Adams is not just against King George III; he opposes all kings everywhere, and he dislikes an aristocracy. He is a frugal person and has few luxuries. With this idea firmly fixed in his head and working with a group of the Sons of Liberty known as the Loyal Nine, he has come to dominate and control the mob that is terrorizing Boston. Adams is what they call the 'mob master.' Even when the two gangs were still acting on their own, Adams has established close relations with the leaders and is aware of what is brewing.

"They say Adams instigated an attack on the lieutenant governor Thomas Hutchinson who is one of the wealthiest men forming the group around the royal governor. He is the holder of many offices, a member of the governor's council, and chief justice of the province as well as lieutenant governor. His mansion was the handsomest in town, and to demonstrate his loyalty, Hutchinson had the crown of England carved in the stone lintel over each window. Hutchinson, no friend of the Stamp Act, is a scholar as well as a statesman; and his history of the Colony of Massachusetts Bay will be, from what I hear, one of the most important documents in history. But for all that he does well, he lacks the common touch, and as the crisis grew, so did the feeling against him."

Bryan said, "A few years ago it was a hot summer night; I think it was in August. It was the hottest night of the year that the mob finally went for Hutchinson. Early in the evening a group had lit a bonfire in King Street near the state house. A restless crowd soon gathered, and in a short time whistles and horns began to sound the mob call, which immediately sent the strong arm squads swarming out of their taverns and garrets. Liquor, always plentiful in such circumstances, became even more plentiful as the mob broke into the houses and cellars of several customs officials. Then the name 'Hutchinson' began to be passed about in the hot darkness, and the cry went up, 'PULL DOWN THE CHIEF JUSTICE'S HOUSE!' Hutchinson was warned that the mob was after him, and he escaped just as the axes began to swing against his front door. The looters and the wreckers stormed their way through the door into the formal ornamented rooms. Everything that could not be carried off was destroyed: family portraits, busts of the king and queen, rugs, clocks, china, books, even the wall paneling. The wine cellar was the first to go. In the garden the flower beds were trampled and the fruit trees leveled. The manuscript of the second volume of Hutchinson's history—the first had just been published a few months earlier—was hurled into the gutter and trampled in the mud along with all the early records of the colony that he had collected. Hutchinson later wrote, 'The hellish crew fell upon my house with the rage of devils.'"

"Wow, Bryan," Joe asked, "how do you know all that?" "I was there," replied Bryan. "You mean they actually tore down the whole house?" "To the ground," said Bryan." "I got caught up in the crowd, but I did not have any part in burning the house down. I found out that the records were later gathered up and returned to Hutchinson, but of his house nothing remained except the floors." Joe asked, "Is this the Adams that is now involved with these gangs?" "The Adams," replied Bryan. "The first reaction of Adams and his Loyal Nine to the night of destruction was sudden uneasiness about what steps the English government might take against this reckless challenge of authority. Adams now called the gutting of Hutchinson's mansion a 'high-handed enormity' and maintained that it had been committed by the vagabond strangers." "You mean that Adams was saying he wasn't a part of that raid?" "Yes," said Bryan, "but I will tell you he was. It was at this point that Adams set out to bring the mobsters under more disciplined control by sending in among them artisans of a 'superior set' to act as controlling noncommissioned officers. They came to be called Adams Mohawks or the Sons of Liberty."

"Well," said Joe, "that sounds like this Adams is the godfather." "The what?" asked Bryan. "The godfather—oh, never mind," said Joe. "The Sons of Liberty and their mob followers became the unofficial rulers of Boston. Governor Francis Bernard and many of his officials thought it wiser to retire to the safety of Castle William in Boston Harbor under the protection of the cannon of British men of war. Customs officials who made any effort to enforce the laws had a rough time," Bryan said. "I will tell you we are in for quite a time." "How do you mean?" asked Todd. "It all started with taxes from England, and the Americans are not standing for it." Joe by now was thinking, "I am here in Boston, and I don't recognize a thing. The damn warehouses are not around; nothing is right. I wonder where the other two are and how they're doing." Finally Joe asked, "What about this Adams? Why is everybody after him?"

"Well," said Bryan, "besides the Hutchinson affair, he is a Boston Patriot that led the resistance to the Tea Act. On the evening of December 16 Bostonians disguised as Indians raided British ships docked in Boston Harbor and dumped their cargoes of tea overboard. The so-called Boston Tea Party enraged King George, Lord North, and the king's other ministers. They wanted the Bostonians punished as a warning to colonists not to challenge British authority." "Yeah," said Todd, "my father was telling me that to avoid paying the Townsend duty on tea colonial merchants smuggled in tea from the Netherlands. England's East India Company had been the chief source of tea for the colonies. The smuggling hurt the company financially, and it asked parliament for help. In 1773 parliament passed the Tea Act, which enabled the East India Company to sell its tea below the price of smuggled tea. Lord North became the king's chief minister in 1770. North believed that the colonists would buy the cheaper British tea and thereby acknowledge parliament's right to tax them. In the process the colonists would lose their argument against taxation without representation.

"The United Kingdom responded to the Boston Tea Party in 1774 by passing several laws that became known in America as the Intolerable Acts. One law closed Boston Harbor and stated that it be reopened only after Bostonians paid for the tea and showed a proper respect for British authority. Another law restricted the activities of the Massachusetts legislature and gave added powers to the post of governor of Massachusetts. Those powers in effect made him a dictator. King George named Lieutenant General Thomas Gage, the commander in chief of the British forces in North America, to be the new governor of Massachusetts." Then Joe said, "What happened then?" "Gage was sent to Boston with troops. Committees of correspondence throughout the colonies warned citizens that the United Kingdom could also disband their legislatures and take away their political rights. Several committees called for a convention of delegates from the colonies to organize resistance to the Intolerable Acts. The convention was later called the Continental Congress."

Joe said, "You mean this whole thing started because of tea and a stamp act?" "And sugar," replied Bryan. "Sugar?" asked Joe. "Yes, sugar. A fellow named George Grenville became King George's chief cabinet minister in 1773. With Grenville's urging, parliament passed the revenue act of 1764 also known as the Sugar Act. The act placed a three-penny tax on each gallon of molasses entering the colonies from ports of the British Empire. Several northern colonies had thriving rum industries that depended on imported molasses. Rum producers angrily protested that the tax would eat up their profits. However, the Stamp Act, an even more unpopular British tax, soon drew the colonists' attention away from the Sugar Act. In 1766 parliament reduced the tax on molasses to a penny a gallon."

Joe said, "You mean that this war started over taxes, tea, stamps, and sugar?" Wow, in the future the wars will be over land, religion, and slavery." "What is this Townsend act anyway?" Bryan replied, "Many members of the British government disliked giving in to the disobedient colonies over the Stamp Act. They included the chancellor of what they call the exchequer, Charles Townsend, who developed a new plan for raising money from the colonies. Townshend convinced parliament that the colonists would find a duty or indirect tax placed on imported goods more agreeable than the Stamp Act, which taxed them directly. Back in 1767 parliament passed the Townshend Acts. One act placed duties on glass, lead, paint, paper, and tea imported into the colonies. Another act set up a customs agency in Boston to collect them efficiently." "Yeah," said Joe, "they still have them now. They are called the Internal Revenue Service." "The what?" said Todd. "Never mind," said Joe.

Bryan then continued, "Seven of the English politicians had to realize that the Stamp Act was unenforceable. Finally the ministry repealed it." "Damn, Bryan, how do you know all this?" asked Joe. "You sound like my old teacher. It sounds like a damn history book." "A what?" Bryan replied. "My family knows the story well. You see, my father and cousins were Tories, and before I left home I learned a lot about what is going on.

"You know," said Bryan, "Adams made it his full-time job to stir up bad feelings against the Red Coats and to make life as painful as possible for them. He published and circulated throughout the colonies a journal of events that gave lurid and for the most part imaginary accounts of British 'atrocities' against the gentle and harmless inhabitants of Boston. No man or woman was safe from the 'bloody-backed rascals.'"

Bryan then continued, "I was there when Adams and one of his men came into the tavern. Whatever happened I don't know, but I will tell you this. A soldier said to one of Adams's men, 'Well, look here. This looks like a rebel, a loser. Pretty soon you rebel bastards will be shining my boots and shoveling my horse's shit.' With that Adams's man said, 'I don't think so. You see, your king is an ass, and the only ones that will be shoveling shit are you Red Coat bastards.' And with that Adams's aide slugged the officer's aide, and a fight broke out. Before you knew it, they were out in the street. The soldiers of the Twenty-ninth Regiment were known for their short tempers and quick fists, and soon they were fighting with Boston's toughest citizens." Bryan said, "It was a hell of a fight in the street and in the alley. Everyone was watching through their doors and windows, and before I knew it, I was in the middle of it, fighting for my life."

It was a moonlit night. A single British soldier stood in his sentry box at the upper end of King Street near the state house. Soon a group of boys gathered across the street and as they often did began to jeer at the "lobster back" and pelt him with rocks and ice chunks. Then a crowd of adults formed a ring and began to close in on the sentry box. The sentry stepped out of the box and amid jeers threatened to run through anyone who came near enough to his bayonet. A small boy darted toward him and received a glancing blow from the Red Coat's musket but not enough to harm him or even to knock him down but enough to set the crowd off. There were shouts that the sentry was murdering the child. There were cries of, "KILL HIM! KILL HIM!" as the three boys were caught up in the crowd with yelling and screaming all around them. Joe said, "I don't like this!" "Neither do I," replied Todd. Then the bell of the Old South Meeting House rang out like a fire alarm, and the fringes of the crowd were suddenly joined by several hundred hard-faced sailors, porters, and rope makers. A mysterious stranger in a red cape and wig looked like Adams. John Adams, Sam's more refined cousin from Braintree, described the mob as 'a motley rabble.'"

The ringleaders were Crispus Attucks, James Caldwell, Samuel Gray, and Patrick Carr—four bullyboys who made a habit of drifting into town and attacking stray Red Coats. Attucks was a dark giant of a man—part Negro, part Indian, part white. Gray was a rope maker, Caldwell was a shipmate, and the Irish-born Carr an old hand at rioting." As the crowd increased and the mob swarmed closer, Joe asked, "What the hell is going on here?" "I don't know," replied Todd, "but it looks like a riot is about to take place." Attucks thrust his club at the "lobster back" and said he would "have off one of his claws" just before threatening hands reached him. The sentry called loudly, "Turn out the main guard."

At once the duty officer captain John Preston stepped out of the guardhouse across the street followed by a guard and seven Red Coats with fixed bayonets. They forced their way through the crowd and formed a semicircle around the sentry. As the threats increased, Preston ordered his men to prime and load. There was a hush while the iron ramrods rattled ominously in the musket barrels. The captain placed himself between the muskets and the crowd to keep his men from firing. Some of the more sensible townspeople tried to urge the others to break it up and go home. Instead the surlier members of the mob pressed forward in a blind rush at the soldiers. Attucks struck Preston with a blow and nearly broke the officer's arm. Then he knocked down the sentry and tried to grab his musket.

"Damn it," said Todd, "this does not look good." The rioters and the soldiers struggled against each other. One soldier grabbed Todd and threw him to the ground. He was about to bayonet him when Bryan hit the guard from behind, knocking the guard to the ground. At this time the fatal command rang out, "FIRE!" No one knew who gave the order, for Preston did not give the order. The shots echoed up and down the narrow street, and the panicking crowd tripped and fought its way back. Trying to get back away from the center where the action was taking place, Todd said, "Let's get the hell out of here!" Captain Preston struggled to push the musket barrels up as he shouted to his men to hold their fire. Attucks, Gray, and Caldwell lay dead. Patrick Carr and Maverick were mortally wounded. Carr lived long enough to confess remorsefully that he and his friends were to blame and that the Red Coats had fired in self-defense. Joe was now thinking to himself, "This is like a gang war I knew in Boston, and we will be lucky to get out of this alive. With the way this is going, I am wondering if we are alive."

The town and the surrounding countryside fumed with indignation. Most people at first thought the soldiers had fired without cause on harmless civilians. Lieutenant Governor Hutchinson had Preston and his men arrested and charged with murder. For Adams the massacre was a gift from heaven. At once his propaganda machine set to work, extolling the King Street dead and calling for vengeance on the "Red Coat butchers." His hot words resounded through the colonies. The dead bullyboys became martyrs to freedom and called themselves Saints of Liberty. The first bloodshed against brute tyranny. Conspicuously absent from the list of martyrs was the name of Patrick Carr. Adams explained that away by calling him an "Irish papist."

"Look," said Bryan, "I think it is time we move on. We were almost caught in a riot with fighting on all sides. We are lucky we did not get ourselves killed." "You are right," said Joe. "Enough of the history of this Adams. He seems like an all-right guy, but I think you are right; we should get going."

The three headed to Charlestown Neck toward Bunker and Breed's Hill. Todd said, "I think we should be safe if we head to Morton's Hill and Morton's Point." When they arrived at Morton's Point they saw one by one the barges ground ashore. The Red Coats with haversacks and muskets splashed through the shallows and up onto the beach. Then the barges returned to Boston for a second load, this time bringing back the Royal Regiment of Artillery and General Howe. The landing well protected by guns of the Royal Navy was made without opposition. A total of 1,550 British troops arrived in the first two waves. "Todd, did I hear you say we would be safe? Are you kidding? Every time we turn around, we are in the middle of a goddamn war."

From the shore Howe observed Stark's and Reed's regiments on the crest of Bunker Hill. As he watched he noticed several detachments hurry down the hill and move into positions along the flat land just above the Mystic River. Howe saw at once that these newcomers would block any chance he might have had to move his troops along the Mystic and seal off the provincials from the rear. About four hundred yards from the rough breastwork, Howe lined up four companies of his light infantry under the protection of a small bank. Then after he had formed up his other troops and pushed three lines of infantry to the top of Morton's, he sent back to Gage to ask for reinforcements. In the interval the men broke ranks, unfastened their knapsacks, took off their helmets, and securely out of rebel range sat down in the grass to eat their dinner.

As he had watched the Red Coats pile ashore Prescott realized that the most vulnerable spot in his lines was the gap where the breastwork ended in the swampy ground short of the Mystic. In the breathing space now given him, he sent Captain Knowlton and his two hundred Connecticut men to close the gap. He also sent Captain Gridley with his field pieces, but as soon as Gridley and his disheartened artillerists were out of sight of the redoubt, they changed direction and headed for the neck. Joe asked Todd, "What the hell is going on here?" Todd replied, "I don't know, but with the way the British are moving, it looks like a battle; and we are going to be right in the middle of it." "Yeah, I know," said Bryan. "I think you are right." "Yeah. Like I said before, we will be right in the middle."

Meanwhile in Cambridge, General Ward learned of the British plans almost by chance when a New Hampshire visitor to Boston managed to sneak away with the news that the Red Coats were preparing advances on Dorchester and Cambridge. Ward and his officers pondered what action to take. Despite desertions, quarrels about rank, and doubts of the Rhode

Islanders about the Vermonters and vice versa, the provincial army was going about its elementary drills and assuming some sort of form. Its remaining volunteers began to feel like soldiers. Luckily food was not yet scarce although almost everything else was. The committee of safety met in Cambridge's Hastings house and decided that "it appears of importance to the safety of this colony that possession of the hill called Bunker's Hill in Charlestown be securely kept and defended."

The committee urged that militiamen be ready to march on the shortest notice completely equipped and having thirty rounds of cartridges per man. Theoretically General Ward now controlled 7,500 men, 1,000 more than the British in Boston. But actually there were no more than five thousand fit for duty, and many of these lacked muskets and ammunition. Colonel William Prescott was ordered to proceed to Bunker Hill and throw up fortifications. Israel Putnam, a burly impetuous Indian fighter known to everyone as Old Put, took it upon himself to visit the Boston Neck fortifications and see what John Thomas commanding the volunteers there could do about seizing Dorchester Heights. Thomas had to admit he could do nothing at all since in a month he had seen the force he commanded dwindle from 6,000 to 2,500. Although reinforced by a detachment of Rhode Islanders under the able Nathaniel Greene, Thomas felt he had all he could cope with in constructing breastworks and defenses in Roxbury.

CHAPTER FIVE

Boston and Charlestown

Another half mile and they reached Charlestown Common following in reverse Paul Revere's midnight route through the marshlands. They reached the crossway where the left road ran to Medford. The lanterns flickered, and Colonel Prescott turned right toward Charlestown Neck and Bunker Hill. Then the men in ranks knew at last where they were headed. Bunker Hill—oval in shape, 300 yards long, and 110 feet high—ran down the center of the mile long Charlestown Peninsula. Beyond it closer to Boston and facing the Charles River was a less conspicuous height of land known as Charlestown or Breed's Hill.

On one side of Breed's Hill lay the now-abandoned village of Charlestown. In front of the hill opposite Boston were broad meadows sloping down to the water's edge with the pastures marked off by stone walls or rail fences. No farmer had dared to cut the hay that spring, and the grass was waist high. On the Mystic riverside of Breed's were swampy ground, some brick kilns, and a thirty-five-feet mound known as Morton's Hill. Prescott and his little staff huddling in the darkness finally decided to fortify Breed's Hill. Whether Prescott misunderstood his instructions or whether he was carried away by Old Put's belligerent enthusiasm, Breed's Hill was his decision—and it was the wrong one. If the crest of Bunker Hill had been fortified with cannon, Prescott could have covered all the approaches to the Charlestown Peninsula while at the time remaining safely out of range of Copp's Hill Fort and the guns of the British fleet. Instead the Americans were to make their challenge on the much less defensible lower level. Todd said, "I have a bad feeling we may be caught and brought into the fight, and if we refuse, we could be shot." Joe replied, "Do not even think of this bullshit. I mean we have to find a way out." Todd replied, "And you better be prepared for anything because we have this war all around us."

While the commanders talked, the men in the ranks grew restless. Finally the word came to move forward. Captain John Nutting and sixty men were sent to scout out abandoned Charlestown. The remainder moved on to occupy Breed's Hill. Colonel Gridley did not think much of the position, but he staked out his fortifications as best as he could in the dark, setting up a box-shaped fort (called a doubt) about forty-five yards on each side with a clear field of fire across the length and breadth of the hill's forward slope.

The men set to with pick and shovel. Farmers for the most part used to such tools worked swiftly, quietly, and efficiently. It was a warm still night with just enough light in the sky for the diggers to glimpse at the outlines of the British ships anchored offshore in the Charles. They saw the *Glasgow* with twenty-four guns, the *Lively* with twenty, the armed transport *Symmetry* with eighteen, and the sloop *Falcon* with sixteen. As the men began their digging, they could hear the Boston clocks across the water tolling midnight and the "all is well" of the ships' sentries. Meanwhile huddled in the tall swamp grass, Bryan was saying, "Something is going to happen. I can feel it, and I don't feel right about it, Todd. It seems sort of eerie listening to those clocks from Boston." Joe then replied, "You fellows don't know what strange is unless you are in my shoes." "What do you mean?" asked Todd. "Oh, never mind," said Joe. "It would be too hard to explain."

Meanwhile, in spite of the skill of the men, there was inevitably an occasional clink of a pick against a stone that would make Prescott catch his breath. Twice he crept down to the water's edge to listen for sounds of British activity. Joe and Todd at this time were trying to get some rest in the tall grass. "This has been a long day. I would like to get some shut-eye," said Joe. Just at that time Joe heard a branch break, and now on their bellies they saw a figure down by the water's edge. "What the hell," said Todd, "is he doing?" "I don't know, but everything right now is so quiet." I will tell you what I think. He must be seeing something or trying to hear something." Nothing broke the silence across the bay but the bells marking the quarter hours and the muffled responses of the sentries. The commander moved up and down the lines among his sweat-stained men, encouraging them with a whispered word here and a pat on the shoulder there. They needed encouraging, for they had not slept in twenty-four hours and had eaten nothing since afternoon. A few became discouraged and drifted away in the direction of the neck among them old Gridley. The rest, now beginning to suffer severely from thirst, kept to their digging. As the blackness in the east shifted into gray and the stars began to fade, the crude redoubt was finished. Prescott sent for Nutting and his men in Charlestown and assembled all his forces within the raw clay rectangle.

In spite of the silence across the Charles, the British had become aware of the night's activities on the peninsula. Some of the sentinels aboard the ships had heard the diggers, but they had not bothered to make a report. General Clinton had been out on a night patrol and had neither heard nor seen the rebels. At once he routed out Gage, Howe, and Burgoyne at province house, urging them to launch a two-pronged attack at daybreak. Howe was agreeable, but Gage finally persuaded the others to wait until after daylight so they could then see better just what the provincials were up to.

Boston and Charlestown and their hills slowly emerged from the shadows, and a few shreds of mist drifted across the placid water. Below Breed's Hill meadowlarks began to sing in the tall grass. The all-too-clear morning light showed Prescott what a fearful mistake he had made in concentrating his forces on such a low unprotected hill. All the British needed to do was ferry troops across the basin to the peninsula and then safely out of musket range march them off either to the Charles or the Mystic until they reached Charlestown Neck. By fortifying this they could bottle up the provincials and starve them out. It was a victory that could have been won without firing a shot. Even the lowliest privates could see the threatening danger, and some of them began to mutter about treachery. By 4:00 a.m. the landscape had brightened enough for the lookout on the *Lively* to spot the fresh earthwork on Breed's Hill. He notified Captain Thomas Bishop who at once warped his ship around to bring her guns to bear on the redoubt. Still smarting from a recent court-martial for neglect of duty, Captain Bishop wasted no time in giving the order to fire. The successive blasts shook Boston's houses and waked the sleeping town.

Drummers were soon beating the call to arms, and the Red Coats poured from their quarters. A boat was lowered from the *Lively*, and its crew pulled hard across the basin toward Boston. Settling in the swamp grass all night when the blast started, Todd and Bryan were awakened by the fire. Joe said, "What the hell is going on?" Bryan replied, "It looks like the firing is coming from that ship in the harbor." Joe stood up, saying,

"What the hell was that?" never really hearing cannon fire like that before. At this point Joe was thinking, "Son of a bitch! In all the time we were trying to rob something, I have never been shot at so much. I really don't know where the hell I am or what the hell I am doing here. This damn thing is getting out of hand, and I can't figure out what the hell to do." Todd said, "It looks like they're firing at that hill over there."

Then for some reason Admiral Graves ordered a letup in the firing. Prescott used the respite to set his men building a protective breastwork from the redoubt straight down the hill toward the Mystic. But before the diggers had really got started, the guns of the whole fleet opened up. "Damn it," said Todd, "it sounds like the whole world is coming to an end!" From water level the cannon could not be elevated high enough to do much damage to the redoubt, but at first the noise and smoke struck fear in the green provincials. Suddenly there was blood on the grass, and the diggers peered down to see the remains of Asa Polard of Bridge's regiment sprawled in the dirt, his head severed by a cannonball. The others dropped their tools and gathered around the body. Prescott kept ordering them to go back to work, but they continued to stand there in dismay. A clergyman stepped forward and offered to perform a burial service. Even as he was praying, more men began to slip away toward the safety of the neck.

In the tall swamp grass Todd and Bryan were watching what was going on. Todd said, "Look, we should go around the other way to the other side and see if we can get a better look at what is going on." Joe said, "I'll stay right here with all this damn shooting. I feel safer here." So Todd and Bryan took off. After about twenty minutes with nothing happening, Joe decided to get a better look. All of a sudden he had a strange feeling. He turned around to see a young British soldier ready to run a fixed bayonet through him. Joe, surprised, said, "Oh shit!" as the soldier made his advance. Suddenly the soldier gasped and fell to the ground with a bowie knife sticking in his back. There stood Bryan and Todd. "You said you didn't want any shooting," said Bryan. "Am I glad to see you! I thought I was a goner! Where did you learn to throw a knife like that?" said Joe. "Another trick I learned at the tavern," Brian replied. Joe said, "All I have to say is that must have been one hell of a tavern!"

By now the sun was well up in the cloudless sky, promising a hot day. Prescott drove his men hard, always digging, giving them no time to brood. Minus his hat and wig, his bald head glistening, he walked with slow deliberation along the parapet. He had taken off his blue tunic and replaced it with a linen smock. As he chatted with his soldiers, a lucky shot from one of the ships destroyed the two hogsheads of water in the redoubt, leaving the men no drink but rum.

Meanwhile at province house Gage prolonged his breakfast conference with his three generals. Clinton still insisted that troops should be embarked at once no time lost before Prescott could complete his fortifications. He wanted the main force under Howe to attack the redoubt from the front while he himself with five hundred troops would go up the Mystic to seize the rebel rear. Although a mill dam blocked a direct landing on the neck from the Charles riverside, Admiral Graves could easily bring up floating batteries and bar the Americans from crossing there, in effect cutting off the Breed's Hill force from both reinforcements and escape. To Howe and Burgoyne, Clinton's plan seemed too complicated merely to drive a crowd of ragamuffins out of their wretched earthworks. The English generals had no respect for the amateur colonial officers. Howe was not even willing to call the prospective engagement a fight. "The provincials," he announced contemptuously, "were to be removed from the redoubt." Breed's Hill was "open and of easy assent and in short would be easily carried."

The British then began their preparation for the assault with a leisurely thoroughness that gave Prescott much-needed time to reinforce his lines toward the Mystic where he felt any attack would probably be made. Since this action was to be technically an expedition, the Red Coats were ordered to take full-regulation field packs. This meant that for a journey of a few hundred yards on one of the hottest days of the year, they would have to carry knapsacks with blankets as well as all their equipment and three days of cooked rations. In all they had about 125 pounds on their backs as they attacked.

Orders poured out of province house: Ten companies of grenadiers and ten of light infantry plus the Fifth and Thirty-eighth Regiments to proceed to Long Wharf for embarkation. The Forty-third and Fifty-second Regiments and the rest of the grenadiers and light infantry were to leave from the North Battery Wharf. These two assault waves numbered about 1,550 men. A reserve detachment, the Forty-seventh Regiment, and part of the Sixty-third and the First and Second Battalions of marines were to stand by at the North Battery. While the British troops were gathering Prescott's men were using stone walls and rail fences to extend the breastwork. The nine-and-twelve pounders of the warships in the basin continued to fire with more noise than damage. By this time the provincials were becoming sufficiently "cannon wise" to duck at the first flash of the muzzles and

watch the iron balls, even those of the twenty-four pounders in the Copp's
Hill battery, arch over their heads harmlessly.

Captain Samuel Gridley managed to get four guns up to the redoubt,
and his artillerists opened fire on Boston. But after a half-dozen shots in
which they missed their targets by a sizeable margin and merely hit a fence
and a house, they quit in discouragement and began to look for some way
of pulling out. There were gaps in the ranks as more of Prescott's men
by twos and threes now slipped away to the Cambridge mainland. Even
those who stayed kept looking toward the neck and grumbling about the
absence of the expected relief. Prescott knew that they were not going to
be relieved at all, but he finally sent Major John Brooks to Cambridge
to ask General Ward for reinforcements. The ailing Ward, who had been
hesitant about the Bunker Hill move from the beginning, at first refused
to consider sending any more men there at all. Anybody could see that
the British were making ready to strike, but where they might strike was
another matter. Suppose they should make a feint at Charlestown and then
advance instead on Cambridge? What would happen to all the collected
provincial stores and ammunition if there were no troops left to protect
them? The Committee of Safety meeting in the Hastings House overruled
General Ward. Aid, they felt, must be sent at once to Prescott.

They ordered out Reed's regiment along with the rest of John Stark's
New Hampshire troops. Each man was issued two flints, a gill of powder,
and a pound of lead cut from the organ of a Cambridge church. This force
set out at just about the time that barges of Red Coats were shoving off
from Boston.

During that explosive morning everyone in Boston whose feet could
carry him made his way to the north side of the town. Roofs and garrets
were crowded with spectators. Rarely has a battle had such a panoramic
view and so many onlookers. General Gage came down to the waterfront
with Abigah Willard, the Tory brother of Prescott's wife, and inspected
the redoubt with his spyglass. Willard pointed out the commanding figure
on the parapet as his brother-in-law. "Will he fight?" Gage asked him. "I
cannot answer for his men," Willard told the general, "but Prescott will
fight you to the gates of hell."

The slam and crash of the ships' guns reverberated as far away as
Braintree, where on Penn's Hill Abigail Adams watched the far-off smoke
of the battle as she held the hand of a little boy who would one day be
the sixth president of the United States. To the watchers on the Boston
rooftops, it was like a pageant. Yet when one of the little antlike figures on

the earthworks opposite them dropped down, he was really dead. Even as the people on the roofs watched a man standing next to Colonel Prescott was torn apart by a chance shot. Each time the big guns belched their orange flashes, the brown figures on Breed's Hill scurried down like insects to let the cannonballs sail over. Black coils of smoke twisted and spread over the placid water. The meadow grass below the redoubt seemed a green sea with here and there a furrow cut by a shell. Joe, Bryan, and Todd watched from the swamp grass off to the side of where the barges were heading.

Then at half past one twenty-eight barges of Red Coats left the shelter of Boston wharves and headed across the channel to Morton's Point on the Charlestown Peninsula. Those who saw that would never forget the clear precise beauty of it. Two parallel lines of fourteen boats moved in clockwork order across the water, white oars flashing in perfect cadence. In each of the leading barges six polished brass six pounders flashed back the sunshine. Todd said, "I've never seen anything like that before!" Bryan said, "You're right. I wonder if we've got a chance of getting out of this."

Joe asked, "What the hell is going on now?" Todd said, "Hit the ground!" Before they could do anything, he was pushed to the ground right into swamp water face down just as a cannonball hit near them. Joe got up and said, "Son of a bitch! What the hell was that?" Todd said, "We were lucky that time." Joe said, "Did you have to push me into the water?" "No choice," said Todd. Bryan said, "Do you think they saw us?" "No," replied Todd, "I just think it was a wild shot."

Joe was now thinking, "How am I going to get out of this? I listened to those other guys and tried to rob a store, and I end up in a goddamn war with people I just met. I'm being shot at with rifles, cannons, and all that bullshit. Everybody keeps saying Boston, and I don't recognize a damn thing, and I have been here all my life!

"One time in school they were teaching about a fight at Bunker Hill, and I remember going on a school trip. This has to be a bad dream, and I don't remember taking any drugs. I mean this is real crazy! I don't even know where I was when I got to the waterfront. I wonder where the hell those other guys are and if they're going through this thing. I think the store owner put a hex on us!"

Then Joe said to Todd and Bryan, "Look at this leaflet I found. For joining the British at Prospect Hill, you get seven dollars a month, fresh provisions, freedom, affluence, and a good farm. They say if you join the Americans at Bunker Hill, you get three pence a day, rotten salt pork, scurvy, slavery, and beggary. What the hell is this!" "Each side wants you to join," replied Todd. Bryan was saying, "We had better stay low in the grass, for we are surrounded by both sides, and I don't think the British are going to treat us to kindly if we are caught."

"What are we going to do?" asked Joe. "Right now I don't know," said Todd. "At this point we should stay still, for the British are heading to Bunker Hill. From what I see, this looks like an all-out war!" Bryan then asked, "What are we staying here for?" "Because right now, if we move, we could be shot by either side. Not a good position to be in. I have a feeling that both sides are trigger-happy and will shoot on sight." One by one the barges ground ashore at Morton's Point. With haversacks and muskets, they splashed through the shallows and up the beach. Then the barges returned to Boston for a second load, this time bringing back the Royal Regiment of Artillery and General Howe.

The landing, well protected by the guns of the Royal Navy, was made without opposition. A total of 1,500 troops arrived in the first two waves. From the shore Howe observed Starks's and Reed's regiments on the crest of Bunker Hill, and as he watched he noticed several detachments hurry downhill and move into positions along the flat land just above the Mystic River. Howe saw at once that these newcomers would block any chance he might have had to move his troops along the Mystic and seal off the provincials from the rear. About four hundred yards from the rough breastwork, Howe lined up four companies of his light infantry under the protection of a small bank. Then, after he had formed up his other troops and pushed three lines of infantry to the top of Morton's Hill, he sent back to Gage to ask for reinforcements.

In the interval the men broke ranks, took off their knapsacks, and out of rebel range sat down in the grass to eat their dinner. As he had watched the Red Coats pile ashore, Prescott realized that the most vulnerable spot in the lines was the gap where the breastwork ended in the swampy ground short of the Mystic. In the breathing space now given him, he sent Captain Knowlton and his two hundred Connecticut men to close the gap. He also sent Captain Gridley with his fieldpieces, but as soon as Gridley and his disheartened artillerists were out of sight of the redoubt, they changed their direction and headed for the neck. Old Put stopped them near Bunker Hill. Gridley's men insisted they were out of ammunition, but the suspicious Putnam inspected the ammunition chests and found them full and angrily ordered the guns back to the firing line. But when he turned his back, the gunners abandoned their pieces and fled the peninsula.

Captain Knowlton was made of sterner stuff. Determined, if somewhat uncertain of his orders, he moved his company to the back of the swamp some six hundred feet behind the breastwork where they extended two hundred yards to the Mystic. His men tore down another fence and set it up just ahead of their own. The space between them filled with grass and brush. There was a gap between the rail fence and the breastwork, a gap taken up by the swamp. Here Knowlton dug three small trenches called fleches. When John Stark, standing atop Bunker Hill, saw how much space Knowlton was attempting to hold with his few men, he at once led his own force down the hill on the double to reinforce them. Stark paused a moment to give his men "a short but animated address" to which the troops answered with three cheers.

They joined Knowlton just about the time that General Howe was landing with the second load of troops. Also at this time Captain Samuel Trevett showed up with two fieldpieces from Cambridge, which he had brought safely through the British fire. At the neck these two guns placed behind the rail provided the only American artillery fire of the day. A British officer remarked that the cannon were "very advantageously planted" and added that the Yankee gunners served them "with the greatest vigor." Trevett's guns and Stark's unit were the last important reinforcements that the defenders of Breed's Hill would receive. Stark, walking along the line of the rail fence, found that it ended at the riverbank. There the bank dropped sharply eight or nine feet to a narrow beach—a perfectly shielded route for the Red Coats to march along and outflank Prescott's whole army. At once Stark ordered "his boys" to pile up stones and make a solid wall on the beach right down to the water's edge. Behind this wall he posted a triple row of marksmen.

Shortly after the alarm sounded in Cambridge, a Dr. Warren started out for Charlestown. He galloped across the neck, disregarding the pounding Royal Navy cannonade, and made his way up Bunker Hill. The provincial Congress had just elected him major general, and Old Put came over and asked the new commander for orders. Warren said he had come to fight as a volunteer in the ranks and not as a general. When he reached the redoubt, Prescott too offered him a command, but Warren said that he had not yet officially received a commission. He borrowed a musket and took his place in line. Seth Pomeroy, a seventy-year old-veteran of the French Wars, also was made a general by Congress. He tramped across the neck and up to Breed's Hill with the musket he had carried thirty years before at the siege of Louisburg. Like Warren he insisted on fighting as a volunteer and joined Starks's men by the fence.

As the climax of the afternoon approached, there were others who showed themselves less courageous. Behind the American lines the confusion was worse than the cannonading. Out of the nine regiments originally dispatched from Cambridge, only five of varying strength arrived at Breed's Hill. Some regiments got lost; some were warned away by the thunder of the guns across the neck; some stopped short at Bunker Hill. While waiting for his reserves and protecting himself from snipers and any surprise attack, Howe ordered Admiral Graves to set fire to Charlestown. The admiral proceeded to bombard the village with red-hot cannonballs, and soon whole rows of buildings burst into flames. The cannonading from the ships increased in tempo as the barges with Howe's reserve detachment landed between Morton's Point and burning Charlestown.

At the time Pigot's men were to come in from the Charles riverside, skirt Charlestown, and attack the redoubt itself. To the provincials listening to the long roll of drums, the scarlet ranks of infantry forming their precise lines were an ominous sight. These soldiers with their peaked helmets and glittering bayonets formed a formidable fighting machine. In open combat they were unequaled as they had proved from Flanders to Quebec. The bayonets were dismaying to those who had none. Private Peter Brown had the feeling that "they advanced toward us in order to swallow us up." Prescott was manning the redoubt and the breastwork with his own men along with bits and pieces of several other regiments, all of them composed of Massachusetts troops. The rail fence was held by Knowlton's Connecticut troops and Reed's New Hampshire men and some of Stark's. Stark himself and the rest of his men guarded the wall by the beach. Three companies protected the Charlestown flank.

Just before the signal for the attack, Howe addressed his men in the formal eighteenth-century manner, telling them he was sure they would "behave like Englishman and become good soldiers." He would not ask one of them "to go a step further than where I go myself at your head." It was a promise he kept. Before moving his infantry, he sent his artillery forward to open fire on the redoubt, the breastwork, and the fence. Unfortunately for him his six pounders had been supplied with twelve-pound shot, and the distance was too great for grapeshot to be effective. There was a further difficulty when the guns bogged down in soggy ground. Gage's chief of artillery was roundly criticized for the ammunition mix-up. An officer sarcastically commented that if the artillery colonel had spent more time attending to business and less time "dallying with the schoolmaster's daughters" in Boston, things might have been different.

While the artillerists tugged at their cannon, the grenadiers and the infantry in the line behind them began their direct advance. Each man was still burdened by the 125-pound pack. Howe felt that they would not need to stop and fire. The cold steel bayonet would be enough. Down Morton's Hill the red lines moved steady and exact, in time to the beat of the drums, across the flat land, and up the lower slope of Breed's Hill. Three hundred abreast they marched as if they were on parade. It was a slow and ponderous advance, and from time to time, the two lines stopped to let the artillery come up. From the hills and roofs of Boston, the slowness of the advance was breathtaking. Against the background of what might have been a fine summer day flame belched from the Copp's Hill battery and the guns of the fleet. Charlestown blazed, buildings crashed with showers of sparks. Against the green meadow the waving red lines moved relentlessly. The smoke from the burning town almost obscured the small brown figures behind the redoubt and the breastwork.

As the red wave of the infantry lapped against the foot of Breed's Hill, the Royal Navy gunners held their fire. The provincials waited behind their rough earthworks and flimsy fences with flintlocks cocked. They could now see the numbered regimental badges of the grenadiers and even the coat buttons. There were no other sounds but the ominous beat of the drums and the heavy tread of advancing feet. American officers paced back and forth behind their troops, urging them to fire slowly and aim low and concentrate on British officers. Prescott passed the word along to his waiting men, "Don't fire until you see the whites of their eyes."

The light infantry that moved off the beach was able to advance more rapidly along the packed sand. Eleven companies were there, marching in columns of four. The Royal Welch Fusiliers were in the lead followed by a company of the King's Own. Their orders were not to stop to fire but to take the wall with the bayonet. Stark's men let them come on until they were fifty feet away and preparing to charge home. Suddenly a row of muskets appeared, and a nasal voice commanded fire, and the wall vanished behind a blaze of flame and curling black smoke. The blast ripped apart the ranks of the fusiliers, dropping some and scattering the rest. The men of the King's Own pushed their way dauntlessly forward only to be met by another hail of bullets stopping them in their tracks. Officers bellowed for the men to reform, but even as they stepped over their dead and wounded, they were cut down. The bodies piled up on the narrow beach that was like a tunnel into which the Americans poured their shot. Some of the Red

Coats fell in the sand and others in the water. Again and again the front ranks dissolved.

Finally, in the face of that withering fire, panic seized the survivors. Even the officers lashing at the men with their swords could no longer rally them. They bolted for the rear, leaving behind ninety-six dead. The first and most important part of Howe's plan to outflank the provincials had failed. Now it was the turn of the grenadiers led by Howe in person as he had promised in a direct frontal attack. The grenadiers were just clambering over their last obstacle when they heard the volleys and the shouting from the beach. Scattered shots came from a few Americans behind the fence, and the Red Coats stopped to return the fire. As they did so, the full provincial fire power from behind the barricades hit them with almost the force that had struck the Royal Welch. Still out of sight Joe was now thinking, "Son of a bitch! How the hell are we going to get out of this fucking situation with all these bullets flying around and we can't move?"

Howe was unhurt, but his staff lay dead all around him, and his grenadiers dropped right and left. The British return fire went high and wide. The Red Coats bunched in the grass made perfect targets for the farmers steadying their muskets on the fence rails. The line of advancing grenadiers was riddled. Never could their thrusting bayonets get close enough for the final charge. As the Red Coats dropped, disorder grew. Even the most disciplined flesh can only stand so much. Finally the British turned and fled out of range of the deadly fire. Pigot's flanking column on the extreme left was also a failure. American snipers, hiding behind rocks and trees and dodging between the burning buildings in Charlestown, nearly drove the Red Coats to distraction. When Pigot saw what happened to Howe, he called his men back before they got anywhere near the redoubt. The Americans cheered and shouted as if victory were already theirs. They had met the terrible regulars and had overcome them.

Prescott knew, however, that the battle was far from won—that the regulars would soon be back. He had few defenders: only 150 now in the redoubt and perhaps another 700 behind the breastwork and the fence. Old Put climbed up Bunker Hill where several hundred provincials were preparing a second line of defense. Though he begged and cursed at them to go forward and aid Prescott, only a few responded. Other reinforcements were still stalled at the neck by the guns of the warships. Within fifteen minutes of his bloody repulse, Howe had rallied his men to launch a second attack. This time he combined the thin ranks of his light infantry and grenadiers to storm the rail fence while he and Pigot threw the rest of their force against the breastwork and the redoubt to within a hundred yards of the American lines. There they formed their line of battle and moved with bayonets at the ready. The provincials let them advance until they were thirty yards away.

By this time Todd and Joe were in the crossfire. Bryan was thirty or forty yards behind them, laying in grass and mud afraid to move. Todd asked, "Where is Bryan?" Joe said, "Behind us somewhere, afraid to move with all the fire around us." Then again there came that withering downhill rain of shot. As the British approached, an incessant stream of fire poured from the rebel lines. It was a continuous sheet of fire for near thirty minutes. The light infantry were served up in companies against the grass fence without being able to penetrate. But how could they penetrate when they had lost so many men? Some companies had only eight or nine men; some had only three, four, or five. On the left Pigot was staggered and actually retreated.

The British lines broke and dissolved into individual Red Coats running pell-mell downhill to get out of the range of the Yankee guns. Howe stood there shocked among the dead and dying a moment he had never felt before. The British wounded who could be gathered up were taken to the boats and ferried to Boston. Howe regrouped his shaken survivors at the bank of the Charles. His remaining officers begged to call off the engagement, but the general was stubbornly determined to make one more attempt. He sent a message over to Clinton who was responsible for the reserves to demand still more men. Clinton dispatched four hundred men of the Sixty-third Regiment and the Second Marine Battalion. He had been watching the engagement from Copp's Hill, and now as he saw Pigot's men huddled leaderless near the Charlestown shore, it was more than he could bear. He himself rowed across, picking up what stragglers and walking wounded he could, and he made his way toward the battleground.

The sharp joy of Prescott's men at the second repulse of the regulars was short-lived when they saw the red lines forming for the third time. Although their casualties had been light, the provincials from the redoubt to the rail fence were almost out of powder and bullets. Men shared what they had with their comrades. Prescott located a few cannon cartridges left behind by Gridley's gunners, broke them open, and distributed this small stock of powder. Still the defenders were far short of what was needed to meet another determined assault. Behind Yankee lines there was the continuing confusing mixture of bravery and cowardice. Hundreds still milled about the neck, taking shelter in the hollows, behind rocks, and behind haystacks. A few went resolutely forward to join the fighting. Others made their way to the rear. Two youngsters hauled water all the way across the neck and up to the battle lines on Breed's Hill. They were warmly greeted by the parched defenders, and the water with rum went very quick.

Hundreds of fresh men wandered aimlessly on the reverse slope of Bunker Hill. Old Put did his profane best (Okay, you sons of bitches, you lazy bastards) to urge them to move down to the redoubt. Turning to an aide, he said, "I cannot drive these dogs." The sun was lowering and the shadows long as the British began the third assault. This time they had brought up artillery with cannonballs that fit.

For the third assault Howe would lead the attack against the breastwork, Clinton and Piggott against the redoubt. Only a handful of troops were to make a feint at the rail fence. Common sense at last won out over military regulations. Howe ordered his men to discard their knapsacks and all other superfluous equipment. Again the drums echoed their sinister rhythm, and again the Red Coats, with their flashing bayonets, came on over the blood-trampled grass where their comrades still lay. This time they advanced in open order in long files, each file twelve feet from the next. When a man dropped, the man behind him took his place, stepping over his body as if it were a log.

The waiting provincials watched the deadly scarlet files moving toward them. One soldier said, "These bastards look too handsome to shoot at. Screw it, I'll shoot them anyway." Joe, looking on said, "I don't believe this. Did you see that we have to find Bryan and get the hell out of here?"

As the British artillery opened up, holes gaped in the breastwork, but still there was no break in Prescott's defenses. Still the provincials' rain of fire cut down the advancing Red Coats, maddened now by the lust of battle that overcame fear. Suddenly a young lieutenant yelled, "Push on, push on!" and the Red Coats advanced with spirit to attack with their small arms. As soon as the rebels perceived this, they rose up and poured in very heavy fire. They kept up the fire until the British were within ten yards of the redoubt. At Pigot's far left the marines were momentarily shattered by fire from the redoubt. Major Pitcairn, unhurt on the retreat from Concord and Lexington, now received a mortal wound while trying to rally his men. Supported by the Forty-seventh the marines recovered their strength and stormed the walls of the redoubt under very heavy fire. The provincials who ran short of bullets fired nails and other pieces of metal they picked up. Others, completely out of ammunition, hurled rocks. Joe was saying to Todd, "They're throwing rocks for Christ's sake at the advancing British columns." For the moment, as the Red Coats poised, the battle lay in the balance. A few of the idle companies from Bunker Hill might have swung that balance to the provincials or a few extra pounds of powder. Prescott realized afterward that one more volley would have pushed the British down the hill. Instead with the last grains of powder exhausted, the American fire spurted out like a candle.

The grenadiers and the marines quickly scrambled over the walls with bayonets thrust forward, with the hoarse traditional victory shout that could be heard as far as Boston. Within the smoky redoubt provincials and Red Coats fought like wild animals, clubbed muskets against bayonets, stones against swords, even fists against fists. Prescott now saw that the end had come and ordered a retreat. The men jammed at the one narrow exit in the rear. So great was the dust and smoke, however, that the Red Coats on the walls did not dare fire into the wild-groping mass for fear of killing their own men. Most of the provincials at last managed to break free. But somewhere in the smoky turmoil Dr. Warren fell with a bullet in his brain.

The resistance at the redoubt was over. Luckily for the desperate provincials Stark's men behind the rail fence managed to cover the retreat before they too withdrew. Old Seth Pomeroy stayed until the end. Clinton found Howe too dazed to continue. His face was blank, his white gaiters red with blood that smeared the long grass. Leaving a hundred men in the redoubt, the younger general at once organized a pursuit. Stark and Knowlton put up a stubborn rear guard defense, their men pausing to deliver a withering fire from behind each wall and fence before falling back. The rebels managed to haul away one of Captain Trevett's two guns, the only American artillery piece to be saved.

At the neck the situation was different. Here more than a thousand exhausted men found the remainder of their courage oozing away as they struggled to cross the thirty-five-yard bottleneck. They had lost more men there than during the battle. The day's casualties for the Americans were 140 killed, 271 wounded, and 30 captured. The British losses were a number of officers picked off by Yankee sharpshooters. The dead numbered 226, and 828 were wounded. Although in possession of the Charlestown Peninsula, the British had neither the will nor the strength to go farther. Clinton sat down and wrote "This was a dear bought victory and another such battle would have ruined us." Night came heavy and overcast, and the Charlestown Neck lay empty. The Americans had withdrawn into the shadows of Cambridge, and the cannon fleet ceased their fire.

On the slopes of Breed's Hill and along the littered beach, stretcher bearers and surgeons moved through the sultry hours, bringing off the wounded, guided in the night by moans and sometimes screams. Back and forth between Morton's Point and Boston's Long Wharf, the barges labored with their loads of broken bodies. The lights of the search parties flickered up and down the peninsula. At Long Wharf coaches, chariots, and even wheelbarrows waited to carry the maimed. The almshouse, the workhouse, and even old factories were taken over for hospitals. Although more than half of the Boston garrison had taken no part in the battle, the spirit had gone out of the whole occupying army. Soon the previously smart Red Coats would be appearing on the streets in sloppy uniforms with soiled gaiters and webbing, unkempt hair, and unpolished boots and badges—a sure sign in any army of disintegrating morale. "The loss we have sustained is greater than we could bear," said General Gage. "I wish this cursed place was burned." To Gage there was nothing left for his penned-up army to do now but to quit Boston.

Howe felt there was nothing to do for the moment but to stay on. Clinton was more aggressive. He wanted to seize Dorchester Heights before the Americans recovered from their defeat. But Gage could not bear the thought of any more offensive action. He would do no more than strengthen the defenses at Boston Neck and enlarge Montresor's works on Bunker Hill. The engagement (as it became known incorrectly) would be seen in its true light as one of the decisive battles of the revolution. Before that bloody afternoon that left British strewn along the slopes of Breed's Hill, it might have been possible even after Concord and Lexington for the colonists to work out some sort of accommodation. But after Bunker Hill, as anger and bitterness raged on both sides, it was no longer possible.

Only gradually as Americans came to understand the significance of the battle did Prescott's valiant fight achieve the symbolism of a heroic act. Practically speaking it was a foolish one. Even if Prescott had seized the higher level of Bunker Hill and established himself there, he lacked the heavy cannon to threaten Boston. From a purely military view, there will always be a question of which side behaved more foolishly. The Americans in setting themselves up in an advanced position that could be easily surrounded or the British who attacked the position head-on. For the rebels the first reaction was the numbness of the defeat. After they had lost the battle and had been thrown off the hill, many of them felt great hostility toward Artemas Ward for staying in Cambridge and issuing no orders during the conflict. The men who fought were bitter about men who did not. Several officers were court-martialed and dismissed from the service.

CHAPTER SIX

The Battle

The most important weapons of the Revolutionary War were the flintlock musket, the rifle, and the cannon. The musket discharged a large lead ball and could fire three or four rounds a minute. A bayonet could be fastened over the muzzle of a musket. Rifles had a much greater accuracy than muskets, but rifles took longer to reload, which made them less efficient in battle. American frontiersmen improved the rifle's value by their skill at rapid loading. Cannons hurled shells to long distances and blasted soldiers at closer range. On the battlefield soldiers lined up shoulder to shoulder two or three rows deep. Their muskets had little accuracy beyond sixty yards for the reason that the attackers advanced as far as possible before shooting. After firing several rounds, the two sides closed in for hand-to-hand combat with bayonets. The battle ended when one side broke through enemy lines or forced the other side to retreat.

In the early years of the war, the Americans had few bayonets, which gave the Red Coats an enormous advantage. Tactically the British had won the victory. But from a larger point of view, the result was a draw. The American colonies entered the Revolutionary War without an army or a navy. Their fighting forces consisted of militia units in the various colonies. The militias were made up of white men from sixteen years old to sixty years old. Those citizen-soldiers were ready to defend their homes and families when danger threatened. The colonies could call up militiamen for periods of service ranging from a few days to a few months. Britain had an army of well-trained, highly disciplined soldiers. Britain also hired professional German soldiers called Hessians because most of them came from the German state of Hesse-Kassel. American Loyalists and Indians also joined British fighting forces during the war. At its peak the British military force in North America numbered about fifty thousand.

George Washington and other Patriot leaders doubted that part-time militias could defeat the British in a long war. Washington worked to build an army made up of disciplined soldiers who had enlisted for several years. However, recruitment for the Continental Army remained a constant problem. Most citizens preferred to serve in local militias and support the Continental Army even when a major battle threatened nearby. Washington rarely commanded as many as fifteen thousand soldiers at a time, and he frequently commanded far fewer. Soldiers often went without pay, food, and proper clothing because the Continental Congress was so poor and the transportation in the colonies was so bad. Yet many poor soldiers stayed in the army because they had been promised free land after the war. They fought as much for economic gain as for political liberty. In time most states permitted blacks to serve in the Continental Army. In all about five thousand blacks fought on the Patriot side in the war. Many were slaves who had been promised freedom in exchange for military service.

Britain's powerful navy loosely blockaded America's Atlantic coast and at times raided port towns. The Americans had a small navy, which was too weak to challenge large British warships. However, the Continental Navy sank or captured many smaller British vessels especially cargo ships. Privately owned American vessels known as privateers also captured enemy cargo ships. The stolen cargoes were then sold with profits going to investors, the ship captains, and the crews.

The Americans were beaten but not shattered. They still had the energy to fortify Winter Hill just beyond Charlestown Neck. The Boston peninsula was still ringed with a chain of fortified hills any one of which the British might find as costly to take as Breed's Hill. "It is all fortification," Burgoyne said. "Driven from one hill you will see the enemy continually retrenching upon the next, and every step we move must be the slow step of a siege." On the other hand, Ward's improvised army was incapable of launching an attack on Boston or challenging the British defenses there. As summer gave way to autumn, the two armies did little more than watch each other warily and wait for reinforcements. As it worked out, the Battle of Bunker Hill's chief fault on the American side was not cowardice but a lack of a proper chain of command. That problem was soon solved. Two days before the battle the Continental Congress sitting in Philadelphia had appointed the Virginia militia colonel George Washington to command all the Continental forces "raised or to be raised for the defense of American liberty." With the arrival of George Washington in Cambridge on July 2 the Massachusetts provincial became the Continental Army of the Thirteen Colonies.

There could not have been a more inspired choice than this tall dignified Virginian. His military experience was large, for he had led expeditions against the French and had served on General Braddock's staff in the ill-fated 1755 campaign against Fort Duquesne. As a Southerner he would draw the support of the Southern colonies. As an aristocrat he would still have the doubts of the conservatives fearful of the firebrand agitators like Adams. As an experienced military officer, he would be able to mold Ward's makeshift force into an army. Washington called this Cambridge army "a mixed multitude of people here under very little discipline or government where confusion and disorder reigned." Washington was not at first discouraged, for he felt that he had the raw material to make into "good stuff." Order and discipline were the first essentials.

The commander in chief began by establishing the necessary if artificial distinction between officers and enlisted men that Americans have always tended to find irksome in all their wars. Since uniforms were not available, in his blue and buff uniform, Washington was one of the few properly dressed officers in the whole army; other and simpler distinctions had to be made. A purple ribbon across the chest marked a major general, pink a brigadier, green a staff officer, majors and colonels wore red or pink cockades in their hats, captains yellow or buff, lieutenants green, sergeants and corporals fastened red and green shoulder knots on their tunics.

Washington's problems were enormous. There was never enough ammunition and powder—those most basic of army commodities. The camp might be temporarily cheered by the arrival of a few companies of frontier riflemen, but the commander in chief was faced with a stern prospect of a coming winter. Where would sufficient supplies, equipment, clothing, and food come from? How could his men be sheltered from the northern blizzards? But his immediate problem was manpower. When he took command he found about thirteen thousand men fit for duty. Many of them had arrived with heroic ideas about war, ready to fight, but scarcely prepared for long boring months of drill, discipline, and fatigue duties. The realization that any army is first a huge housekeeping establishment was too much for many of them.

As the weather turned colder, desertions increased. Ward had persuaded the original volunteers to sign up until the end of 1775 except

for the men from Connecticut who were engaged only until December
10. When January came, these veterans would be free to go home, and
most of them decided that they were going. They felt they had fulfilled
their promise, done their share, volunteered their lives, and served their
time. Now let somebody else perch uncomfortably on the hills around
Boston! Of the 7,000 men in the eleven old regiments only 966 could be
persuaded to reenlist for an additional year. At one point Washington was
so discouraged that he wrote, "Could I have foreseen what I have and am
likely to experience, no consideration on earth should have induced me to
accept this command."

After much cajoling of the newer men, about a quarter of the whole
army agreed to stay on. Massachusetts and New Hampshire began to raise
additional militia units. The Connecticut men were asked to stay until
the new soldiers arrived, but they flatly refused. Recruits still continued to
trickle in, however, this time from all over New England. On New Year's
Day 1776 the new Continental flag was hoisted over the American camp.
The crosses of St. George and St. Andrew graced the blue field where the
stars were now arranged and the stripes of red and white for the thirteen
colonies.

In spite of the cold desertions and reluctant soldiers, Washington
gradually managed to build up his army to about ten thousand men, a
mixture of veterans, raw recruits, and short-term militia. Those who had
left took their muskets with them.

But worse than a lack of men in the army was a lack of weapons above
all artillery. Three hundred miles away at Fort Ticonderoga artillery was
in plentiful supply. This key fortress on Lake Champlain between Canada
and British North America had fallen into neglect and half-ruin at the end
of the French Wars. Three weeks after Concord and Lexington, an oddly
matched pair—dapper elegant Benedict Arnold and rough-and-ready
Ethan Allen—had led a detachment of eighty-three homespun Vermonters
that surprised and captured Ticonderoga's small British garrison. Only one
sentry was wounded in this slightly comic engagement. Allen, sword in
hand, demanded the fort's surrender from a British officer who donned his
uniform so hastily that he had not time to put on his breeches.

From the ruins of the fort Arnold and Allen secured seventy-eight
serviceable cannons from four to twenty pounders as well as quantities of
cannonballs and powder. In mid-November Washington decided to try
to bring some of the captured weapons to Boston even though it meant
carting them by oxen-drawn sledges down the Hudson Valley and over

the steep snowy barrier of the Berkshires. For this grueling task, he picked twenty-five-year-old artillery officer Henry Knox. Knox was a full-faced, florid, good-natured man and enthusiastic amateur soldier. Tall and stoutly built, he weighed 280 pounds. A few years earlier, his London Book Store, where he sold all the latest books from England, had been an informal intellectual center in Boston. Knox himself read a lot. His hobby was military science, and from military books and his membership in Boston's Ancient and Honorable Artillery Company, he had made himself into a capable artillery officer. He arrived at Ticonderoga to undertake his great task on December 5, 1775.

In the meantime, as discouraging as life could be for Washington's Continentals, ringing Boston life within the town was equally bleak for the occupying British. Smallpox raged. The lack of fresh vegetables soon brought scurvy to the reinforced but still demoralized army. Supplies of all kinds, from meat to fuel, had to be shipped from England. The British government sent out massive cargoes to the beleaguered town: five thousand oxen, fourteen thousand sheep, vast numbers of hogs, ten thousand butts of strong beer, and thousands of bushels of coal. Few of these essentials ever arrived. Ships sent from England in the period of autumnal storms floundered or went off course. Animals died at sea. Many a cargo ship was captured by prowling American privateers. By early autumn Gage's three colleagues agreed that Boston should be abandoned and the bottled-up army evacuated. There was no question of making any more attacks on the Americans when each assault might turn into another Breed's Hill.

On October 11, Gage set sail for London, his career in ruins. Howe now commanded all British forces in the thirteen colonies. He would have to quit the town at once, but he felt that since he lacked sufficient ships, his troops would have to sit it out until spring. While the sullen Red Coats wandered about in Boston's narrow streets—scrounging whatever they could and breaking up wharves, old ships, fences, barns, and sometimes even houses for fuel—the British officers did their makeshift best to amuse themselves. In this they were assisted as much as possible by the local Tories. Daughters of prominent Loyalists took female parts in plays that the British officers put on in Faneuil Hall, the old "cradle of liberty," which they had made into a theater. Voltaire's *Zara* was produced there during the winter as well as General Burgoyne's newly written *The Blockade of Boston*, which ridiculed Washington as a country bumpkin. There were sleighing parties, dances, and dinner parties. Pulpit and pews were torn out of the Old South Meeting House, the floor covered with tanbark, and the building used by the officers as a riding ring with the gallery serving as a refreshment room.

Other Tories took a more active part in the siege. On the very day of Lexington and Concord, several hundred Loyalist tradesmen and merchants had offered their services to Gage as gentlemen volunteers. During the summer and autumn such Loyalists formed themselves into three volunteer companies: Loyal American Association; Royal Fencible Americans; and, strange as it might seem, the Loyal Irish Volunteers. The Loyal Americans were commanded by Timothy Ruggles who had presided over the Stamp Act Congress ten years before and who had the reputation of being one of the best soldiers in the colonies.

Except for minor skirmishes the winter stalemate remained unbroken. In February Boston Harbor froze over, and for a while Washington toyed with the idea of a direct assault on Boston until this military council persuaded him to give it up. The situation changed abruptly at month's end when Knox arrived with the Ticonderoga cannon. He had accomplished a prodigious feat in the bitterest of weather, hauling his loads on forty-three sledges he had constructed and pulled by eighty yoke of oxen. Now he presented his commander with what was indeed "a noble train of artillery": forty-three cannon, fourteen mortars, and two howitzers.

Washington finally had long-range weapons to fortify Dorchester Heights. These heights just across the bay to the southeast of Boston were as vital to the safety of the town as was Bunker Hill to the north. If Washington could plant his heavy cannon there, he would dominate the town, the fleet, Castle William in the harbor, and the defenses on Boston Neck. Unless Howe could drive the Americans off these heights, he would be forced out of Boston. Washington made careful and thorough preparations to occupy the heights by surprise before the British caught on to what he was doing. Even with planning and equipment, it would be a much more difficult task to accomplish in one night than was Prescott's since the earth was now frozen to a depth of a foot and a half.

To throw the Red Coats off the track, Washington's artillery began to cannonade Boston from the surrounding hills for three nights. Extra militiamen were called up, and after dark a working party of 1,200 men under John Thomas left Roxbury for Dorchester Heights. Escorting them was a force of eight hundred troops. Hay was piled along the road to screen three hundred and sixty oxcarts traveling back and forth with equipment. With steaming breath and numb fingers, Thomas's men toiled through the night, setting up heavy timber frames into which they placed previously prepared bundles of sticks called fascines. In font of these fascines they set up barrels filled with earth. There was a bright moon, but a haze hung over the harbor to conceal the operation from the enemy, and the thunder of big guns from the farther hills covered up all sounds. As picks reached below the frost line, the work became easier. By morning two small redoubts were complete and mounted with a cannon and fully manned and out of range of British artillery. Only a direct assault could drive out the Continentals now. At dawn's early light General Howe was astonished and dismayed. The rebels did in one night what his whole army could have done in months. Yet the surprise need not have been so complete. Some of the British had become aware during the evening of what was going on. A lieutenant colonel Campbell had reported to Colonel Francis Smith at ten o'clock that "the rebels were at work on Dorchester Heights." Smith, who seems to have learned from his experience at Lexington and Concord, characteristically did nothing. Although Howe had long since determined to quit Boston, his first reaction to Washington's bold stroke was a pugnacious one. He would drive the Continentals from their heights at bayonet point.

He ordered five regiments of 2,200 regulars to embark at once from Long Wharf for Castle William. The soldiers had a day's food supply and canteens filled with rum and water. Their muskets were unloaded; this was to be a matter of cold steel. From Castle William they were to assault the first redoubt while two more regiments were to attack the second. An American watching the Red Coats leave Long Wharf observed that they looked "pale and dejected," and one said to another, 'It would be another Bunker Hill affair or worse.' Fortunately, for the gloomy rank and file, Howe's attack plans were interrupted by a howling windstorm, a "hurricane," as one Bostonian put it. Then on that evening Howe countermanded his hasty orders. Under the threat of Washington's cannon, there was no choice left now for the British but to withdraw.

Howe gave orders to evacuate the city and began his preparations for moving stores and equipment. Days of confusion and plunder followed. What could not be taken was to be destroyed. Not only were 9,000 soldiers to be transported but an additional 1,100 Tories who would not or could not make peace with their opposing countrymen demanded passage. Their names included many honored names since the early settlement of New England—names like Apthorp, Boylston, Bradstreet, Brattle, Dudley, Faneuil, Hallowell, Lechmere, Pepperell, Putnam, Quincy, Ruggles, Saltonstall, Sewall, Vassall, Willard, and Winslow. But the Tory emigrants were not rich and wellborn. There were many Loyalists of modest means, farmers and mechanics, who had endured much for their allegiance to the king and who were now about to lose almost everything. Some managed to get a few of their most precious household possessions aboard ship, but at the last hour Howe ordered all furniture and other "useless luggage" overboard.

Officially Howe refused to hold any communication with the rebel Washington, but unofficially both sides agreed to a truce. If Howe would withdraw and not burn the town, Washington, in turn, would hold his fire and do nothing to impede the embarkation of the Red Coats.

At nine o'clock on Sunday morning—it was now St. Patrick's Day—the last of the British garrison and the Tory exiles filed aboard the ships of the fleet. Boston's streets were left strewn with debris and almost deserted. A few Red Coats still lingered at Castle William to prepare mines for blowing up fortifications. During the day they exchanged a few shots with the Americans across the bay, but by evening they too had embarked. As the last British outposts withdrew from the defenses at Boston Neck, a lieutenant Adair of the marines was sent to scatter crow's feet (sharp four-pointed irons that always landed with one point up) in the no-man's—land beyond the gate. "Being an Irishman," as one man said, he began by scattering the crow's feet about from the gate toward the enemy, and of course, he had to walk over them to return. It took him so long that he was almost taken prisoner. Bunker Hill was apparently still manned, but the Red Coats in that stronghold seemed suspiciously motionless. Brigadier General John Sullivan and two other American officers cautiously making their way up the hill found nothing but dummy sentinels with horseshoes for gorgers and ruffles of paper. One of the scarecrow soldiers had a sign pinned on his chest, reading, "WELCOME, BROTHER JONATHAN."

After weighing anchor the British fleet hove to in Nantucket Roads five miles below Boston, and the sailors spent an additional ten days adjusting the hastily loaded cargoes and taking on water. Finally they put to sea, bound for Halifax, Nova Scotia. From Penn's Hill Abigail Adams watched as the sails billowed in the breeze. "We have a view of the largest fleet ever seen in America," she said. "You may count upward of a hundred and seventy sails." And so the British rule in Boston ended with white sails moving across the blue water like a curtain coming down at the end of a play.

The three boys were still in the marsh. Joe said, "You know, we haven't eaten in twenty-four hours, and after being shot at with these damn cannons, what the hell are we going to do?" "I don't know," said Todd, "but this swamp and these bugs are beginning to get to me." Bryan said, "You know it seems quiet, like the shooting has stopped." "Maybe they're just taking a rest," Todd said. "I don't think so. Let's move out and head toward the river and see what happens." "See what happens! What the hell do you mean see what happens?" asked Joe. Todd said, "Maybe we can work our way to the river then to Charlestown and then to Boston."

As they moved out and toward the river, stepping over dead soldiers on both sides down to the riverside, the three picked up some rifles and food from the knapsacks. They then moved to Charlestown after hours of cautiously moving around the abandoned redoubt and headed for Boston. When they arrived in Boston, they looked amazed as the three stood there staring at all the buildings burning. "I'll be damned," he said. "I never saw anything like this." Shops, churches, and private houses burned in flames that reached to the sky. Todd said, "Let's head for the waterfront." "Good idea," said Joe "maybe I will recognize something."

As they came to the waterfront, they saw a ship: a British ship. There was a tavern still standing on the pier near the ship. There were a lot of British soldiers in the tavern. Bryan said, "Let's hold for a minute." "Why?" asked Joe. "Let's see, right now it looks dangerous." Meanwhile, on the ship the captain was saying to his men, "Men, you did a good job in bombarding these American bastards and before we sail home; we will leave two guards, and the rest of us will go to the tavern for a farewell drink."

Everybody left the ship for the tavern—everybody but for the two guards and the men headed for the tavern. When they got to the tavern, they began to sing English songs. There was a little wind, but the night had a full moon, which outlined this tall ship in the harbor. "Bryan, you know we could do our part by burning that ship." "Are you crazy?" said Joe. "No, I think this is a good idea," said Todd. "I think you are crazy. Why the hell would we burn the ship when we are trying to get these bastards out of here anyway?" "Doing our part," said Bryan. So Bryan and Todd headed toward the ship with Joe following. "I still think you two crazy bastards have a death wish," said Joe.

With the guards walking back and forth, the three got on the ship and huddled behind cargo. Joe whispered, "Now what the hell are we going to do?" Bryan and Todd then got some knives; silently came up behind the guards; and stuck them in the backs, killing both of them. Joe was saying, "Oh great, here we go again." Todd said, "Let's get these lanterns and get the fire started on the cargo." Bryan was saying, "It's only the damn Tories' belongings anyway." So they broke the lanterns, and the fire started on the ship, and then it began to really blaze. Meanwhile one of sailors came out of the tavern for air and saw the fire and yelled to his shipmates, "The ship is on fire." The tavern then emptied out, and they headed out for the ship. The three jumped off the ship into the water with the ship in full blaze. In the background buildings in Boston were still burning to the ground. The captain was the first to the ship, ran up the ramp, and after he found the two dead guards, he yelled out, "Those sons of bitches, those bastards." He told his men to get back, and he jumped to the pier. "Those damn Americans, they burned the ship. Let's see if we can find them and kill them."

The three swam ashore, turned around, and watched the ship burning with flames going to the sky. "All right, Dick Tracy, now what the hell are we going to do?" asked Joe. "Let me think," said Todd. Joe was thinking, "Now I have the damn British navy after me. Is this damn nightmare ever going to end?" The men from the ship set out looking for whoever torched the ship. With Boston and Charlestown still burning and the ship in the harbor burning as well, it was quite a sight. Heading down the side streets, they found two horses in front of a house that was still standing. "These bastards must be Tories," said Todd. "Let's burn them out," said Bryan. "Bullshit," said Joe. "Let's get the hell out of here. We have the British navy after us." Todd said, "Can you ride?" "Ride what?" asked Joe. "Those horses? You are going to steal those damn horses?" "Yes," said Todd. Then Todd and Bryan set out to steal the horses. "They have no saddles, and besides, I don't know how to ride a damn horse." They jumped on the horses, and Bryan rode past Joe and said, "Okay, jump on. Let's get the hell out of here." Joe jumped on the back of the horse and said, "Damn this! I hate this." They rode to safety up past the Charlestown Common to Charlestown Neck and on past Bunker Hill to Morton's Hill. "Where the hell did you learn to ride like that?" asked Joe. Todd said, "On our farm we had an Indian, and he taught me to ride Indian style. What about you, Bryan?" "Oh, another lesson from the tavern." Joe said, "Like I said before, that must have been some tavern."

"Look," said Bryan, "this is where I have to leave you." "What do you mean?" asked Todd. "I am going back to join that general George Washington. He looks like a man I would like to fight with." Todd said, "We can't talk you out of this?" "No," said Bryan, "I have been thinking about this for some time now. Would you fellows like to join me?" "No," said Todd. "I think we will be heading west." "Well, I will miss you guys," said Bryan. Joe said, "We will miss you too. It has been interesting." "Yeah, it sure has," said Todd. "I guess all we can say is good-bye, good luck, and keep yourself safe. Hope we meet again." As Bryan rode off, Todd waved good-bye. Joe then said, "Good call. I did not feel like going back into a fight. I sort of had enough." The two headed west toward Worcester. "I am sure glad we are getting away from Boston. The only thing I ever got around here is being shot at by cops and the British. It will be good to get away from here. I will sure miss Bryan," said Todd. "I will too," replied Joe. "He was a good guy. I hope he remains safe like some of my other buddies." "Other buddies?" asked Todd. "Yeah," Joe said, "we got split up in Boston about the time I met you.

"You know, Todd, I know how this thing with the British is going to turn out." "You do! How do you know that?" replied Todd. "Kind of hard to explain. I am still trying to figure that out myself. Let's rest and get something to eat," said Joe. Todd said, "I know of a place about an hour away; it is a tavern and a roadhouse. You know, we are going to have to get another horse, wagon, or something." "Damn it," said Joe. "We are not into stealing another horse, are we?" Todd just smiled.

In about an hour Todd and Joe arrived at the tavern, and once inside they sat down. The tavern was dark with candles on the tables. The tavern keeper came over and said, "Can I help you?" "Yes," said Todd. "I will have a steak and ale." Joe said, "The same for me." Joe bellowed out, "Cook mine well." "Did you see those horses and wagon?" "Yeah, what about it?" said Joe. "Well, it looks like just what we need." "Damn it," Joe said. "What the hell are you talking about? There are only a few people in this place. Are you trying to get us killed?" "Look," said Todd, "we need a ride; one horse will not do it. After we finish, I will sneak around the back and let the horses loose. You jump in the wagon, and we are out of here." When Joe and Todd finished and paid for their food and drink, they walked out. Todd said, "Look, Joe, you get in the wagon; and when you hear the horses scatter, take off in that direction." Then Todd left for the back of the tavern. All of a sudden horses started scattering, so Joe grabbed the reins, and the wagon took off. By now Todd was running alongside and then jumped in the wagon. A patron walked out just in time to see the wagon taking off. "Damn," he yelled back into the tavern," "they are taking off with the wagon and horses." The tavern owner came out with a shotgun and shot at the wagon, which by now was out of range. "Damn it, Todd. I'll be a son of a bitch. Here is another idea of yours, and we are being shot at again. When and if they catch us, they will hang us." Todd said, "It will be quite, for they have to get their horses first."

They rode most of the night looking over their shoulders to see if they were being followed. Todd said, "The horses seem to be doing all right, so we will head south toward New York and get out of this area." "New York! I have never been to New York," said Joe. "Anyway I wonder if those fellows back there rounded up their horses and are taking off after us." "I don't know," said Todd, "but we have a good head start on them, and all we have to do is keep going. I think if we keep going, we will be in New York by morning." At dawn they were in New York territory, heading toward Saratoga. Todd was saying, "You are going to love this place. I was here years ago, and it was a very peaceful place to be."

While Howe was moving on, Philadelphia "gentleman Johnny" Burgoyne, a fifty-five-year-old fashion plate, was making himself unpopular in Upstate New York. Burgoyne had a play produced in London and greatly admired his own writing ability. He published a long and flowery statement trying to explain his march toward Albany. But Burgoyne's fancy phrases backfired. Instead of soothing or even scaring the Americans, his statement made them furious. The Green Mountain Boys of Vermont came out to fight and joined with the New Hampshire men who hurried to enlist. From Fort Ticonderoga, which he captured, Burgoyne continued south toward Fort Edward on the Hudson River. His troops hacked their way from the southern end of Lake Champlain through twenty-three swampy miles of giant pines and hemlocks. In his strong 7,500-man-army Burgoyne had not only British and German regulars but 250 Canadians and 400 Indians.

Two days before Burgoyne occupied Fort Edward, which General Schuyler had abandoned, the chiefs of His Majesty's European forces and of the princes, his allies, esteem you as brothers in the war; emulous in glory and in friendship, we will endeavor reciprocally to give and to receive examples; we know how to value, and we will strive to imitate your perseverance in enterprise, and your constancy to resist hunger, weariness and pain. Be our task, from the dictates of our religion, the laws of our warfare and the principles and interest of our policy, to regulate your passions when they overbear, to point out where it is nobler to spare then to revenge, to discriminate degrees of guilt, to suspend the uplifted stroke, to chastise and not destroy.

A group of Indian scouts committed a shocking murder and gave American recruiting officers additional anti-Burgoyne fuel to throw on the fire. The victim's name was Jane McCrea. She was twenty-three and engaged to marry David Jones, a Tory who had fled to Canada to fight for the British. When Burgoyne's Indian scouts found her, Jane was staying with an elderly lady named Mrs. McNeil near Fort Edward, and waiting she hoped to meet David. The Indian promised to lead the two ladies to the British. But they had not gone far before one of the Indians quarreled with another Indian over which one was Jane's guard. He shot her, scalped her, and tore the clothes off her body. Burgoyne's first thought was to execute the Indian whose name was Wyandot Panther. But he changed his mind, fearing that if he did so, the rest of the Indians would desert. It was a poor decision. Within a short time Burgoyne's Indians deserted anyhow. Thousands of New Englanders, outraged by stories of Jane's unavenged murder, marched toward Albany in order to reinforce the northern army. At the same time the two boys are in New York, heading toward Albany. Todd was saying to Joe, "I think we will have to find a roadhouse to get something to eat and get some sleep." "Yeah," said Joe, "it will be nice to go a day without being shot at."

When they arrived at the roadhouse, they parked the wagon, tied up the horses, and headed for the tavern. When they went in, there was some rumbling among the patrons. Hearing some of the conversation from the next table, one man was saying they should shoot all the damn British and their friends for what they did to Jane McCrea. "Who is Jane McCrea?" asked Joe. "I don't know," said Todd, "but whoever she was and whatever happened, this place is sure angry." Todd asked one of the men who Jane McCrea was. He responded, "She was a pretty twenty-three-year-old girl that the Indians scalped and murdered with the help of the British. I hope those bastards get what is coming to them." "The Indians!" said Joe. "What Indians?" "The Indians that fight with the British," said the man. "You have to watch out; this is their territory." "Son of a bitch! Now you're telling me that we will now be shot at by the damn Indians?" asked Joe.

After they had eaten, they checked in for the night and went upstairs. Joe started thinking, "This thing is out of control. I wake up, and I am in this time lapse. I must be in hell. I mean this is one war after another with no television, no radio—nothing to know what the hell is going on. I don't know if this is punishment for that damn robbery. This damn nightmare. Everybody is telling me I am in 1775. Son of a bitch, what happened to 1984?

"I carried a gun when we did the robbery, but I never shot a gun. Now everybody is shooting at me or trying to bayonet me. Man, you talk about a bad dream." The next morning—a great morning—they had breakfast and went on their way, heading toward the Hudson and then to Saratoga. When they arrived at the Hudson on the other side of the river, they noticed a large movement of British soldiers undercover and in the woods. "Look at that," said Todd. "Those troops are heading north. I wonder what is going on." "What is going on you ask? I'll tell you what the hell is going on," said Joe. "It looks like the damn thing that went on in Boston." Todd said, "I have a feeling you are right. Let's follow the troops and see what happens." "Follow the troops? What the hell do you mean follow the troops?" Joe said. "With the damn British, I will tell you what happens. If we are in the wrong place again, we get shot at. That's what the hell happens." "Bullshit," Joe was now saying to himself, "here we go again." So Todd and Joe started out driving their wagon along a dirt road, heading toward Saratoga.

Just before they got there, they pulled their wagon over. "There," said Todd. "What?" said Joe. "Look over to the left a few yards [about two hundred yards]." What they saw was a band of thirty Indians. "Here we go," said Joe. "We haven't seen anybody on our side." All we seen was the damn British and now the damn Indians. And yes, throw in the damn Germans." "Look," said Todd. "let's get our wagon over to the side into the woods and see if we can get closer to the action and see what is happening." "Get closer?" said Joe. "What the hell do you mean get closer? Are you trying to get us killed?"

Burgoyne made another mistake. His German cavalry, dressed in stiff leather trousers and huge coked hats, had been having a miserable time for an understandable reason: they had no horses. Once the British reached Fort Edward, Burgoyne decided to send the Germans east to Vermont to steal some supplies. Lieutenant Colonel Baum, the leader of this raid, neither spoke nor understood English. This was a serious handicap because, in addition to stealing horses, cattle, and wagons, Baum was supposed to enlist any Tories he might find. Bennington, Vermont Baum's first objective, was protected by a New Hampshire brigade, which had just been raised under the command of the veteran John Stark who had served at Bunker Hill, Trenton, and Princeton. He was tall sinewy, cantankerous man and a born troop leader who was furious at the Continental Congress because for political reasons it had failed to promote him.

CHAPTER SEVEN

Burgoyne's Indians

After hearing the news that Burgoyne's Indians ranging ahead of Baum were terrorizing the civilians between the Hudson and Bennington, Stark marched forward to meet the intruders. Four miles west of Bennington, just inside what in later years became the New York State line, the two forces came to a halt with the Walloomsac River and a bridge between them. Although Baum did not know it but the Americans outnumbered him by more than two to one, and Colonel Seth Warner's three hundred and thirty Vermonters were marching south to reinforce Stark. At about noon two small American detachments started to swing wide around both German flanks. Stark, with his main strength, stayed in front, waiting for the encirclement to be completed. When the flanking parties approached the German rear, they looked like farmers, not soldiers. Baum had hoped they were Tories seeking protection perhaps or coming to join the British. Since the German-speaking officer could not question the Americans, he ordered his sentries to let them alone. The New Hampshire soldiers carefully worked themselves into position. Then they opened fire. In front of Baum's position Stark gave the order to attack: "THERE THEY ARE! WE'LL BEAT THEM BEFORE THE NIGHT, OR MOLLY STARK WILL BE A WIDOW!" The Americans rushed the Germans from all sides, driving them together onto a small hill. Baum's men were brave. They stood their ground for two hours, and when their ammunition ran out, they drew their sword's, hoping to chop their way out of the American trap. They didn't give up until Baum fell.

When Burgoyne finally left Skenesborough, his progress was slow, thanks to Schuyler's scorched earth policy. Burdened with fifty-two pieces of artillery and gallons of champagne, he took five days for the relatively short trip to Fort Edward. Another seven days had gone before he reached Fort Miller, a crumbling little post across the Hudson from Saratoga. Burgoyne, however, had sent reinforcements: a force of Germans under Lieutenant Colonel Breymann that was almost as big as Baum's party. They were a day late in getting to the battlefield. When they did approach Bennington, Stark's men were scattered all over. The New Hampshire recruits were given a chance to take anything they wanted from Baum's outfit, and they were combing the German campsite for loot. Stark was caught off guard. Luckily Warner's reinforcements from Vermont arrived just in time. Breymann, like Baum, mistook the Americans for farmers. Or did at least until a squad of New Hampshire men fired at the German column and killed Breymann's horse. The Germans attacked Stark's and Warner's combined force and found to their dismay that however unprofessional the Americans appeared they wouldn't let themselves get outflanked. And on the firing line, they gave as good as they got or better. Breymann was forced to retreat. His drummers beat a signal for a surrender conference. But the Americans who were more farmer than soldier didn't know what the drums were supposed to mean. They kept on shooting, and the German retreat turned into a rout. When the final score on the two battles at Bennington was added up, the Germans had lost 207 killed and about 700 prisoners. The Americans had thirty killed and forty wounded. The Continental Congress in gratitude finally appointed Stark a brigadier general in the Continental Army.

Burgoyne's plan for the conquest of New York had two prongs. Besides his own main drive down Lake Champlain to the Hudson River, a second smaller British expedition commanded by Colonel Barry St. Leger was supposed to move on Albany from the northwest. From Oswego on the shore of Lake Ontario, they were to proceed down the Mohawk River, which joins the Hudson just above Albany.

St. Leger, an experienced officer, was optimistic. Only one obstacle stood in his path. That was Fort Stanwix, a wilderness post where the city of Rome, New York, now stands. It was held by the Third New York Continentals commanded by twenty-eight-year-old Peter Gansevoort. When St. Leger reached Fort Stanwix, he expected Colonel Gansevoort to surrender at the sight of his dazzlingly well-equipped army. The Americans, although outnumbered by more than two to one, had no such intention. A fifty-five-year-old local landowner Nicholas Herkimer, a brigadier general in the militia, was marching to Stanwix with eight hundred volunteers to help Colonel Gansevoort. But six miles from the fort at a village called Oriskany Herkimer's column marched into an Indian ambush arranged by St. Leger. When the savage hand-to-hand struggle was over, Herkimer had lost two hundred men, and many more were wounded. He himself had received his death wounds. It was lucky that there were any American survivors at all. No reinforcements got through, but Herkimer's effort helped in another way. For while St. Leger's men were too busy at Oriskany, Gansevoort's second in command, Lieutenant Colonel Marinus Willett, led a highly successful raid on an almost-empty British camp. Willett's men made off with twenty-one wagonloads of muskets, ammunition, camp kettles, blankets, and clothes. They stripped the Indians' tents of everything they contained, hoping to make the braves think about the wisdom of assisting King George. Despite Willett's raid, the British went on preparing to destroy Fort Stanwix, and it looked as if they would it unless Gansevoort got help.

At Stillwater just north of Albany, General Schuyler heard about the plight of the Stanwix garrison. Most of Schuyler's officers opposed sending a detachment to rescue Gansevoort. They felt that the American army in front of Albany had more than it could do to hold off Burgoyne. Schuyler was outraged. He called for a brigadier to command the relief. Benedict Arnold, a major general and Schuyler's second in command, volunteered for a job far below his rank. Arnold was off marching as fast as he could with 950 volunteers who were glad to follow him. But he knew when he started for Stanwix that his rescue party was too small to beat St. Leger by force alone. He thought of an ingenious trick. The Americans held a Tory sentenced to be hanged for recruiting for the British. This prisoner named Hon Yost Schuyler was at least half insane and therefore regarded with great respect by the Indians, who thought that madmen were divinely inspired. Arnold made a bargain with Hon Yost. He promised him a pardon if he would go ahead and tell St. Leger's Indians surrounding Fort Stanwix that a huge party of Americans were about to descend on them. Hon Yost agreed and played his part to perfection. The Indians, believing him, mutinied and seized St. Leger's officers' liquor. Two hundred of them drunk and then ran off into the forests. The boys were still in the woods, observing what was going on. Then all of a sudden a lot of Indians started heading for the woods. "Son of a bitch," said Joe, "what the hell is going on? Now this bunch of Indians is coming our way, and from the looks of it, they are all drunk." "I think our wagon is safe. Let's pull over in this gully and see what happens." "See what happens?" Joe replied. "We have what looks like two to three hundred drunk Indians heading our way. and you want to see what happens?

"Like I said awhile back, I think you have a death wish, and I kind of not like to be a part of it." "Don't worry," said Todd, "I think we are safe here in this gully, in the brush. Like you said, Joe, if they are drunk, then I don't think they will see us. It looks like they are just getting the hell out of here." "First time I heard you say 'hell,'" said Joe. "Yes, I got it from you." In their hurry to retreat, the Indians passed by the two in the gully without even seeing them.

As they were waiting for the Indians to pass, they slowly came up from the gully, looked around, and went to pick up the wagon. They started untying their horses when they heard a click. Looking around at three farmers and looking down the barrel of three rifles, Joe said, "Oh shit, what the hell is this now?" One of the men said, "Who are you fighting for?" Joe asked, "Who are you fighting for?" "The Americans," said one of the men. "So are we," said Todd. "Good," said the leader, "then you can come fight with us." "Fight with you!" said Joe. "What do you mean fight with you? Just what I said," the leader replied.

"We are part of the Vermont regiment, and we also can use your wagon." "I am sorry, sir," said Todd, "but we cannot join you." "You can't or won't?" replied the leader. "No," replied Todd. "You see, we are working for General Moore out of Massachusetts, and we are scouting the British." "Did you ever hear of Captain Moore?" the leader said to one of his men. "No, I have not" was his reply. "Well, sir, he works very closely with General Washington, and our job is a very important one." The leader thought for a moment and said, "In that case, good luck. If this mission is for General Washington, then be on your way. We have to be undercover and stay for a while to see what is going on. So good luck to you." After the men from Vermont left, Joe said, "Who the hell is General Moore?" "How the hell do I know? I used to drink with a George Moore." "Oh great," said Joe, "that's just great."

The chiefs of those Indians who remained insisted that St. Leger give the order to retreat since the Indians were more than half the force. There was nothing else St. Leger could do. Burgoyne's plans were not working too well.

The chiefs of His Majesty's European forces and of the princes, his allies, esteem you as brothers in war; emulous in glory and friendship, we will endeavor reciprocally and to give and to receive examples; we know how to value, and we will strive to imitate your perseverance in enterprise, and your constancy to resist hunger, weariness and pain. Be it our task, from the dictates of our religion the laws of our warfare and the principles and interest of our policy, to regulate your passions when they overbear, to point out where it is nobler to spare then to revenge to discriminate degrees of guilt, to suspend the uplifted stroke, to chastise and not destroy. This war to my friends, is new, Upon all former occasions, in taking the field, you held yourselves authorized to destroy wherever you came, because everywhere you fond an enemy.

The case now was very different. The king had many faithful subjects dispersed in the provinces; consequently you have many brothers there and these people are more to be pitied that they are persecuted or imprisoned wherever they are discovered or suspected, and dissemble, to a generous mind, is a yet more grievous punishment. Persuaded that your magnanimity of character, joined to your principles of affection to the king, will give me fuller control over your minds then the military rank with which I am invested, I enjoin your most serious attention to the rules which I hereby proclaim for your invariable observation during the campaign I positively forbid bloodshed, when you're not opposed in arms. Aged men, women, children and prisoners must be held sacred from the knife or hatchet, even in the time of actual conflict. You shall receive compensation for the prisoners you take, but you shall be called to account for scalps. In conformity and indulgence of your customs, which have affixed an idea of honor to such badges of victory, you have affixed an idea of honor to such badges of victory, you shall be allowed to take the scalps of the dead when killed by your fire and in fair opposition ; but on no account, or pretence, or subtlety, or prevarication, are they to be taken from the wounded or even the dying; and still less pardonable, if possible, will be held to kill men in that condition on purpose, and upon a supposition that this protection to the wounded would be thereby evaded. Base, lurking assassins, incendiaries, ravagers and plunderers of the country to whatever army they may belong, shall be treated with less reserve ; but the latitude must be given you by order, and I must be judge on occasion. Should the enemy, on their parts, dare to countenance acts of barbarity towards those who may fall into their hands, it shall be yours also to retaliate ; but till this severity be thus compelled, bear immoveable in your hearts this solid maxim—it cannot be too deeply impressed: that the great essential reward, the worthy service of your alliance, the sincerity of your zeal to the king, your father and never—failing protector, will be examined and judged upon the test only of your steady and uniform adherence to the orders and counsels of those to whom his majesty has entrusted the direction and honor of his arms sincerely general John Burgoyne }

He had learned that Howe was not sailing up the Hudson to join him. He had lost nine hundred men in the Bennington battles. Now he had to face the fact that St. Leger's expedition, the whole western wing of his attack, had collapsed. To make matters worse for Burgoyne, the strength of the American force that stood between him and Albany had been growing especially after the word spread of the murder of Jane McCrea. It was becoming a pretty good army too. It included some Continental regiments, Daniel Morgan's riflemen, among them some first-class militia outfit.

Its commander in chief was General Horatio Gates who had replaced Schuyler. Gates, a jolly fifty-year-old former English officer who had lived in Virginia before the war, was an expert on army administration and paperwork. He had both ambition and ability. But on the other hand, it had been a long time since he had commanded on the battlefield. When General Arnold got back from Stanwix, the Americans picked Bemis Heights, overlooking the river road on the west side of the Hudson, as the place to dig in and stand off Burgoyne's attack. Bemis Heights, about ten miles south of the town of Saratoga (now called Schuylerville), had only one serious fault. There was a higher hill slightly west of the bluffs that the Americans failed to occupy. If Burgoyne could seize it, his gunners would be able to shoot down from above the American trenches.

The British started from their camp four miles up the river in a bright morning sun. They were divided into three sections: one to march down the river road; one to move slightly inland toward Bemis Heights; and the third to sweep around through the woods, trying to surprise the Americans and capture the unoccupied hill. As the first two British sections approached, the Americans could easily see them coming. Their Red Coats were brilliant. Their polished steel bayonets glistened in the sunlight. For three hours, while the British attack shaped up, Gates did nothing at all. Arnold, his second in command, begged to be allowed to advance to meet Burgoyne's assault. But Gates seemed to think that the Americans were safe inside their crude fortifications. Finally he woke up. He realized that there might be some threat to the American left flank; therefore, he ordered Morgan's riflemen and Henry Dearborn's light infantry to guard against it. If they ran into trouble, they could call on Arnold's other men for help.

Morgan's sharpshooters attacked using a flanking maneuver on Freeman's farm. A furious fight developed. Arnold's men hurried to help. The battle raged across, clearing woods of some twenty acres. The Americans had the best of the shooting, but every time they drove the British from the field, Burgoyne's men returned by charging with their bayonets. Arnold, who was directing the battle, felt sure that with more American troops he could break the British line. Gates, still sitting in the fortifications, refused to give him the men.

The Americans retreated to their fortifications. The Americans had won a victory—their casualties were only half as much as Burgoyne's—but not a decisive one. The British camped on the battlefield. That ended the first half of the Battle of Saratoga.

More than two weeks passed before Burgoyne struck again. He waited because he hoped that General Sir Henry Clinton far to the south might be able to help him. Clinton, who had been left behind in New York City when Howe went to Philadelphia, attacked and captured two American forts (Clinton and Montgomery) on the west bank of the Hudson at Bear Mountain. But having done so, he went back to New York City. Burgoyne waited in vain. On the American side in the meantime Gates and Arnold had a falling out. Gates, in writing his report to Congress, did not even mention the name of Arnold, the man who had won the battle for him. The two had a bitter quarrel. Gates relieved Arnold of his command and excluded him from headquarters. Arnold, an officer without a job, stayed in the Bemis Heights camp. Burgoyne felt he could no longer wait to hear from Clinton. He had to capture Albany before winter.

Since he wasn't quite sure what to do, Burgoyne planned a strong reconnaissance by more than 1,500 of the British to see if the Americans had occupied the high hill west of Bemis Heights. They had. Burgoyne's reconnaissance had barely started before the American outpost guards spotted it. This time Gates reacted quickly. Morgan's riflemen and General Enoch Poor's brigade promptly threw themselves against the British column. Dearborn' light infantry was right on Morgan's heels. Both ends of the British line were beaten back, and Burgoyne had sent his aide to order a general retreat. Before he could deliver the command, he was shot and captured. At this moment Benedict Arnold, riding a huge brown horse, galloped into the field. He had no command, but he could not bear to stay in camp, doing nothing with a fight in progress. The first soldiers Arnold met were part of Poor's brigade and happened to be militiamen from Norwich, Connecticut, his hometown. They gave him a rousing cheer. Arnold raced on, overtook the head of General Ebenezer Learned's brigade, and led three of its regiments in a charge against German troops in the center of the British line. But the troops were led by General Simon Fraser, as brave and inspiring a field officer as Arnold himself.

Fraser dashed up and down the line, rallying the British troops. It was not until Fraser fell, picked off by one of Morgan's marksmen, that the British gave up. The entire line gave way and fell back to their entrenchments immediately north of Freeman's Farm. That seemed to end the battle. But Arnold was not done. He was not satisfied with winning the field. He wanted a smashing victory. Arnold led one party in a furious charge against a section of the British fortifications. Then he rode straight across the line of fire and organized another attack on a redoubt full of German soldiers led by Lieutenant Colonel Breymann who had been beaten at Bennington. Arnold galloped around to the back of the strong point and into it. His brown horse was shot, and Arnold was hit in the leg with a bullet that broke his thigh bone in the same leg that was wounded at Quebec. He had to be carried off the field victorious but lamed for life. A week later at Saratoga, Burgoyne, having thought over his losses, surrendered. It was a tremendous American victory. When Burgoyne handed Gates his sword in surrender, the tally of the defeat was shocking: King George's fighting forces lost seven British generals, three hundred other officers, and more than five thousand enlisted men along with five thousand muskets, twenty-seven cannons, and stores of all kinds of equipment. By this time, however, Gates's reputation was ruined.

The autumn dusk was thickening into night before the firing ceased, and the British, six hundred of their men dead, began a slow retreat in the direction of Saratoga. "This moment," Baroness Von Riedesel would remember, "was the beginning of our unhappiness!" Ten days latter Burgoyne surrendered. The terms of surrender, a document known as a convention, did not compel the defeated British general to turn over his troops, five thousand in all, but agreed to let him ship them to England. Quickly realizing that every soldier returned to the homeland would release one to fight in America, the Continental Congress contrived by various quibbles to ignore this part of the convention. In later years attempts would be made to whitewash this action, but to be blunt "the honorable Congress" went back on its word. In time Burgoyne and his officers, Von Riedesel included, would be allowed to go home. Not so for the private soldiers. For they would be confined near Boston after which they would be moved in turn to Charlottesville, Virginia, to Lancaster, Pennsylvania, and to other places. A few would be exchanged back to their own army, but at war's end the bulk of those who had survived would melt into the American population.

CHAPTER EIGHT

George Washington and Benedict Arnold

George Washington began looking for a post that his dashing officer (Benedict Arnold) could manage in spite of his wounded leg. He made Arnold military governor of Philadelphia; in no time at all Arnold and Pennsylvania's civilian authorities were at each other's throats. Arnold was arrogant and unwilling to try to compromise with the civilian point of view. The Philadelphians were suspicious of military men, and they thought Arnold was too lenient with Tories and war profiteers. They disapproved of his courting Peggy Shippen, a girl twenty years his junior and who had danced with British officers in Philadelphia. Arnold and the Pennsylvania government were practically at war. Pennsylvania complained to the Continental Congress, and the Congress ordered Arnold to face court-martial. While awaiting trial, confident that he would be cleared, Arnold married Ms. Shippen. Then came the first step toward treason. Mrs. Arnold knew a handsome young British officer, Major John Andre, who had been stationed in Philadelphia and was now on Clinton's staff in New York City. The Arnolds wrote secretly to Andre, offering to Washington to give an official reprimand. Arnold was furious. The truth is that he had been involved in several shady deals. Washington, who respected the man's great fighting ability, made the reprimand as mild as possible. But because he had not been completely cleared, Arnold was ready to close his bargain with the British. He agreed to more than change sides. Arnold promised to betray the fort at West Point and at least three thousand soldiers for twenty thousand dollars and a high command in the British. Then he asked Washington, who had done his best to keep from hurting Arnold's feelings, to give him the command at West Point. Washington did so.

There remained one last step: a face-to-face conference between Arnold and some British army representative to settle details of the betrayal. Ambitious major Andre, who had been working on a plot for more than a year, insisted on going to meet Arnold himself. A British warship, the *Vulture*, took Andre up the Hudson and rowed ashore in the dark by two tenants on the estate of Joshua Smith near Haverstraw. There Andre and Arnold sat on the riverbank, talking from midnight until dawn. Arnold produced a packet of secret papers possibly to convince Andre of his sincerity. The papers were all highly damaging to the rebel cause. One described the unfinished condition of West Point: "redoubt no. 3, a slight woodwork three feet thick, very dry, no bomb proof, easily set on fire, no cannon," and so on. Another document revealed the disposition of the troops at the fort. Yet another was a copy of Washington's last council of war, which described help expected from France and included a plan for a diversionary attack on British-held Jamaica to ease pressure on the colonies.

At daybreak they moved into Smith's house because it seemed too dangerous to row Andre back to the *Vulture* when he might be seen. Arnold gave Andre the plans to West Point and some other secret papers. Then he returned to his West Point headquarters while Andre hid for the day in Smith's attic. American shore batteries fired on the *Vulture*, and Smith decided that even at night it would be too dangerous to row Andre back to his ship. He thought Andre should return to New York City by land, and he offered to guide Andre through the American lines if Andre would take off his British uniform and disguise himself in civilian clothes. It was a dreadful risk for Andre to take, for that made him a spy. If captured he would surely be hanged. Andre called himself "John Anderson" and carried a pass in that name signed by Arnold. The secret papers were hidden in his stocking. He got safely past the southernmost American post when three young men stopped him. They meant to rob him.

They made Andre take off his clothes to make sure he was not hiding any money, and they found the papers in his stocking. Whatever else they may have been, the three young men were Patriots. When they saw the plans of West Point they escorted Andre back to the American army post at North Castle. Lieutenant Colonel Jameson who commanded there was suspicious. He noticed that secret papers were in the same handwriting as the pass: Benedict Arnold's. Instead of sending both documents and the strange prisoner back to West Point, as his standing orders demanded, Jameson forwarded the papers to George Washington. To protect himself and before sending Andre under guard to Arnold, he sent a note to Arnold, telling him what had happened and what he had done. By coincidence Washington was on his way to inspect West Point. Sitting at a table Arnold wrote out three passes. The first gave Smith permission for a boat on the way to New York. They met the *Vulture* on the river. The second allowed Smith to go to White Plains, the northernmost British outpost.

The Arnolds were spending a quiet Monday morning. Peggy was still in her bedchamber. Two young officers had gone to a nearby orchard to fetch peaches for her, and she was sitting up in bed, awaiting her breakfast treat. The general was sitting downstairs at the breakfast table, chatting with Majors Samuel Shaw and James McHenry. They had arrived only moments before to announce that the commander in chief would be delayed and to start breakfast without him about ten o'clock. Lieutenant Solomon Allen, dusty and sweaty from a long ride, appeared with a letter from Lieutenant Colonel Jameson. As soon as the note from Jameson arrived, excusing himself, Arnold took the letter and broke the seal. Arnold's face had shock and disbelief and then the chilling realization that his plot had been discovered. By now even Washington must know of his dealings with the British, so Arnold now realized that the game was up. Controlling himself he told Allen to wait for an answer. Quickly he bolted out of the house and into the stable yard, ordered his horse saddled, and the pistols in the saddle holsters loaded. He sent a servant down to the river with orders for his barge to stand by. Then as fast as his bad leg would carry him, he went back to the house through the dining room and up the stairs to his wife's room. McHenry noticed Arnold was in "embarrassment and agitation so unusual that he knew not to what attribute it." Arnold told Peggy of Andre's capture. But he had time for no more than a few hasty words. A knock sounded. His secretary David Franks called through the door that the commander in chief's two servants had just arrived to report that His Excellency is nigh at hand. Peggy fainted. Arnold bolted from the room and almost knocked Franks down, limping down the stairs and out to the stable yard. He leaped on his waiting horse then immediately drew in on the reins.

Around the corner of the stable appeared four of Washington's light horsemen. Arnold's hands went for his loaded pistols, but one of the officers saluted respectfully and said the commander in chief was coming up the road immediately behind them. So Washington hadn't as yet received Jameson's letter. There was still time. Arnold told the four to stable their horses and go in to the house for breakfast. Then galloped across the yard and down a sharp drop to the Hudson and reined up at his barge. He ordered the crew to row hard for Sandy Point. He was in a hurry, he said, because he was "anxious to return to His Excellency." At Stony Point Arnold told his crew he had changed his mind. He now wanted to go to the *Vulture* where he had "particular business from His Excellency" with the *Vulture* captain. The crew looked at each other. The *Vulture* was an enemy ship. Arnold saw their hesitation. Quickly he promised them two gallons of rum at this offer.

The prospect seemed brighter but not for long. As the barge bumped alongside the sloop of war, Arnold leaped over the rail, pulled pistols, and pointed them at the crew. He had recognized the failings of the rebel cause, he announced to the startled bargemen. He was returning to his rightful allegiance to the crown and was now a British officer. They were, he declared, prisoners of war. Numbly the barge crew climbed over the rail and was herded below. As Arnold escaped to the *Vulture*, Washington arrived at Arnold's house. He waited for Arnold. The messenger with the secret had missed him on the road, and Washington suspected nothing until the afternoon when the rider carrying the telltale evidence against Arnold finally delivered it.

Arnold reached New York City and the safety of the British just after the capture of New York City. Hale was caught behind the British lines dressed as a civilian. He was in a British camp. Andre was tried by court-martial and was hanged as a spy. He died bravely, and all over America those who felt sorry for him—and many of them did—told the stories of his charm and courage. Andre's death was tragic. So had been the death of Nathan Hale who was hanged by the British, arrested one day and hanged the next. This is not to say that one death canceled out another or that Andre was hanged because Hale had been hanged. But only that in war the fate of spies who are caught is tragically certain.

Todd and Joe in their wagon set out for Saratoga. "If anybody else asks about what," replied Todd, "next time we could be shot on the spot." The two decided that they won't use the spy thing. Joe said, "I think you may be right. Stop at the next roadhouse and inn." They tied their horse to a hitching post and went into the tavern. They found a table and then sat down. An older woman came over, and they both ordered an ale. While waiting Joe asked Todd, "You know, I know how this is all going to turn out." "What do you mean?" Todd asked. "Look, suppose I told you that you will be able to go cross-country in an airplane in about five hours, and there will be cars with motors that you could go as fast as ninety miles an hour and fast food restaurants, Burger King and McDonald's. You could pick up a hamburger real fast." Todd replied, "What do you mean across country to where? An aero what? What king are you talking about, and what is a hamburger? You keep saying you know how this is going to turn out. If you do, who will win this fight?" "The Americans," replied Joe. "That's good," said Todd. "At least the right side is going to win," Todd remarked while sipping his ale and looking at Joe in a funny way.

Two gentlemen approached the table and said, "How are you two fellows doing?" "Fine," said Joe. "How are you?" "You know, you two fellows look like you could use some money." "What do you mean?" asked Todd. "Well, how would you two like to make one thousand dollars?" "One thousand dollars! Who do we have to kill for that?" Joe said jokingly. "Benedict Arnold," replied the man. "Benedict Arnold?" replied Todd. "You mean the fellow that was the hero up north of Saratoga?" "The word is coming down that he is a traitor, and we have a group that would like to stop him before he can do any damage." Joe said, "Why don't you have the soldiers do it?" "Well, he has a lot of loyal people that won't believe this, and this proposition could very well backfire." Joe said, "Could me and my partner talk about this?" "Sure," said the man. "We will give you an answer in the morning." The two men went back to their table. Todd said, "That's a lot of money." "Look," said Joe, "they don't know us at all, and they give us that offer. Just suppose we take that offer and we try to do this. What is to keep them from killing us? Nobody knows the better. The money is good, but it just does not seem right. Maybe I have been on the street too long." "What street?" said Todd. "Never mind. We will tell them we well give them their answer in the morning and try to get out of here without them seeing us." Todd said, "That's an awful lot of money." "Yeah, I know," said Joe, "but I don't think we will ever get it."

In the morning the two went down to eat breakfast, and the two men were waiting for them. "Well now, good morning," said one of the men. "Good morning," said Todd. "Did you think over what I said?" "Yes, we did," said Joe, "and I think we will pass." "Are you sure?" said the other fellow. "Yes," said Todd. As they went to their wagon, the men followed them to the wagon. In the back of the wagon under a blanket there was a rifle; so as the two men approached, Joe went for the rifle, pulled it out, and said, "Is there anything we can do for you?" Looking surprised they said no and headed back for the tavern. "See what I mean?" said Joe. "If we don't have a rifle, we have trouble." "I think they were planning to give us trouble. Let's watch them just to be safe." The two then headed out of town, still looking behind them. Joe said to Todd, "Where do you think we should head now?" "Well," Todd replied, "I think we should head back to the Saratoga area. I think the battle is over in that area. At least I hope it is."

The moon was bright as the wagon headed down a dirt road by a part of the river. Todd said, "I think we could camp here for the night." "Where?" said Joe. "At that opening," replied Todd. They got off the wagon, took their blankets out of the wagon, and tied the horses. Todd said, "I hope there are no wild animals around here." "Wild animals?" replied Joe. "What do you mean wild animals?" "Oh, bears or cougars or such." "Oh great," said Joe. "That's all we need."

They found some dry logs, and Todd started a fire. Joe said, "How did you start that fire?" "With sticks and stones. I really took some matches from that last tavern." "Did I ever tell you how this is going to turn out?" "You said something awhile ago," replied Todd. "Well, in the end the British are going to lose this fight." "How do you know this?" asked Todd. "I just know." "And you will have cars, airplanes, trains, boats, and cars?" "Yes, cars, with motors—and not horses—that will go ninety or one hundred miles an hour; airplanes that will travel three thousand miles in five hours; and fast food restaurants, Burger King, Mc Donald's, and Wendy's where they sell hamburgers. I wish I was back there now." Todd was now looking at him as if he were crazy. "What are you talking about?" "What king and what is a hamburger?" "Look," Joe replied, "it's kind of hard to explain. If I tried to, I don't think I could." Todd by now was not too sure what Joe was talking about. Todd said, "Joe, I think you are tired. I think all this is getting to you. Let's try to get some sleep, and maybe you will feel better in the morning." "Yeah," said Joe. "I guess you are right."

Todd was now sleeping. Joe was thinking, "What the hell am I doing, trying to explain this? I don't know how I got here. I can't explain how I got here. If I can't explain it to myself, how the hell can I do it with somebody else?" The next morning when they woke up they gathered their belongings and put them in the wagon. "How do you feel this morning?" Todd asked Joe. "Pretty good," replied Joe. "I did not get much sleep, though." "Oh, by the way," said Todd, "I was thinking about what you said, about the British losing the war. If we ever get captured or somebody has a gun on us, you can tell them to give it up because they're going to lose the war anyway," said Todd with a smile. "Yeah," said Joe, "I guess you are right."

They started toward Saratoga. "One thing I will tell you since I met you, Todd. I have been shot and almost captured. This thing is like a bad movie." "What's a movie?" asked Todd. "Never mind," Joe replied as the wagon headed to the next town and breakfast. As they came upon a town with dirt streets and saw a tavern, Todd said, "Let's see if we can get some breakfast." They pulled their wagon over and then went into the roadhouse/ tavern. When they went inside, there were a few people that were talking and buzzing. Joe said, "I wonder what is going on." A person came over to the table. "What is going on?" said Joe. "People are talking about Benedict Arnold going over to the British side." Todd, surprised, said, "You mean he became a traitor?" "Seems like I read about that one time," Joe said. "Read about it?" said Todd. "Where did you read about it?" "Let's say I heard about it," said Joe. Todd said, "Let's go and head toward Saratoga."

When they arrived at the outskirts of Saratoga, there were soldiers all around the place. Todd said, "I wonder what is going on." "I don't know," said Joe. "It looks like there is going to be another battle, and this is just what we don't need. Let's this time stay way out of the way and see what happens." "Good idea," Todd said, looking at all the Americans dressed like farmers with rifles, muskets, and bayonets. Joe was saying, "But it looks like they are just there. You know, it doesn't look like at this point that there is anything going on, any fighting or anything. They're just milling around. I don't know what is happening." Dressed the same as the farmers, Todd and Joe mingled among the soldiers. Todd went over to one of them and said, "What is going on?" The soldier said, "Who are you?" "Well," said Todd, "we have been fighting down South with General Washington and sort of coming this way to find out what is going on." "General Washington . . . oh," said the soldier, looking at Todd like he did not believe him. "Well," said the soldier, "it looks like the British general Burgoyne is about to surrender; at least that is the word." Joe said, "What do you mean surrender? Do you mean this is over?" "I doubt it," said one of the men. "Getting rid of this bastard is just one battle won.

"The way it looks, this fight is far from over." Todd said, "Let's get out of here." "Where to?" said Joe. "I don't know," replied Todd. "Somewhere where we won't be shot at." Joe was thinking to himself, "I wonder if I should tell Todd about what is happening and about this dream I think I am in. I mean I start out in 1984, and in one night I end up in 1775, wars and people shooting at us. In a couple of wars that I only read about, I wonder if that is it. This is just a dream about what I once read about, but shit, these are real bullets and arrows and cannonballs. This is too real.

I think I will hold off for now. If I say anything, he will think I have gone mad. If I give him a story like that, I don't know what is going on. I am in damn action. Where Benedict Arnold is involved, I think I will keep my mouth shut for and see how it plays out."

Todd said, "Why don't we gather up our stuff in the wagon and head out?" "Good idea," Joe replied. "You know, Todd," Joe said, "I wonder if those men we grabbed this wagon from are still looking for us." Todd replied, "I don't know. It's a big country. They might be. I mean they left rifles in the back. I don't imagine they were too happy. If they ever do see us, they will most likely shoot at us." "Great," said Joe. "In that case I hope they never find us." They continued on, and after about an hour they came upon an abandoned cabin. "This looks safe enough for the night," Todd said. "We will stay here for the night and leave early in the morning. We have enough to eat, so let's build a fire. We should be all right."

Sitting around the fire, Todd said to Joe, "You know, every once in awhile, you come up with some sayings that baffle me." "What do you mean?" replied Joe. "Well, like you say you know how this war is going to turn out. What do you mean when you say that?" "Well," said Joe, "if I told you, you would not believe me." "What do you mean?" asked Todd. "Well, I have two other friends, and we were separated in Boston just before I met you. Just say I am from another time." "Another time?" asked Todd. "Yeah," replied Joe. "Another place in my time Boston will have more convenience stores, but besides the shooting, I am not sure a better place exists. Right now you have something to look forward to such as freedom and a new world. But let me tell you in the future the people will screw all that up. You will have more wars. You will win this one against the British, but that is only the beginning; and to tell you the truth, I have no idea how I got to this point."

"The two others—what happened to them?" asked Todd. "I don't know. We were being chased by the British and split up. We were to meet down by the wharf in Boston, but when we went back in that Bunker Hill fight, I could not find the place. Right now if I say any more, you will think I have really gone out of my mind." Todd looked at Joe like he already came to that conclusion. "Okay," said Todd, "let's get some sleep and leave at dawn." Putting the fire out, the two went to sleep for the night. The next morning the two woke up as the sun came up over a lake. Joe was thinking, "What a peaceful sight. This is like heaven compared to the hell I have been living in." Todd said, "Let's get our stuff together and get ready to go. After getting into the wagon and heading down a dirt road through the forest and with the sun coming down through the trees, Joe was saying to himself, "Hell, I don't want to leave this place." About two hours later they came upon a settlement with a roadhouse, a tavern, and eating place, a quiet place with women and children going about their business.

"On a nice warm morning, with trees shading the center like a common, doesn't anybody go to school?" Joe was saying to Todd. At one end children were playing hide-and-seek in the common. Five kids were playing tag, and some were playing chuckers (a game played where you stand a distance away and "chuck" a penny into a hole). Most young children had a few toys: a top, a whistle, or a doll. Most toys were made at home but could be bought at a store or from a peddler. An older boy usually carried a jack knife, which was a handy carving tool as well as a toy. Little girls played with dolls made from rags or straw. Joe was thinking, "A jackknife as a toy. Boy, have times changed. Anybody with a jackknife where I come from is used as a weapon. This is great for the kids." They asked a little girl, "What other games do the other kids play?" The little girl, looking at sort of funny, said, "Oh, sometimes we play scotch hopping [hopscotch] and topspin [spinning a top like marbles, skilled players could toss a top and send it spinning into another and knock it out of the way], and we play graces [throw a hoop using two sticks; to catch the hoop, you hold the stick straight up. To throw the hoop, they crossed the sticks like scissors]. Another thing we do is bilboquet." "What is that?" asked Joe. "Well," said the little girl, "you try to throw a ball up into the air and try to catch it in a cup. Here I will show you." After the little girl showed that, she then said, "We also play ring around the rosie and frog." "What the heck is frog?" "Well, somebody sits on a chair in the middle, and other kids form a ring around her, and the person tries to tag someone without leaving their seat. Is that all?" said the little girl. "Yeah," said Joe. "You know, you ask a simple question, and twenty minutes later I think you get an answer. I wonder what do the grown-ups do." Todd said, "Let's go and get something to eat, and maybe we will ask somebody what they do around here." "Good idea," replied Joe.

As they entered the roadhouse eating area, they sat down. A server came over and said, "What would you like?" Joe said, "Since it is midday a couple of brews." Todd said, "Two lamb stews please." "Lamb stew?" "Yeah," said Todd. "Had it once and it was good." Two men were sitting at the next table, so Joe asked, "What do adults do in this town?" "Well," said one man, "sometimes we have hunting parties, and sometimes we bet on cockfights. We have wrestling contests and tug-of-war when the local fairs come in, and a great many play boules [a form of lawn bowling] and also billiards."

The brews came to the table, and while Joe and Todd were sipping, young locals came in, singing, "Burgoyne's surrender" and followed with "Clinton's retreat." "Strange-sounding songs," Joe was thinking. A rowdy man came in and in a loud voice said, "Those goddamn Indians, we should kill all the bastards. They are fighting for the British, and they are paying the Indians to kill women and children in the country. Those sons of bitches are murdering settlers remote from military support from the Continental Army [the raids had little military value for the Brits]. They should kill every one of those bastards and burn the villages." "Wow," said Joe, "what the hell is this all about?" The man in the next table said, "All I can say is that if you see an Indian, don't say hello. Just shoot the son of a bitch." The other man laughed. "So much for the peaceful town," said Todd. "Let's finish our meal and get out of here."

When they left, they saw a man sitting on a porch, reading a book. Joe asked where they could buy supplies. The man put his book down and said, "You go to the end of the street, and it is on the left-hand side where there is a general store." When they arrived at the store, they went in. Todd said, "I will pick up what we need." As Joe looked around, he saw a girl about seventeen, looking at a book. Joe walked over and asked, "What are you reading?" The girl looked up and smiled. "I am looking at a book called *Common Sense*. It is by Thomas Paine [common sense words fired up the American Revolution and revolutions as far away as Poland, Greece, and France. There was even a rumor that King George's own son, Crown Prince George, was reading the book]." Todd said, "Let's go." "As they put the stuff into wagon, Joe was thinking, "I hate to leave here. It's a hell of a lot better here than where I come from in Boston."

As they drove their wagon out of town, they saw two men following them on horseback. Joe, looking back, said to Todd, "What the hell are these guys doing? They have been following us since we left town." "Highwaymen," said Todd. "What the hell is a highwayman?" asked Joe. "Most are robbers or murderers," Todd replied. "Great! What the hell do we do now?" Todd said, "In the back of the seat, there is my pistol; and if they try anything, shoot them. Remember, shoot to kill, not to wound." "Great," said Joe. "That's just great." Todd started slowing down the wagon. "Now what the hell are you doing?" asked Joe. "I want them to catch up." "You do?" "Yes, and then we will see what they will do." "What do you mean see what they do?" "Look," said Todd, "they both have their left hand on the reins, and if they do anything with their right hand, start shooting." As the two men came closer, Joe did not wait. He pulled his pistol and pointed at one of the men. They looked at Joe and with the pistol on them said, "Good afternoon, gentlemen, we were just wondering how far it is to the next town." Joe said, "You did not have to follow us for two hours to ask that question, and besides, we don't know." One man said, "We will be going." "I guess you better," said Joe. As the two rode by, Todd said, "I don't trust them. They may try to ambush us later on up the road. Get the shotgun from the side of the wagon just in case." "I think they saw us in town and pegged us as a mark," said Joe. "A mark?" asked Todd. "Yes, figuring we would be easy to take. So from here to the next town, we will have to be on guard."

As the wagon headed down the road, Joe was looking around and was very nervous about the two men coming back or going to ambush them. By this time it was early evening, and they came upon a place called the Fox Tavern. They pulled their wagon to the side of the tavern, tied the horses, grabbed their guns, and went in for the night. "Are you hungry?" asked Todd. "Not really," said Joe. "Me neither. We will check in and get a bed for the night." When they went in, a seedy man with a Southern accent said, "What can I do for you?" "We would like a couple of rooms for the night." The man said, "Sign the register," and started fumbling around, looking for keys. "Oh, here you are. Good night, gentlemen." The two went upstairs to their rooms. After about twenty minutes, as Joe was dozing off, there came a knock on the door. Joe was saying to himself, "Now what the hell is it?" and opened the door. There stood Todd. "Now what?" asked Joe as Todd went past him into the room. Todd said, "There is something wrong here." "What are you talking about?" "Look," said Todd, "most of these taverns in towns are run by women, and the man downstairs had a different talk, which I have not heard around these parts." "So?" said Joe. "I don't like this. I have a feeling there is something wrong." "What?" asked Joe. "I don't know. I will stay in this room." "Suit yourself," said Joe as he fell back upon his bed and closed his eyes.

Downstairs there were four men who had killed the barkeep and the women who ran the place. They were pillaging the place and getting supplies when one man said, "What are we going to do with those two upstairs?" The leader said, "We will kill them and take what they have." "But they have guns. Didn't you see that? "We will go upstairs for they are most likely asleep, break down the door, and shoot them before they have a chance. But they are in two different rooms, so when the other comes out, we get him."

So the four men headed upstairs, trying to be quiet. As they started up, one hit a squeaky stair. Todd, hearing this, woke Joe. "I hear something." Joe listened. "I don't hear nothing." "I do," said Todd. "Look, get your gun, go out on the roof to my window, and see what happens. If they break in, shoot. I will stay here just in case they come in this room." Joe went to the roof [second floor] and then to Todd's window. In a short while the four men broke down the door and rushed into the room only to be met by Joe's fire, killing the first two men. The others went for the hallway only to be met by Todd's fire, killing the last two. "Holy shit," said Joe. "I thought for once I was at the okay corral." "What?" asked Todd. "Never mind," replied Joe. "How the hell did you know this was going to happen?" "Just had a feeling. Now we get some sleep. I don't think anybody will be here before morning," said Todd. "I am not going to sleep in either of those rooms." "Well, it looks like we have our pick."

The next morning the two went downstairs to find the dead barkeep and the women. Joe and Todd gathered up some more provisions and loaded their wagon. Joe said, "Whoever comes here this morning will be surprised to find everybody dead."

What a way to start a morning. They started out for open country and Indian country. As they started, Joe was noticing that on some trees there were signs

TO BE SOLD ON BOARD THE SHIP hey BANCE. YLAND ON TUEFDAY ON THE 6TH OF MAY NEXT, A CHOICE OF ABOUT 250 FINE HEATLTHY NEGROES just arrived from the windward & Rice Croft. The utmost care has been taken and shall be continued to keep them free from leaf danger of being infected with SMALL-POX. No boat having been on board and all other communication with people from Charlestown prevented.

signed Aufsin, Laurens, & Appleby. (a sign in 1775).

Joe said to Todd, "What the hell are these signs?" "I guess it is about selling slaves." "Todd, what do you think about that?" Todd replied, "To tell the truth, never thought about it. Too busy going about my own business."

"You know in the future that slavery will end." "That will be good," replied Todd.

As they were riding, they came upon a farm. On a fence surrounding the farm, there was a Help Wanted sign. "What do you think?" said Todd. "We could be here for a few days and pick up some extra money and get some eats and rest for a little while." The wagon pulled up to the farmhouse. Todd walked up to the front doorway, knocked, and a woman answered. "Hello," she said, "is there anything I can do for you?" "Yes, my name is Todd. My friend Joe and I were looking for work, and we saw your sign. We would like to get some work for a few days." "Come in. My name is Ann Schmidt and in the other room my husband, Hans." Ann called her husband. "We have some boys here about our help sign." Hans came into the room. He was about six feet two inches and 223 pounds (a big man in 1775). "So you want to work, do you?" "Yes," said Todd. "Well, we pay three dollars a day and food." "You have to be kidding," said Joe. "That is pretty good," said Todd. "We will take it." "Good," said Hans. "I will need a good day's work, and we have a side room where you can stay." As they went to the room, Joe said, "What the hell are we doing for three dollars a day? I could work at Burger King for six dollars an hour." "That's fine," said Todd. "Are there any of those around here?"

"We had better get to bed early because we will be up early." The next morning came, and Hans said, "I have a shed about fifty yards toward the backwoods, big enough to put your horses and wagon. Then you can go to the north field. I have some fences to be fixed." The two put their wagon in the shed, fed their horses, and then went to work for about six and a half hours, fixing fences and other things. "Son of a bitch," Joe was thinking, "this is more work than I ever did." After their day's work, the two headed back for the house. When they got there, Hans was done with his work and sitting in his chair with a brandy. As Joe and Todd came in, Hans asked, "Well, how did you do?" "Pretty good," said Todd. "Hmm," replied Hans, "I will check your work in the morning." Just then the Schmidts' two children came in. "Kids," Joe whispered to Todd. "I didn't know they had any kids," so said Todd. "Oh, nothing" said Joe. Mrs. Schmidt said, "Dinner is ready."

Joe and Todd went in to the table. Dinner consisted of neck of mutton and vegetables and apple pie with beer, wine, and "flip" (flip, a mixture of rum and cider), which was popular with the children. Joe was now thinking, "Rum and cider. Hell, these kids will be shitfaced before the night is over." After dinner everybody retired to the living room where there was coffee and hot chocolate. By now Hans, with his favorite wine, was sitting back and relaxing while Mrs. Schmidt put the children to bed. "You know," said Hans, "this is part of Indian country. We do our best to coexist with them as best we can. Do you know anything about the Indians?" asked Hans. "The Cleveland Indians," replied Joe. "What tribe are they?" asked Hans. "Only kidding." said Joe. Todd looked funny at Joe. Hans said, "Let me tell you about the Indians. There are a lot of them who are friends of the settlers. They taught us a lot how to grow corn and plant fruit trees. We have the Mohawks and Penobscot. There are some that are rogues because we have taken their land. They fight, kill, and kidnap some children. Those are the ones that are dangerous and the ones you have to watch out for. For example, do you see under that rug, that bulge?" "Yeah," said Joe. "Lift the rug," said Hans. Joe did it. "A trap door," said Hans, "and under that door there is a tunnel that was dug over the years to escape Indians, highwaymen, and whoever tries to attack us. I think it is about time we went to bed, for we have another early morning and busy day."

The next day everybody was up at dawn and ready for breakfast. "Ready for work?" Joe said to Todd. "You know, I wonder what would happen if we happen to run into some rogue Indians." "We had better take our guns just in case."

The day went without an incident, and when they finished, they went back to the house for dinner and rest. After dinner Hans said to the two, "Do you know anything about the Indians, how they live, what their habits are?" Joe said, "Should we know?" "You never know when the information will come in handy. There are good and bad Indians, but you should know who your friends and your enemies are. It is best to know as much about them as possible. We did, and for the most part, we survived all the trouble. Take the Iroquois and the Mohawks, for instance. I have learned that both the French and the English believed that the Iroquois held the balance of the power on the continent. Their allegiance could determine the fate of empires in North America. Some Iroquois and particularly the Mohawks would fight for the British." "What the hell. Don't these people live in tents or on the ground or something like that and live off fish on the river?" Hans smiled. "Let me tell you something. They live in some structures that are fifty to two hundred feet long and twenty-five feet wide. They were homey by the fact that many families occupied one building. The men built the framework of elm wood and the facings and the roof of elm bark. A man lives with his wife's family. Smoke from the cook fires lit the dim escapes through staggered holes in the roof; there are also outdoor fireplaces that they could use in good weather." Joe said, "That was the original outdoor barbecue." "The what?" asked Hans. "Never mind," said Joe. Hans went on to say that in heavy rain or winter snow the smoke holes would be partially closed by a series of shutters. Even though the roofs were high, eyes would sting from the smoke. No doubt the steam from the soup kettles and the variety of smells from babies, bear grease, soot, tobacco, and an assorted humanity combined to create a special atmosphere; but at least it is warm and dry. On each side wall widely divided by central corridors were raised platforms separated for privacy by skin curtains. Here an entire family could sleep snugly among a variety of furs. Above their heads were deep shelves for storage. Every pole, beam, and rafter carried its load of drying foods: peppers, squash, apples, corns, and herbs of all kinds. "So you see, they did more than live in tents and catch fish in the river. In fact, some of the old ones showed me how to grow corn and other ways to farm. But there are some of these young Indians who are more wild and dangerous, and they are the ones you have to watch out for. Let's go to bed and get ready for a busy day tomorrow."

The next morning everybody was up at 5:30 a.m. and ready for work. Hans headed for the barn. Todd and Joe headed for the field by the woods to mend some fence and dig holes for posts. About noon, as they were working, Todd noticed that there were some Indians riding and skirting on the side of the land and heading for the woods. "I wonder what is up with this," said Todd to Joe. "What do you mean?" asked Joe. "I don't know. But I have a bad feeling about this. Just stay near the wagon and be ready just in case we have trouble." Joe was thinking to himself, "Son of a bitch, here we go again. Now we are going to fight Indians." But the rest of the day nothing happened. So when they got to the house late in the day, they said to Hans, "You know, working in the fields we saw a few Indians, maybe about fifteen or twenty of them," said Todd. "Hmm, is that so?" said Hans. "Are they still there?" "Think so," said Todd. "I am going out through the woods and see what is going on." Todd said, "I will go with you." Joe said, "I will pass on this one." Mrs. Schmidt said, "Be careful. They may be trouble." The two headed out through the back. "Be quiet," said Hans. "They are sensitive. You break a branch, and they can hear it." So moving out to the backwoods carefully, they came upon where they were camping. Hans said, "They look like a war party. Let's get back to the house and wait to see what happens." When they got back to the house, Mrs. Schmidt asked, "What happened?" "Nothing," said Hans, looking at Todd as if to say nothing. Hans then said, "Let's have some dinner."

After dinner they went to the den, and while everybody was sitting and talking, Todd was standing by the window. That night the moon was bright—so bright that you could see everything: the fields and the woods. The moon was shining through the trees. Todd was thinking, "What a beautiful sight." He turned around and noticed some movement and shadows in the trees. He turned to Hans and said, "I don't like this." "What?" said Hans. "There is something happening out there." Hans said, "The Indians don't usually attack at night." Joe now was looking out the window. "Yeah, tell them that," he said. Hans said, "Get the kids." Todd rolled up the rug and opened the trap door to the tunnel. Hans, Todd, and Joe grabbed their weapons; broke the windows, and started firing toward the woods. Their fire was returned, and pretty soon they were under attack from all sides. Arrows with flames were hitting the house, and by this time the house was burning. Quickly Joe, Todd, Hans, and the entire family were in the tunnel and heading for safety. When they got to the end of the tunnel and were outside, they just stood there and watched their house burning. The Indians thought they killed everybody when the house burned to the ground and left. Mrs. Schmidt was crying, and the children were scared. Joe said, "I guess these Indians were the bastards, right, Hans?" Hans had no answer. Hans said, "Boys, I thank you for your help. I will pay you for two weeks."

Todd went to get the wagon, which was still there. Through all the action, the horses had not moved. When Todd came back, he said, "Can we take you anywhere?" "Yes, if you don't mind, we have friends about five miles down the road." They got into the wagon and headed out, looking back at the charred remains of their house. When they arrived at Han's family friend's house, they dropped everybody off. The next afternoon Todd said, "Is there anything else we can do for you?" "No," said Hans. "You have done plenty, and I thank you. Good luck, and from now on, have a safe trip."

Todd and Joe started out. Joe said, "Do you think they will be all right?" "They were fine people. They will be just fine," replied Todd—just fine as their wagon headed down the dirt road into an open field with the sun setting behind the hills. Joe was thinking of the damn British, the Indians, and the highwaymen. "This is a nice place to be—no police, no slums, no smog from smoke. What the hell am I saying? I do miss people, the television, and ball games. I wish now I didn't get involved with that damn robbery, and somehow I am paying the price." Todd broke into Joe's thoughts, "What are you thinking?" "Oh, nothing," said Joe, "nothing." After about three hours, it was getting dark, and they were in the woods with the wagon on a narrow dirt road with deep woods on both sides. "Damn it. Can hardly see anything," said Joe. "I know," said Todd. "You know, this is a little scary. I mean we could be sitting targets for anybody—highwaymen or Indians." Joe grabbed his gun just in case, and after they came upon an opening. There was a cabin silhouetted by the full moon around a lake. "This is something," said Joe. "I mean we came from the deep woods where you could hardly see anything to this. You could see the whole lake and the stars in the sky. I mean wow," said Joe. "Yes," said Todd. "Let's see what this cabin looks like." They walked into the cabin and looked around. There were two beds and provisions, but it looked like nobody lived there for weeks. "This looks like a story I once read about the three bears. I hope they don't come to this cabin," Joe said, joking. "The three what!" said Todd. "Never mind," Joe replied. "Well, we could stay here for the night." "Sounds good to me, Todd."

After getting into bed, Todd went to sleep, but Joe could not. He got up out of bed, walked, and continued down by the lake where he saw a boat. "Hmm," he said as he got into the boat and rowed to the middle of the lake. There he was sitting in the boat by himself with the lake fully lit by the moonlight. Joe was saying to himself, "Wow. This is something. I have never in my life felt such peace." While Joe was looking around the lake at the starry sky and the surrounding woods, he was thinking, "I never had anything like this in the city. I heard about kids going to camp, and they would tell me about something like this. I wish now I went to camp with them. The one good thing about this time is that if I were sitting out on a lake not fishing or anything, they would think I am crazy or something. But not this time. In Boston we had gangs and cops. We got lazy and wanted to make money the easy way. If I had this to do over again, I would go a different way. But here we have Indians and wars that I once read about or sort of. Somehow I am now living history. It's sort of like looking at a movie and knowing the ending."

Rowing back to shore, he pulled the boat up on the edge of the lake and looked back over the lake. He then turned around and headed back toward the cabin. He went into the cabin and found Todd was still asleep. Since there with no lights on, he felt his way back to bed, lay down, and went to sleep. When the next morning came, Todd said, "Did you go out last night? "Yes, I did, for I was alone and able to think." "Well," said Todd, "you are lucky that you didn't get killed. I mean you could have run into Indians or even the person whoever it is that owns this cabin." Todd looked around and said, "I guess there is nobody around. Let's get our stuff into the wagon and get out of here." Looking at the lake, which they had just passed by, Joe said, "This is another place I hate to leave.

"This was a very good time." "What do you mean a good time?" said Todd. "Look," Joe said, "as I said before, if I told you, you would not understand what I was talking about." As they rode by the river, Todd said, "Hold it." "What?" said Joe. "Look at that over the other side of the river." "Indians! I wonder if they are friendly or not." "I am pulling over toward these woods and see what happens. I don't want to find out." "Let's sit here watch and see what happens." They pulled over where they could not be seen and watched. "Look, these Indians are like deer; they're so sensitive they can almost smell you. I don't know what tribe they are, so let's move out slowly. Try to stay low and move in these trees along the river." They moved out, keeping an eye across the river. "Damn it," said Joe. "I hope they don't see us. The last thing I want at this point is to have an encounter with the Indians." "I know," said Todd. "If we take our time, I think we will be all right." They continued down the side of the river without being seen. "You know," said Todd, "I think we are in the middle of Indian territory, and to tell you, I don't know whether they are hostile or not. So let's not take a chance and stay out of their way." "Good idea," said Joe.

They waited until dusk then proceeded down the river and away from the Indian camp without being seen. "That was too close. I am glad we didn't run to a scout or anything like that." "Yes," said Todd, "but we don't know whether they were friendly or not, but I am glad we didn't find out." "Yeah," said Joe. "Let's go slowly just in case." "You know," Todd said, "this wagon sure did come in handy."

They rode into town and tied up their horses down by the stable. Then they looked around and saw a bustling village where people were milling around. They went into the tavern and sat down. Todd said, "I could use an ale. How about you?" "I sure could," said Joe. Sitting down and relaxing, the two were talking about the day. Todd said, "Every once in a while, you talk about knowing what is going to happen. Just how do you have this great knowledge?" "It's kind of hard to explain," Joe answered. "You would think I was from the TV show *The Lost Planet* or something." "*The Lost Planet*! What is that?" asked Todd. "Look, Todd, I am from a different time. How I got to this time, I don't know." Todd by this time was looking at Joe really funny like he had just lost his mind. "The way you are looking at me is just what I am talking about." "Look," said Todd, "if you know what is going to happen, why don't you stop the things from happening?"

"Look, Todd, I can't foresee our situation. What I am saying is that I know how the war with the British will turn out and how things will be, but as far as things in the next hour, no, I really don't have any idea of the outcome." "What do you mean?" said Todd. "Look, Todd, I don't remember whether I told you or not, but things will change. There will not be any horse and wagon. There will be cars that will go a hundred miles an hour and planes that will go from Boston to California in five hours. There will be trains with tracks, television, radio, and sports to watch and listen to. There will be tall buildings in Boston and New York. You will get from Boston to New York in three to four hours, not like in days, which is the way we have to travel." Todd, listening to this, said, "Where is California?" Sitting back, looking at Todd, Joe said, "That is what I mean. That is why I can't tell you, for it is no use."

CHAPTER NINE

Joe, Todd, and the Indians

While they were sitting there, a dark man walked in and sat down next to them. Somehow he got into a conversation with them and ordered ale. They introduced themselves. "My name is Todd, and this is my friend Joe." "My name is Ron Two Hawks." "Two Hawks is an Indian name," Joe was now thinking. "Oh shit, a damn Indian. First I am running from them; now I am sitting down and drinking ale with them. From what I hear, they go crazy when they drink."

"We saw a tribe up the river. Are you with them?" "Yes, I am," said Ron, "and they are a peaceful tribe." After a few drinks Ron said, "Would you like to go back to camp with me and meet some of my people?" "Sure," said Todd. After they finished they headed out. On the way out Joe said, "How do you know the son of a bitch isn't going to scalp us?" Todd replied, "I don't know that, but if they do, I will make sure you go first." "To hell with you, Todd. I am staying here and wait for you to get back." "I am only kidding," said Todd. "Look, we drank with this person, and I can tell he is all right." "You can tell you are not from Boston," said Joe.

They got into their wagon and followed Ron Two Hawks back up the other side of the river to the Indian camp. When they arrived, the chief was not too happy with Ron. "What is the matter with him?" said Joe. "I don't know," said Todd, to which Ron replied, "He usually is not happy with me and my lifestyle. You see, I used to sneak out and meet with a white settler and his son. I learned a lot from him, and we became friendly. He does not approve of my lifestyle, but I know both ways of life." As they got out of the wagon, Joe said to Todd, "Look, this is crazy. We are in an

Indian camp." "I might add that the chief does not like white men or his son for being around white men. This is where I got the name Ron; it was just Two Hawks."

"This is great. If he gets pissed off, what the hell chance have we got?" "Don't worry," said Todd. "Ron is still his son, and he is in camp. Nobody has got hurt yet." "Yet," answered Joe. Ron came over and said, "It is time to turn in, for tomorrow will be a busy day," as they were shown where they were to sleep. Joe said to Todd, "'Turn in'—what Indian says 'to turn in'? I will tell you I am not going to sleep tonight."

In the morning, when they got up, the day was bright and warm. Todd said to Joe, "How did you sleep last night?" "Are you kidding? Not much I'll tell you. I had one eye open all night." Ron said, "Good morning." Yeah, good morning," said Joe, still half asleep. Todd asked, "What are they doing down by the river?" "Building a canoe. Would you like to see how they do it?" "Yes," said Todd. "Wonderful," said Joe sarcastically.

The Indians were laying out gunwales, which made the shape of the canoe. This was done by simply placing two long pieces of white cedar on the ground, binding the ends together with tough roots of black spruce and forming the shape by forcing the long cedar pieces apart with suitable widths of cedar planks. Stakes were then driven into the ground, outlining and securing the shape. The stakes were then pulled up and laid alongside with their ends left in place by the holes outlining the shape. The cedar frame was lifted off, and strips of birch bark unrolled to cover the outline. The framework was then very carefully put back in place, and stones were left on the crossbars to weigh it down. The bark was then fitted to form the sides of the vessel. Longitudinal strips were added. The outer stakes were pounded back into their holes, and smaller stakes on the inside of the frame were tied to the outer ones to act as clamps to hold the bark in place. Once rising and securing the bark was complete, the stones were removed and the gunwales raised to a proper height.

The women then began the delicate task of fastening bark around the gunwales by punching holes in the bark with awls and using split ends of spruce root as binders. They were able to lace the birch bark securely as the spruce root laces were kept wet for flexibility. After the lacing was complete, all the stakes were removed, and the canoe was turned over. Then the women repaired the patch wherever necessary. They tied the endpoints together with more root lashings. The canoe was then turned right side up, and the seams and cracks were sealed with hot black spruce gum. Finally the men reinforced the interior with long strips of white cedar laid in lengthwise. These were held in place by shorter pieces of bent wet cedar, fitting crosswise, and tucked under the gunwales. The crosswise pieces were further reinforced by sewing them to the gunwales with spruce root.

"Wow," said Todd, "I always wondered how you did that. Didn't you, Joe?" Yeah. Say, do they eat breakfast around here?" "Yes," said Ron. "We have trout." "Trout!" said Joe. "No pancakes, sausage, or anything like that?" Ron and Todd looked at one another. "What is pancakes?" Joe said, "Damn it, it's no use." The chief came over and said something to Ron. Joe said, "I wonder what they are talking about." "I don't know," said Todd.

Everybody was excited down by the river. "There is a moose," said Ron. "What is a moose doing this far down country?" "Come with me." They all went down by the river, and sure enough there in the middle was a large moose. Ron said, "Get a canoe, jump in, and grab a spear." "What do you mean jump in and grab a spear?" said Joe. Todd said, "Don't waste time; just jump in." Joe struggled to get into the canoe. Once in the canoe they started out with four other canoes after the moose. "What are we going to do? What the hell are we doing?"

The moose started moving faster. Billy was upfront where he was ready to kill the moose, for the canoes were coming up fast with the flow of the river. "Son of a bitch," said Joe. "I feel like Captain Ahab of *Moby Dick*." "What did you say?" "Nothing," said Joe. Ron's canoe reached the moose first. Ron thrust the spear into the moose. Todd followed suit, killing the moose. Then they tied up the moose in the water and dragged it ashore. When they got there, the others helped them get the moose ashore. Once ashore the chief came over and said something. "What did he say?" Ron said, "All he said was it was a fine meal." "Great," said Joe to Todd. "Look, I am not into eating moose. Let's get the hell out of here." "Not right now." Todd said to Ron, "What tribe is this?" Ron replied, "We are Mohawk.

"We are here because we split from our regular people. This is mostly the Iroquois land, and some are trouble, and some are not. But we have had no trouble with them. You see, we all belong to the confederacy—which would be Mohawk, Oneida, Onondaga, Cayuga, Seneca—and they say the Tuscarora Iroquois confederacy." "What the hell is that?" Best known of all Iroquois nations were the five nations of the Haudenosaunee, whose confederacy took its name from the longhouses from which they lived. These five nations came to think of themselves as embodying an enormous longhouse that stretched two hundred and fifty miles across, which is now New York State. The Onondaga—who lived in the center of the region, near the Haudenosaunee Trail, their principal communication route—were said to represent the central corridor of the great longhouse and were the fire keepers for all five nations. The Seneca were the keepers of the western door, and the Mohawks were keepers of the eastern door. Together with the Oneida and the Cayuga, these five groups formed the Iroquois confederacy and later expanded to include the Tuscarora; all this was done before Columbus's arrival.

Tribes created the confederation as a means for the peaceful resolution of conflict among member nations. Before the existence of the league of the Iroquois, when a man murdered someone from another nation, the victim's people sought revenge through raids, which often erupted into war between the nations. Deganawidah, a Huron spiritual leader, had a vision of a great spruce tree that reached through the sky to communicate with the Great Spirit. His vision also showed him how to put these ideals into practical application through great law, a set of rules, and procedures for settling hostilities. Yet few people accepted his message perhaps because of Deganawidah's speech impediment. In his travels he met the compelling Mohawk orator Hiawatha. Together Hiawatha and Deganawidah were able to communicate effectively the Great Spirit's message of peace, unity, and clear thinking to the five nations.

After they finally convinced the nations to relinquish warfare among themselves, they planted the Great Tree of Peace on Onondaga land near present-day Syracuse, New York. The Iroquois put these ideas into practice by forming a confederacy of forty-nine chiefs. These representatives settled their disputes peacefully through agreements and ceremonies at annual gatherings with each decision requiring unanimous consensus among all member nations.

The women of each matrilineal clan chose their most respected to be clan mother who, in turn, chose a clan chief called a sachem to represent the lineage on the basis of his integrity, wisdom, vision, and oratorical ability. The clan mother also had the power to depose the chief if he did not conform to the will of his lineage and the Iroquoian values of unity, democracy, and liberty.

The effective ways in which the nations of the confederacy put these ideas into action quickly attracted the attention of American leaders of the revolution. These leaders sought the help of the Iroquois in their attempt to replace the British monarchy with a democratic alternative: in 1775 they formulated the Albany plan of union based on Iroquoian ideals. In Philadelphia, in May and June 1776, American leaders asked Iroquois chiefs to attend the weeks of debate on the Declaration of Independence.

Impressed with the sincere efforts of the Americans an Onondaga sachem gave John Hancock, who presided over the debates, the name Karanduawn, which means "the Great Tree."

In 1790 Thomas Jefferson led others in a toast to the United States Constitution as a ("Iroquois") tree of peace that sheltered the Americans "with its branches of the union." In 1777 the Iroquois confederacy allowed each nation of the league to follow its own path in the war between the British and the Americans. This division of allegiance ended the league's military power.

Todd walked down by the riverside. There were squaws washing garments. When he caught one looking at him, Todd looked back with a flirting eye. Ron came by to say hello to Todd. Ron was smiling. "I like her. She is nice." "Yes, she is," said Ron. "What is her name?" "Bright Water." "Hmm, that's a nice name." "But to let you know, she is that warrior's squaw. He is Crazy Fox, and he is jealous." Joe was nearby and could not help hearing the conversation. Joe got Todd aside. "Are you crazy, man? Look, you get into it with this Crazy Fox or whatever the hell his name is, and this son of a bitch kills you. That leaves me with a bunch of these crazy featherheads." Todd said, "Her name is Bright Water." "Look, I don't give a damn if it is Running Water, shit Bright Water, Crazy Fox, and a damn Indian with a white man's first name. His father is pissed off because he took that first name. It is all nice, but let's get the hell out of here before we can't."

Todd said, "Let's stay a few more days. This is very interesting the way they live. I had a different idea about Indians like they are not all bad." Joe said, "Interesting my ass. Look, you just want to see that squaw. Let me tell you something, partner. We are on the wrong street corner for this bullshit. You just want to see Running Water, and that can get us killed." "It's Bright Water," replied Todd. "Whatever! Just let's think about getting out of here before it is too late." "We will," said Todd. "Let's just wait a day or so and just see what happens."

"Ron, is this a renegade?" "No," said Ron, "this is a Mohawk. You see the Huron. They lived in longhouses." "I thought they told us the Iroquois lived in the longhouses." "Some do, but the Huron are the ones who, for the most part, live in the longhouses. They are made with saplings bent and tied together at the top, creating a tall framework with curved roof and sides. This framework is then covered with slabs of bark. A central corridor is dotted with fire pits and mat curtains form cubicles along the sides. Bunks built along the walls did double service as seats and beds while storage spaces were located under the bunks on shelves and in pits dug into the floor. Many hooks and pegs were available for hanging garments, bags, baskets, and assorted paraphernalia for family living. Plant foods were hung from the rafters to dry in the heat and smoke that rose from the fire pits.

"Because the Huron were a matrilineal society, mothers and daughters lived in the longhouse. Each family occupied a compartment along one side of the central aisle where the cooking fires burned. Everyone snacked from the more or less communal clay pots during the day, but families ate together at mealtimes. The senior women of each household dished out the food, and as a gesture of respect to the protectors of her family, she made sure that the men ate before the women. The leadership of each clan segments rested with a particular household whose eldest able-bodied woman was the clan matron and the coordinator of the clan's domestic needs. From among her male relatives, she chose two men to lead the clan: a civil chief and a war captain.

"Married men lived in the households of their wives. Yet because a married man's primary relationship was with his own clan [that of his mother and sisters] rather than with his wife or wives, marriages tended to be short-lived. Indeed when it came to raising couple's children, it was the brothers of the wives who assumed the role that the fathers usually take in other societies, for they and their sisters belonged to the clan. And so brothers of wives had the responsibility of raising their nieces and nephews to be proper adults, knowledgeable about clan heritage and affairs. However, since men were often away for long periods—trading, raiding, or visiting—the day-to-day rearing of children was usually preformed by related women.

"You know, the Hurons were divided into eight matrilineal clans distributed among a confederacy of four tribes. But with the arrival of the Europeans and the inevitable disease-borne death toll that followed, two of these tribes respectively joined together their reduced numbers for mutual protection against inter tribal warfare. Because members had to marry into a clan different from their own, most clans were represented in every village. During ceremonies clans were grouped into three clan clusters known as the Wolves, Turtles, and Deer. In addition to these kinship-based links, other forms of bonding developed.

"The various healing or curing fraternities, with strong spiritual significance and the interclan councils that deliberated over general clan welfare, were groupings that required the cooperation of unrelated neighbors and thereby helped to fuse each town into a cohesive community.

"The Iroquois people lived in a huge rectangle extending from the Hudson River to Lake Erie. Calling themselves the people of the longhouse, the Iroquois divided their homeland into five north—south strips, each area watered by its own lake or river, and they are surrounded by their enemies: the Algonquian tribe."

"Well, this is all well and good," said Joe. "It seems like I heard this before awhile ago or something like it. But what the hell is this doing for us now? Look, Ron, I am trying to get Todd out of here before something happens. He likes—what's her name?" "Bright Water," replied Ron. "Yes, but this Crazy Fox is going to cause trouble, and I would like to get out of here before anything happens." "When you leave, I will have to go with you," said Ron, "because I brought you here. If I stay alone, there will be trouble for me too." "You said your father is chief. How the hell could you be in trouble?" "He disowned me when I left." "Oh, that is just great," said Joe, "just great. By the way how did you come up with the name Ron?" "When I left and lived with a white family, they gave me the first name and educated me with schooling and the ways of the white man and also religion. You see, he was a minister, so I know a little of both cultures." "You do? Well, maybe you can tell me about this thing with this Indian girl. What the hell we can do?" Ron replied, "There will be trouble with Crazy Fox and also the chief. So like me you think we should get out of here while the getting is good in a manner of speaking," said Ron.

"What the hell do you mean in a manner of speaking? Yes or no?" Ron said yes. "Well, we had better get the stars out of Todd's eyes before he gets us all killed, and I think we had better come up with some ideas fast." That night as they turned in, he went to the wagon and took his rifle back with him to his living quarters, a bark wigwam. Once he got back, he felt a little safer, and Todd was already asleep; so therefore, it was too late at this time to talk to Todd about anything.

"Boy, this is something I worry about getting killed, and I don't know whether I am in purgatory or hell or if this is heaven. Heaven? Forget that, but I wish it could be explained to me how I got from 1984 to here. I guess it's better than the city, in a way a little more freedom but a different kind of danger. I wonder how Jim and Dave are making out."

The next morning when everybody got up Joe said, "Look, Todd, I was talking to Ron, and like me he thinks we should get the hell out of here. I don't know what is going on with you and this Indian girl, but let me tell you it is dangerous." Todd said, "We have had trouble before." "Yeah, I know," said Joe, "but in most cases we had a way out, and right now we are in the middle. Ron thinks the same, and on top of that, he wants to go with us." "He does!" "Yes, he says that the situation can get very bad. I mean he can't trust his own people, and he says he has to leave with us, or his life is in danger even with his father as chief."

As they walked, they noticed three Indians with clubs. Joe said, "What the hell is this?" "Don't worry, they are after rabbits. They have a makeshift fence to head them off, and then they hit the rabbits, killing them; and that is for dinner tonight." Todd said to Ron, "It is real interesting. Like how do the kids learn?" "There are no schools," Ron said. "You don't go to a formal school; you learn by watching grown-ups. You hunt, farm, tan hides, and carve bowls. You make bows and arrows and breaded moccasins and create and build other things. You learned about Iroquois history and the founding of the Great League when elders told the story of the peacemaker and Hiawatha at the festivals. During the long winter months, children sat around fires and listened as their elders told fabulous tales. There were tales about good people and very foolish ones. Some of the stories were funny, some were sad, and some were very scary. All had a meaning you could think about.

"Until the boys are eight or nine years old, they stay with their sisters, mothers, and aunts. When they grow older, they spent some time with their fathers. But often their most important teachers are their mother's brothers because from these older men boys learned the ways of the forest: how to hunt, make tools, and build longhouses and canoes. Girls learned many things from their mothers and aunts: how to make clothing, cultivate the soil, plant seeds, and bring in the harvest. You also learn from your own experiences. As teenagers both and girls went into the forest alone. You stay in a small hut, and you don't eat any food for days. And they have a vision or a special dream. You dream about your guardian, a spirit you believe will protect and watch over life."

"What do these people do when they grow up?" "We do everything. For example, if you work today in basket making, you might do only one thing such as prepare the base. But an Iroquois girl or woman did the whole thing. She made the tools she needed for the work. She gathered and prepared the materials and then actually made the whole basket. There is no such thing as a job that people looked down on, for every job was respected."

Todd then said, "How do you tell the time?" "What the hell do you mean how do you tell time?" said Joe. "When it's dark, it's night; when it's light, it's day. Now let's think about getting out of here." "No," said Ron, "but you are almost right; the Iroquois tell time by the rising and setting of the sun and the changes of the moon. It takes about a month for the moon to go through its various phases depending upon the times of the year and on what is happening in nature. The Mohawk names for the April and May moon is Oneratoka or promise of nature. The September moon is Saskekowa, last warning for the harvest. And the December-January moon is Tsotorha, starting to freeze, and that is when the Midwinter Festival would begin.

"When they were away from home, hunters watched for a group of seven stars that only appear in the eastern sky after the first frost. The Pleiades set in the west around the time of the last frost is half over. That was the sign that the Midwinter Festival would occur five days after the next new moon. We live our lives in unison as the world goes on around us."

Todd said, "What are these women doing with corn?" Ron replied, "You see, corn has many uses. Dried corn kernels are used for beads for decoration and also mats to sit and sleep on like the ones you were sleeping on." "You mean I was sleeping on a mat that was made of corn?" "Yes, outside of deer hide, some moccasins, kindling, baskets, medicine masks, and dolls, corn silks were used as tubes to hold medicines. Green corn leaves are sometimes used as bandages. And corn silk is used to make medicines. Also, corns were thrown on the fire for smoking skins and the different ways that we cook corn."

Todd said, "What do you do if someone steals something?" Joe looked at Todd in a sort of funny way. "Well," Ron said, "there not many crimes. We have no jails like the white man does, for nobody steals anything. There are no locks on longhouse doors. A pole or a stick leaning across the door is a sign that there is nobody home and others should stay out. Inside the longhouse all possessions were stored in open areas. Stealing, however, was so shameful that everyone looked down on a thief. And that in itself was considered a very strong punishment.

"A few crimes are severely punished. Murder, the worst crime of all, was punishable by death. When a murder occurred the nations or clans involved held meetings to try to prevent revenge attacks. The murderer's family might send a white wampum to the victim's family. This was a sign of confession and asking for forgiveness. If the wampum was accepted, the murder was forgiven. If it wasn't accepted, the victim's family had a right to punish the murderer."

Joe said, "This is all well and good. I will tell you. What about those Iroquois and Mohawks and Seneca bastards that launched that raid with the British that massacred thirty-three innocent people? Sixteen soldiers were killed. One good thing, even some Tories and those sons of bitches—they may have gotten what was coming to them for helping the damn British. From what I hear the slaughter and wanton cruelty committed by those bloodthirsty savage bastards was unnecessary." "Yes," said Ron, "but there is enough killing on both sides to go around." "Bullshit," said Joe. "There was a Seneca chief Cornplanter who was opposed to breaking the treaty of neutrality made with the Americans. But when the Seneca decided to join the British, Cornplanter was chosen to lead the war chiefs into war with the Americans." Joe said, "They should have planted that bastard."

Todd said, "If you were going to be married or something like that to an Indian, how would you go about it?" Joe said, "That does it. What the hell are you talking about married? Look, the father doesn't like you, and her boyfriend wants to scalp us both. Hell, his own son wants to leave with us because he screwed up and brought us here. Look, Todd, take a cold shower. No, shower here, jump in the river, cool off, and let's get the hell out of here like I have said over a hundred times."

Ron said, "You have to get permission from the family, and then there are rituals you have to go through. It will take time, and besides you have Crazy Wolf to think about. He is not a pleasant person." "Yeah," said Joe, "we should do what we do in Boston." "What is that?" said Ron. "Walk up and punch the son of a bitch in the jaw." Todd and Ron looked at each other.

Todd said, "What do you do if you get sick for there are no doctors that I see?" "No," said Ron. "We have different kinds of healers who could treat you depending on your illness. You could become ill from bad water or air or catching someone else's disease. But they also believe you could become sick because of witchcraft by bad people or the work of evil spirits. Sometimes when you are sick, the false faces or one of the other medicine societies would try to heal you.

"These medicine groups preformed special rituals that are an important part of the religion, and we believe that other people should not know about these ceremonies." Todd asked, "How do you pay these healers?" "You pay them with tobacco and give them the food they like. The false faces favor a certain kind of pudding. Another medicine group, the little water society, loved boiled bear's head and corn syrup. If you were cured, you became a member of the society and help to treat others. If you broke your leg or arm, you would be treated by a surgeon. The Iroquois are excellent surgeons who not only set broken bones but also were great at keeping wounds clean. Not many white doctors practice cleanliness."

"I want to know how long it will be before we get the hell out of here." The next morning there was a lot of excitement—a lot of yelling. "What is going on?" "Ron said we have a game going on." "What kind of a game?" "There were eight players on each side lined up in two rows facing each other, and each player had a bat. The ball was dropped between the two lines, and each team fought for possession. You'd run with the ball in the bat's netting until you were blocked. Then you'd hurl the ball to another team player. If you carried the ball through your team's own gate a set number of times, your team would win. As with all Iroquois team games, individual players weren't thought of as stars. It was the team's victory that was important."

"We also have runners," said Ron. "Runners carried information from one village or nation to another. It's not surprising that a sport-trained runner often competed at festivals. Sometimes a race would be entertainment, often ending one of the grand council meetings. You know," said Ron, "the Iroquois loved games. They bet on the outcome of any contest. One favorite was a game played with beans made of polished elk horn. They were about an inch in diameter and burned on one side to make them dark colored. You'd put them in a bowl and toss them. If six turned up one color, you got two points; less than six, no points; seven, four points; all the same color, twenty points. There was a pile of extra beans on the side. The winner received a bean for every point. A similar game was played with six peach stones blackened on one side and shaken in a bowl. The peach stone game is often played on the last day of green corn harvest and New Year's festivals.

"When they go to war, each of the Iroquois have its own council, a legislature to run local affairs. Now these councils could declare war involving only their own nations, though warriors from any nation were welcome to get into the scrap. Even when the league council declare war, its concern with the matter stopped at that; no troops are mustered, no strategy planned. Anyone who wants to fight might do so, but there is no compulsion. When war is declared, a hatchet painted red and decorated with red feathers and black wampum is struck into the war post in each village. The local war chief that is elected sounded a whoop among the longhouses and starts a war dance at the post. The men who join the dance are automatically enlisted. Their wives immediately pack maple sugar and parched corn for rations.

"The war party leaves when the dance is over. Parched corn was boiled first and then dried by slow roasting. Now I will tell you that the warriors walk the trail in Indian file, and they travel fast. You know that a party can manage a hundred-mile trip in only a few days. Some trails were well established. The principal one connecting the larger villages of the five nations and branching to the smaller ones ran crooked course from the Hudson to Lake Erie. They say it's reported to have a foot and a half wide and worn six inches into the ground.

"On the trail war parties meet, but each group still remains under its own chief who isn't subject to any higher military authority. War tactics with the Indians are chiefly surprise, strike, and run. I will tell you what is different about the Iroquois is their ferocity. As far as scalping is concerned, I don't know who started it, but the French and English forces requested scalps as well as head and hands as proof of death. In itself scalping isn't always fatal, though a lot of people resisted the removal of their hair to the point of death.

"The Iroquois brought captured enemies home to be inspected by the community. If a family had lost a man, a captive might be adopted to replace him. He first had to run the gantlet between lines of women and children. If he comes through with his head up, he was treated well and became an Iroquois. Captives who were not adopted were tied to a post and turned over to the women for torture. The stoical endurance of pain was a kind of final grace to the Indian. He schooled himself to it from childhood. Pairs of little boys would rub their foreheads together until one yielded. A warrior in the course of treatment too dreadful for description would chat calmly with his captors on matters of topical interest to prove his bravery."

Joe got Todd aside and said, "All this bullshit is fine, but what has this to do with us? Look, Todd, I am telling you we have to get out of here; and if we split up, we will not make it in this country. Now what the hell is going on with that adult with the kid, and what is that mask he is wearing?" Ron said, "If a young one does something bad, you are never spanked like the Americans do; that man will throw water on you or dunk you into a stream. If you are really bad, you know 'the long nose will come after you.' He will threaten to carry you off unless you promise to be good." "What the hell is a long nose?" asked Joe. "Well," said Ron "a long nose is an adult, usually a relative, who wears a special mask that every child knows and fears. When a long nose comes after you, they always promise to change their behavior. That mask scares me with that ugly look and long nose."

Todd said, "That is why they call it a long nose." Okay, I had enough. Look, Todd, let's get out of here tonight.

"This Crazy Fox—I don't trust him or his friends." "Yes," said Todd, "but I would like to see Bright Water before I leave." "Oh great," said Joe. "What are you going to tell her? That you are leaving? That will give this clan a chance to kill us, which they would have done if we had not been here with Ron."

Walking back to the wagon, they noticed a bunch of teenagers and turned to Ron who was behind them. "What is going on?" Ron replied, "They are turning them out into the woods where they will survive or die. They will have no provisions, and when they survive, they will be warriors." "Damn, you have to be kidding." "No," said Ron, "that is custom." "Did you have to go through that?" "Yes," said Ron, "I did. I survived and kept going and ended up in with those farmers I told you about. That is part of what my father the chief doesn't like and has trouble talking about. He expected me to come back and become a warrior." "Wise choice. You would have done great in Boston in my time." "Your time?" said Ron. "Yeah, never mind," said Joe.

Going back to the wagon, they wanted to make sure that everything is ready to go just in case they decide to leave. Ron, walking through the center of the camp, noticed that Crazy Fox and his friends were working on something. Getting closer and standing behind a tree, he saw that they were working on bows with their own shape. The middle was a reverse curve, and the arrows were three feet long and feathered spirally. From what Ron saw, they were dipping the ends in poison, which was made from a berry. They also had clubs, which were handsome and deadly implements. There were two kinds of clubs: one was made of dense heavy ironwood. It was about two feet long and had a one-inch ball at one end. The other was the same length, but a four-inch spur of deer horn set in the lower edge replaced the ball. Both kinds were usually decorated with patterns and feathers. This was mainly used for hunting, but from what Ron saw, the prey was going to be Todd and Joe.

Ron headed back to where they were standing right next to the wagon. Ron said, "Crazy Fox and his friends are about ready to move on you and Todd. If we are about ready to move, it had better be tonight." "Why? What is happening?" asked Joe. "Well," said Ron, "what they are doing is mixing poison berry, a mix they put on the tip of an arrows. It kills animals and people, and I think Crazy Fox and his friends have you and Todd in mind." "Great!" said Joe. "Why don't I just grab this rifle and shoot the son of a bitch?" "No good," said Ron, "then we will have the whole camp down on us." "Well," said Joe, "we have to get the lovesick one off his ass and see if we can get out of here. But I don't know how we will do that." Ron said, "We will have to create a diversion." Yeah," said Joe, "how do we do that?" "Well," said Ron, "there is some dry grass behind our teepee. We set fire to the grass, and it catches our teepee. The Indians here are scared of fire and will put their attention on putting the fire out. That will give us a little time to move, but I will tell you we had better move very fast."

"Todd is down with Bright Water," said Joe. "Ron, you had better go down and tell Todd, and I will try to get our belongings into the wagon slowly while nobody is looking." Ron went down where Todd was talking to Bright Water, pulled Todd aside, and told him what was happening. "Look, Todd, this is serious; this group will try to kill you." "Why?" said Todd. "Because of Bright Water?" "That is one reason; the other is they don't like white men. This is what will happen tonight, so say good-bye. Don't tell Bright Water anything. Maybe someday you will come back, but I tell you we had better get out of here tonight."

As dusk was falling, Ron and Joe went back to the grass and started a fire. Pretty soon the blaze caught their teepee and started rising toward the sky, and then trees caught fire. The Indians came out and turned their attention to putting out the fire. Ron, Joe, and Todd by this time were in their wagon. Their horses were jittery with one of them raising up on its hind legs. Therefore, they started out with the wagon's horses at full gallop. Joe had his rifle out just in case.

In all the commotion Crazy Fox, seeing this, screamed out a war whoop, went for his bow and arrow, and raised it to shoot. Joe shot his rifle, hitting and killing Crazy Fox as their wagon headed out of the camp and down the side of the river, noticing the camp was in a full blaze in the background. "Damn it," said Todd, "I thought we were going to start a little fire, not burn down the whole goddamn camp. I hope Bright Water is all right." "Bright Water? What do you mean Bright Water?" said Joe. "Look, Todd, between the fire and all the commotion, I think I shot Crazy Fox. Let's get as far away as possible and then think about it."

They followed the road down the river and arrived at the town where they met Two Hawks. "Wow! What a ride that was," said Joe. "Let's stay here. I would like to sleep in a bed for a change." "I agree," said Todd. "What about you, Ron?" "I will go to where I was staying, and I will see you tomorrow." "Okay," said Joe. Todd said, "I could use ale. What about you, Joe?" "Yeah, but if we meet another Indian, let's stay away from him. I don't want another journey like that one again." "Yes, I know," said Todd. Joe said, "I wonder where Ron went." "I don't know."

"You know, Todd, I wonder where they come up with those names: Ron Two Hawks, Bright Water, Crazy-whatever-the-hell-his-name-was." "It was Crazy Fox," replied Todd, "but they probably think Davis is a funny name too." "Yeah, I guess so," replied Joe. "Let's go and get ale. I sure could use one." After awhile Joe said, "I think I will turn in. I will see you tomorrow, Todd." "Okay, bright and early, and then we will see what we will do."

The next morning, when they woke up, they found a beautiful day with the sun shining. Todd left his room first and went over to knock on Joe's door. Joe answered. "Good morning," said Todd, "it's a great day." "Yeah," said Joe. "I didn't get much sleep last night. It was too damn warm and humid. I wish they had an air conditioner in here." "A what?" said Todd. "A damn air conditioner," replied Joe. Todd said, "I don't know what you are talking about; you should have just opened the window." "Giving up the conversation, Joe said, "I will meet you downstairs."

When Joe came downstairs, Todd was sitting down, having a conversation with two men. Joe was thinking, "Here we go again. I wonder what kind of trouble we are going to have this time?" He walked over to the table, and Todd said, "This is Joseph and Seth. They are from Long Island down near New York." "Yeah," said Joe, "I know where Long Island is. So what?" "They say George Washington is there, and the British are moving in, and it looks like there will be trouble down there." "Look, Todd," said Joe, "do you think we should go down there? I mean it will be Bunker Hill all over again." Seth said, "There are some things we have to do." "Then why aren't you down there?" asked Joe. Joseph said, "We are on a mission from General Washington to see if we can get some men." "Oh, recruiting are you?" said Joe. "Is this an uncle kind of thing?" "Uncle who?" said Todd. "Uncle Sam, you know. You don't know. Forget it," Joe said.

After the two finished their meal, they went to meet Ron Two Hawks. "Look," said Todd, "we will travel inland for a couple of days to see what we can find out about this war that is happening down in Long Island. I am not sure what is going to happen, but if the British are involved, I know there will be trouble. Do you want to come with us, Ron?" Ron replied, "No, I will stay here." "Okay," said Todd. "If nothing happens, we will be back in a few days." Then the two got into their wagon with some provisions and headed out of town west.

About a day out they came upon a fort, and it was getting late in the afternoon. As they rode up to the fort, a guard yelled halt and came over with a rifle pointed at the two. Todd and Joe looked at each other. The guard asked, "Where are you going?" "Well," said Todd, "it is getting late, and we were wondering if you had any place where we could stay for the night." The guard with the rifle, stilled trained on the two, replied, "I will take you to our commander Clark." The guard said, "If you are British or Tory, you can consider yourself dead because Colonel Clark hates British, Indians, and Tories." "This is just great," said Joe. "We have to depend on how this guy feels at the moment."

As they went into the commander's office, they saw a giant of a man in about his midtwenties. "Where are you from?" asked Clark. "We are from Boston," said Joe. "What are you doing out this far?" "Well," said Joe, "we were just getting away from the British. We fought at Breed's Hill and Bunker Hill, and between the British and the Tories, we felt it was time to get out." "Yes," said Clark, "you fellows had a tough time at Bunker Hill." "Yes, we did," said Joe. "Since you are not with the British, you can stay for the night. Sergeant Collins, show these two to their quarters down in back." "Yes, sir. Come with me."

They took their wagon to their quarters, tied their horses to the post, and took their belongings inside. "What do you think of this guy, Todd?" "I don't know, but I will tell you one thing. I would not want to be against him." "I mean how about that guard?" "If you are a Tory or British, you are dead." "You know," said Joe, "it doesn't matter which side you are on, for they are both viscous bastards." "I guess you are right," said Todd, "but to get your freedom, sometimes I guess you have to be that way."

There was a knock on the door; Joe answered. "Yes, how can we help you?" The man looked around nervously. "Can I come in?" Joe looked at Todd. Todd said, "All right, but what do you want?" When the man came in, he said, "You fellows will be leaving here. Can you take something with you?" "What?" said Joe. The man pulled out a letter consisting of three sheets of paper and said, "Something happened last week, and I would like someone from outside this fort to know about it. I can't stay here any longer. If we get caught, we will both be shot." The man headed out the door.

Joe said, "What the hell do you mean shot?" The man did not answer and quickly opened the letter.

There is a very good crop in these parts, but soon comes desolation. Wherever we march, we keep our horses in the fields among the corn and oats so that the enemy if they gain the ground may have poor fare for them and their horses. And the Tories are very troublesome here. Many of them are taking up arms against us and lurk in the woods with the Indians, waiting for a scalp. The Tories have scalped many of their countrymen as there is a premium from the British for scalps. They are taken in by our scouts, and I believe some of them will swing very soon. The Indians treat both sexes with the same barbarity. They have killed whole families together: men, women, and children. A few days ago I rode a little distance from the camp where we had a few men stationed to guard the sick. I had just passed a place where a party of Indians happened to lay in waiting. I stopped at the first house and talked with an officer. As I sat upon my horse, out rushed those Indians and fired at some men swimming in the water and chased some as they were passing. Seeing this I screamed to a guard to pursue them and rode toward them. They discharged their pieces toward us and fired one ball into a house not far from the door where I was. Immediately upon our pursuing them they ran into the woods and escaped. They were in such haste that they had no time to get a scalp. They killed two: one was shot in the water; the other got out and ran a considerable distance before he fell. Since then they have cut off more of our men. One hundred Indians in the woods do more harm than one thousand troops and have been the death of many brave fellows.

Our colonel Clark has a dislike for Indians and Tories. He attacked a party of Indians returning from a scouting expedition. His men killed two Indians and wounded one. The rest were surrounded and taken bounded to the village, and after being placed in the street opposite the fort gate, they were put to death. Notwithstanding a truce that existed.

One of them was tomahawked immediately. The rest sitting on the ground in a ring and bound saw the fate of their comrades. What did they expect? The next Indian on his left sung his death song and was, in turn, tomahawked. The rest underwent the same. Only one was saved by the intercession of a rebel officer who pleaded for him. Telling Colonel Clark that the savage's father had formerly saved his life. The chief of this party, after having a hatchet stuck in his head, took it out himself and delivered it to the inhuman monster who struck him first. He repeated his stroke a second and a third time, after which the miserable spectacle was dragged by a rope around his neck to the river, thrown in, and suffered to spend still a few moments of his life in fruitless struggling.

Colonel Clark, reeking with the blood of these unhappy victims, came to the esplanade before the fort gate, where it was agreed to meet him and treat of the surrender of the garrison. He spoke with rapture of his late achievement while he washed the blood from his hands stained in this inhuman sacrifice.

Sincerely,
Henry Hamilton

Joe said, "Do you believe this son of a bitch? I knew there was something crazy about him. It's a good thing Ron did not come with us, for he would no doubt have killed us all. Look, Todd, tomorrow we will say thank you for his hospitality and get the hell out of here as fast as possible before he changes his mind and decides he doesn't like us for some reason, as if this crazy bastard needs a reason." Todd looked at the notes, still in disbelief. "I thought I heard something about this awhile ago, but you are right; we will get out and go back to town."

Joe said, "In reading history you never hear about the slaughter on both sides." "In reading history?" asked Todd. "Yeah, we'll talk about that some other time. Right now who does this guy want us to give this letter to?" Todd said, "I don't know, but let's get out of here early tomorrow." "Do you think this guy is some sort of a nut?" Todd said, "I don't think so. I thought I was rather involved with people that heard about this, but we will take this with us because I don't trust this Clark fellow. I would say for a colonel, he is unstable; and if he decides to go off, I don't want to be around." "I am with you," said Joe.

The next morning they woke up; gathered their belongings, loaded their wagon; and headed out of the fort, passing the sentry. Todd said, "Thank Colonel Clark for his hospitality." After they passed the gate and were out of the fort, Joe said, "This is like passing out of the gates of hell."

They headed back to town. "You know," said Joe, "first we are running from Indians so they won't scalp us; now we are heading back to town to warn Ron so he can go back to the Indians and warn them." Todd said, "You know, you can't paint everybody with the same brush." "I guess so," said Joe. "We had better tell Ron about what happened and find out who to give this letter to." "Yes," said Todd, "no matter what you think of the Indians, what this colonel Clark did was wrong. I can understand with the massacre what the Indians are doing, but this letter is too much; in this case Clark was wrong."

Arriving back in town they went to find Ron Two Hawks. Todd and Joe went to the tavern but did not find him there. They finally found Ron at the stable. Todd yelled over at Ron, "Hey, Ron, can we see you?" Ron came over. Joe said, "Ron, we were at a fort last night, and they have a colonel Clark. I will tell you I think he is a psycho; he does not like Indians. One guard said if you are an Indian or British, you are dead. I think he may be heading in the direction of your camp." "If you are right, I think I will take a ride back and see how they are doing. Check out where this Clarke is and what he is doing."

"What do you think your father will do?" "Well, like it or not, he will have to listen. Well, fellows," said Ron, "I will have to leave you good luck." Todd said, "Tell Bright Water that I hope she stays well." Ron smiled. "I will," he said. Ron got up upon his horse, waved, and rode toward the river.

"What are we going to do now?" Todd said, "We will head down the Hudson toward New York." "I heard there is trouble down there." "I know there is, but I think we should go down and find out." "Yeah," said Joe, "but I don't want to go through another Bunker Hill again." "I know," said Todd, "but if we can do our part to defeat, the British—" "Yeah," said Joe, "but I'll tell you even if we don't go, we will still beat the British." "You keep saying that," said Todd, "and I keep asking how do you know? Then you keep saying if you tell me I won't understand." "Look, Todd, if I told you I was from another time in the future, would you understand?" "No," said Todd. "Case closed," said Joe. "What do you mean case closed?" asked Todd. "Look, Todd," said Joe, "if I told you that in 1984 there will be little appreciation for what you are doing here.

"Yeah, you are fighting for your freedom; but kids will be listening to rock and roll, smoking pot, and in some cases robbing people. Some grown-ups are more interested in baseball standings and football standings and what the odds are on teams but will have no idea how they got to where they are." "You mean they bet on things the way the Iroquois did?" "Same thing, different time." "We have to do what we have to do in this time," said Todd. "So I think I will head down to New York." "I will go with you," said Joe, "against my better judgment." And so they loaded up their wagon and headed south toward New York.

As they rode down the Hudson, they saw a lot of British troops, and many barges were heading toward New York City. "I wonder what is going on," said Todd. "I don't know," said Joe, "but with all these Red Coats, it sure doesn't look good." "This looks worse than Bunker Hill," Joe was thinking to himself. "If these kids only knew what this revolution was really all about."

John Adams stood in the statehouse in Philadelphia and, among his fellow delegates to the second Continental Congress, began a suspenseful nomination for a commander in chief, deliberately withholding a name. Adams suddenly mentioned that his choice was "a gentleman from Virginia." His words elicited simultaneous but opposite reactions from two of the wealthiest men in the colonies; President John Hancock of Massachusetts, with his expectations of the command shattered, flushed and in "mortification and resentment." Virginia delegate George Washington, who wore the red and blue uniform of a militia colonel, dashed into the library adjoining the chamber "from his usual modesty."

The next day the Congress unanimously elected Washington, and the tall Virginian stood before the suavely resigned Hancock and with slow dignity read his speech of acceptance:

Mr. President, though I am truly sensible of the high honor done me in this appointment, yet I feel great distress from a consciousness that my abilities and military experience may not be equal to the extensive and important trust. However, as the Congress desires, I will enter upon the momentous duty and exert every power I possess in their service for the support of the glorious cause. I beg they will accept my most cordial thanks for this distinguished testimony of their approbation. But lest some unlucky event should happen unfavorable to my reputation, I beg it be remembered by every gentleman in the room that I this declare with the utmost sincerity I do not think myself equal to the command I am honored with. As to pay, sir, beg leave to assure the Congress that as no pecuniary consideration could have tempted me to have accepted this arduous employment at the expense of my domestic ease and happiness. I do not wish to make any profit from it; I will keep an exact account of my expenses; those I doubt not they will discharge, and that is all I desire.

Washington probably had hoped to lead the Virginia forces. At forty-three he had not soldiered actively for eighteen years, and his entire military experience consisted of five years of leading small units in wilderness fighting. He turned to Patrick Henry who he confided, "Remember, Mr. Henry, what I tell you. From the day I enter upon the command of the American armies, I date my fall and the ruin of my reputation." He then departed for Cambridge and entered upon his command two weeks after the Battle of Bunker Hill.

The predominant military effort was under the commanders in chief Washington and Howe. Opposed one another the Americans saved Boston and held the South but lost New York, Canada, and most of New Jersey and a vast amount of munitions and supplies. The British strategic design for the year was threefold. First, Boston was to be evacuated. Howe was to establish his new base in New York City where the advantages were a strong Loyalist population and a superb harbor for the all-powerful navy, which would control the Hudson River and so isolate New England from the other colonies. Second, General Carleton in Canada was to drive out the Americans still besieging Quebec (since their failure to capture it in 1775) and perhaps unite with Howe in New York. Third, a limited force of regulars was to accompany a cadre corps of officers to the south for the purpose of creating an army from among the king's supporters in the Carolinas.

General Clinton left Boston for North Carolina. At Cape Fear, Clinton learned of the Loyalists' defeat at Moiré's Creek Bridge, North Carolina, and consequently selected South Carolina as a more promising field to assist a Loyalist uprising. He struck at Charleston. Although reinforced from Ireland by troops under General Charles Cornwallis and a fleet under Commodore Peter Parker, Clinton's attack failed. The entire expeditionary force joined Howe on Staten Island, New York, and the South saw no Red Coats for two years. When Howe pulled out of Boston, he went to Halifax, Nova Scotia, which was an unsatisfactory rest camp. Two months later he sailed for New York and landed on Staten Island where reinforcements from England reached him. He had assembled thirty-two thousand troops and an enormous fleet of transports and warships. The British army retired behind their entrenchment.

The British army took their position directly in front of Washington's position in full array of the American entrenchment, which was so weak that it is lucky the British general did not attempt to storm the American troops. General Washington was fully aware of the perilous situation of the division of his army, so he immediately convened a council of war at which the propriety of retiring to New York was decided on.

After sustaining incessant fatigue and constant watchfulness for two days and nights—attended by heavy rain, exposed every moment to an attack from a vastly superior force in front and to be cut off from the possibility of a retreat to New York by the fleet, which might enter the East River at night—General Washington commenced recrossing. To move so large a body of troops with all their necessary appendages across a river a full mile wide with a rapid current in the face of a victorious, well-disciplined army nearly three times as numerous as Washington's and a fleet capable of stopping the navigation so that not a boat could have passed over seemed to present a big problem.

But in the face of these difficulties, the commander in chief so arranged his business that at ten o'clock at night his troops began to retire from the lines in such a manner that no chasm was made in the lines. As one regiment left their station on guard, the remaining troops moved to the right and left and filled up the vacancies. General Washington took his station at the ferry and superintended the embarkation of the troops. It was one of the most anxious busy nights. As the dawn of the next day approached, troops in the trenches became very anxious for their safety. When the dawn appeared there were several regiments still on duty. At this time a very dense fog began to rise, and it seemed to settle in a peculiar manner over both encampments. The fog was so dense that you could scarcely see a man six yards ahead. When the sun rose, the orders were to leave the lines before they reached the ferry. The commander in chief sent one of his aides to order the regiment to repair again to their former station on the lines.

Colonel Chester immediately faced to the right about and returned where men tarried until the sun had risen, but the fog remained as dense as ever. Finally, the second order arrived for the regiment to retire, and they very joyfully bid those trenches a long adieu. When the men reached Brooklyn ferry the boats had not returned from their last trip. But they very soon appeared and took the whole regiment over to New York. General Washington was on the ferry stairs when he stepped into one of the last boats.

CHAPTER TEN

New York and Brooklyn

The boats were well on their way to New York when the British reached Brooklyn. Todd and Joe were pulling into New York just as the ferries were pulling in to New York. "Holy shit," said Joe, not finishing his sentence. "Look at the water and all those boats. I wonder what is happening." "I don't know," said Todd. As they moved toward the docks, watching soldiers disembark, they were amazed as a tall man stepped off the boat. "Son of a bitch, that's George Washington. I can't believe this. I used to see his picture in history books in school. I'll tell you this. He looks better than he did in the books."

Todd said, "What are you talking about?" "History books! Look out farther. Those are British boats. This does not look good. I think we will be under attack soon." "Look," said Todd, "let's put this wagon somewhere and see what is going on." "Okay," said Joe. Todd said, "Look at this fog coming off the water." "Yes," said Joe, "let's walk down toward the water." "We had better watch out," said Todd. "There are a lot of Tories in this area, a lot of enemies around here. I feel that is why there are a lot of British soldiers.

"It will be interesting to see what happens." "Interesting my ass," said Joe. "We could be right in another Bunker Hill or Saratoga where we almost got shot a couple of times." Todd said, "We are dressed like a lot of the locals, so maybe we can find out something and report it to the Americans." "Damn, you mean like spies?" Todd replied, "Something like that." "I don't think so," said Joe. "Are you crazy? We have no idea what the hell we would be doing. From what I gather right now, we don't know who the hell our friends or enemies are. If we don't know what we are doing we could be shot by either side." Todd said, "We could sort of feel out the situation and see what happens." "Look, Todd, what do you mean feel out the situation? The way this feels and looking at those ships out in the harbor, we could be in a war very shortly." "Yes," said Todd, "but if we can help in any way, I think we should.

"After all, when we started, we were going to do all we could to help fight the British. Those bastards were stealing the living of the residents with their taxes so that bastard the king could sit fat and happy on his fat ass on that big throne in England." "Look, Todd, what makes you think years from now it will be any different except it will be politicians that will be stealing your taxes? If you could see in the future, you will see that money graft and all those wonderful things will not change. It will just be different."

As they walked down the street, they saw a pub. They walked in and looked around. Todd said, "Let's see if we can get ale and listen and see what is going on." They sat down and listened to two men talking. One was saying to another, "I hear enlistments are down and conscription out of the question. England is looking beyond their shores for soldiers to fight here. Lord North, the prime minister, first tried to hire twenty thousand mercenaries from Empress Catherine of Russia who rejected his overtures without 'civility to answer in her own hand.' When the Dutch declined any part of a deal, North turned to Germany, traditionally Europe's stock farm manpower. Frederick the Great of Prussia scornfully denounced the practice of selling men like cattle. That left some three hundred petty German princes, all of them greedy for England's blood money.

"'Treaties' were signed with various courts: Brunswick, Hesse-Cassel, Hesse-Hanau, Waldeck, Anspach, Bayreuth, and Anhalt-Zerbst. All together, thirty thousand Germans will fight this war. They call them Hessians because the best and most [sixteen thousand] soldiers come from Hesse-Cassel, which is in conformity with this contract between King George III and Frederick II, the landgrave."

"See what I mean about that bastard king trying to hire thugs to grind us under with Germans?" "Yeah," said Joe, "but down the line that will not be the only time. We will have trouble with the Germans, believe me. In the future they will be worse."

In the far corner they began to sing the song of the day "Yankee Doodle." They sang "Nankey Doodle came to town riding on a pony with a feather in his hat upon a macaroni."

A surgeon in the British army at Albany in 1775 composed a song to that air, which was in derision of the uncouth appearance of the New England troops assembled there and called it "Yankee "instead of Nankey Doodle." The air was popular as martial music. The change in spelling of "Yankee" was not made until after the revolution.

While the British were still in Boston and after the arrival of Washington at Cambridge in 1775, some poet wrote the following piece. In derision of the New England people, this original "Yankee Doodle" was the song of the revolution.

There began to be tension in the room because there were some Tories and some British soldiers and some Americans. Joe said, "Never mind, we could have a war right here." "I don't think so, Joe; they're letting off a little steam." "Yeah, but I don't want to get In the middle of that steam," as they went back into a corner and sat down at a table with two young men.

They looked over at the corner where the men were singing, but the two men were not paying attention; instead they were talking about a student at Yale, David Bushnell, who had demonstrated that gunpowder could be exploded underwater.

"Considering Bushnell's machine as the first of its kind, I think it will be pronounced to be remarkably complete throughout in its construction and that such an invention furnishes evidence of those resources and creative powers that rank him as a mechanical genius of the first order. I shall first attend to a description of this machine and afterward to a relation of the enterprise now." One man said, "How is the damn thing made?" The other man said, "It is composed of several pieces of large oak timber, scooped out and fitted together, and its shape compares to that of a round clam.

"It was bound around thoroughly with iron bands, the seams were corked, and the whole was smeared over with tar so as to prevent the possibility of the admission of water inside. It has a capacity to contain one engineer, who might stand or sit and enjoy sufficient elbowroom for its proper management. The top or head is made of a metallic composition, exactly suited to its body, so as to be watertight; this opened upon hinges and formed the entrance to the machine.

"Six small pieces of thick glass were inserted in this head for the admission of light: in a clear day and clear seawater, says my informer, he can see to read at a depth of three fathoms. To keep it upright and properly balanced, seven hundred pounds of lead were fastened to its bottom, two hundred pounds of which were so contrived as to be discharged at any moment to increase the buoyancy of the machine. But to enable the navigator when underwater to rise or sink at pleasure, there were two forcing pumps, by which water could be pressed out at the bottom and also a spring by applying the foot to which a passage was formed for the admission of water. If the pumps should get deranged, then resort was had to letting off the lead ballast from the bottom.

"The navigator steered by a rudder, the tiller of which passed through the back of the machine at a water joint. In one side was fixed a small pocket compass with two pieces of shining wood [sometimes called foxfire] crossed upon its north point and a single piece upon the last point. In the night, when no light entered through the head, this compass thus lighted was all that served to guide the helmsman in his course.

"This ingenious inventor also provided a method for determining the depth of water at which the machine might be at any time. This was achieved by means of a glass tube twelve inches in length and about four in diameter, which was also attached to the side of the machine. This tube enclosed a piece of cork that rose with the descent of the machine and fell with its ascent. One inch rise of cork denoted a depth of about one fathom, the principle upon which such a result was produced.

"The principle upon which such a result was produced and also the mechanical contrivance of this tube entirely escaped the observation of Mr. Lee, amid the hurry and constant anxiety attendant upon such a perilous navigation. But not the least ingenious part of this curious machine was that by which the horizontal motion was communicated to it. The object was effected by means of two oars or paddles, formed precisely like the arms of a windmill, which revolved perpendicularly upon an axletree that projected in front. This axletree passed into the machine at a water joint and was furnished with a crank by which it was turned. The navigator being seated inside with one hand labored at the crank and with the other steered by the tiller.

"The effect of the paddles so constructed and turned in the manner stated by propelling or rather drawing a body after them underwater will readily occur to anyone without explanation. These paddles were but twelve inches long, and about four wide two smaller paddles of the description also projected near the head provided with a crank inside by which the ascent of the machine could be assisted. By vigorous turning of the crank, the machine could be propelled at a rate of about three miles an hour in still water. "When beyond the reach of danger or observation of an enemy, the machine was suffered to float with its head just rising from the water's surface; and while in this situation, air was constantly admitted through three small orifices in the head, which were closed when a descent was commenced. The efficient part of this engine of devastation, its magazine, remains to be spoken of.

"This was separate and distinct from the machine. It was shaped like an egg, and like the machine itself was composed of solid pieces of oak scooped out and in the same manner fitted together and secured by iron bands. One hundred and thirty pounds of gunpowder, a clock, and a gun lock provided with a good flint that would not miss fire were the apparatus, which it enclosed. This magazine was attached to the back of the machine a little above the rudder by means of a screw. One end of which passed into the magazine, and there operated as a stop upon the movements of the clock while its other end entered the machine. This screw could be withdrawn from the magazine by which the latter was immediately detached and the clock commenced going.

"The clock was set for running twenty or thirty minutes at the end of which time the lock struck and fired the powder, and in the meantime the man can escape. But the most difficult point of all to be gained was to fasten this magazine to the bottom of a ship; here they are saying difficulty can arise, which, and which alone, as will appear in the ensuing narrative, could defeat the successful operations of this warlike apparatus.

"They say Mr. Bushnell contrived this very sharp iron screw was made to pass out from the top of the machine, communicating inside by a water joint. It was provided with a crank at its lower end by which the engineer was to force it into the ship's bottom. This screw was next to be disengaged from the machine and left adhering to the ship's bottom.

"A line leading from this screw to the magazine kept the latter in its destined position for blowing up the vessel. Mr. Bushnell said I shall now proceed to the account of the first attempt that will be made to destroy a ship of war, all the facts of which are already stated. I received from the bold adventurer himself."

"Wow," said Joe, "can you believe this conversation? It sounds like they are talking about a damn submarine. I'll be damned."

"Admiral Howe lay with a formidable British fleet in New York Bay a little above the narrows, and a numerous British force upon Staten Island, commanded by General Howe, threatened annihilation to the troops under George Washington. Mr. Bushnell requested General Parsons of the American army to furnish him with two or three men to learn the navigation of his new machine with a view of destroying some of the enemy's shipping. General Parsons immediately sent for Lee, then a sergeant, and two others who had offered their services to go on board of a fireship, and on Bushnell's request being made known to them, they enlisted themselves under him for this novel piece of service.

"The party went up to Long Island Sound with the machine and made various experiments with it in the different harbors along shore. After having become pretty thoroughly acquainted with the mode of navigating it, they returned through the sound, but during their absence the enemy had got possession of Long Island and Governor's Island.

"They therefore had the machine conveyed by land across from New Rochelle to the Hudson River and afterward arrived with it at New York. The British fleets now lay to the north of Staten Island with a large number of transports and were the objects against which this new mode of warfare was destined to act. The first serene night was fixed upon for the execution of this perilous enterprise, and Sergeant Lee was to be the engineer. After a lapse of a few days, a favorable night arrived. At eleven o'clock a party embarked in two or three whaleboats with Bushnell's boat machine in tow. They rowed down as near the fleet as they dared; when Sergeant Lee entered the machine, he was cast off, and the boats returned.

"Lee now found the ebb tide rather too strong and, before he was aware, had drifted down past the men of war. He, however, immediately got the machine about, and by hard labor at the crank for the space of five glasses by the ship's bells [two and one half hours], he arrived under the stern of one of the ships at about slack water.

"Day had now dawned, and by the light of the moon, he could see people on board and heard their conversation. This was the moment for diving and accordingly closed the overhead, let in the water, and descended under the ship's bottom. He next paddled along to a different part of her bottom, but in this maneuver he made a deviation and instantly arose to the water's surface on the east side of the ship, exposed to the increasing light of morning and in imminent hazard of being discovered.

"He immediately made another descent with a view of making one more trial, but the fast approach of day—which would expose him to the enemy's boats and render his escape difficult, if not impossible—deterred him. He concluded that the best generalship would be to commence an immediate retreat. He now had before him a distance of more than four miles to traverse, but the tide was favorable.

"At Governor's Island great danger awaited him, for his compass having got out of order, he was under the necessity of looking out from the top of the machine very frequently to ascertain his course and at best made a very irregular zigzag track.

"The soldiers at Governor's Island spied the machine, and curiosity drew several hundreds upon the parapet to watch its motions. At last a party came down to the beach, shoved off a barge, and rowed toward it. At that moment Sergeant Lee thought he saw his certain destruction and as a last act of defense let go the magazine, expecting that they would seize that likewise and thus all would be blown to hell together.

"Providence, however, otherwise decreed it. The enemy, after approaching within fifty or sixty yards of the machine and seeing the magazine detached, began to suspect a Yankee trick, took alarm, and returned to the island.

"Approaching the city he soon made a signal; the boats came to him and brought him safe and sound to the shore. The magazine, meanwhile, had drifted past Governor's Island into the East River where it exploded with tremendous violence, throwing large waves and pieces of wood that composed it high into the air. General Putnam, with many officers, stood onshore spectators of this explosion.

"In a few days the American army evacuated New York, and the machine was taken up the North River. Lee afterward made another attempt upon a frigate that lay opposite Bloomingdale. His object now was to fasten the magazine to the stern of the ship, close at the water's edge. But while attempting this, the watch discovered him, raised an alarm, and compelled him to abandon his enterprise. He then endeavored to get under the frigate's bottom, but in this he failed, having descended too deep. This terminated his experiments."

"Wow," said Joe, "this sounds like a movie. I can't believe a submarine with all this stuff going on in whatever time I am in." Todd said, "What's a movie?" "Never mind," said Joe. Todd said, "That is something we should try." "What do you mean try?" said Joe. "I can hardly swim. I did not want to go on that damn canoe ride with those Indians chasing that moose. Now you are talking about going underwater. Are you crazy?"

As they left the tavern and walked down the street, it was now dusk. Todd said, "Look, I will be right back. You stay here, for I just want to get the feel of just what is going on." After about twenty minutes Joe was now thinking, "I wonder what is going on. Todd should be back by now. He has his pistol with him, and since I haven't heard any shots, so I guess he is all right."

Joe then he heard something behind him. "Well, now what do we have here?" He quickly turned around and saw a man with a pistol aimed right at him. "Who the hell are you?" asked Joe. "A damn American." "What do you know, I am your executioner." "My what?" said Joe.

"We have been shooting Americans. You know that you are traitors to the king." Before he could say anything, the man pointed the gun at Joe's head and ready to pull the trigger. A shot rang out. The man's eyes rolled, and he fell to the ground dead. Standing behind them stood Todd with a smoking pistol.

Joe looked at himself to see if he was shot but found he had not. Todd asked what that was all about. "I don't know," said Joe. "All I know is that the man came up behind me, and the asshole was going to kill me. He probably was one of those damn Tories or something." Todd said, "Let's see if he had any papers or identification on him." They rolled the body over, and out fell a letter.

Friends, I am now in New York where I promised to write you a chapter about pretty girls. Before, however, reading my narrative to a lady, examine it carefully so as to see if there is any danger of causing future trouble between my dear countrywomen and me. Should you decide against it, have mercy on me and upset the ink stand on the entire chapter! The ladies of this vicinity and as far as Boston and New York are slender of erect carriage and without being strong and plump. They have small pretty feet, good hands and arms, a very white skin, and a healthy color in the face, which requires no further embellishment. I have seen a few disfigured pockmarks for inoculation against small pox, which has been in vogue for many years.

They have also exceedingly white teeth, pretty lips, and sparkling laughing eyes. In connection with these charms, they have a natural bearing, essentially unrestrained, with open frank countenances, and much native assurance. They are great admirers of cleanliness and keep themselves well shod. They frizz their hair every day and gather it up on the back of the head into a chignon, at the time puffing it up in front. They generally walk about with their heads uncovered and sometimes but not often wear some light fabric on their hair. Now and some country nymph has her hair flowing down behind her, braiding it with a piece of ribbon. Should they go out even though they are living in a hut, they throw a silk wrap about themselves and put on gloves.

They have a charming way of wearing this wrap by means of which they manage to show a portion of small white elbow. They also put on some well-made and stylish sun bonnet from beneath, which their roguish eyes have a most fascinating way of meeting yours. In the English colonies the beauties have fallen in love with red silk or woolen wraps. Dressed in this manner a girl will walk, run, dance about you, and bid you a friendly good morning or give you a saucy answer according to what you may have said to her.

At all the places through which we passed dozens of girls were met on the road who either laughed at us mockingly or now and then roguishly offered us an apple accompanied by a little courtesy. At first we thought they were girls from the city or at least from the middle classes, but lo and behold! They were daughters of poor farmers. Notwithstanding the many pretty things I have said about the gender sex in this country, I must still give my loved countrywomen the credit of possessing certain gentle, lovable, and languishing qualities, which lend additional attractions to their charms but which are entirely lacking in the beauties to be found here.

Most perfectly formed and beautiful nymphs are to be seen on all sides, but to find one endowed with all the attractions of one of the graces is a very difficult thing. Enough of this, however.

"What do you think?" Todd asked. "This is a German son of a bitch. They are here. I think they have landed this fellow here, and I believe he is a scout. I think the action will soon begin." Todd then shot the man again in the head. "What the hell did you do that for? The man is already dead." Todd said in a low voice, "Just making sure."

Admiral Howe reached New York "Black Dick Howe," brother of the general, arriving in New York from England with supplies and reinforcements, having first put in at deserted Halifax. With the troops from Charleston defeated he joined Howe on Staten Island. The principal part of the fleet carrying 7,800 "German mercenaries" arrived in New York from England, swelling the troops under General Howe to approximately 32,000, the largest expeditionary force of the eighteenth century.

Washington, anticipating the attack on New York, had moved nineteen thousand troops into the area. Howe won Long Island in a day's fighting and after two battles on Manhattan forced Washington to retreat into action, fought on the southern tip of the island. Howe expertly mounted a frontal assault against the enemy's right flank and then circled his left. Panicked the Americans fled to prepared positions at Brooklyn Heights.

Howe defeated a small portion (about 5,000) of the American army. Estimated casualties: Americans, 200 killed and wounded, 812 prisoners, including Generals Alexander and Sullivan; British, 377 killed or wounded.

Howe refused to storm their works despite the pleadings of his advance troops. The Germans acquired a reputation for cruelty by bayoneting surrendered Americans.

Washington moved to Westchester to avoid being flanked. At White Plains Washington moved back five miles. At this time Howe resumed the offensive by landing nine thousand troops at Kip's Bay (Thirty-fourth Street). By nightfall the British control the southern half of Manhattan Kip's Bay estimated casualties: Americans, 35 killed and wounded, 300 prisoners; British, 3 killed 18 wounded.

After a naval bombardment routed the American defenders from their flimsy earthworks the American general Israel Putnam evacuated New York City and brought undetected 3,500 troops north to join the rest of the army at fortified Harlem Heights (125th Street). A hot two-hour battle began as an American reconnaissance mission climaxed in a buckwheat field where 1,300 Americans compelled 5,000 British before Washington called a halt, fearing the onset of a general engagement for which he was ill prepared. The victory boosted American morale and impressed upon Howe the enemy's ability to fight in the open as well as behind defenses.

Joe and Todd were now in the middle of the navy bombardment. As they were trying to make it through the streets, a shell from the navy ship hit a building, causing a big explosion with the whole building blowing up in a ball of fire. Two houses blew up with pieces of debris flying everywhere. Joe and Todd were running for their lives with cannon fire from the ships and fire and destruction all around them as the Germans hit the shore.

Some soldiers, seeing Joe and Todd, started shooting. They darted behind houses and fences. Two soldiers were following us. "Son of a bitch," said Joe, "let's shoot back. There are only two of them and two of us." "We will," said Todd, "when we get far away from the rest of this force that is hitting shore."

As the invasion was starting, the British and Germans were hitting the shore in full force with fire from the ships backing them up. With buildings blowing up and the two Germans chasing them, Todd and Joe were now in smoke from the fires and fog from the weather. At this point they could hardly see each other.

"Damn it, Todd, will you shoot?" "How the hell am I going to shoot when I can hardly see anything?" said Todd. Just then they heard something. One of the Germans saw an outline and fired. Seeing the flash Todd shot back, mortality wounding one of them; the other man turned and ran. The two walked toward where they thought the shooting came from and found the dead soldier with the other one gone. They thought he would come back. Todd said, "I don't think so because he must have been a young German soldier. If he wasn't, he would of stayed and come after us. Anyway we had better get out of here." "I am with you," said Joe.

They headed out with the smoke and fog as much undercover as possible. Now the battle was in full force; trading shots from both sides could be heard in the streets. Todd said, "Let's see if we can get back to the wagon if the horses haven't taken off by now." "Right," said Joe.

There were people scurrying everywhere as they moved from one place to another. Bullets were ricocheting off the buildings and fences. Todd said, "I think we should try to get back to see if we can find where Washington's line is." Joe replied, "Why don't we stay away from either line? That way we know how we stand." Todd said, "The only problem is that if we do that, we won't know which side that is coming down on us. If we are alone, that leaves us suspect to the Tories, to the British, and to the Americans. This way we will know who are friends are."

The two were now heading for Westchester to see if they could connect with Washington's men. Joe was thinking, "I always wanted to go to New York to see the Red Sox and the Yankees play or the place they call Radio City or go to the rock places. I finally made it, and where the hell am I? In a war with George Washington and the damn British!"

Todd said, "Let's see if we can find our wagon if the horses haven't taken off by now or somebody hasn't stolen the damn thing." They finally found the wagon and horses intact. "I'll tell you one thing, Todd," said Joe. "These horses must have seen a lot of action because we have been in three battles and raids, and they are still where we left them each time."

As they climbed into the wagon, "Hold on there" was the command they heard. Todd and Joe looked around only to see two men with rifles pointed at them. "Get down, you two. That wagon is now ours." Two men approached the wagon; got real close; and as one man was about to climb up onto the wagon, Joe let go with a punch, knocking the man to the ground. Todd grabbed the reins; the horses reared up, knocking the other man to the ground with his rifle firing in the air as he was falling. Joe and Todd raced off, leaving the two would-be bandits on the ground stunned.

Racing to head north the horses were at full speed with buildings on fire and cannons and rifle shots everywhere. Todd said, "I hope we get out of this alive." "Yeah," said Joe. "Sometimes with this adventure I wonder if I am alive." "What do you mean if you are alive?" "Never mind," said Joe, "Just keep going. Right now everything is so crazy around here with these damn shells from those ships and the bullets from the people onshore. You know, Todd, I have been in a lot of trouble in my life, but I have never been shot at so much or chased as I have since I have come to this time and place.

"How I got here I don't know; sometimes it so peaceful. I have never seen anything like it. Another time it is like one ongoing nightmare. With our luck the sons of bitches we stole the wagon from will show up, and they will start shooting at us too." Todd said, "We will have to be careful from now on because we won't know who our enemies or our friends are." "Wonderful," replied Joe, "just wonderful."

Todd said, "It looks like the American army is retreating the way the British are coming onshore. This looks like Boston all over again," said Joe. Todd said, "The way things turned out, the Americans won that battle or at least drove a lot of the British out, but this situation looks different. This looks like we may lose this battle. It looks like there are too many British sympathizers around here, and with the Germans it looks like they are hitting this area with full force.

"I have to figure this out," said Todd. "If we ride too fast, we may attract attention and be shot because they will think that we are the enemy or stole something. If we get stopped, we better have some good answers, or we will be shot. If we do get stopped, we had better act like Tories and say something about the king, and we must win against the Americans or something like that." "I would rather shoot the bastards," said Joe. "We may have to do that if it is one person. If the odds are against us, you will do as I say unless you have a better idea." "No," said Joe, "I don't." Todd said, "From now on until we get back to the American lines, we will have to watch our step along the way and not trust anybody. If we can get back to the American lines, we will be okay."

"Right now I feel surrounded by these damn people, and if we run into the Germans first, those bastards will shoot first and forget about asking any questions." Joe was thinking, "We have had a lot of fights with the Germans shooting at us now and in World War One. I could really write a history book. If I wrote this, they would not believe it anyhow." "A history book," replied Todd, "what do you mean a history book?" "Well," said Joe, "you know, for the future." "The future," said Todd. "If we don't get moving, we will have no future. It looks like the British forces are going to overrun this town.

"I wonder what General Washington is going to do. Now I mean there's fighting going on, but I will tell you right now it does not look like we are winning." "I guess you are right," replied Joe. "I hope we get out of this one."

Howe saw an opportunity to trap a large number of Patriot troops in Brooklyn. In August British troops landed on Long Island in front of American lines. Howe surrounded the patriots' forward positions in the Battle of Long Island. However, the slow-moving Howe paused before attacking again, enabling the remainder of the Americans to escape. In September, Washington sent Captain Nathan Hale behind British lines to obtain information about British positions on Long Island. (Hale was caught and hanged for spying. But before being hanged, he reportedly said, "I only regret that I have but one life to lose for my country.")

As the two were riding slowly, they saw a number of solders. They did not look like British, so they pulled up to them causally as if to be ready for whichever side they would encounter. One of the groups saw them and approached them with a rifle trained on them. Joe said, "Oh shit, here we go." The soldier said, "Where are you two going?" "Well," said Todd, "you look like Americans." "We do. Do we? Well, you are right.

"We are and under General Washington's orders. We are to defend Fort Washington. Like I said before, where are you going?" "Well," said Todd, "we were heading north to see if we could get to the American lines." "Why? Are you with Washington's army?" "No," replied Todd, "but we are Americans, and we would like to help if we could." "You would! You come to the right place, for we need all the volunteers we could find. So get some grub and come with us."

"Where are we going?" said Todd. "To Fort Washington," said the soldier, "and we could use your wagon to transport some supplies." "This is great," said Joe. "We were just trying to get to the front to be safe, and now we are in the fucking army going to defend the fort something." "Great idea," Todd stopped Joe. "If we don't go along with them, we will probably be shot for spying." "I will tell you, Todd, I don't like it one damn bit."

The soldiers started for Fort Washington along with Joe, Todd, and their wagon loaded with supplies. Joe said to Todd, "What the hell is going on here? We are heading in the wrong direction. Aren't we supposed to be heading more north than this?" Joe was right; the two were in their wagon loaded with supplies thrown on by the soldiers and were heading toward Fort Washington. Surrounded by soldiers and their captain as they came upon the fort, Todd had a bad feeling. He said to Joe, "I don't like this. It looks like we are the only troops." "Yeah," said Joe, "but it looks like by looking around at least a thousand people in this party." "Still I don't know," replied Todd.

As the wagon headed for Fort Washington, Todd said, "I think we are going to be in the middle of a battle, and I have a feeling we are going to be outnumbered." The wagon pulled up to the front of the fort; they encountered a guard. Then the gates opened, and the forces moved in with two soldiers riding alongside of the wagon. Todd said, "Now I really don't like this." "What the hell are we in for?" Todd said, "You know, I think we are in for a lot of trouble because I think this is going to be the front line for the attack." Joe asked, "Where the hell is Washington?" "The way things are beginning to look, it appears that this garrison is going to hold off the attack while Washington retreats. These people will either fight to the death or be captured." Joe said, "You are kidding, aren't you?" "No," said Todd, "right now that is the way it looks. Just take a look around. We saw in the water there were a lot of ships and on the ground there are a lot of British and Germans. We sure don't see our full army, and we don't see Washington and his forces. What I see is a lot of trouble." Joe said, "Shit, we could have another Alamo." "Another what?" said Todd. "Never mind," said Joe, "but it isn't good."

The captain then said, "Attention, soldiers, we are here to make sure that we hold off the British forces. It will be a long fight. I might not be able to say this again, but good luck; and if we don't come out of this, I want to tell you, you are all good men, and it was a pleasure fighting with you." "What the hell does he mean if we don't get out of this?" said Todd. "Like I said, another Alamo," said Joe. "There you go again. What is an Alamo?" asked Todd. "In another time, another fort, another war, and when the fight ended nobody in the fort made it out alive. What the hell are we going to do?" asked Joe. "I don't know at this point, but we have to get ourselves the wagon out of here somehow."

Meanwhile General Howe walked into his quarters and said, "Gentlemen I think that an attack on the fort as soon as possible will give us an advantage and will drive Washington to surrender or will defeat his troops and end this thing right here." One of his captains said, "General, if we take this fort, what will we gain?" "I think I just told you what we will gain. So get your troops ready, so we get this thing proceeding as fast as we can."

The British forces started its attack on Fort Washington. The battle had begun, and by this time the battle had inflicted a crushing defeat on Washington's army. To escape the onslaught Washington withdrew his colonel forces from Brooklyn Heights to Manhattan. Less than two weeks later he decided to evacuate New York City rather than be trapped in Lower Manhattan. However, before he withdrew from the city Washington prepared fortifications in Upper Manhattan and was able to repulse the British army in the Battle of Harlem Heights.

In the face of the advancing British forces of General Howe, Washington evacuated his main force from Manhattan Island, leaving behind a garrison at Fort Washington, and marched to White Plains. In the Battle of White Plains the British inflicted heavy casualties on Washington's army, whereupon Washington slipped away westward to North Castle.

The battle was now becoming heavy. Todd and Joe were shooting from the wall, trying to figure a way out. Joe said, "Look, Todd, there's the wagon over by the side wall." Todd said, "I will be right back." With fighting all around him Todd headed for the wagon. When he got there, he found everything still intact: the two rifles and pistols, which in their haste the soldiers failed to touch. Todd returned to the wall and said, "Everything's still there. The soldiers grabbed all the equipment of theirs off the wagon and did not touch anything of ours."

Howe's forces were now driving toward the fort. With all the action going on, Todd and Joe started slowly toward the wagon. In their hurry the soldiers did not even unhitch the horses. Todd said, "I don't know what we are going to do now. I feel like we are going to be deserting." "Deserting? What the hell do you mean deserting? We never even asked to join this group, never even volunteered. They volunteered us. I will tell you as plain as I can, Todd. I want to get the hell out of here."

By now Howe's forces were at the front gates. Todd and Joe got slowly up on the wagon seat, and with so much action going on no one even noticed. "Now what?" said Joe. "I don't know yet," said Todd, "but I will tell you one thing: whatever we are going to do, we better do it fast."

Joe said, "So far these horses have not moved or gone crazy or anything like that." "Like I said, Joe, they must have been used to a lot of action because most of the action we have been in, they for the most part have been good, quiet, and have not run away." Just then a gate was blown open, and the fighting was now inside the fort. Todd started the wagon slowly and then at full gallop heading for the open gate. There was shooting and hand—to-hand combat as the wagon moved through the gates. Then soldiers started to shoot at them. One soldier said, "Those little traitor bastards, shoot them." With shots flying all around them, ducking so they would not be hit, they ran into a British force. Raising their hands Todd said, "We are Tories. We were held captive by those Americans." The British soldier said, "Get the hell out of here," and yelled, "Let them go; they are on our side."

Howe was beginning to drive Washington's forces from New York City and slowly pursued the Americans as they retreated toward White Plains, New York. His hesitation cost the British a chance to crush Washington's army. But other Patriots' forces remained on Manhattan Island to defend Fort Washington. The fort fell to Howe and the United Kingdom. They captured nearly three thousand Americans. New York City remained in British hands until the war ended. When Washington shifted his forces to New York City after, the Red Coats withdrew from Boston.

He did not expect to win New York City, but he wanted to make the British fight for it. To defend the city Patriot troops fortified Brooklyn Heights, an area of high ground on the western tip of Long Island. After Howe had seized a hill the British general, unable to bring his Bunker Hill to a decisive battle, moved south and captured Forts Washington and Lee on the Hudson, preliminary to an invasion of New Jersey. Washington attempted a defense but was compelled to flee across to New Jersey while his army dwindled to five thousand and less when these ragged Patriots crossed the Delaware River into Pennsylvania. Howe confidently closed the campaign.

Joe said to Todd, "How did we pull that one off? I thought we were goners." Joe said, "Look back at that fort. I think the British will take that fort and everybody in it in a few hours. We have to head north and see if we can find Washington's troops. This time let's not have anybody talk us into joining anything until we know what the hell we are getting into."

They continued to move slowly through New York City again, not sure which side they will run into. Joe was thinking, "This must be a dream; otherwise, there is no way we get out of that fort, for we are the luckiest damn two that ever lived." Joe was thinking, "What a sight with British ships in the harbor and smoke billowing up into the sky from burning buildings. I don't know what the hell is going on, but let's try to outrun the British and see if we can catch George Washington's troops.

"This whole damn thing is crazy. If we ever get off this crazy merry-go-round, I will have to someday get back to the harbor in Boston and see if I can find the other two." Looking around Todd said, "Don't look now, but there are two men following us." "Yeah," said Joe, "I wonder what side they are on."

At this time Todd had a pistol under his jacket hidden in his belt. Joe asked, "What are you going to do with that pistol?" "Just in case," replied Todd. "Just in case what?" asked Joe. "If we run into trouble with this bunch," replied Todd. Joe then asked, "What the hell are you going to do with that damn thing?" "In that case," said Todd, "I will have to take down one person and see what happens." "Oh, that is just fine." Joe was thinking, "I hope we don't find any trouble. I know that is asking too much the way things have been going."

As they turned and headed toward the river, the two men kept going past them. "Great," said Joe. "At least this time we didn't have to shoot anybody or have anybody shoot at us. This time let's see if we can stay on track and get out of New York and get to where we are going."

The two were now heading toward White Plains and following Washington's retreat. They drove the wagon to a stream to let the horses drink and rest. "What do you think?" asked Todd. "About what?" replied Joe. "Oh, about the situation," replied Todd. "I really don't know what to say. You know, Todd, I have two buddies. We were sort of split up awhile ago, and we were supposed to meet in Boston, but things sort of changed, and I don't know what happened. This was before I met you, and right now I don't know where anybody is or what happened to them?" "What do you mean what happened to them?" asked Todd.

"Look, Todd, I told you I am from a different place and that I know how this is all going to turn out. As I said, I can't explain how this happened because I don't know myself. At times I think this is a dream until the bullets start whizzing over our heads. I'll tell you, Todd, this is the worst thing I have ever been through." "What do you mean?" asked Todd. "I have tried to tell you. To tell you the truth, Todd, we set out to commit a crime. It didn't work out; and we were chased by the police, got away, and hid until the next morning. We wake up, and here we are. I am with new friends and still being shot at, but this time it's history that I sort of read about George Washington and the like.

"Really, I have no idea what the hell is going on and really haven't since the day we met." "The police were chasing you? What are the police?" Todd asked. "Are they like the British soldiers?" Joe was slumbering down by a tree, saying under his breath, "What is the use?" "You know," said Todd, "this reminds me of my house looking down on the river. Sometimes I wish I was back there, maybe someday." "Yeah," said Joe, "I know what you mean. It is very nice here; but I miss the baseball games, the football games and family outings, cookouts, and such. I thought because I was born I was owed everything, so I went to drugs and stealing. How I got here I don't know, but if I didn't, I probably be in Walpole State Prison or shot.

"I wish I could go back." "Go back to where?" said Todd. "I don't know. Back to Boston I guess. Maybe someday and start over, and this time listen to my folks. Anyway, enough of that," said Joe. "What is our plan now?" "I don't know yet," said Todd, "but we had better come up with something fast before it gets dark. I don't want to be traveling in the dark because of Indians, the British, or highwaymen. Some of them not only rob you but kill you too. So when you are ready, we will get going as far as we can."

Loading some of their belongings back on to the wagon to go north along the River Hudson, they continued going north to see if they could catch Washington's troops. "You know," said Joe, "we are trying to catch Washington's troops. What the hell do we do if we do catch up with them? Are we going to be in another fight, be volunteered for another duty with troops that are trying to protect Washington's retreat so he can fight another day? I tell you the damn British are going to lose this war. I know it doesn't look like that now, but I'll tell you that's what is going to happen." "Okay," said Todd, "let's see if we can get away from New York City and then see what happens."

They rode until nightfall down a path until they came upon a lake, and there they decided to spend the night. When they woke up the next morning, it was cloudy, misty, and windy; so the lake had white caps, and the trees were blowing. "We had better move on," said Todd.

They covered their things in the back of the wagon and started to move on. They moved as fast as they could down the path toward the main road with branches blowing off the trees since the wind was blowing so hard even some small trees were falling to the ground. "When they came to the main road, the rain was coming down sideways. Joe said, "I hope we can find some shelter soon." Now sort of muttering, "If this is a dream, I am sure getting soaked." Todd had the horses going at a faster pace to see if they could find some shelter fast.

As they rode northeast, they came upon a settlement called Mount Vernon. They were wet and cold and then suddenly noticed a roadhouse. "I think we have enough money to stay here, take a bath, and rest for a while." They secured their horses and headed for the roadhouse. With the rain still driving hard, the two headed down a dirt street and toward the front door of the roadhouse.

When they walked through the door, there was a warm fire going, and four people sat by candlelight with ale sitting in front of them. A woman came forward and said, "You boys look cold and wet." "Yes, we are," said Todd, "and would like a bath, some food, and some hot rum please." "Okay," said the woman upstairs, "we have a place where you can bathe, and when you are ready, you can come downstairs for your rum." By now the wind was blowing so hard you could hear the shutters banging on the side of the building. With two bathtubs with heated water, the two got into the tubs, finished, and dried themselves. They got their extra clothes from their roll bags, got dressed, and went downstairs for a meal and some hot rum. When they reached the bottom of the stairs, they went to their table. The women came over and said, "Well, you boys look a lot better than you did ago." Todd said, "Yeah, and drier too."

She said, "What would you like to eat?" "Yes, a dish of mutton and hot rum," said Todd. Before she asked Joe, he said, "I will have the same." Joe said, "I wonder how it is outside." Todd said, "I don't know. Why don't you go out and see?" "Good idea," said Joe as he left the table and went outside. The rain was still coming down, but the wind was not as bad. He went back to the table. "It's still raining, but the wind is not that bad. I hope this is not a northeasterner." "What is that?" asked Todd. "A three-day rain," said Joe.

Then they settled down to a meal and hot rum. "Well," said Todd, "this has been quite a day." "Yes, it has," said Joe. "With this wind and rain, it felt like a hurricane." "A what?" said Todd. "A heavy wind," said Joe. "Let's see now if we can get some sleep since I did not sleep that well by the lake." "Good idea," said Todd. Joe said, "It looks like at least the wind died down, so I think we can get some sleep and not hear those damn shutters banging around."

As they finished their rum, one person came over to the table from the other table and said, "Hello, how are you?" "The question is, who are you?" asked Joe. "Oh, we are travelers, and we were talking about the war. Seeing we are on neither side, we were wondering which side you are on." "Like yourself," said Todd, "we are travelers and not on either side. Excuse us but we are tired and need of rest." Joe and Todd got up and headed upstairs.

"What do you think that was all about?" "I'll tell you what I think," said Todd. "I think they are British spies and think they were just testing us." "They didn't look very trustworthy," Joe said. "I hope that's the last we hear of them." "I hope so," said Todd, "but I don't think so. Let's see what happens."

Joe and Todd went upstairs, and the man returned to his table. Once Todd and Joe made it to the top of the stairs, they both looked down to see if one of the men at the other table was about to follow them. "I don't know," said Joe. "I think they are all right." "I still don't know," said Todd, "but I will tell you one thing. I am keeping an eye open tonight." "I guess you are right," said Joe.

"It is funny that in this time all the treachery and double-crossing that goes on. Hell, you don't know who is at times fighting for the British or who is fighting for the Americans." "What a crazy time! A lot of times they smile and a short time later they are trying to cut your throat. I wonder where the Washington troops are now." "I don't know," said Todd, "but in the morning we had better keep moving."

In the night, when everybody was asleep, the four men who were at the table met downstairs and moved up to the rooms where Joe and Todd were half asleep. Then they broke through the door of Joe's room. Because he was first in going for his gun, Joe didn't have a chance, With their guns drawn, they put a gun to Joe's head who was now on the floor with another man's foot on his back. Todd, hearing the commotion, ran into Joe's room with his gun. He asked, "What the hell is going on here?" Not seeing a man at his back, Todd then felt a gun at his head.

"Never mind," said one man. "What I heard I did not like the answer you gave downstairs. I think both of you bastards are American spies with Washington's army. We will take you to our commander, and if proven guilty of spying, you will be hanged." By this time both Todd and Joe had their hands tied behind their backs. As they were brought downstairs, the women who ran the place woke up and came to the bottom of the stairs. "What is going on?" she demanded. "Never mind," said one man, "go back to bed, keep your husband happy, and stay out of our business."

As they were pushing the two out the door, Joe said Todd, "If we get out of this, I want to take this son of a bitch out. I don't care what happens, but I am killing this bastard." "Take it easy," said Todd. "Let's see how this plays out."

The men took the two and put them in a coach, which they had waiting outside. Two got into the coach, and the other two got up on the top to drive the coach. Joe said, "What the hell is going on here?" "Never mind," said one man, "sit back and shut up. We don't want to hear from you the rest of the ride." "No," said the other man. "We figure you as American spies." "Oh yeah," said Joe, "and just how did you come to that conclusion?" "When you were sitting down at the table, we heard you talking about Washington, and we knew right then who you were." "Oh," said Joe, "how did you know that we weren't talking against Washington?

"There is no way you could hear our full conversation from where you were." "Well," said the man, "we will let the British figure that out." Joe said, "You sons of bitches have nothing to do with the British. You bastards are bounty hunters, selling whoever to the British for money. You don't care whether we are Americans or not." The other man said, "I told you to shut up and sit quietly, or I will shoot you right here."

When they arrived at their destination, the two men threw both Joe and Todd to the ground. As they looked up, they saw a British officer looking down at them. "Well," said the officer, "what do we have here?" "I believe we have a couple of traitors or spies. We caught them down in the roadhouse a few miles back." As Joe and Todd were brought to their feet, the officer said, "What do you have to say for yourself?" Joe said, "Bullshit! That is what I have to say. We were sitting in a table across the room, and these two assholes claimed that they heard our conversation; they said they were travelers, and we told them that is what we were, and then they pull this."

The officer said, "We have a stockade for the prisoners. I will talk to the captain, and we will see what we will do with them." As they were taken to the stockade Joe said to Todd, "This is where I came in, being thrown into a stockade. Maybe this is where this damn nightmare will end."

The officer went to the captain and said, "We have two men that our friends brought us, and we think they are spies." The captain replied, "Are they?" "I don't know," replied the officer. "It is hard to tell." "Well," said the captain, "I don't have time for this. I am trying to find where Washington is retreating to. Why don't we hang them? That way we will be sure." The officer said, No trial?" "No," said the captain.

The officer walked out to the sergeant and said, "We will have to take the two we just brought in and hang them. Pay off the bounty hunters." "No trial?" said the sergeant. "No trial," said the officer. "Wow," said the sergeant, "that has not been done before." "I know," said the officer. "I guess this is what they mean when they say there is always a first time.

"Get them ready and bring them to the field since the gallows have been dismantled for firewood. Get a detail, bring them out, and hang them. I will pay off the bounty hunters." The officer returned to the office where the four men were waiting. The officer went to the safe and said, "Here is your money." "Thank you," said one of the men, "it is nice doing business with you." The officer looked at the men with disgust. "Hey," said one of the men, "you are trying to win this war, and all we are doing is helping you." The officer said, "Yeah, we are doing this for England, and all you are doing this for is money. You don't care which side wins or who you capture or shoot. You are in it is just for the money, and that's what the difference is between you and I." The other man said, "We have our money. Let's go." The men left.

The officer said to the sergeant, "Okay, get the two men you brought in, get them to the field, and hang them." The sergeant said, "This is wrong. No trial and we are taking the word of those bounty hunter bastards." The officer said, "I know, but follow orders." "Yes, sir," said the sergeant. He took four men to the stockade. When they got there, Todd's and Joe's hands were still tied. "Okay," said one of the soldiers, "get up." "Where are we going?" said Joe. "We have a date in the field," as they got Joe and Todd up and pushed them through the door. Todd said to Joe, "These bastards are going to hang us." Joe said, "I hope we can think of something before we get to the field." They put Todd and Joe in the back of the wagon and with their hands still tied the wagon then left for the field with four soldiers.

In about thirty minutes they reached the field. They came to two trees, so one of the soldiers put the noose around Joe's and Todd's heads and threw the ropes over the strong branches above. The sergeant said, "Do you have any last words?" Joe said, "Yeah, go fuck yourself. We did not do anything wrong, and what trial did we have?" "Well, if that is your last word, okay, fellows, get them up on the wagon." They had Joe and Todd standing up in the wagon. Just as the sergeant was about to secure the rope, a shot rang out. A bullet hit the sergeant in the chest, killing him instantly. The four other soldiers turned to fight, and the wagon took off, throwing Joe and Todd to the ground. Seeing the ropes were not secure, they fell to the ground and were not hurt. The gun battle continued, and in the end one of the shooters was wounded, and all the other soldiers were killed.

"What the hell was that?" said Joe. "I don't know," said Todd. Seven people headed their way. "Oh man," said Joe, "what the hell is this now?" As the seven surrounded the two, Joe looked up and to his surprise saw the woman from the roadhouse. "Hello, boys, it looks like you are doing fine." "Who are you?" said Todd. "We are fighting with the Americans," replied one of the men, "and when they took you, we were looking for what was going to happen. We had someone watching you all the time." "You did?" said Joe. "Well, I guess it is a good thing they didn't put us before a firing squad." "I guess you are right," said the woman.

"My husband and myself have been helping the Americans work their way north, but this the first time we had to do this. But there was no other way. By the way, we were trying to figure out how to get you out." "They played into our hands." "But how come they did not try to hang you inside?" Todd said, "They burned the hanging scalpel for firewood, and according to the soldiers, the headman was worried about Washington. I guess they did not have time or didn't want to waste any bullets on us." "Okay," said Joe, "let's get back to the tavern and pick up our wagon if it's still around. If those bastards come back, I have a score to settle with that one son of a bitch." "Don't worry about your wagon; we have it right here," as they untied their hands. "We also have your guns that they left in their hurry. They left them on the floor. I guess they were in a hurry to get you back to the British."

The woman said, "Besides, I don't think it a very good idea to go back to the roadhouse." Joe said, "Do you know who those sons of bitches are?" "They are bounty hunters. That's who those bastards are, and they were not part of the British army. They were not even spies," the woman said. "Here is your wagon. Nothing has been touched, and the horses have been fed." Joe said, "I want to go back. I have a score to settle." The woman said, "That is not a good idea. We did not know they were bounty hunters. When and if they come back, we will take care of them. If you come back, you will compromise our position, and we will not be able to do our job. Go north and Godspeed." "What is your name?" said Joe. "No names," said the woman. "It is better that way. Now go before the soldiers miss these men and come looking for them."

The woman said to her men, "Load the bodies on our wagon, and we had better get going," and turned to Joe and Todd. "You had better get going yourself." "Yeah," said Todd, "and good luck to you." Joe and Todd got up on their wagon and started out. Todd said, "That was some lady." "Yeah," said Joe, "but I will tell you one thing. I am glad she was on our side because I would not want her as an enemy." "Boy, you are right," as the two wagons took off in different directions.

On the way Joe was thinking, "Boy this is something. This has to be a dream or a nightmare or something because these situations we keep getting in and out of. I don't know if I am either in a nightmare, a dream, or dead and in some other world; but why the Revolutionary War? Why this time? I don't know if this is something like out of *The Twilight Zone*, an old TV show I used to watch as a kid. I don't know. It's all so real. I can hear the rain and the wind and hear the bullets ricocheting off rocks and trees when being shot at. I really don't know what the hell is going on." Todd asked, "What are you thinking about?" "Oh, nothing Todd, really nothing." Todd then said, "Well, you were thinking of nothing for a long time now." "Yeah, guess so," said Joe. "I was thinking how lucky we are getting in and out of trouble without getting shot or really hurt. I mean like that last episode where we were about to be hanged with the rope around our necks and out of nowhere comes that lady, and her men save us." "Yeah," said Todd, "just lucky I guess." Todd said, "Now we have to look over our shoulder and not trust anybody and see if we can get to the north and see if we can catch Washington's troops."

"Look," said Joe, "let's say we do catch Washington's troops. Are we supposed to join them? Hell, as far as we know, they are retreating. It looks like this time the British are beating them." Todd said, "I thought you knew how this was going to turn out." "Yeah," said Joe, "but I don't know how this moment is going to turn out, just the results of the damn war."

As the wagon headed toward New Rochelle, Todd said, "If we can join the troops, maybe we can protect ourselves with numbers." Joe said, "What the hell are you talking about numbers if they are retreating? Like we think it could be in a lot of cases, every man for himself. Remember awhile ago in whatever battle when we heard that Washington had a tough time keeping his men together. If he is retreating and this is happening again, how do you figure we will be safe?" "Well," said Todd, "we have to keep going, and I guess see what happens.

"You know," said Todd, "back there I was wondering what will happen when those soldiers that had us captured go to the field and find nobody, no bodies—nothing. I have a feeling that they will think the soldiers deserted. The group that saved us were covering their tracks pretty good. It looks like they have done this before, for they were pretty good on that attack. They were fast, swift, and they took all the bodies with them. So if the soldiers get there, they will find nothing." Joe said, "Let's hope that we are well out of the way before they find out that anything happened." "You have that right," replied Todd.

Meanwhile the officer in charge asked one of his men, "I have been looking for three of our men and the sergeant. Did you see what happened to them?" "Yes, sir," replied the soldier. "About three hours ago under the captain's orders, they took two men out to be hanged, but they haven't come back yet." "What do you mean they haven't come back yet? Where did they go?" "Out to the field, sir." The officer said, "Get a detail and go out to the field and see what happened. By the way, soldier, what were they supposed to be hanged for?" "I don't know, sir. I think they thought they were spies. Sir, the detail is ready to go out and find the men."

The horses were mounted, and the detail took off, looking for the soldiers. Riding for about thirty minutes the soldiers came upon the scene. One of the soldiers got off his mount and looked around. "It looks like something happened here; there are two ropes, no bodies. It doesn't look like any tracks. Okay, fellows, let's look around and see what happened. They took the two out here in a wagon. There is no wagon and no bodies—nothing. There has to be something." One of the soldiers said, "Do you think the men deserted?" "I don't know what happened' all I know is if they hanged the two, they would have had to bring the bodies back or buried them or something. What we have here is a big nothing."

One of the soldiers called out from about two hundred yards. "Come over here. I think I found something." The soldiers walked over. "Look, wagon wheels." One of the soldiers kneeled down. "Now whatever happened here, they covered their tracks. Pretty good, but it looks like they made one mistake. Okay, men, let's get our mounts and follow these tracks and see where they lead."

The soldiers continued to follow the lead's tracks and broke tree branches. One soldier said, "They did a pretty good job of covering their tracks. They probably felt that they went so far that they did not have to cover them anymore. Let's just keep going and see where it leads." In about an hour, they came upon the wagon; it was set afire with bodies in the back burned beyond recognition. "Son of a bitch," said one of the soldiers, "who could have done this?" "I don't know," said the other soldier. "I wonder if it could be Indians, and I wonder what happened to the two that was supposed to have been hanged?" Looking around the leader said, "We had better get back to the fort and see what the captain says." "Yes," said the other soldier, "we can't do anything with this wagon."

They then got back upon their horses and rode back to the fort. When they got to the fort, two of the soldiers went to the officer's quarters and reported what they found. The officer then went to the captain's office. "Yes," Denton said, the captain. "Sir, we have a problem." "What is that?" said the captain. "The men that you sent out to hang those two that were captured." "Yes," said the captain, "what about them?" "Well, sir, we found the men—all of them—killed and then burned." "WHAT!" shouted the captain. "What about the two that were supposed to be hanged?" "I don't know, sir. All the bodies were burned beyond recognition. We don't know."

"I'll tell you," said the captain, "it's those goddamn Americans. I bet they were some of Washington's men. I said both of those bastards were spies. I knew it. I'll bet he sent some of his troops to see if he could knock off some of our scouts and then got lucky when they saw our men and killed two birds with one stone."

CHAPTER ELEVEN

General Washington and General Howe

"Washington, that son of a bitch, I'll bet he is doubling back and coming back to New York. Send a message to General Howe. He should be very interested." "So what will we do?" "Okay," said the captain, "send a wagon to get the men and well-armed guards just in case those who did this come back. It has to be Washington's men. We have had no trouble before. The problem with these damn Americans is that there wear no uniforms. A lot of them are dressed like farmers; you just don't know whether you're shooting at a damn rebel or one of the Tories that are on our side. Okay, I don't know what we do. I thought Washington was retreating, but with this action I don't know. Send some troops south to see if anybody has seen any American troops."

While some men went to the wagon, others went to the south. When they came to the roadhouse where Todd and Joe were captured, the British soldiers saw the roadhouse. They rode up, got off their horses, and walked into the tavern. They saw the woman working, cleaning tables and around the bar. One soldier asked in an abrupt manner, "Did you see any strangers around?" The woman said, "Not lately. Ago we had some strangers around." "Oh," said the soldier. "Yes, but four men took them prisoner, but that is about it. I think the four men were British soldiers, and they took two people out and put them in a wagon. I really did not know what was going on." "Have you seen either the four men or the other two?" "No," said the woman. "Okay, if you see them, you make sure you let us know." "I will," said the woman.

"We have a peaceful place here for travelers and have not really been involved in the war with the British or anybody else." As the soldiers walked back to their horses, one soldier said, "What do you think?" The leader said, "I think they are all right. She did not look smart enough to tell anything but the truth." As the soldiers got up upon their horses, the husband came out of the back room and said, "That was a close call." "Yes," she said, "that was close. It is a good we did not have a smarter soldier. We will have to watch ourselves from now on. Tell the others to watch themselves. We should have covered our tracks better."

"I think we were lucky. I'll bet they thought it was Washington's troops or rebels. We will have to watch ourselves closer next time. What we will have to watch out for are those four bounty hunters in case they come back. In fact, from now on we will have to watch all our costumers very closely," said the wife. "Yeah," said the husband, "I hope those two got away." The wife said, "They did; otherwise, the soldiers would not of come here, but at least they are heading in the right direction." "What do you mean?" said the husband. "South," replied the wife. They both laughed, turned, and went back inside.

Meanwhile while the soldiers were heading south looking for Todd and Joe, they were heading north, trying to find where Washington's men were. Hoping to find some friendly forces for a change and seeing in some small way if they could help. "You know," said Todd, "I hope that those soldiers don't go down to that roadhouse for that woman." "I don't think so," replied Joe. "Even if they find tracks, I don't think that it will lead to that woman. She's too smart." "That was a good setup. They never let on that they were involved in any way. I would just like to shoot that one bastard of a bounty hunter. I would like to run into him someday." "The way you feel, I hope not. Nothing would be accomplished doing that. We are free, and let's be grateful for that."

As they continued north and riding most of the day, they passed Throggs Neck and heading toward Pell's Point. Todd and Joe came upon two men also riding in a wagon dressed like farmers. "What do you think?" asked Joe. "I don't know," replied Todd. "They could be British dressed up as farmers, or they could be fighting for the Americans." "It looks like we are coming upon them. Say hello and let them do much of the talking."

As the two wagons came upon each other, one of the men in the other wagon said politely, "How are you fellows doing today?" "All right," said Todd. The other man said, "It sure is nice looking out on the bay, very peaceful." "Yeah, it is," said Todd. "What are you fellows doing?" asked the man in the other wagon. "Well," said Todd, "we are riding just like you are." The other fellow said, "It looks like the British, from what we hear, are trouncing the Americans in New York." Todd said, "I wouldn't know about that. You see, our family owns a farm up north, and we are sort of are skirting around the edges of the war. We don't want to become involved." "That is good," said the other man. "It could be dangerous on either side. We are doing the same thing; we are not on any side. We just wish this damn thing was over so we know which side wins. But from what we hear, the British are pushing north and chasing Washington toward White Plains, so we are heading south. Have a good day, gentlemen."

As the other wagon continued on its way, Joe asked, "What do you think?" "I don't know," replied Todd. "They looked like they were in the middle and to be with whichever side wins; they don't care. But at least we know that Washington is heading toward the White Plains area, so let's head in that direction."

Meanwhile in the battle the Americans were getting beaten badly. A lot of Americans were retreating, swimming for their lives across Gowanus Creek, with the Long Island battle going with the First Maryland Regiment bravely covering the withdrawal. Approaching New York, General Howe established a base on Staten Island then landed twenty thousand troops on Long Island. He outflanked Washington with his night march, defeated him roundly, and forced him back northward with his weakened army.

In the wagon Todd and Joe continued slowly toward the north until they came upon three men setting up camp for the night. As the wagon started to go by, one man stepped out: a tall man with sharp features, jet-black hair, and rugged but slim, with a pistol and a shotgun by his side. "Shit," said Joe, "what the hell now?" "I don't know," said Todd, "but let's stay calm until we find out what he wants." The man came forward. "Hello," said the man, looking over Todd and Joe very carefully. "Hello," said Todd. "Where are you fellows headed?" "Oh, we are just farmers headed north." "Come join us," said the man. "I don't think so," said Todd. "You see, we are in a little bit of a hurry."

"I would like to have you join us," the man demanded. Joe, looking around, saw two rifles pointed at them, so Joe nudged Todd. "Look," said Joe. Todd turned around. Todd said, "Well, maybe for a while." They both came down off the wagon. "Why do you have your guns pointed at us?" "Well," the man said, "we would like to know who you really are. Now if we find out you are with the British, we will kill you right here." The guns were stilled trained on Joe and Todd while one man searched them.

"Just to let you know before we kill you, we want you to know that we are with Washington's army." "There are clean, nothing on them," said one man. "That's great," said Todd. The man looked puzzled. "We didn't know whether you were with the British or not."

"My name is Todd, and this is Joe, and we were heading north to see if we could catch the Washington troops. I will tell you that for a while we were being chased by the British and in and out of a few wars." Joe said, "How do we know that you are not with the British, trying to trap us?" "Have no fear," said the man. "You don't know how close you came to being shot." So Joe said, "What is happening?" "We have been trying to escape to the north; we lost touch on what is happening."

"By the way," said the man, "my name is Carl, and to answer your question, it is not good. I was down there, and from my information Sir William Howe—" Joe said, "Yeah, we heard of him." "Well," said Carl, "he came down from up north where he left his Loyalist refugees; refit his ships; took on supplies; and then came south to Sandy Hook, New Jersey, where the Atlantic Ocean feeds into the lower bay of New York.

"We saw 52 British warships and 426 transports. At night in Staten Island, a hilly landmass separating the lower bay from the upper one, you could see the campfires. They had as far as we could see an estimated thirty-two thousand Tommies and German Hessians. It was cold that night, and they were under blankets; and to tell you, so were we." "So what you are telling us is that you are spies for Washington?" "You could say that," said Carl. "The way it is that if we get caught, we will be hanged or shot by the British. That is why if we found out that you were on the British side, we would have killed you two right here."

Again at Washington's headquarters the commander in chief ruminated on the difficulties of his position. He had no sea power to throw against the heavily armored vessels off the docks of New York. Washington's men counted twenty thousand effectives among his forces. It was the largest army he would ever command, but it was not his best. Most of his men were green. Discipline was as much of a problem as it had been in his days at Cambridge. When two British men of war entered the North River (the lower Hudson) and began cannonading the city, his orders to man the shore batteries were largely ignored. Drunkenness was prevalent among those artillerists who did report. Their fire made no impression on the sturdy oak of the invading warships. The town that Washington had been called on to hold could have been tucked into a corner of today's metropolis. It occupied only the lower tip of a thirteen-mile long island later known as Manhattan.

North of where city hall now stands lay mostly open country with here and there a lonely farm or a backwoods village. Militarily Washington's chances of defending the seaport were slim. Politically, he had no choice but to defend it. The loss of New York would be a staggering blow to a nation so young that it measured its existence in weeks. Carl continued, "We have information that deserters have left enemy vessels, and we were trying to find out when the British would attack. And they said soon. That could mean tomorrow.

The possible places were so numerous as to make an adequate fortification of all of them impossibility. At the northern end of the island, Kingsbridge, a small wooden span over Harlem River, provided the only link between Manhattan and lower Westchester country on the mainland. On neighboring Long Island, across the East River to the south, loomed Brooklyn Heights. Strike by the British at Kingsbridge could imprison the American forces on Manhattan. Enemy cannons implanted on Brooklyn Heights could do to New York City what the American field guns on Dorchester Heights had done to Boston. Eighteenth-century military textbooks spoke of doom awaiting the general who divided his forces, but terrain, not textbooks, guided Washington's preparations.

Up Manhattan went General Heath and one thousand troops with instructions to encamp on both sides of Harlem River at Kingsbridge. So across the East River went nine thousand soldiers to complete the chain of forts already started on Brooklyn Heights to guard the Long Island shore where it bulged westward into the slender channel of water the narrows that divided it from British-held Staten Island. Both of the rivers flanking the city itself received attention, especially the Hudson, as its broad waters constituted Washington's only direct communication with General Schuyler at Albany.

Near where the George Washington Bridge now goes across the Hudson, toiling soldiers sank large stone-laden frames called chevaux-de-frise. Atop these bulky objects were protruding points capable of cracking the hulls of vessels. Even as these ambitious structures were being lowered, some of the timbers joining their elements separated, creating a passage. A few weeks later two British warships and three tenders felt their way up the river, found the opening, and moved through. In still another effort to deny the Hudson to the enemy, the Americans threw up a five-sided earthwork on a dark limestone hill slightly north of where 180th Street now meets the river.

Sir William Howe and his brother, the admiral, came to New York with instructions to perform a double mission. Their orders made them at one and the same time the leaders of the British invasion and peace commissioners. As peace commissioners, they were authorized to offer the Americans certain concessions provided they laid down their arms.

On a torrid July morning a British naval officer docked at New York under a flag of truce. In his hand was a message inviting the American commander in chief to confer with the British peace commissioners. Washington's aides noted that the message was addressed to George Washington, Esq., etc." They refused it, saying that if the letter was from Commissioner Howe they must send a message so addressed. A few days later a second officer came, bringing a second message. If Howe wished to communicate with "His Excellency General Washington," they must send another message so addressed. A few days later another officer came, bringing another message addressed to "George Washington, Esq." This too was refused. Finally a high-ranking British officer arranged to lay the British peace proposal before General Washington in person.

The commander in chief heard him out and shook his head. He failed to see any peace in the British offer. He pointed out that the powers of the Commissioners Howe and Howe were severely limited. They offered pardons to the rebels only on condition that they stop rebelling. Washington said that the Americans were not rebelling. They were defending their liberties; for this they needed no pardons.

Commissioners Howe and Howe could not lay their peace proposals before the Congress. In the British eyes that organization had no legal status, but in London Admiral Lord Howe and Ben Franklin had become friends and had played chess together at each other's homes. The admiral described the peace proposals in a letter to Franklin. Congress informed of its contents and authorized Franklin, John Adams, and Edward Rutledge of South Carolina (brother of the governor) to confer with Lord Howe at his headquarters on Staten Island The three-hour conference ran a genial and soft-spoken course. The delegates from Philadelphia said that when England recognized American independence, the war would end. Until then it would go on.

Admiral Howe looked pained. He said that he always loved America as he would a brother. "If she would fall—" "My lord," said Franklin with a smile, "we will use our utmost endeavors to save your lordship that mortification." On this note the peace conference ended. Meanwhile, the war continued.

Joe said, "You were there?" "Yes, we were." Todd then said, "How did we get in this position when it looks like we are losing the battle in this area?" "Here is how this happened. It was a wind-lashed morning. A Lord Cornwallis and fifteen thousand Red Coats landed along the Gravesend section of Long Island. Two days later General Leopold von Heister and five thousand blue-coated Hessians followed. Cornwallis pierced inland, swiftly flushing out the American sharpshooters, whose hiding places in the cornfields of Flatbush had been revealed to them by local Loyalists. Von Heister lunged north in the direction of the rebel works on Brooklyn Heights." "How did you guys get out?" "We were lucky, I guess, but I don't know for how long.

"On the British side the bloody encounter was brilliantly executed. Sir William Howe, in overall command of the British invasion, had learned a lesson at Breed's and Bunker Hill. He avoided direct confrontation with the defenders. He attained his ends by a series of flanking maneuvers.

"On the American side it was marked by ineptitude, by a recurrent failure of communication among the commanding generals, Israel Putnam, John Sullivan of New Hampshire, and William Alexander of New Jersey, more often addressed as Lord Stirling because of his claim to lapsed Scottish earldom. By noon fifteen hundred Americans were dead or captured. The others fell back to the fortifications on Brooklyn Heights. From New York Washington rushed four thousand troops to their assistance only to realize immediately that even with reinforcements the situation on Long Island was hopeless."

"Okay," said Joe, "what are we going to do now? We are on the outer rim of this action." "Behind and below the now almost twelve thousand Americans in the forts of Brooklyn Heights lay the East River. In front of them stretched the British camp only six hundred yards away. Sir William Howe's generals urged him to attack the American survivors at once. Howe refused. A direct assault on the entrapped Americans was bound to succeed but only at a terrible cost in lives.

"Okay," said Carl, "we are out of here. It looks like the British are making their move. We are going back to the American lines. Do you two want to come with us?" "It looks like we have no choice," said Todd. "I guess you are right," said Joe. "Okay, fellows, we are out of here. Gather your belongings." Carl then turned to the two and said, "You don't mind if we use your wagon for some of our equipment?" "No, I guess not," said

Todd. "Okay, put some of our nonessential belongings into the wagon," Carl ordered one of his men. "Let's get the hell out of here," as they could hear cannon fire coming closer to their position. Todd turned to Joe and said, "It looks like now we really have no choice." "Yeah, goddamn it. Here we go again," said Joe. Todd said to Carl, "Where are we going?" "Well, you fellows wanted to catch up to Washington's lines, so that's where we are going. It looks like the whole company is getting out." "Whatever it is," said Joe. "I hope so because I am getting pretty sick of these damn wars. If I was brought back to this time, why the hell could I have not got married and had a damn farm or something?" "Okay, guys, let's get going. Joe, what are you mumbling about?" "Nothing, nothing," said Joe.

The British commander opted for a siegelike procedure. He began laying down parallels (series of trenches) with the idea of gradually closing in on the Americans, eventually forcing them to surrender. Behind this humane decision was Howe's conviction that he had plenty of time and that the men holed up on Brooklyn Heights could not possibly get away. But they did. Washington saw to that, and as with Dorchester Heights, the elements came to his aid.

The night was one of a heavy rain and gusty winds and very black skies. All through the dark hours and into a murky dawn, rowboats manned by Washington's troops chased downed a British ship and Colonel John Glover's Marblehead fishermen plied the East River between New York and the foot of Brooklyn Heights. It was 4:30 a.m. before the British realized that their prey was escaping. It was 7:00 a.m. before a red jacketed patrol reached the shore just in time to see the last rowboat vanish northward into a rolling fog. A round of British musketry was ineffective happily for the American cause as the last man to leave Long Island that morning was George Washington.

In a splendidly planned and coordinated maneuver, he had snatched more than half of his army from certain capture, but Washington could not save New York. Reluctantly he let it be known that the city was to be evacuated. Todd and Joe arrived as Washington was speaking. "Wow," said Joe, "George Washington is standing there speaking. I have read about him. He a little taller than I thought he was. If I ever got his autograph and if I get back, I could be rich. Hell, my father waited for Mickey Mantle, Whitey Ford, and Elston Howard for hours. Here I am standing forty yards from George Washington. I'll be damned."

Todd said, "Joe, what are you thinking about?" "Nothing this time. You would not believe me if I told you and probably would not even know what the hell I was talking about anyway." "Well," said Todd, "we wanted to get to Washington's lines. Well, here we are."

"What the hell is going on?" said Joe. "I don't know, replied Todd. "What all these people are doing?" Thousands of people took off, taking their belongings with them and thus stripping the city of the conveyances needed to transport the army's cannon and stores. When the British arrived, they would fall heir to most of Washington's heavier equipment and much of his gunpowder. Todd said, "I guess this is the finial retreat that we were hearing about." A lot of people were moving out, and by now Joe and Todd were engulfed in the mass of all the people that were getting out of New York. "Wow," said Joe, "I have never seen anything like this. People moving everywhere, trying to escape."

On the whole the soldiers exhibited as little dignity as the citizens. Many of them departed without waiting for orders to do so. For three days the highways running up the island were a creeping jam of wagons loaded with household goods of distraught civilians and of fleeing soldiers. Joe was saying, "This is like 128 at rush hour." Todd was not about to ask what the hell 128 was.

Terror and confusion were everywhere when under the searing midday sun, the British landed from the East River at Kip's Bay and probed westward along a line roughly parallel with what is now East Twenty-third Street. Panic seized the Connecticut militiamen assigned to the American trenches in the Kip's Bay area. Some fled while others froze. Washington, suddenly appearing in the vicinity, was seen to fall into a rage. He ripped his three-cornered hat from his head and slammed it to earth. He was heard to shout, "Are these the men with whom I am to defend America!" Blinded with fury he might have been seized by the invaders had not a fellow officer hustled him away.

Joe, looking in amazement, said, "Wow, I never read Washington had a temper like that. No wonder a lot of men followed him. You know, Todd, if that officer had not taken him, he probably would have stood up to the British all by himself." Todd said, "I don't know about that, but I am glad the officer whisked him away."

A few American units were caught south of the invasion line. Most escaped to Paulus Hook (Jersey City). On the western bank of the Hudson, one unit, including a company of artillery under Captain Alexander Hamilton, made its way up Manhattan along hidden woodland pathways guided by a handsome twenty-year-old major named Aaron Burr. On

Harlem Heights, Washington emplaced his men in Vanguard of the invasion force and pursued as far as Van Dewater (now Morningside) Heights.

"Okay," heard Todd and Joe, "you two get ready; we are about to fight. Todd said, "What do you mean fight? I thought everybody was retreating." "All civilians," said the soldier. "What the hell do you think we are?" "Right now you are going to fight." "Does that mean we are volunteering again?" "Now you two you go with the Connecticut group." "But—" said Joe. "Never mind the but," said the soldier angrily, "You get with that group, or I will shoot you right here." Todd turned to Joe, "Can he do that?" Joe replied, "I guess he can, seeing he has his rifle pointed at us."

The soldier said, "Now get going. I don't want to have to tell you again." As the two headed for the Connecticut group, Joe said, "In my time this is what we called getting drafted. They reported to the head of the group." "Fine," said the captain, "we need all the help we can get. Fall in with that group over there."

Nightfall of the fifteenth found the two armies within hallooing distance of each other, separated only by the Hollow Way, the then-wooded ravine where West124th and 125th streets now run. Shortly after dawn the next morning a battalion of the Connecticut Rangers, 150 men under Lieutenant Colonel Thomas Knowlton, slipped into the Hollow Way and prodded westward. Their orders were to encircle the British encampment and determine the disposition of its outposts. As Knowlton and his rangers trooped toward the Hudson, two enemy battalions were seen coming toward them across the slope (that now supports the tomb of General Ulysses S. Grant). Buglers marching with the British blew the fox hunter's call that tells the members of the hunt that their prey has gone to earth.

On Harlem Heights Washington's recently appointed adjutant, Colonel Joseph Reed of Philadelphia, was "mortified" at this melodic insult. He begged Washington to send reinforcements to aid Knowlton and his now-threatened battalion "reluctantly," according to Reed; the commander in chief said no. Later he put men into motion that during the afternoon lured a large detachment of British into a disastrous ambush. In his official report General Howe described the six-hour clash that ensued as a mere "scrape" an "affair of outposts." More accurate was the American term for it: "the Battle of Harlem Heights." Within an hour 4,900 Americans and somewhat larger number of British Red Coats and green-clad German jaegers were engaged. The hostilities ranged widely from the shores of the Hudson eastward into the fields of buckwheat ripening in the valley (where later the tenements of Harlem section of New York would rise).

Heretofore, the Americans had done practically all their fighting from behind barricades. Now for the first time they faced the best that England could offer in open combat. On Long Island the inexperienced defenders of New York had fumbled every opportunity and fallen into every British trap. At Kip's Bay they had turned tail. Here on the plains of Harlem the spirit was that of men determined to atone for past weaknesses. The fighting was by now hand to hand at the point where Todd and Joe were. They had by now rifles with bayonets. Some men next to them were shot and dropping. A British soldier coming in on Todd was about to bayonet him when Joe, seeing this, bayoneted the soldier in the back, killing him instantly. "Thanks," said Todd. "Don't mention it," said Joe.

The battle was long and bloody. "Hey, you two guys." "Yes," said Todd. "We have some wounded. Get them back to where we have doctors. They are not that bad, but they can't fight, so put them in that wagon and get them out of here." They helped get the wounded back in the wagon and moved them back away from the action. "That was lucky they picked the two of us." "Yeah, let's see if we can get them back." "This is like a damn movie, and I am in it." "A what?" said Todd. "A movie, a damn movie," replied Joe as the wagon was moving to the back of the lines with the wounded.

"One of these men is hurting," said Todd. "I hope we get back to a doctor. If we don't get there, he will be in trouble. I hope he doesn't lose his leg." "I hope he doesn't," said Joe, "because I don't want to watch that." When they got back into camp, Joe asked, "Where is the hospital?" "Over there," said one soldier. "Over where?" said Joe. "Over there," the soldier replied. "That's a damn tent." "That is where the doctors are working." "Holy shit," said Joe, "that is where they will be operating on these men," as they drove the wagon toward the tents.

"You know, Todd, if I have a chance, I am going to get out of here and see if I can get back to Boston." "I am with you," said Todd, "because I think Washington will lose here, and I don't want to die in a losing war." By this time the job was not to win battles but to preserve a disorganized army from the clutches of a superior force.

Sir William Howe was shaken by the outcome. It could be that the excessive caution, which marred his conduct of the English campaigns in America, was born that day, a typical product of the leisurely and gentlemanly war, making of eighteenth-century Europe outcome. It could be that in the months ahead, he would exhibit more timidity than ever. To Washington the small victory in the buckwheat fields of Harlem was heaven-sent. It gave him a badly needed breather for a few weeks in which to put his ragged forces in order.

It was a frustrating period for the British. They came close to losing the city they had seized to a fire that gutted hundreds of homes and was probably set by the Patriots still in New York. An inkling of Howe's troubled state of mind is found in an incident on the following day. When on Long Island his soldiers picked up a Connecticut captain disguised as a teamster; the British commander acted with uncharacteristic harshness. He ordered the captured spy hanged at once and without trial. The British troops summoned to witness the execution, say, they were impressed by the young American's claim as he walked to his doom. His last words sped northward to be repeated with awe by Washington's soldiers and cherished by their descendants.

"I only regret," said Nathan Hale as the noose draped his shoulders, "that I have but one life to lose for my country." The word spread to the camp about the hanging without trial. Upon hearing it Joe said to Todd, "Does that sound familiar, Todd, hanging without trial? You know, you read about these times, and you think, 'Boy, it sure would be good to live in these times with no hustle and bustle, to see fields and trees, birds, and streams where there are now housing projects and crime. Peace when there are no ambulances, police sirens, no traffic jams, maybe except for that one when everybody was trying to get out of New York City.' The trade-off is the damn British are firing at you, people getting hanging without trial, and you don't know who is going to cut your throat."

Todd was just staring at Joe, wondering what the hell he was talking about. "What do you hear about Washington?" Todd asked a soldier. The soldier looked around cautiously and said, "I hear where Washington and his troops will be going to New Jersey across the river." "I don't know about you, Todd," said Joe, "but I am not going to New Jersey." "I am not either," said Todd. "So," said Joe, "when we have a chance, let's get away and head north."

With the troops beginning to move away from the British front, the windswept fires now raged through British-held New York with flames burning through 493 buildings. Even many Americans blamed Patriot arsonists. (Historians believe the fire started accidentally.) The Red Coats rounded up suspects by the score, some bayonet at point. John Adams best analyzed the Battle of Long Island: (In general, our generals were outgeneraled.) The fight for New York had already been settled with the loss of Long Island. But for political reasons the second largest city had to be defended. "I could wish to maintain it," Washington wrote Congress, but he knew even the attempt might be "fatal." British ships moved into the East River and pounded Kip's Bay. General Howe landed his troops and found no opposition. The bombardment had erased the American earthworks, and the defenders had fled. "Demons of fear and disorder seemed to take full possession," one American private said. "Take the walls," roared General Washington astride his horse. "Take the cornfield!" A few soldiers responded, but the panic was almost complete. "Used every means in my power to get them into some order, but Washington's attempts were fruitless."

Suddenly about sixty British soldiers appeared leaving; Washington and his aides were left to face them without so much as a musket to escape at a gallop, furious and humiliated. Kip's Bay cost the British three dead and some eighteen wounded. With those casualties they purchased New York.

CHAPTER TWELVE

Washington's Battles: Long Island, Brooklyn Heights, Manhattan, and Harlem Heights

One day the scene was wild. General Howe, fearing an American trick attack, refused at first to spare his troops to fight the flames. The Britons blamed the Yankees, and even Washington suspected that perhaps "some good honest fellow" had set the fire to deny the British winter quarters. In Long Island the casualty figures tell the story: seventy British and Hessians killed and two hundred wounded as against thirty Americans dead and ninety wounded. By midafternoon Howe's Red Coats and jaegers were fleeing to their lines. George Washington, observing the action from Harlem Heights, felt his spirits and his faith, reviving in "the men with whom I am to defend America." As the afternoon waned, he called his triumphant troops home. At this point his job was not to win battles but to preserve a disorganized army from the clutches of a superior force.

Sir William Howe was shaken by the outcome. It could be that the excessive caution, which marred his conduct of the English campaigns in America, was born that day. During the final days in the Battle of Long Island Howe inflicted a crushing defeat on Washington's army. To escape the onslaught Washington withdrew his colonial forces from Brooklyn Heights to Manhattan. Less than two weeks later he decided to evacuate New York City rather than be trapped in Lower Manhattan. However, before he withdrew from the city, Washington prepared fortifications in Upper Manhattan and was again able to repulse the British army in the Battle of Harlem Heights. In the face of the advancing general Howe,

Washington evacuated his main force from Manhattan Island and marched to White Plains.

In the Battle of White Plains the British inflicted heavy casualties on Washington's army while Washington slipped away westward to North Castle. After deciding to abandon the New York area, Washington moved his forces across the Hudson River and into New Jersey joined by General Greene's troops at Hackensack. They retreated together toward the Delaware River with General Cornwallis at their heels. (Most historians agree that if General Howe had capitalized on his victories over Washington's army as shown on historic maps, it would have been the turning point in the Revolutionary War.) Were it not for Washington's skill as a tactician, his courage, and his daring against overwhelming odds and the inspiration he gave his troops, England may well have won the war.

Joe and Todd by now were at their wagon, loading their belongings. "You know," said Joe, "Washington's army is heading toward New Jersey. I think this is a good time for us to head north." "Yeah," said Todd, "I think you are right." "You know, Todd," said Joe, "I still can't believe that with all the cannon shots and the battles, it is a wonder that these horses aren't headed back to Boston or wherever they came from." "Yeah," said Todd, "I know. When we stole the wagon, I thought that we would have trouble. But for the most time, it has been lucky for us."

The two headed north as most of the action was heading toward New Jersey. They headed toward Connecticut. "You know," said Joe, "this should be good. Maybe this time we will be able to get somewhere without getting shot at or being hanged or anything like that." "Well," said Todd, "shall we head back to where we came from? Tell me, will you be happy to get back to Boston to see if you can find your other friends?" "Does that mean you believe me?" Joe asked. "I don't know, Joe, but I will tell you one thing: hanging with you for the most part has been weird. Like you said, just when it looked like we were going to die, all of a sudden we are out and free. I am beginning to know what you mean about being in a dream."

"You know, Todd, so far this has been some adventure. I mean with highwaymen, Indians, the British, and George Washington damn forty yards from him. You know, Todd, I don't know whether you were born too early or I was born to late, but you know, I now miss my parents more than ever. They weren't bad. I just thought I knew it all and went my way. I wish I could go back and start over. What about you, Todd?"

"Yeah, I would like to see my parents again. I hope they are all right. They were on the British side—at least my father was, and my mother—I don't know. Like I told you, they took over the farm, so I hope they are all right. It would be funny if they got into a battle with the Americans. After all we have been through fighting with the Americans.

"Well, we might as well get going," Joe said. "I guess you are right," said Todd, as they got into the wagon and headed north. "You know," said Todd, "we are not out of the woods yet." "What do you mean?" said Joe. "Well, even though Washington retreated to New Jersey and the British are still in pursuit, it doesn't mean that just because we left, we are still not in danger. We still have the Tories and the Loyalist to the British cause." "You are right," replied Joe.

Joe said, "I will tell you that I know I keep repeating myself about not knowing how I got here, but people in the future, even though they read about these times, could not know how tough it was to win this country from the British. Our travels have shown the brutality from all sides not only from the British but the Indians and, yes, the Americans. Just think about all that these people went through with all the killing and persecution. Guess what? The people in the future, for the most part, won't give a damn. From what I see, freedom will give a lot of people things they won't appreciate. You know, years from now, where you have beautiful sunrises and sunsets over these fields, there will be tenement houses, drugs, fire engines, and police sirens. No open spaces, people living on top of one another so much so that their patience keeps running thin. You know, when they talk about progress sometimes I wonder."

As they continued heading north they were riding along a high rise and enjoying the panorama of the river below. "Beautiful clouds," Joe said. "This is really heaven. Wow, what a sight!"

All of a sudden they heard some commotion, and as they looked around, they saw a small group of British soldiers. When the soldiers saw them, they started shooting and started to give chase. Joe said, "Let's move." The wagon was now at full speed with Todd at the reins. Joe by now was in the back lying down and shooting back at the soldiers. The chase was going along the side of the cliff. The horses were moving fast. Todd, now realizing that they were coming fast to the cliff's edge, yelled "Damn, damn." "What?" yelled Joe. Todd jumped down between the horses and unleashed them; he jumped back on the wagon before the horses took off. Joe said, "What the hell are you doing?"

Before Todd could answer the wagon went off the cliff and was in midair with the river below. The wagon went into the deepest part of the river, crashing to pieces with Todd and Joe going underwater. Meanwhile on the top of the cliff the soldiers, thinking they were dead, turned around and headed back. Down below Todd and Joe came to the surface with debris from the wagon all around them. Swimming to shore Joe said, "Todd, what the hell did you do?" Todd replied, "Look, we were going so fast there was nothing I could do. I had to let the horses go, or we would have lost them." "Then why the hell didn't you say something? For Christ's sake, we could of jumped." "I had to take the chance." Joe said, "You had to take the chance. What the hell do you mean you had to take the chance? Son of a bitch, I wonder why we didn't get killed."

"Look," Todd said, "if we hadn't jumped, those soldiers would have surely killed us." "Shit," said Joe, "I am so damn wet. Did we save anything?" "Well, I had two guns under my shirt and a billfold with some money, but that is about all." "Now what the hell are we going to do? For the first time we don't have a wagon or horses. What now?" Todd looked at the river's edge and saw that the roll bags washed up on the river's edge. He walked over and said, "What do you think of this? Both bags washed up, and they're in pretty good shape. "Yeah," said Joe.

Todd opened one of the roll bags. "Look." said Todd, "didn't you say you lost your billfold? Here it is in the roll bag. Isn't that something?" said Joe. "Okay, we have no horses, no wagon—what the hell are we going to do?" "I don't know," said Todd, "but whatever it is, we will have to do it fast."

After they dried off a little, Joe, looking up to where they fell, said, "See what the hell I mean? We should have been killed with that damn fall." Todd said, "Just lucky I guess." "Lucky you are damn right. I will tell you what, Todd, I am beginning to wonder about you. You didn't even get a scratch either. I don't know with all the shooting and that damn wagon going over that cliff, you have no broken arms or legs or bullet holes. On top of that, being chased by the British, Indians, highwaymen, and people just pissed off at us—all that and not a scratch. Oh yes, I forgot almost being hanged." Todd, listening to Joe's rambling, looked at Joe. "Like I said, just lucky."

"Lucky, huh?" said Joe. "Well, I will tell you what if this is not a dream and if I get out of this and get back, I am going to wonderland dog track? If I am this lucky I will spend days there." "What track?" said Todd. "Damn it, Todd, never mind. Let's get going. I don't know how far I can walk, so let's see if we can come up with something fast." They gathered up their belongings and started to walk, rest, and walk again.

Soon it became dark; the moon was large and bright. Todd said, "Let's head over here and see where it leads." As they continued they found themselves walking through a graveyard. "Oh great," said Joe. "What are we doing here?" Todd said, "Just watch your step." "Yeah, where is Stephen King when you need him?" "Stephen who?" asked Todd. "A writer." "What does he write? Something like Thomas Paine?" "No, Todd, never mind. Let's get the hell out of here as fast as we can. This is really creepy."

Leaving the graveyard they came upon a road. Todd said, "We will go as far as we can and try to sleep somewhere." Just then over a rise with a full and big moon behind it as background came a coach. Sitting on top the driver had a high hat. The two waited for them to pass. "Son of a bitch, it looks like something that Dracula would be in." As the coach stopped, the driver said "Would you like a ride?" Todd said sure. Joe said, "I don't know." Todd said, "Do you want to walk all night?" "No," said Joe.

They got into the coach were there were two men. One was a man with a three-cornered hat and a large coat with his face partially covered. The other had no hat and was in his late twenties. "Where are you going?" asked the younger man. "As far as we can." "Well, this coach will be going to Connecticut." "That's fine," said Todd. "Well, Mr. Arnold, we have company for the rest of the way." The man looked with a cold stare at the other man. Both boys sat back speechless. "Holy damn," Joe was now thinking. "Benedict Arnold! Damn, this has to be the guy they wanted to shoot." The rest of the trip there was nothing but small talk.

They continued until they got to Connecticut. The coach stopped around (what is now the center of New Haven). "Sorry, fellows, this is where the ride ends." Todd said thank you. After the two got out, the coach started down toward the east. "Damn, Todd," said Joe, "do you know who I thought that was?" "Yeah," said Todd, "I'll bet that was Benedict Arnold. I am sure glad we didn't say anything." "You are right," said Joe. "Well, Todd, we will have to find our way back to Boston." "Yes," said Todd, "I would sure like to know how this is going to end." "Well, we have some money, so maybe we can get a coach. Let's see if we can find a place to sleep, for I did not sleep too well in that coach."

After four hours of walking and sleeping on the ground, they came upon a roadhouse and tavern, went inside, and went to the bar. "Could we have a hot rum? We are a little bit cold." The person said, "All right, you can sit over at that table. I will get your rum." When the man came over to the table, Todd asked, "Will there be a stagecoach to the Boston area soon?" "Yes," said the waiter, "in about forty minutes." "Good," said Todd.

The innkeeper came over, and Todd asked, "How is the war going?" "Well," said the innkeeper, "most of the action, from what I hear, is down in New York-New Jersey area. We hear that Washington has retreated to the New Jersey area, Hackensack, or around there. We still have hard feelings around here between some Loyalist and the Americans. Between you and me, I hope this damn war stops soon. It is tough having two sides coming in here. So far so good. No problems. But you never know."

In a little while a stagecoach pulled up in front of the roadhouse. The driver hopped off, went into the tavern, and said, "Hello, Joseph, I would like to have an ale. Do you have any riders today?" "Yes, we have those two." The driver walked over to the two. "Where are you going?" Joe said, "We would like to go to the Boston area if we could." "Well," said the driver, "let me finish my ale, and we can be on our way." After they finished the driver said, "Okay, boys, let's go." The two got into the wagon, and the coach headed north.

They finally were back to the Boston area when the stagecoach stopped. "Okay, fellows, we are in Boston." "Well, Todd, here we are, back where we started from." "Yes," said Todd, "what are you going to do now?" "I don't know," said Joe. "Go back to the waterfront, see what happens, and see if I can find my friends. Do you want to come with me?" "No," said Todd, "it looks like there is still some of the war going on. I think I will go back home, see what happened, and maybe someday go back to the Indian camp. You remember Bright Water, don't you?" "Yeah," said Joe. "I am glad I met you. It was sure some adventure, and you turned out to be some friend. I will miss you. I did miss Bryan too. I wonder what happened to him since he was going to join Washington. I hope he is all right." "Yes, so do I. Well, I guess this is good-bye," said Todd. "Yeah, I guess it is. Like I said, Todd, I really want to go with you, but I can't." "I understand. Whatever happens have a good life, and I will miss you." Joe was saying, "Oh, never mind when I ask you a question," as Todd left.

Joe felt alone again as he headed for the waterfront to see if he could pick up where he left off. After about three days of looking around and finding food where he could, he started to get a fever. He was sweating heavily, very weak and coughing. Joe was asking around if there was a doctor. He finally found one and went to his door.

The older doctor said, "Can I help you?" "Yes, doctor, in the last few days I have felt very sick. I have had fever, sweating, and coughing." "Come in. Let me see." After looking at Joe, the doctor said, "Son, your lungs seemed to filled up. It seems like you have this sickness called pneumonia.

I will tell you are not going to leave here for a while. We will have to find a place for you to stay." As Joe lay down the doctor went to his wife. They closed the door. "I don't know what is going to happen. It does not look good for this boy." The wife said, "Is he going to die?" "I don't know; it looks like it is too far gone, but right now it looks like he is."

(Part taken from LEXINGTON Concord and Bunker Hill, (first came the Indians, Indian warriors and their weapons) Felicity's world 1775, (The American Revolution, if you were there in 1776)

Chapter Thirteen

Dave and the Pirates

Dave, leaving Joe and Jim, headed toward Boston, hoping to get back to the waterfront to see if he could find the place where they were caught. Maybe he could find the warehouse where they hid and try to find out what happened. There were a lot of British soldiers, so with a lot of people out and around the area, he blended in. He finally made his way to the waterfront, but when he arrived, he found that nothing was the same. As he walked to the water, there were a lot of British warships with their sails up. All he could think was it was awesome. As he looked around, there were no buildings, just some houses; and nothing was the same. He was thinking, "I don't know. It is confusing. I used to know these streets, but now I don't know what to do.

"If Jim and Joe show up, where the hell are they going to meet me? Nothing is the same—no warehouses, no nothing—the only thing I can see in the distance is long wharf." As he walked over to the edge of the water to sit down, he looked out over the ocean to try to figure out what to do next. After he got up, he headed up the street only to find a lot of British soldiers milling around in pairs. Looking a little farther he now saw a group of soldiers, so he now moved in behind a building. At this point, he was hoping not to get caught.

He waited for hours and still no Joe or Jim. "I wonder if they got lost. They should have been here by now." Dave was now thinking, "I have to sit down. The one thing I can't do is get caught. I'll have to move out of here. I hope Jim and Joe are taking care of themselves."

Dave walked a few blocks, moved up Battery Marsh toward Milk Street near the fort hill area, and headed away from the waterfront area. While he was walking, he saw a tavern, and looking in his pocket, he had money. But he didn't know if he could spend it since, however he got to this place, his money had not changed. He was wondering if he could spend it.

So he walked in to the tavern. There were quite a few people; and the tavern was dingy, smoky, and a mixture of British soldiers and sailors, with regular citizens as well. The local people were loud, and some were singing popular songs of the day. So Dave walked up to the bar, ordered ale, stood back, and looked around. People standing nearby were talking. One man was saying to another, "What do you think of these damn upstart Americans?" The other said, "Yes, they want to fight the king, and the bastards are causing a lot of trouble up in the Concord area." "But I am sure the soldiers will take care of that," said one man.

Not wanting to get into a conversation, Dave walked away from the bar so far so good. The bartender looked funny at the money, but he had a few of his own drinks and was in a merry mood, singing with everybody else. Dave moved toward the back and against a wall where he could see everybody and see if he could figure out his next move. He looked around, saw a table, went over, and sat down. Pretty soon another man walked into the tavern, saw a waitress, ordered, looked around, and saw that the only table that was open was the one that Dave was sitting at. He walked over and said, "This looks like the only table. Do you mind if I sit here?" Dave looked and said no. At this point, not knowing if he was with the British or just coming in for a drink, the man said, "It sure is busy tonight." "Yes," said Dave. "By the way, my name is Dave Baker. What is yours?" "Charles Cole. People just call me Cole, and I like that just fine."

"What do you do?" asked Dave. Cole answered, "I work the waters." "What do you mean? Are you a British sailor? I will tell you that those ships in the harbor, I have never seen anything like them." Cole looked at Dave a little coldly and said, "I am hardly with the British. Are you with the British?" asked Cole. "No," said Dave with caution, "I just came in for ale." Not knowing whether he was a spy, Dave was not quite sure.

"Where are you from?" asked Dave. Cole said, "I am up from south of here." "South? What do you mean South?" "Oh, down around the Bedford area. Sometimes I work on ships, sometimes do other things." "What other things?" asked Dave. Cole did not answer and pretended he did not hear. So Dave let it go and with a feeling that maybe this was something that he didn't want to hear. Cole, in turn, turned to Dave and asked, "So what do you do?" "Right now nothing," replied Dave. "How would you like to work with me?" "What doing?" asked Dave. "Well, we always need help on our ship. It's hard work, but you eat and get paid on whatever we catch." You mean work on a boat? I have never done anything like that." "You will have to change your clothes, but don't worry, you will be all right."

Dave asked Cole, "You didn't come in here to recruit, did you?" Cole answered, "Not really, but we are always looking for some good men." Dave was thinking, "Well, Joe and Jim are not here by now, so I might do this and see if I can make some money on a trip and come back maybe in a week or so. I'll come back and see if I can meet up hopefully with Jim and Joe. I hope they didn't get caught." Cole said, "Do you have enough money to carry you over for the night?" "Yes," said Dave. "Good," said Cole, "then we can leave in the morning." Dave was saying to himself, "I hope this is all right. Hell, he comes in here; and after a short conversation, he is giving me a job, and we are going to the New Bedford area. Man, I hope this is all right; but if anything, it will get me away from these damn British around here."

The next morning, when Dave had awakened, he met Cole who had a wagon and two horses and supplies inside. "Where did you get the wagon?" Dave inquired. "This is what I came up with; it belongs to the firm that I work with." "Well," said Dave, "it looks like you have enough supplies. Did you expect to have more men with you?" Cole looked and just smiled as they headed south toward Roxbury flats. Finally they got to the Dartmouth area; the land is owned by the Joseph Russell family.

"This is quite something a beautiful place, isn't it? Is this the place where they go whaling?" "Whaling?" replied Cole. "Yes," said Dave, "you know, where they go after whales." "Well," said Cole, "the Indians go after whales with small boats. They wait for them to thin out and go after the smaller ones." Just then they heard a lot of shooting. "What is happening?" asked Dave. "We are down near the water, so let's see if we can find out."

At that time the British landed at Clark's Point and marched through Bedford to Acushnet and back to Fairhaven, burning wharves, buildings, and ships. The waterfront suffered complete devastation. "What the hell is going on?" asked Dave. "They are burning everything. Look at those buildings, the flames; it looks like they are destroying everything." "Holy cow, look at the ships," said Dave. "There are even burning them. I wonder if they are burning any of the ships you are working on." "I don't think so," said Cole. "Our ships are pretty well hidden." "What do you mean hidden?" asked Dave. "Well, you see, Dave, we sort of have our own business." "Business? What do you mean business?" asked Dave. "Well, let's say we sort of take care of things on the seas." "What things?" "We relieve some British ships of their belongings."

"What the hell do you mean? You mean to tell me that you are pirates?" asked Dave. "Well, we like to be called privateers." "Like I said," Dave replied, "pirates." "And which privateer would be the choice of the volunteer?" Ask this and he would answer with his own question. "Who's the skipper?"

Few towns in the revolutionary America were more than one hundred miles from the sea, and every local newspaper made haste to announce the latest privateering exploits. Tavern talk and wagging tongues made point of the string of prizes brought in by each captain. The greater the number, the greater his reputation. It followed that the lucky vessel could most part chose his own crew. They would only be as successful as its commander.

The captain drummed up recruits by having a band play stirring martial tunes, flags flying and also giving patriotic speeches. Such inducements were the practice of the thin-ranked naval service. Privateering caught the fancy of a red-blooded man with a yen for the sea. He would have less discipline and shorter cruises than the navy and more jingle in his pockets if the hunt took some worthwhile prizes. There would be no wages paid to the captain or the crew in any event, but the chance for sudden riches was just over the horizon.

"So like I said, we have a job for you, and we get paid for what prizes we take in." Dave was thinking, "I don't know where I am, but whatever dream I am in, I am stealing again. I don't believe it."

There is a gap in America's Revolutionary War history about as big as the Atlantic Ocean on this watery highway. The mightiest naval power in the world carried soldiers and supplies enough to crush her rebellious American subjects. At the outset of the conflict, there was not a single Continental vessel to annoy the English shipping. By 1777 there were but thirty-four cruisers afloat, and in 1782 their number had been whittled to seven. Yet no enemy vessel was safe on the high seas! A sort of civilian navy had evened the odds.

The privateers were men outfitted at the shipowners' expense and commissioned by the new states and Congress to attack and take enemy vessels. They made a mighty contribution to America's independence. Over two thousand privately armed vessels, large and small, carried eighteen thousand cannon and seventy thousand men into battle. Their efforts brought back a grand total of sixteen warships and two thousand nine hundred and eighty British merchant vessels. Valuewise, these prizes paid off fifty million dollars to the shipowners and the volunteers making the captures.

Washington's hard-pressed army received much of the war booty while King George gained nothing but grief. And there lies the gap in our early history, for relatively little is known of these Yankees who combined patriotism with profit. Such private and highly individualistic cruises rarely found their way into official records. Many old ships' logs filled with the excitement of the chase still remain undiscovered in the attics of the descendants.

Gleanings come from the occasional diaries and journals letters from shipboard or prison, as well as contemporary newspapers reporting privateer actions or prize sales. British-scale drawings of captured sharp-sailing craft and eighteenth-century texts used in gunnery, navigation, and surgery. When these fragments were gathered, sorted, and spliced into the following pages, the privateer's man of two hundred plus years ago stands tall among his liberty-loving countrymen. He is well worth it. (This is from a foreword from revolution's privateers.)

Dave said, "What am I to do? You want me to go on this ship with you? What do I do on this ship? I mean outside of one time I was invited on a Boston Harbor cruise, I have never really been on a ship." Cole said, "What kind of a cruise?" Looking around Dave thought he could never explain and said, "Oh, nothing." Dave said, "Let me get this right. What we are going to be doing is stealing their goods. Now what happens if we lose a battle or get caught?" Cole said, "Well, there are three things that could happen." "What is that?" said Dave. "We could die In a fight, go to prison, or be hanged." "Oh great," said Dave, muttering under his breath.

The captain Elisha Hinman stood up on the top deck. "Gentlemen," he said with a gruff voice, "you are now under my command. That means if you disobey my commands, you will be punished; otherwise, you hold up your end, and everything will be all right. Okay, let's set sail," said the captain. When they were out on the water, the captain said, "Now here will be the breakdown of this trip." The captain shares will be eight; first lieutenant will be four; second lieutenant, four; master, four; surgeon, four; officer of marines, two; prize master, two; carpenter, two; gunner, two; boatswain; two; master's mates, two; captain clerks, two; steward shares, two; sail maker, two; gunner's mate one and a half; boatswain's mate, one and a half; carpenter's mates, one and a half; cooper, one and a half;

surgeon's mate, one and a half; armorer, two; sergeant marines, two; cook, two; gentlemen volunteers, one; and boys under sixteen years, half.

"Where do I fall in this?" Dave asked. Cole said, "We will find something, but for now we have to get you some clothing. Let's see, we have what we call sailcloth, mostly from Europe [there were no mills until the first at Beverly, Massachusetts, in 1788]. I will tell you that no privateer would put out to see without an extra 'suit' of sails. Well, here is one that I think will fit you; you can go into that room and try them on." Dave came out after awhile and said, "I will tell you one thing. These are different; they feel sort of funny." "Don't worry," said Cole, "they look fine.

"Do you know anything about these ships?" "No," said Dave. "Well, that one over there they call a schooner, for they are fast and maneuverable. It carries two or three masts with fore and aft sails, fore and aft staysails on a square rigger, the spanker on gaff, and boom is aft. Now over here we have a sloop, a smaller single-mast sister to the swift schooner." As they continued, the brig has two masts and square rigged, brigantine foremast was square rigged, and the main mast was fore and aft rigged. Dave was listening, shaking his head but had no idea what the hell he was talking about.

"Tell me, Cole, that group of people over there—who are they?" Cole replied, "Oh, them. They are landlubbers." "Landlubbers? What the hell are they?" "Well, a lot of them are country boys stolen off during the night, leaving their distressed parents a 'gone a privateering' note. Doctors, ministers, lawyers, shopkeepers, farmers, runaway Negro slaves.

"Dave, I will tell you one thing. You are all expected to get all your sea legs in short order. As part of the outsized crew [privately armed ships were always crowded], they were needed as sailors, gunners, moving captured cargo, prisoner guards, carpenter's helpers to repair damage; and as prize crews the latter might strip the vessel down to one-tenth of the able-bodied seamen aboard. This was to be expected on a successful cruise, for each prize crew was made up of between twelve to twenty men."

The captain came over and said, "Hello, Cole, how are you?" "Fine," said Cole, "I have a friend here. This will be his first time on board." "Well, Cole," said the captain, "you know you will be picked. As far as your friend, all I can say is that he better pull his weight." The captain turned around and headed for the ship. Dave said sarcastically to Cole, "A real pleasant fellow, isn't he?" Cole said, "He is tough, but most of the time he is fair." "Most of the time?" replied Dave.

Most privateers wore no uniforms. The clothes that were worn back on the farm, the shop, or fishing vessel were good enough. Still it made some sense to wear some of the gear that had proved useful over long years of sea. Hats, the conventional wide-brim hat, was worn three cornered or coked, turned up all around, turned up on one side or both sides. There was a sailor's flat-brimmed hat made from a piece of the ship's canvas and waterproofed with tar or a paint knit cap black to hide the dirt. A neckerchief originally called a sweat rag was worn about the neck or forehead. Peacoat was seaman's top coat for cold weather. "Pilot clothes" were bell-bottomed trousers that could be easily rolled up when scrubbing decks or wading ashore.

The skins were kept aboard in brine; each was rolled up and secured at the top with ribbon and bow.

"Okay, Dave, here is your ditty bag." "My what?" asked Dave. "Just look," said Cole. So he was given a canvas sack. Looking in it Dave had wrought scissors-drawn four-fifths-size sewing gear, jack knife, wooden shaving dish, and razor. "Okay, everybody, aboard" was the call. Once everybody was aboard, the second in command from the top deck said, "Okay, we have different watches: midwatch, midnight to 4:00 a.m.; morning watch, 4:08 a.m. to 8:00 a.m.; forenoon watch, 8:00 a.m. to noon; afternoon watch, noon to 4:00 p.m.; first dog watch, 4:00 p.m. to 6:00 p.m.; second dog watch, 6:00 p.m. to 8:00 p.m.; and night watch, 8:00 p.m. to midnight.

Anchor watch in port was reduced to but three or four men. The ship's belled one bell, 12:30 a.m.; two bells, 1:00 a.m.; three bells, 1:30 a.m.; four bells, 2:00 a.m.; five bells, 2:30 a.m.; six bells, 3:00 a.m.; seven bells, 3:30 a.m.; and eight bells, 4:00 a.m.

All time was kept by sandglasses, and on the half hour the glass was turned. This procedure was repeated each watch with the quartermaster striking the bell when the glass was capsized. The weary welcomed the eight bells' strike that sent them back to their hammocks.

"Okay, Dave, you take the 6:00 p.m. watch." Dave asked, "What am I watching for?" "Well, anything: oncoming vessels, bad weather, or the British. Okay, Dave, you have to go up there." "Up where?" asked Dave. "Up there," said Cole. Looking up Dave was looking at a perch about a hundred feet above deck. "You are shitting me," said Dave. "No," said Cole. "How the hell do you expect me to get up there?" Cole said to a crew member, "Come over here." The crewman came over and said, "Yes, sir." "Yes, show this man how to get up on the top for lookout."

"Well, you climb the square openings in the windward rigging and never but never let go of one rope until another is firmly in hand. Always remember one hand for yourself and another for the ship. So when you get to the top platform, a man falling overboard from aloft has little chance unless lines break his fall and the distance to the sea is no more than forty feet.

"If your fate is the water and you're alive enough to know it, keep cool, steady, and turn away from the wind and swim. Every now and then, raise your arm to direct the rescue boat. Don't waste your energy by shouting or trying to swim back to the ship. Even in high seas you can remain afloat for half an hour, plenty of time for a small boat to heave you to safely aboard.

"After your first trek to the tops, you must pay your footing. All hands must be treated to a mug of rum." Now Dave began his climb, trying not to look down. After he got to the top, he now worked his way over to the loft and got to look down at the ocean below. He said to himself, "I can't believe I did this. Son of a bitch, I am up here for two or three hours. I hope I don't get sick, but at least looking out on the ocean from the top was a beautiful sight."

As the ship continued sailing, nothing happened on Dave's watch. After Dave got back down on deck, Cole said, "You owe everybody rum." "I don't have that much." "Well, if we get a prize ship, we will get it then." After the rum party Dave headed for his hammock for the night. Falling asleep, slowly listening to the waves coming up against the ship, he was thinking, "This damn thing is driving me crazy.

"We tried to rob the store, and the crazy owner comes up with a shotgun. I think we escaped, and I end up in this mess in 1775 on a damn ship with pirates yet. I am tired, for I just want to go to sleep."

The next morning, the captain called out, "Okay, everybody, to the crews' quarters." Dave arose and saw Cole. "How did you sleep?" asked Cole. "Not bad," replied Dave. "I thought it would be worse sleeping on a hammock, but when you are tired, I guess you could sleep on a picket fence." Sitting down Dave asked, "What do they eat?" "Ah," said Cole, "we follow the Massachusetts State Navy orders, which are subscribed by the ship's owners, which is one pound of bread, one pound of pork beef, one grill of rice and one grill of rum, a half a pound of peas or beans, one pound of potatoes or turnip [might be substituted for the rice], and three quarters of a pound of butter. One-half a pint of vinegar was allowed weekly."

The necessity of preserving meats in brine soon snuffed out any resemblance to home cooking. The finest side of beef became a soggy, leathery mess of fibers—"salt junk," it was called, for junk was an old rope. The similarity needed no elaboration for those with timid stomachs, of course; the brine must first be removed by a thorough watering in a "steep tub" before boiling. The ship's cook could redeem himself by a frequent offering of lobscouse; dried potato slices resembling wood chips, and soaked salt beef were hashed together. Dried peas and beans, both more likely ammunition for a musket, and pieces of unyielding hardtack were often added to the mush and cooked well. And from these unlikely ingredients came meat that no mariner could resist. The makings for the last-mentioned hard tack—or if one washed he could use the less realistic name of sea biscuit or ship's bread—were as unappetizing as the result. For hard tack they mixed one teaspoon of salt with one pound of flour, ship enough water to make a very stiff dough, cut the whole into four-inch sections, and punch it with holes, and bake on a flat pan at 250 degrees for two or three hours.

After eating Dave said, "You know, Cole, this food is really bad, and this bread is awful. By the way what the hell do I hear?" Cole said, "Singing." "Singing?" asked Dave. As they walked up on deck, the songs were for the purpose pulling. These songs had a single aim to have all hands haul the halyard. Single-pull chantries called for one great effort followed by a breathing spell before the next pull. The pull came on the last syllable and then the solo, and the chorus repeated until the chore was done. Solo: "We'll haul the bowline so early in the morning." Chorus: "We'll haul the bowline, the bowline haul!" Double-pull chants for long pulls. All hands pulled twice on each chorus.

Solo: "A Yankee ship came down the river." Chorus: "Blow, boys, blow." Solo: "And all her sails they shone like silver." Chorus: "Blow, my bully boy's blow. (In the twentieth-century songbooks it was known as "Blow the Man Down.")

Cole said to Dave, "You know, when the time comes, you will have to fight. A lot of these British ships do not give up easily, so I just want you to know what may be coming. We are out here for one reason, and that is to relieve these ships of their goods." Dave was now thinking to himself, "Some job I was offered. Here I am out on the water, stealing from ships that will fight, and people could get killed. What the hell did I get myself into now?"

Dave said, "We have been out for about three hours, and we haven't seen a ship yet. When do you think we will see a ship, and how long do you think we will be out here?" Cole replied, "As long as it takes. The people that back this trip—you know, the shipowners—want to make sure we better come back with something." The day went by without any incidents, so after dinner everybody bedded down for the night. It was a little cool, so Dave got some blankets and went to sleep.

The next morning, when all awoke and headed for the crews' quarters, Dave met with Cole, and they had some coffee. Cole said, "How do like the coffee this morning?" "Well," replied Dave, "it's not Dunkin' Donuts, but it will do." "Dunkin' what?" said Cole. "Never mind. When we finished we can go up to the deck and see what is going on," replied Dave.

When they arrived on deck, there was a heavy fog. "Wow," said Dave, "this is something. This fog is so thick you can hardly see ten feet around you." "Yeah," said Cole, "we will have to wait a couple of hours till this thing clears. While we are waiting for it to clear, let me show you a few things. There will be things you must know if and when we do get into battle."

Cole said, "Let me go over a few things for the gunners: [1] cast off lashings when action unlikely; gun is secured to eyebolts above gun port. [2] Power monkeys hoist powder and shot up at main hatch from the shot locker. [Small tackles whips of a single rope in block does the job.] [3] Haul gun inboard with train tackle, [4] remove tampion from muzzle of your gun, [5] raise gun port, and [6] observe wind and lay the budge barrel [powder barrel] or cartridges [cylindrical flannel bags filled with gunpowder] to the windward of your piece and the match staff or linstock to the leeward. [7] Touchhole with pick. [8] Sponge her well and strike the sponge on the muzzle with several blows to rid it of foulness. [9] Stand to the right side of the gun and ram powder cartridge down full length of the bore, or if powder ladle is used instead, have the powder barrel held aslope. Thrust in your ladle, give a shag, then strike off heaped powder. Put your ladle home in the chamber, turn the ladle staff until your thumbs be under it, and give a sturdy shake to clear the powder off the ladle, draw it out, keeping an upward pressure so that no powder is removed. Ram the powder home quietly to pack and make the powder fire the better. Put home a good wad with two or three strokes; your assistant should have his thumb on the touch hole all the while. [10] Take a ball from the shot rack and put it home with a rammer, follow it with a good wad of rope yarn rammed home so that no space between the powders, the first wad, the shot, and the last wad. [12] Stand to the windward and prime the touchhole with fine powder, letting it fill the base ring. If a cartridge is used first, prick it open so that the priming will set off the charge. [13]

Run your carriage forward with the side tackle. Muzzle will project well beyond the gun port to prevent fire, taking hold of the dry ship's timbers; train tackle will prevent the carriage from rolling too far forward. [14] Aim your gun up or down, lever your handspike against a carriage step, and heave up the weighty barrel breech the quoin that wooden wedge with side elevation markings is slid forward on its bed to the estimated elevation or depression. [15] Take up your linstock and blow on the slow match to raise a spark standing to the right. Touch the powder in the base ring and not the touchhole, for the upward flame would otherwise douse your slow match. The explosion in the chamber should be instantaneous. While the ball seeks its mark, the force will drive the cannon carriage backward; the heavy breeching rope will stop its motion. [16] Swab out the bore with your wet sheepskin sponge to extinguish any sparks before reloading.

"A good crew will load and fire in less than a minute." "Son of a bitch, Cole, you gave me about sixteen things I am supposed to remember. And you are saying that this crew can do this in less than a minute. This being a pirate is tougher than I thought." "What do you mean?" Cole asked. "Well, I mean I thought like in the movies you get into a battle, you jump on the ship and get a beautiful woman, the gold, and a parrot on your shoulder." Cole asked, "Dave, what the hell are you talking about?" "Nothing," said Dave, "nothing. Forget it."

"Well, the next lesson you have to know the enemy. The privateers' man seeking out the plump merchantman was well aware of the quarry's habits. They had two ways of going to sea. Often one hundred and sometimes as many as six hundred merchantmen would sail under the protection of English warships. Collecting such a number of vessels took such time and effort that word had reached sharp Yankee ears before the mass of ships had weighed anchor.

"The formation was predictable. The van ship of a large fleet, a powerful ship of the line commanded by no lesser rank than admiral, led her brood like a mother duck. She would hoist signals frequently for the faster vessels to shorten sail to let the dull sailors catch up to the rest. Sloops and brigs of war doing guard duty on the flanks also did service by towing laggards up to the others.

"Nightfall was a particularly dangerous time for the convoy, and at the close broiler signal all merchantmen would cluster as close to the van ship's stern as possible. Here cooperation between several privateering vessels paid off. While one enticed a guard ship away, the other would cut out a laggard. The prize crew would then board and sheer her off to leeward with a zigzag course. Once the privateers' men and the prize had scattered, the guard ships had little enthusiasm to chase and leave the flanks of the fleet unprotected. Darkness, fog, or foul weather worked to the privateer's advantage. Merchantmen could become scattered and fall easy prey.

"Swift-sailing merchantmen, not all cargo-carrying ships, were floating tubs with sails atop. Some had faster lines, could crowd more canvas, and carried cannon and crew enough to take their chances alone. These lone sailors usually carried goods of considerable worth, and so were eagerly sought by the Yankee captains one could secure the vessel for their own.

"Now, Dave, we have to tell you about the boarding ships. A collision at sea is a ready-made boarding opportunity or a disaster for the attacking ship. If you can foul the enemy's bowsprit in your main shrouds, you can rake his length at your pleasure. As a rule of thumb, get a bit to the leeward. When you are one or two ship lengths ahead [depending on your speed], shiver your sails—that is, spill the wind by huffing your canvas or laying them flat against the mast. Put your helm hard a lee, and you have his bow locked in your rigging; she's yours for the taking.

"To chase and board, a captain intuitively keeps his keel at an efficient angle to the wind. He might put it this way. A vessel cannot sail into the eye of the wind. Fore and aft rigs can point into the wind no more than forty degrees, when close hauled no better than fifty-five degrees. However, a wise seaman never sails as close to the wind as possible. This 'pinching' will give the lowest speed, and the lower the speed, the greater the side drift. Therefore, you must point as high as possible while keeping good-speed 'running' with the wind astern, which is best done with the wind within thirty degrees of either side for the aft sails.

"Now you have to keep close to the weather quarter of the enemy; then you have to worry her with a blanket of fire. Boarders away! Now if she tacks to windward, your speed, being better on the weather side, permits you to make a tight arc. You shortly will be on her stern. But if the enemy tacks to windward, you have a chance to rake her stern. Luff sails when going windward to keep astern. Board on her leeward. If you come about too fast to the wind, shorten your sail and rake her as you pass.

"Now, Dave, if we get into a fight, the captain will take care of most of this, but you will have to know what is going on. If you don't know it, it could kill you. So I know it is boring, but listen to me. It could save your life. Now if we become prisoners, take it easy. Check out the situation. If the captain is a bastard, don't start anything because if you do, they could throw you overboard. If we capture any prisoners, we will have to watch out.

"I read in the *Boston Gazette* on December 9 where a letter by an Englishman was quoted concerning the capture of the American privateer sloop *Yankee*, which had nine guns and sixty men. Henry Johnson, commanding the capture of the ship, was solely owing to the ill-judged lenity and brotherly kindness of Captain Johnson who not considering his English prisoners in the same light that he would Frenchmen or Spaniards put them under no sort of confinement but permitted them to walk the decks as freely as his own people at all times.

"Taking advantage of this indulgence, the prisoners, one day watching their opportunity when most of the privateer's people were below and asleep, shut down the hatches and took the vessel without force." "Wow," said Dave, "talk about being stupid." "Yeah," said Cole.

All of a sudden there was a call—a ship—and it looked like a British ship. All hands started to get into position. Cole turned to Dave. "This looks like this is it," handing Dave a sword and a pistol. "If this is a fight and we get separated, good luck and may the gods be with you." Dave, standing there stunned, was thinking, "What the hell is this? I have a sword and this damn gun. Now what?"

The gunners were taking their position at the cannons. The captain turned to his first mate and said, "Do you think we are faster?" "I don't know," said the first mate, "but we have to get on the same tack and course as them. Hoist the same sail. Now set her position in your compass. If our sharp-hulled craft is faster, their sails will soon draw a point aft. If both are equal sailors, she will keep the same compass point. But if she draws points forward, a chase will be pointless. Now remember to chase to the windward. If we have the faster vessel, we must set the same course as the other ship."

Dave was now saying to himself, "Shit. I hope we don't catch that other ship because I am not ready to fight. There is no place to run here. I just want to get back to shore, and the hell with this pirate thing."

The ships were now coming upon each other. It was getting tense. Dave was beginning to feel like he was getting a little sick, feeling like there was not any place he could go. If a fight started, all he had were the confines of the ship, not like on land like in Boston where there were plenty of places to escape.

Just then a cannon shot fired at the ship. Dave said, "What the hell was that?" Cole said, "They are firing at us. Get ready," as both ships came upon each other. Men were boarding from each ship with swordfights, fistfights, and shots being fired. One sailor, seeing Dave, started at him with his sword flashing. Dave, seeing the man coming at him, shot off his gun and missed, taking off Cole's hat. Cole was in a swordfight and, after running it through the sailor he was fighting, turned to Dave and said, "What the hell are you doing?" Dave said, "Sorry, I just missed."

Meanwhile the other sailor, swinging his sword at Dave, knocked the sword out of Dave's hand and by now was on the top deck, chasing Dave, with Dave throwing things at him and the man ducking. Dave tripped, and the sailor was about to run Dave through with his sword when all of a sudden a shot rang out, and the sailor fell. Standing behind Dave was Cole. "Get the hell up. Here is your sword. Don't drop it, or next time I might not be here. And for Christ's sake next time you shoot, make sure you hit something and not me."

The fight was now everywhere with even the two captains involved. Dave by now was moving onto the next ship with everyone around in knife and swordfights or shooting at one another, neither side giving up easily. Dave was thinking, "This is crazy fighting in the middle of the ocean." Just then a shot was fired. It missed Dave with the bullet lodging in a barrel and let some liquid out pouring it over the deck, around, and over Dave. Dave, agitated, said, "Son of a bitch, it's rum." Dave was talking not really to anyone in particular. After hours of fighting Dave's ship finally won out, and the enemy ship was captured. The enemy captain and remaining crew became prisoners and were put in leg irons.

"Well," said Cole, "not bad. You fought pretty good when you didn't have somebody chasing you. By the way, what do I smell?" Dave said, "It's damn rum. I have the stuff all over me." "Well," said Cole, "you won't have to worry about drinking it, for you have it in your hair and all over you." Cole, still smiling, said, "You won't have to worry about money, for our split of the bounty looks pretty good." "Yeah, I can't wait to get back to shore. These damn things are great for the movies only." "The what?" said Cole. "Nothing," said Dave.

"By the way, what happens to the prisoners?" "Oh, they will be all right. They will be brought to prison ships, which will be taking them to prisons on land. But let me tell you about how the British treat their prisoners. A story that was told to me about the treatment of the American captives was just shy of hanging. Nathaniel Fanning in his *Narrative* gave a fairly characteristic picture of the heavy-handed British.

"Fanning had sailed as a prize master from Boston on the newly constructed privateer brig *Angelica* [sixteen guns, ninety-eight men, and boys, with William Dennis commanding]. He was captured and placed on board the British frigate *Androineda*. They were first paraded on the quarter deck in the presence of their great and mighty general, the celebrated general Howe of Bunker Hill memory. The general asked us a number of insignificant questions, among which was if we were willing to engage in His Majesty's service. We have answered pretty unanimously in the negative; he then upbraided us with these words, 'You are a set of rebels, and it is more than probable that you will be hanged on our arrival at Portsmouth.' Following this welcome aboard, this master at arms and some crewmen made a pretext of searching the privateer's baggage for concealed knives. The baggage was never seen again.

"On the way to the ship's hold, some of the jack-tars ordered the prisoners to halt and begin to strip them of their clothes, saying, 'Come, shipmates, these fine things will only be a plague to you. The climate is very hot where you are bound [meaning the ships hold.' They were given frocks and trousers and sent into the hold. There they received no food for twenty hours, thereafter but two-thirds the usual prisoner-of-war allowance.

"The captain and General Howe were deaf to complaints and answered that we were treated with too much lenity being considered as rebels, whose crimes were of such an aggravated kind, that we should be shown no mercy. Mercy was not entirely wanting. However, once every twenty-four hours, the prisoners were allowed on deck one at a time. Then sent back to the oven pit of the ship, hot enough for most of the men to go stark naked. There the closely packed privateers' men stewed in their own juices until the boiling point was reached.

"The enterprising and liberty-loving Yankees laid plans to take over the ship, one of Her Majesty's mighty men of war, but word reached enemy ears before the plot could be hatched. The food was just enough to keep a man alive: half a pint of water per man each day. The prisoners remedied their hunger pangs by prying a plank from a partition that led to the general's store room. The menu was a handsome catch of wines, liquors, white biscuit, raisins, dried fruit, tongues, hams, and beef. The Americans were soon 'drunk' over the general's excellent Madeira wine, and so they lived like 'hearty fellows' until the anchorage at Portsmouth, England, all the while keeping suspicions down by snatching at the few scraps brought to them.

"The general, captain, and officers were astonished to find the prisoners all brave and hearty. General Howe was heard to say, 'What! Are none of those goddamn Yankees sick? Damn them. There is nothing but thunder and lightning that will kill them.'

"Once onshore each prisoner faced a battery of detailed questions from two civil magistrates. The grilling was repeated and the answers compared; in this way the British authorities hoped to ferret out any and all British subjects serving on American vessels. A noose would be their fate, while their American shipmates marched off to an indefinite confinement."

"Well, I hope we get to land pretty soon. And by the way, Cole, thanks for the job, but I think this will end my pirate career when I get back. I want to stay on land from now on." Pretty soon they saw land as boats went out to guide the ships into their landing. "You know," said Dave, "I wish you would have let me know what job you were giving me. I might have stayed back in Boston and took my chance with the British." Cole just smiled. Finally they came ashore. Dave was the first one to jump onto land.

"I will tell you one thing, Cole. I am glad that that victory was ours. I would have not liked to have been the one that was captured. Now I will have to find some way to get this sticky rum off me." When Dave was all cleaned up, he met Cole, and they both went to a tavern for ale. "Well, now," said Cole, "that looks better." "Yeah," said Dave, "that feels better too."

"Well," asked Cole, "you said you don't want to go out on the water again." "You are right there," answered Dave, "for that was not exactly a luxury cruise, you know." "Well, what are you going to do?" "I don't know," said Dave, "but what I received from the bounty will keep me for a while. I think I will head south and see what happens." "You know," said Cole, "I have been out on about ten of these missions, and believe it or not, this was the easiest of them all." "You have to be kidding," said Dave. "No," replied Cole, "so I think I will skip the next one and tag along with you—that is, if you don't mind." "No, I don't. I would like to have the company."

"By the way, Cole, I have to ask this question. When you said the ship's owners, you mean they get their cut, and some goes to George Washington?" "Yes," said Cole. "That tells me that the haul must have been something." "Yes, it was," replied Cole. "So some of this helps the fight against the British." "Yes."

"You know, Cole, with some screwy laws we have in Massachusetts, the father of our country could have been arrested for receiving stolen goods."

Cole said, "What are you talking about and what laws? The only laws that anybody is talking about are the British laws, and anything you do is against their laws." "Yeah, you are right, Cole. I am still trying to figure out how I got here. But tell me, Cole, about the owners."

"Well, most of them, believe it or not, are owned by American families, and there is a number investing their money in privateering. It is honorable, patriotic, and profitable venture. Half of all the prize monies would go to the owners. Indeed many of these gentlemen gained in respect and ability as their fortunes increased. If one could measure such a quality. But make no mistake; it was a gamble. No matter how scrappy or swift a vessel, the might of the British navy was ranging along the coastline. If the vessel were taken, not a farthing would come from the pockets of the hard-pressed taxpayers.

"With a converted merchantman or sharp new vessel nearing completion, a captain must be chosen. Family titles, friends, and backslappers stood no chance with hardheaded Yankee businessmen. They would choose a man with a reputation for seamanship, a respected leader of his crew, a sea chest full of initiative, and an incurable itch for action. Such a man would already be well-known among America's bustling seaports.

"Now you know, Dave," said Cole, "that the privateering was in a lot of things." Sort of jacks-of-all trades," said Dave. "I guess you could say that," replied Cole, looking at Dave with a quizzical look. Cole continued, "Not all privateer engagements were on the high seas. For example, one of the fastest sailors in New England, the *General Putnam*, with twenty-nine ponders and one hundred and fifty men and Captain Harmon commanding, had taken fourteen prizes earlier in the war. Her fleetness was of little use, however, when she was driven into a harbor [present-day Saco, Maine] by a frigate.

"The British came to anchor to wait their quarry. Not one to collect barnacles in port, Captain Harmon hauled one of his guns ashore and up to a point on land. The frigate was fired upon, and the warship answered with broadsides. But before the woods could be leveled by British cannonballs, the American gun cut away the others' forestay. She was obliged to come to sail and put to sea.

"Down the coast, the tiny boat *Speedwell*, which had two guns and twenty men, and Captain Levi Barlow commanding was forced into Nantucket Harbor by a privateer schooner of superior force manned by Tory refugees and sheep stealers from New York. Barlow and his crew landed by a wharf. There they hove up a breastwork and made ready for attack. But an assault came from an unexpected quarter when they were driven off by some less than patriotic islanders. These people had profited from their trading with the enemy and had little affection for Captain Barlow who had recently taken a number of their kind prisoners.

"While the Tory privateer made splinters of the *Speedwell,* Barlow and his men made their way to the Massachusetts mainland and held a hurried meeting with Captain Lot Dimmick of Falmouth. Several small boats were borrowed, and the two captains with a part of their crews made their way for Nantucket. The enemy vessel still lazed off the island. Commandeering a sloop at anchor, the Yankees sailed into a warm welcome from swivels and musketry and were able to board and take the vessel. The twenty-eight prisoners were taken to the friendlier port of Falmouth.

"Commando-like raids on British towns were no rarity. You know, the privateer trail went from Halifax, Nova Scotia; to Lunenburg, Annapolis Royal; Saco, Maine; Boston; Nantucket Island; Falmouth; and Newport. There is a story that a lieutenant Barteman waded through heavy musket fire in the northwest part of town. The garrison retreated to the south blockhouse where they returned a brisk fire. Their enthusiasm ended when the Americans closed the contest with a few balls from a four-pound cannon.

"Care was taken to observe 'the strictest decorum' toward the civilians with their clothing and furniture inviolably preserved for their use. The royal magazine was stored in the hold of the *Scamtnel* along with quantities of dry goods; twenty puncheons of good West Indian rum; and the king's beef, pork, and flour. Other cargo included the British colonel and some of the principal citizens. The town was ransomed for a thousand pounds sterling.

"On the side of the brave sons of liberty, three were wounded slightly and one dangerously; on the part of the abettors of oppression and despotism, the number of slain and wounded were unknown with only one of their slain being found." "Cole, you mean they ransomed the whole town?" asked Dave. "That is what they say."

"In May the privateer *Lady Washington*'s four guns, six crew, and Captain Joseph Cunningham commanding, and the schooner *Franklin*—several two pounders and swivels, twenty-one men, and Captain James Mugford commanding—sailed from Boston Harbor. Their departure was duly noted by enemy shipping when the *Franklin* ran aground in the *Gut.* Thirteen or more British boats, many with swivels, and two hundred marines and sailors pushed off under cover of darkness. Between nine and ten o'clock the *Lady*

Washington anchored near the *Franklin* and discovered the raiding party. Challenged they shouted that they were from Boston. Captain Mugford immediately fired, and his crew followed with a volley.

"By cutting the cable, the *Franklin* was able to bring a broadside to bear. The charges loaded with musket balls cut into the enemy. Before the cannon could be reloaded, two or three of the boats were alongside. Within minutes there were eight or nine boatloads attempting to board, but the attacks were repulsed with muskets and boarding pikes. Two boats were sunk with no survivors.

"Meanwhile the *Lady Washington* was set upon by the remaining four or five boats. Captain Cunningham and six of his men with their swivels, blunderbusses, and muskets were able to drive off the British. But there was no celebration that night, for Captain Mugford had met his death by a musket ball."

Cole said, "I was on a couple of expeditions where we got into a lot of trouble with some British ships but somehow lucked out even though we did have a fight. Our last trip in open water was one of our easier ones." "You have to be kidding," said Dave. "I could have been killed out there with all that fighting. I mean the shooting and that son of a bitch trying to stick me with a sword." "Yes," said Cole, "but you made a good profit, and the worst thing that happened is you ended up with a hair full of rum." "Very funny," said Dave. "Well," said Dave, "we should be on our way. Are you sure you still want to come?" Cole said, "Yeah, I will go with you and get away from pirating, for there should be some interesting places and maybe some bounty." "Best of all, somewhere along the way, we can make some British pissed off." "Is that the way you put it, Dave?" "Yeah," replied Dave, "I guess so."

"Where will we head now?" "Well," said Dave, "let's get out of this area and see what happens." "Can you ride a horse?" Cole asked Dave. "No," replied Dave. "Well, we will have to be able to get some sort of transportation." "What do you suggest?" asked Dave. "The shipyard has a coach something." "Like a stagecoach?" asked Dave. "No more open than one of those. I think I can work something since a shipmate of mine works there." Cole came back. "Okay, Dave, we have a wagon and two horses. The man owed me a lot." "Great," said Dave.

"Well, we have everything. Shall we go?" said Dave. "Yes," said Cole. "Where are we going?" "Well," said Dave "let's head south toward New York." While they were riding, Dave had a chance to start thinking about things that were happening. Like how he got to this place and what Jim and Joe were doing. Wondering if they were going through the same thing. "How weird. This was 1775 and 1776. Whatever the hell was going on?" Dave was thinking about saying something but not at this point. He was afraid that Cole would think he was crazy or something.

"Are you okay?" asked Cole. "Yes," said Dave. "Why?" "Well, you looked like you were somewhere else. Shall we go now?" said Cole. So the two started off and headed towered New York, not knowing that there was a battle going on in that area.

Swiftly and hopelessly General Washington was driven out of New York City, then out of New York State, then across New Jersey, and finally into Philadelphia. When at last he had the remnants of his dwindling army safely over the Delaware River, the general finally began to do something he should have done much earlier. He set up intelligence nets. He established one net in New Jersey where he expected to attack the enemy in a few weeks. He set up another around Philadelphia where he feared the enemy might attack him.

For these espionage systems he had to have new American spies who were familiar enough with the local people to know who was a Whig and who was a Tory and who understood local geography, customs, and habits. These new secret agents were to supply the Continental Army with constant and accurate military intelligence no matter where the army went, no matter what the enemy was doing. General Washington set up his new intelligence system in New Jersey where his army's immediate need was greatest, then inside and around New York City, the British base, and then around Philadelphia. It was certain to be fighting sooner or later.

Within a very short time American espionage in New York City was much increased. By November 1776 General Mercer who had failed to get an agent to Staten Island was able to send into New York City itself a skilled observer. To this day no one knows who he was; but he came back with a full report of British intentions, troop movements, losses, and reinforcements. When the Americans were forced back beyond New Brunswick, New Jersey, on the first day or two other daring secret agents were quietly dropped off in preparation for eighteen months of undetected espionage. Still other new spies were soon at work. A screen of additional secret agents spread out onto New Jersey far beyond the American front.

Two of the men helping direct this espionage, Joshua and John Mersereau, always believed they saved Washington's weakened army from total destruction. They may have been justified. Too weak to face British forces, Washington, after retreating into Pennsylvania, had tried to seize all boats on the Delaware. If he could lay hands on all of them, the British could not cross to attack him. Some of the local Tories, seeing what Washington was doing, had sunk boats in the river, thus concealing them. They meant to raise them from the water when General Howe's men arrived and needed ferries.

But Joshua Mersereau ran a ferry himself and owned a boatyard, which built small craft. He knew all about such tricks. The two brothers found the boats where the Tories had hidden them and took them all away. The Red Coats could not cross. Thanks to these two men, General Washington had a chance to rest and reorganize his army. After that he was able to cross the Delaware himself and defeat the Red Coats.

After days of travel Cole and Dave arrived into New York. By this time the British had taken over New York and Long Island. "Ah, this is very interesting," said Cole. "What is that?" said Dave. "I don't know," replied Cole, "but it looks like there are a lot of British soldiers around here. I thought George Washington was around this area, and from what I heard, there was supposed to have been a lot of fighting around here. Let's see if we can get a place to eat, rest, and see what we can find out about what is happening."

They finally found a place where they could rest in New York City. They walked into a tavern. Above the walkway was a sign, and the sign said, "Welcome to the Happy Bull." "The Happy Bull," said Dave. "What the hell kind of a name is that for a tavern?" "I don't know," said Cole. Dave was now thinking, "You know, that would not be a bad name for a bar and grill." They sat down for ale and something to eat. There were quite a number of people in the tavern.

Cole said, "We have to watch our step and what we say. I think about 90 percent of the people here are British or Tories, and if we say the wrong word, we could be in a lot of trouble." So they sat down and looked around. "I will tell you, Cole, it is hard to see who the good guys are and who the bad guys are." "I know," said Cole, "but I thought it was going to be better than this. There are plenty of British around. I was under the impression from what I heard that Washington was doing pretty well around here. I hope I didn't make a mistake leaving the ship because from what it looks like, this place has nothing but British or Tories around here."

British spies in New York City always watched this matter carefully. They knew the Americans could not attack Long Island or Manhattan unless General Washington had enough boats to carry hundreds of soldiers across at the same time. General Washington had the same idea about the

British. "You know, Dave, we had better move out of here." "Where the hell are we going to go?" Cole said, "We have enough money, more than enough to get to the Virginia area; and besides, if things really go wrong, there are always ships off the coast we could join."

"Let me put it this way," replied Dave. "In that case I hope we stay out of trouble because you will never get me on a goddamn ship fighting again. And Virginia—what makes you think of Virginia?" "I don't know," said Cole. "It seems like all the fighting is up in this area." "Well," said Dave, "it seems to me that I read somewhere there was fighting in the South." "Where did you read that?" asked Cole. "I know I read it somewhere." "Well," said Cole, "it beats staying around here because we might be able tell the difference down there. Not like here where we don't know who the hell would be on our side. We can't tell who is on whose side: the British, Tories, Americans, or spies on either side."

"I know one thing. If we get caught up on the wrong side, we get hanged, and let me tell you there will be no trial. And if we say the wrong thing, we are in trouble." "How do you know if we are talking to an American spy or a British spy? To tell you the truth, Cole, this getting to be too much. First it's a damn pirate ship and then its spies. I will tell you this has to be a dream or a nightmare or something." "Well, I will tell you, Dave, this is no dream. If we don't get going, we, will be like I said before, will have a lot of trouble. And besides, from what I hear, Washington is heading for the New Jersey area; so the only ones here are troops in the rear working their way out or Tories."

"We should make our way across to Jersey and then head south. So how are we going to get there?" "I don't know yet. I tell you what, from the sun it looks like around midday. Let's see if we can find a tavern." "I don't know what good that is going to do, Cole, but I do like your thinking." Dave was thinking, "I wish that when I started, those British bastards didn't take my belongings. I bet they still can't figure out that wristwatch."

They found a tavern, went inside, and sat down at a table. The waiter came over, but on his way over, he said to another table, "Hey, Seith, how's the boatyard coming?" "Okay" was the reply. "A boatyard," Cole started thinking. Then he said to Dave, "Let's wait until those guys leave and follow them." "Why?" asked Dave. "Because if we don't let them know which side we are on, we may possibly have some transportation." "What do you mean transportation?" asked Dave. "Well," Cole said, "the man said he ran a shipyard, and if we can see what side he is on, maybe he can find something that we can get across the river with."

Dave asked, "What do you mean across the river? With what are we going across the river?" "Maybe he has a raft or a ferry or something." Dave then asked, "A raft, a ferry? Cole, what the hell are you talking about? What are we going to do with the wagon?" "Coach," replied Cole.

"Cole, look, I don't give a damn coach, wagon, or what the hell. How would we take a wagon with horses across the river on a raft?" "Very carefully," replied Cole, smiling.

The two walked down to the boatyard where they saw some men working. Cole said hello. "Yeah," said the man, "what can I do for you?" "Is Seith around?" asked Cole. "Why? Do you know him?" "No," said Cole, "but a man said if I needed anything to ask for Seith." "He did, did he? I will see if I can find him." Finley Seith came over and said, "What can I do for you?" in a gruff voice. He stood about six feet and looked weather-beaten.

Cole said, "We would like to get across the river over to the Jersey side." "You would, would you? What are you going to do over the other side?" "Well," said Cole, "we are travelers, and we are heading south to Virginia. We figure the shortest way is if you have a ferry so we can transport our wagon and our horse." Seith said, "I don't think so. We are not letting any ferries going out today." "But, sir—" "Damn it, didn't you hear me? You are probably spies anyway. Now get the hell out of here."

"Now what are we going to do with the horse and wagon?" asked Dave. "Coach," replied Cole. "Let me think a minute." Looking down by the river, Cole saw a young man working on one of the ferries and said to Dave, "Take the horse and carriage down by the ferry." "What are you going to do?" "Never mind," said Cole, "just bring them down there." Cole went to the young man and said, "How are you doing?" The young man looked up and said, "Fine. Is there anything I can do for you?" "Yes," said Cole, "as a matter of fact, there is. We would like to take this ferry with our horse and wagon across the river, and it looks like this boat could handle that."

"Yes, sir," said the young man. We carry heavy loads on this boat, but I can't do it unless I get an okay from the boss." "It's okay. We had already asked him." "Well, I will have to ask him if you don't mind." As the man started to get off the boat, Cole pulled a pistol on the man, pointed it at the man's head, and said, "Get this thing going, or I am afraid I will have to kill you on this spot." "Oh yeah?" said the young man. "If you do, the whole shipyard will be down on you." "Ah yes," said Cole with a cold look, "but that will not do you any good because you will be dead. It is kind of hard to know what is going on with a bullet in your head.

"Okay, Dave, move the coach on the boat and loosen the rope tied to that post." As they moved the coach on the boat, the horse got a little jumpy, but everything got on safely. With a gun still to the man's head, they started to move on to the water. Just as they were quite a way's out, one man working at the yard yelled, "There is a boat heading out!" Seith commanded, "Get your guns and let's get those bastards. Get to your boats and catch them. If we can catch them, shoot them."

So the men in the boatyard gathered their weapons and started for their boats. But by the time they had realized that Cole and Dave's boat was on the water, they had quite a head start. Cole said to the man, "I see where your boys are starting to chase us, but on the water your buddies are in our territory. So, my friend, I see the Jersey shore; so if you want to live, you had better make sure that we get there. You let us off, and you turn around and head back quickly."

They made it to the Jersey shore, and when they did, Cole quickly jumped on to the landing, hurriedly grabbed the rope, and tied it securely. Dave by now was in the wagon. The gate was dropped and the horse, still a little jumpy, but they got it off the boat. The man on the boat stood there a little stunned as Cole untied the boat and pushed it off. Cole said, "Get going," but the man just stood there. Cole fired a shot over the man's head. The man started back, but the men chasing them were still quite a ways away, so Cole and Dave escaped.

Now on the Jersey side they started south, for the men chasing them did not arrive to the shore on time. Catching the other boat coming as it was back to them, Seith said, "What the hell did you do?" The man answered, "Sir, they had a gun to my head." Seith, steaming mad at this point, had no way of catching them. "Those bastards! I hope I meet up with them again."

Sir Henry Clinton was bored and frustrated. Ever since the Battle of Monmouth, the war had come to a standstill in the north. His army was bottled up in New York City as General Gage's army had been bottled up in Boston after Bunker Hill. The British position was too strong to be stormed, but their force was too weak to risk a decisive battle with George Washington's. Thus, New York became a prison in which Clinton amused himself by "fox hunting." A cavalryman would race through the streets, trailing a bone on a rope, followed by a yelping dog, while the general and his staff galloped them, shouting, "Tally-ho!" But the war couldn't be won by chasing dogs. To win Clinton believed that a new front had to be opened in the South. Although large the South was a thinly settled region. Still it was vital to the rebel cause.

The tobacco raised there allowed Congress to buy foreign war supplies. The cities of New England and the middle states, cut off from the world by the British fleet, received much of their food from their farms. Losing these resources would be a crippling blow to the rebels. Besides, the South was supposed to be filled with Tories eager to join in a crusade against the rebels. A British invasion would bring the Southern Tories into the fight. From then on, it would be easy to seize Georgia, the Carolinas, and Virginia, thus attacking Washington's army from the "back door."

A start had already been made with the capture of Savannah, Georgia. This was followed by an assault on Charleston, South Carolina, the best seaport south of Philadelphia. The attack was carried out by a hundred vessels and 8,700 troops led by Clinton in person. An earlier attack had failed, but this time the fleet forced its way past the harbor forts to bombard the city from the sea while the army cut it off by land.

General Benjamin Lincoln defended Charleston with 5,500 troops. They fought bravely and well but against impossible odds. The British landed siege guns and began to tear the place apart. The sky was streaked with red-hot cannonballs. Bursting shells showered the earth with silvery fragments of metal. At last Lincoln surrendered after a six-week siege. (Not until the fall of Bataan in the Philippines in 1942 would so many American soldiers are captured at one time.)

Lord Cornwallis, who took command when Clinton returned to his New York headquarters, lost no time in following up the Charleston victory. He sent fast-moving cavalry units inland to raid plantations. In one place after another, they arrested those sympathetic to Congress and terrorized civilians. Even women weren't safe. (Eliza Wilkinson remembered how sweaty, rough-looking men rode up to her plantation house in a cloud of dust. "The horses of the inhuman Britons seemed to tear up the earth and the riders at the same time bellowing out the most curses imaginable. which chilled my whole frame." They broke down the front door, shouting, "Where're these women rebels?" Eliza was robbed of everything valuable, including the dresses out of her closet and the buckles off her shoes. When she begged to be allowed to keep her wedding ring, a red-faced brute put a pistol to her face and swore he'd pull the trigger if she didn't give it up instantly. Luckily, they didn't burn the plantation as they did with others in the neighborhood. The world turned upside down.)

But not all Southerners dreaded Cornwallis's raiders. The plantation slaves welcomed them as liberators. The British announced that any slave who escaped from a rebel master was automatically free. That took a lot of courage, for runaways were punished harshly. Recaptured slaves might be whipped, branded, or sold to West Indian sugar plantations where most died of overwork or hanged. Yet the desire to be free was stronger than any fear, and thousands joined the British wherever they appeared including some slaves from Mount Vernon. Unfortunately the offer of freedom applied only to runaways. Slaves taken during raids on plantations were treated as ordinary loot and sold for their captor's profit.

Black people served the British in many ways. Black women followed the army doing camp chores alongside Red Coats' wives. Black men enlisted in British regiments, knowing that capture meant certain death. Others served as spies and guides. At Savannah Quamino Dolly led British troops through a swamp to the rear of the rebel positions, enabling them to capture the town easily. Most blacks, however, never saw combat but used the skills learned in slavery to help the British. Thousands worked as axmen, ditchdiggers, road builders, skilled carpenters, and blacksmiths. Although several hundred free blacks joined the Continental Army, they were never allowed to serve in the South for fear of setting a "bad example" for slaves.

CHAPTER FOURTEEN

The Virginia Battle

After weeks of driving, stopping here and there to feed and water the horse, and picking up another horse, they arrived in Virginia. Dave said, "This is something. Where the hell is an airplane when you need one?" "A what?" said Cole. "Never mind," said Dave, "someday I will tell you something. I would tell you now, but you wouldn't believe me." "Tell me what?" said Cole. "Never mind," replied Dave.

New York, Pennsylvania, and Southern Tories organized into Tarleton's Loyal Legion, which were the most feared raiders in the South. The legion's commander and only British officer was Colonel Banastre Tarleton, twenty-six, a handsome man who liked skintight uniforms, high boots, and bearskin hats. Yet this dandy was a hell of leather cavalryman who was happiest in battle. Clever and cruel, Tarleton wanted to spread terror so that the Americans wouldn't care resist him.

His chance came two weeks after the fall of Charleston. Colonel Abraham Buford was leading nearly four hundred Virginia Continentals toward the city when he learned of its capture. Buford turned back, but Tarleton's cavalrymen caught up with them in the Waxhaws wilderness near the North Carolina border. Tarleton's Loyal Legion came on a gallop, cheering and shouting as if nothing could stop them. The Virginians held their ground, turning away the first charge and sending Tarleton hurtling to the ground when his horse was shot from under him. The colonel was furious at losing his favorite mount, which he valued more than rebel lives. So furious, in fact, that he did nothing to prevent the tragedy that followed.

The Loyal Legion charged a second time, breaking through the rebel line. Seeing that further resistance was useless, the colonel ordered his men to lay down their weapons and sent someone forward with a white surrender flag. Tarleton ignored the flag, and the man carrying it was shot in cold blood. That was the signal for his dismounted troopers to open fire and charge with bayonets while mounted men plowed into the huddled crowd with sabers. "No quarter!" they shouted. "No mercy!" Now began a massacre of Americans by Americans. For fifteen minutes Tories stabbed and hacked at the defenseless Continentals, literally cutting them to pieces. No one was spared. Tories went over the ground, plunging bayonets into anyone who showed signs of life. Where the dead and wounded had fallen one on top of the other, Tories used bayonets as pitchforks, throwing off the topmost bodies to reach those beneath. By the time order was restored, 113 Virginians were dead and another 150 so badly wounded that they were left to die on the battlefield.

Soon Southerners were speaking of "Tarleton's quarter" war without mercy. Through clenched teeth people called him "Bloody Ban," "Butchering Ban," Tarleton. However, he didn't care what people called him so long as he struck terror into their hearts. But he also inspired hatred, a fierce hatred, that cried for revenge. General Horatio Gates, the new commander in the South, tried to repeat his Saratoga victory at Camden, South Carolina, but that was not to be because everything went wrong from the moment he arrived. Gate's troops were walking skeletons who'd been getting along for weeks on green corn and nearly raw meat. The night before the battle, the general issued each man a pint of watered-down molasses. That alone was enough to cause defeat. By morning half the army had diarrhea and cramps that felt as if their guts were tied in knots. They were in no condition to meet Cornwallis's veterans.

The Battle of Camden began badly for the Americans and quickly became a disaster. Bloody Ban Tarleton's cavalry broke their line, opening the way for the Red Coats and their bayonets. The Americans might have recovered had their general kept his head. But Gates panicked. He leaped on a fast horse and galloped away out of the war and into disgraced retirement.

Meanwhile Southern columns with Ferguson's Americans were moving far in land on the left wing. The only Englishman in this thousand-man regiment was its commander, Major Patrick Ferguson. Meanwhile back at the Waxhaws two scouts came back to find all their men slaughtered including Colonel Buford. The two scouts walked among the dead and saw the man with the white flag. One of the scouts said, "This is the work of only one man: that son of a bitch Tarleton. If we ever meet this son of a bitch, I want to be the one to cut his head off with a dull ax. I mean these soldiers surrendered, and they still massacred them. We have to see if we can find a friendly regiment and report this."

Meanwhile Dave and Cole, riding South, were avoiding minor skirmishes of fighting between a small band of British and rebels. "This is unbelievable," said Dave. "What?" said Cole. "How long it takes to get from one place to another." "I thought we are making pretty good time." "You mean weeks to get to here is pretty good time?" asked Dave. "Yeah, I think so," replied Cole. "I wonder just where we are." "Somewhere in Southern Virginia I would say," said Cole. "I say we rest by this river." "Okay," said Dave, so they pulled their wagon by a tree and sat down.

"This is so peaceful," said Dave, "that you would hardly believe all this is going on around us." "Where you originally from Boston, or did you come over on a ship from England?" "No," said Dave, "you can believe I am from a different place." "What do you mean?" said Cole. "I can't explain. I have to try to figure it out myself. You see, Cole, there are things I can't say because there are unexplainable. Some time when I can, I will tell you. Everything has been happening so fast since we first met that I haven't had much time to think." Cole, listening to Dave, just kept staring.

All of a sudden they heard rustling in the woods. They were grabbing for their guns when the two scouts came out of the woods with their guns drawn. "This looks like a Mexican standoff." Cole said, "What the hell are you talking about?" One of the scouts asked, "Are you with the British?" "Are you?" asked Cole as the two scouts cocked their guns. "No, we are not," said Dave at this point not sure what was going to happen. "We are not either. Our troops got massacred as we were out scouting. We came back and found everybody dead and are trying to get back and see if we can find some American troops."

After hearing the story, Dave said, "This is crazy. Hop in the wagon and we will see if we can get you to where you want to go." As they were loading, Cole said, "This is a coach, not a wagon." "Yeah, whatever," said Dave.

Major Ferguson at Brandywine, who he prevented a sniper from shooting George Washington in the back and despite his gallantry there, could be as ruthless and as bloody as Ban himself. During his march northward, his men looted and burned Patriots' houses. This work gave them much pleasure.

Tarleton called an aid and said, "We have some people in the west, and we should warn them that if they continued with their attitude and that if they decide to help the Americans, I will send troops over and kill every damn one of them and their families. Make sure every one of those ignorant bastards understand that." But the word of Ferguson and Tarleton's action's traveled over the Blue Ridge Mountains into what is now Tennessee.

As Cole and their passengers were heading toward the American lines, they came upon a soldier. "Watch out," said Cole. "This looks like a British soldier." As they came closer to the soldier, Cole said, "How are you doing?" "Who are you?" asked the soldier. "Oh, we are Tories, and we are just traveling." "You are, are you?" "Well, you dress like seamen." "Why do you say that?" asked Cole. "Because," said the soldier, "I have friend who is on a ship with the British navy off the coast of South Carolina." "Oh," said Cole. "Well, we came from the coast and helped the navy." "Were you with the navy?" asked the soldier. "You don't have navy apparel." "No," replied Cole. "We helped them sometimes, so this is why we have these clothes."

Cole, changing the conversation, said, "Where are you headed?" The soldier replied, "I am heading over the mountains to give a message to the people over there." "What message?" asked Cole. "If they side with the American rebels, then they will be attacked, and no mercy will be given." Cole said, "I think we will go with you for a while." "Why would you want to do that?" asked the soldier. "Well," said Cole, "we will feel safer." "Okay," said the soldier.

The two soldiers in the back of the wagon kept quiet as the group headed for the Blue Ridge Mountains. When they finally arrived at a settlement, they found their leader by the name of Big Red. The messenger said, "Ferguson is sending you a message. If you side with the American rebels, you will feel his full retribution, meaning that unless you stop the ambushes, he would cross the mountains to hang the settlers and burn their farms." Big Red answered, "I will tell you that if you and your partners don't get out of here fast, you will not leave at all." "All right," said the soldier, "I will give your message to Ferguson and Tarleton." "Oh, you mean the Bloody Butcher. Well, you tell him to go to hell."

The soldier turned around and said to Cole, "Are you fellows coming?" Cole said, "Maybe later." "Suit yourself," said the soldier. Red said, "Aren't you fellows going with that soldier?" Then the two men jumped off the wagon. "We were with the Virginia regiment that was wiped out by Tarleton, and we would like to fight with you if we can." Red replied, "You came in with that soldier." "Yes, but we poised as Tories." "Yeah," said Red, "if I thought you were really with the British, I would have you hanged right here and now."

Over mountain men didn't take kindly to threats, for a threat to them was a challenge to fight. They always tried to land the first blow. Soon within days over a thousand men were steaming across the Blue Ridge. They were led by experienced Indian fighters such as "Nolichucky Jack" Sevier and Colonel William Campbell a rawboned giant with a fist as big as hams. Each man was mounted and carried a long rifle. He wore boots, a fringed buckskinned hunting shirt, and a coonskin cap. He carried his own rations, a bag of corn sweetened with maple syrup and could fight for weeks on this, and a canteen of water.

Now Major Ferguson had no intention of running from this "rabble," as he called them. He took up position at Kings Mountain on the border of the two Carolinas, a flat-topped hill rising sixty feet above the surrounding plain and its steep wooded sides strewn with boulders. Kings Mountain was a natural fortress, and Ferguson felt sure he could hold it against "God Almighty and all the rebels out of hell."

The Overmountain Men arrived in the morning and got down to business. Gathering in groups they listened to pep talks by their commanders. Private James Collins, a sixteen-year-old, was listening to his commanders yelling, "All cowards, leave immediately so as not to infect the others with your cowardice." Young Collins was scared and would like to have run away; so swallowing hard, he made up his mind that whatever happened, he'd act like a man.

Big Red said to Cole, "You and your partner, bring that wagon over here and keep it here just in case we need it for ammunition or wounded or any of our needs." "Son of a bitch, Cole," asked Dave, "what the hell are we doing?" Cole replied, "It looks like we are going to battle to the finish." "What do you mean, Cole?" "I mean the way it looks, the side we are on wants revenge. On their side it is power and control. I think a lot of people will be killed here today." "Oh great, replied Dave."

When the speeches ended, the commander gave the day's password: "BUFORD." The men then put four or five bullets in their mouths to quench the thirst and make reloading easier. Then they started up the hillside. Cole came back to Dave and said, "I think we are in real trouble." "What do you mean?" asked Dave. Cole said, "This is a divided command with the Americans on one side and the mountaineers on the other." Both commands started up the mountain. Ferguson's men started firing, but the Overmountain Men knew how to take cover. They moved like Indians, darting from rock to rock, tree to tree, stopping only to fire, reload, and fire again.

Moving up the mountainside Dave was leading with Cole following. Cole looked to the side and from a rock on top saw a man drawing down on Dave. Just as the man was going to shoot, Cole shot the man, killing him. As soon as the men reached the hilltop Colonel Campbell's voice boomed over the crackling rifles, "Here they are, boys! Shout like hell and fight like devils!" That's just what they did.

They pinned down the Tories at the center of the hilltop. Several Tories raised their white surrender flags, but Major Ferguson cut them down as soon as they appeared. He fought bravely, trying to rally his men, until he was shot from his saddle. Ferguson's death ended the Battle of Kings Mountain as far as the Tories were concerned. Yet they were mistaken if they expected their surrender flags to be honored. Immediately they were mistaken. Too much blood lay between the two sides for that to happen. Now that the Overmountain Men had them in their power, they wanted revenge. As the Tories huddled around their surrender flags, the Overmountain Men's anger got out of control. Shouting "Buford! Buford! Tarleton's quarter!" they opened fire at point-blank range. They all would have massacred their prisoners had Colonel Campbell not begged them not to become murderers.

Only two hundred of Ferguson's men escaped. One soldier called a sixteen-year-old over, gave him a gun, and said, "See that man over there?" "Yes," said the boy. "Shoot him." "But, sir—" "Shoot him." The boy aimed the gun and trembling shot the man dead. Dave, looking at this in horror, said to Cole, "Damn it, Cole. Did you see that?" "I know," said Cole.

The prisoners received rough justice. Nine were tried for crimes against civilians and hanged on the spot. The twenty-eight American dead were sent home for proper burial. The three hundred Tory dead were dumped into shallow pits. Dave and Cole headed for their wagon. They heard a call, turned around, and there stood Big Red. "Damn," said Dave, "I wonder what he wants." As the big man came over, he said, "Thanks. You fought well, and today we taught these bastards a lesson. Where will you be heading?" Dave said, "We will be heading South." They both got up onto their wagon. "Thanks again," said Red. As the wagon started off, Cole said to Dave, "Quite a man." "Yes," said Dave, "I would be fighting with him instead of against him."

The bodies at Kings Hill shallow graves did not stay private very long. Collins returned a few weeks later and found thousands of bones scattered about the hilltop. Wolves had dug up the bones and scattered them about the hilltop. Wolves that had dug up the bodies grew so bold from eating flesh that they lost their fear of humans, thus making it dangerous for settlers to venture out at night. Although no one knew it at the time but Ferguson's defeat was the turning point of the war in the South.

Before Kings Mountain the Patriots seemed unable to do anything right. Despite terrible hardships and setbacks, they never lost a major battle after Kings Mountain. The tide began to turn when Nathanael Green took over from Gates. This thirty-eight-year-old Rhode Islander was a remarkable man, having taught himself the art of war by reading everything he could find on the subject. He learned well rising from private to major general in less than five years. George Washington called him "Brother Nat." He was his favorite field officer as bold as Benedict Arnold and a better man.

Although Washington couldn't spare many reinforcements, Greene's aides were first-rate. His second in command was the "Old Wagoner" Daniel Morgan. His cavalry commanders were "Light Horse" Harry Lee and William Washington, the general's cousin. Thaddeus Kosciusko served as chief engineer. Brother Nat had no plan in mind when he came South in December. He didn't want to challenge Cornwallis in an all-out battle but to keep him off balance, steadily wearing him down. Greene alone would decide when and where to give battle. He'd attack Cornwallis's supply lines, forcing him to chase him through the Carolinas, but fight only on his own terms. This wasn't a strategy that allowed the enemy room for error. Every time he made a mistake, Greene would be there ready to pounce.

Greene split his forces between himself and Dan Morgan. A strange tactic, for generals weren't supposed to divide their strength in the face of a superior enemy. Yet this was a good plan, for he'd actually given the enemy two choices, both of them unpleasant. If Cornwallis struck at Greene, Morgan could slip past to strike British outposts in South Carolina. But if he went after Morgan, Greene could attack Charleston. Cornwallis decided that he had to split his own force.

While he went after Greene, Bloody Ban Tarleton would deal with Morgan. Tarleton caught up with the Americans near Cowpens, a clearing west of Kings Mountain where cattle were fattened before sale in coastal towns. Morgan made camp. After dark a fine rain was falling as his troops huddled around campfires to cook supper and dry their clothes. They were jittery as men are before battle. Morgan tried to cheer them on as best he could. He went from campfire to campfire, checking on their weapons and joking about whatever came to mind.

The Old Wagoner would crack his whip over Bloody Ban in the morning, he promised. If every man did his duty, "the old folks will bless you, and the girls will kiss you for your gallant conduct!" The armies, each about eleven hundred strong, met in the morning. Tarleton, as usual, opened the battle with a slashing attack. His cavalry, mostly dismounted and fighting as infantry, charged the waiting Americans. As the human wave rolled forward, Morgan ordered his men to fall back and reform. It was no retreat, but Tarleton's troops, thinking they'd already won, broke ranks and came on as fast as their legs could carry them. That's when the Old Wagoner cracked his whip. The Americans had been running up the slope of a low hill when they suddenly turned. Hundreds of muskets spoke at once. Tories fell dead by the dozen.

The wounded littered the ground, thrashing and screaming in pain. Sergeants were shouting for survivors to reform their ranks when a cry rose from the American line, "Give them the bayonet!" Panic swept Tarleton's army as Morgan's infantry rushed down the slope, gaining momentum with each step. Hundreds threw away their weapons and begged for mercy on bent knees. The Americans, knowing what would have happened had the battle gone the other way, roared "Tarleton's quarter!" It took every ounce of their officers' energy to prevent a massacre.

Tarleton himself was lucky to escape with his life. He was riding away with two officers when William Washington's cavalry charged from behind the hill. The moment Washington saw Tarleton, he led his officers toward him with drawn sabers. Washington slashed at one officer, but his saber broke off at the handle. The officer was about to crack Washington's skull with his own saber when a fourteen-year-old bugler shot him with a pistol. A sergeant drove off the other officer while Tarlatan went for Washington, who turned away the blow with his broken saber. Tarleton escaped, but his legion was destroyed as a fighting force, losing all but a hundred of its men in less than an hour. Morgan had sixty killed.

Despite this defeat Lord Cornwallis was determined to destroy the rebels. He met Greene's and Morgan's combined forces at Guilford Courthouse, North Carolina. The battle lasted for hours, reaching its climax in a meadow where armies went at each other with bayonets and rifle butts. The fighting was so fierce that His Lordship ordered his gunners to fire grapeshot through the ranks of his own Red Coats to halt the American charge. He called this slaughter "victory," because Greene finally retreated. But what a price he'd paid! Cornwallis lost 532 killed and wounded nearly a third of his force and more than twice the American losses.

Apart from Bunker Hill, Guilford Courthouse was the bloodiest battle of the revolution. During the months that followed, Greene fought two other battles in South Carolina, Hobkirk's Hill and Eutaw Springs, and lost them both. But losing didn't matter. What mattered was being able to keep on fighting and to hurt the enemy at little cost to himself. As Greene wrote to a friend, "We fight, get beat, rise, and fight again." Strange as it seems, the Americans won by losing.

Yet Greene's army didn't fight alone. Every farmhouse looted every Patriot murdered after surrendering, which turned ordinary folks against the enemy. Southerners resisted in countless ways. You didn't have to fire a gun to hurt the enemy. You might play stupid when a British officer asked for directions or give wrong directions, sending a patrol miles and hours out of its way. You might also help bridges collapse, and trees fall "accidentally" across roads used by enemy supply columns. Your neighbors, however, might be very violent indeed. There were hundreds of square miles in the Carolinas where the local people could never be trusted.

One British report reads like an American report from Vietnam two centuries later. The soldiers were received with smiles one moment and the following instant butchered by a set of people who by their clothing and appointments cannot be distinguished from the quiet inhabitants of the country. The night belonged to the Patriots who operated in twos and threes that knife sentries and snipe at outposts. Soldiers who wandered from camp were never again seen alive. Military messengers went with large cavalry escorts; otherwise, they were fair game even for women.

One night Grace and Rachel Martin, wives of American soldiers, put on their husbands' clothes to ambush a messenger escorted by two officers. The British were tearing along a deserted road when the women rode out of the shadows, blocking the way. Surprised with pistols aimed at their heads, the British meekly surrendered their papers, which were sent to Brother Nat. People also joined the guerrillas.

By this time, Cole and Dave were in with guerrillas under Captain Jake and fighting on the edge of the Carolina swamps. "You know, Cole, you were right. This is just as bad as up north. I think if we can get out of this. Let's head back north." Cole said, "I am with you. We are fighting in a terrain, which at times I have no idea when we are. When we have a chance, we will leave here and head north."

The war was fought by roving bands operating enemy lines. The bands were less than a hundred fighters. Being small they could hide easily, move quickly, and hit the enemy when least expected. They might ambush a wagon train here, wipe out a patrol there, and make nuisances of themselves everywhere. If they met strong resistance they broke contact, fleeing to mountains and swamps until ready to strike elsewhere. Traveling lightly they lived off game or gifts from friendly people. It was essential to be on good terms with the locals who often provided valuable information about the enemy. The most feared guerrilla leaders were South Carolinians.

Andrew Pickens formed a guerrilla band after Tories burned his plantation. A somber man—it was said no one ever saw him smile—Pickens led hundreds of hit-and-run raids. The father of the United States Army's Special Forces was Francis Marion. He was a quiet strong man whose favorite drink was vinegar mixed with water. Marion knew the swamps of Clarendon County, South Carolina, like the back of his hand. And he knew about Indians—their ways of fighting and surviving in the wilderness. Putting the two together and adding ideas of his own, he built the best guerrilla band in the South.

The British were bewildered by Marion's tactics. Whenever he planned a raid, he kept the target to himself until the last moment. Marching at night from one forest or swamp to another, he made camp before dawn and rested his men until getting under way again at sunset. He never used the same campsite twice. If a bridge had to be crossed near an enemy outpost, it was covered with blankets to muffle the clatter of horse's hooves. Scouts, who always went ahead to prevent ambushes, hid in the thick tops of trees, signaling with a shrill whistle that carried for miles. Tarleton chased Marion's band into the swamps several times. But after splashing around in the mud and giving the mosquitoes a feast, he gave up the hunt each time only a few days. "As for this damned old fox," grumbled Bloody Ban, "the devil himself could not catch him!" The Americans were amused that their hero was compared to a fox, and that's why we remember Francis Marion as "the Swamp Fox."

Cole and Dave headed away from the action of Tarleton and the Swamp Fox. When they were over in the Virginia border, they passed a farm. When they emerged from the woods to an open field, shooting started from the farmhouse. The two started firing back as they were diving in back of rocks and behind drinking troughs. After the shooting stopped, slowly the two started for the farmhouse. They went up onto the porch, trying to be quiet. Suddenly they broke through the door, and on the floor lay a man and women dead. Dave said, "I wonder why they started shooting at us." "I hope that they were Tories," replied Cole. Cole said, "Let's see if they had a wagon, seeing that our coach broke down out in the woods."

They went to the back of the farmhouse. "There we can fetch horses and a bigger wagon. We can hitch them up. Go back and get the rest of the stuff out of the other coach," said Cole. "Now, Cole," asked Dave, "is this a coach or a wagon?" "A wagon," replied Cole, and so the two headed north. After avoiding minor skirmishes, in about a week and a half, they arrived well into the Virginia area. They stopped off at a roadhouse where there were people drinking and listening to a person on a harpsichord, playing the latest favored tunes of the day.

Dave was saying, "Where is Elvis Presley when you need him?" "Elvis who?" asked Cole. "You know, Cole," said Dave, "I have not had a chance to tell you when I met you in Boston that I was really looking for two of my friends. We were supposed to have met down by the waterfront." "What happened?" asked Cole. "Well, I don't know. We split up awhile ago. Cole, I will tell you it is hard to explain, but I will tell you I am from another place. I have read a little history and know how this will turn out. Don't worry, the Americans will win this war with the Tories and the British." Cole asked, "What do you mean another time?" "Well, the last I remember was the year 1984, and we got into this situation. I don't know how or whether I am in a dream or dead. What I do know is that when I woke up, I was in 1775. How the hell that happened I don't know."

Cole by this time was looking at Dave a little funny, like just staring, as Dave was talking. Dave continued, You know, all this fighting and killing is trying to win our freedom. In 1984 there will be more conveniences, but I will tell you that years from now there will be wars, killing, poverty, and crime. You will win the battle, but I am not sure we will win the war. These people had a purpose. The people in the future will take these wars for granted. They will read about wars but really will have no idea of their consequences.

"Cole, as far as crime, I am afraid that I was a part of a lot of the crime part myself. That's what makes this so damn confusing. I wasn't shot or anything. So how," asked Dave, "the hell did I end up here?" Cole by this time was looking at Dave dumbfounded. Cole said, "I know you have been under a little pressure because you have not been in battle before. But let me tell you these are real bullets and swords we have been up against. If you say this is a dream, then how the hell did I get into it?" "I don't know," said Dave.

Lord Cornwallis retreated to Wilmington, South Carolina, to await reinforcements and plan future operations. Uncle Nat and guerrilla chiefs had fought him to a standstill after only Charleston and a few other ports were secure, thanks to the Royal Navy's guns and supplies. He knew that without this access to the sea, the Americans would wear him down, forcing him to surrender sooner or later. Yet there was still a chance to win and win quickly. If he could conquer Old Dominion, Virginia, everything else would fall into place. He believed Georgia and the Carolinas couldn't survive without Virginia's men and supplies or Washington's army based in New York City.

Cole said, "You know, Dave, that we are doing our part. For instance, I heard that as the American and British troops were battling in the back country, a small Patriot navy won a few spectacular victories at sea. On two occasions a small American squadron captured a port in a place called Nassau, the Bahamas." "That is now a resort." "What?" asked Cole. "Nothing," said Dave.

By now Benedict Arnold had led sixteen hundred Red Coats, Hessians, and Tories on a rampage through the eastern part of the state. Moving up the James River, he destroyed precious supplies, wrecked Virginia's largest cannon foundry, and burned much of the city of Richmond. Governor Jefferson offered a reward for his capture dead or alive, and soon Virginia riflemen were sharpening their aim on targets representing his head. George Washington only wanted the traitor dead. Furious that Arnold should be ravaging his home state, he sent Lafayette after him with eight hundred men. There needn't be any trial. Lafayette's orders were clear. "If he should fall into your hands, you will execute him in the most summary way."

Reinforcements under Anthony Wayne Baron von Steuben followed several weeks later. These reinforcements were Northerners who now had their first glimpse of plantation slavery. The Northern troops were greeted near Richmond by white women wrapped in linen against the burning sun. (Lieutenant William Feltman was shocked at their servants: boy slaves in their teens. They will have a number of blacks about them all naked, nothing to hide their nakedness. Equally shocking was a black man's head stuck on a tree on one side of the road and his right hand tied to a tree on the other side. He'd been hanged and cut to pieces for killing his master. "Incidents like these encouraged many of the Northerners to demand abolition of slavery in their home states.")

In the meantime Cornwallis planned to join forces with Arnold in Virginia. Although Arnold was soon recalled to New York, Cornwallis went ahead with the invasion. Early in May, after leaving a covering force in the Carolinas, he marched into Virginia. During the next months he spread terror: looting, raping, burning, and killing. Once he nearly captured the entire state legislature including Governor Jefferson in Richmond. Lafayette was powerless to stop him, but he kept on his trail, hoping to slow him down and get him to make a mistake. He was helped by one of Cornwallis's own servants, a "runaway slave" named James. James really was a slave who had volunteered for dangerous mission. For months he sent Lafayette details of Cornwallis's plans. (After the war he took the name James Lafayette, and the Virginia legislature bought him from his master and set him free with a forty dollars a year veteran's pension.)

Meanwhile Cole and Dave were still heading north and by now were on the outskirts of the battles in Virginia. "There is a lot of talk about this Benedict Arnold fellow who is a traitor. He was a hero for our side and then went over to the British," said Cole. "Yeah," said Dave, "I read about him once." "Read about him?" said Cole. "Yeah," said Dave, "once in school I read about him." Dave said, "I have tried to tell you about what is happening, but I can't get it across, and that is why I have to get back to Boston."

"Why do you want to go back to Boston?" asked Cole. "Well," said Dave, "that is where this all started, and maybe I will catch up with my other friends. Although you have been a pretty good guy and we have gone through a lot things together, I still wish I could maybe get out of this dream or nightmare or whatever the hell this is."

They continued to go north, came into town, and found a gathering where soldiers and civilians were partying and talking. Cole looked over and saw a beautiful redhead. "Come on," said Cole, "let's go over and talk to that woman." "I don't know," said Dave. "That could be trouble." "I don't think so," said Cole. So they walked over to the woman and said, "Hello what is your name?" Looking at the men, she smiled and said, "Eileen Dumont," and asked, "What is yours?" "Mine is Cole, and this is Dave. What is going on?" asked Cole. "Oh, nothing, just a little celebration and entertainment." "What kind of entertainment?" "Oh, just music from the battlefield and other popular songs. Would you like to come in and hear some?" "Not really," said Dave. "We sure would," said Cole.

So they went into the large mansion, and there was a man sitting at a harpsichord, a man playing the flute, and people listening to the songs. Dave said, "Like I said before, where is Elvis when you need him?" The songs they were playing were the top songs of 1775. They were playing "Devil's Dream," "Soldier's Joy," Mozart 478, Mozart minuet, and concerto for the clarinet by Wolfgang Amadeus Mozart. By this time, Cole was dancing with Eileen; and Dave was leaning against the wall, saying to himself,

"Wonderful, just wonderful. I hope we don't get attacked while he is on the dance floor." Cole came off the dance floor. He said, "Dave, I think I will stay here for a while. I think I am very fond of this woman." Dave said, "You are kidding, right?" "No," replied Cole. "How the hell do you know which side she is on?" "Does not matter," said Cole. "If it doesn't work out, I will go back to the sea." Dave looked at Cole in disbelief.

"It was a good trip and an exciting one, but I think I want to see how this works out. Would you like to stay here and see what happens?" "No," said Dave, "I think I will head back to Boston and see if I can catch up with my friends somehow." "Well, good luck, and I will take my stuff, and you can have the wagon." And so alone again Dave said to Cole, "Like you said, it was exciting, and you watch yourself." Dave rode away and was thinking, "What a crazy son of a bitch and a great guy. I hope she is not married, and the poor bastard doesn't get into a dual or something like that."

At this point Dave was at his loneliness for the first time in quite awhile. He was alone and now trying to get back to Boston alone. After about a week and a half, he was back; he ran into the French that left Newport to join the Americans near Dobbs Ferry on the Hudson.

Each army came with an imaginary picture of the other that was both true and false. Their meeting surprised everyone. The Continentals had pictured their allies as overdressed dandies who ate frogs and spent hours combing their hair. They were colorful as peacocks. Their uniforms were of white linen with regimental colors—pink, blue, yellow, rose, scarlet, green—on the collars and lapels. Americans gasped as cavalrymen in tall fur hats rode by on black horses with tiger skin saddlecloths, each man armed with pistols, a curved saber, and an eight-feet lance. Their encampments hummed with music, as bands played and soldiers danced in pairs. Americans, overcoming their shyness, joined in. "Officers, soldiers, and the Americans mix and dance together," It was a feast of equality, the first fruits of the alliance. Yet there was another side to these dandies. They marched smartly, handled their weapons easily, and many had horrible scars on their faces. They were fighters.

The French were also surprised. They'd expected to find the neatly dressed, disciplined soldiers mentioned in European newspaper accounts of the war. But at first glance they thought them to be no soldiers at all. The uniformed Continentals seen in old drawings and paintings existed only in the artist's minds. Nearly all the men the French met wore homespun or sweat-stained hunting shirts. Most went barefoot and hadn't had a barber's attention for months. They carried light packs and slept on the ground or in four-man tents on branches covered with dirty blankets. Many were boys of twelve or thirteen and old men. Yet their muskets gleamed, and they knew how to use them. One man said, "I cannot insist too strongly how I was surprised by the army composed of old men, children, and Negroes and how well they performed under fire," Dave was thinking, "No American army." A French officer wrote after a skirmish, "It is truly incredible that troops almost naked and poorly paid matter."

"Wherever I go I am always in a war. This is the worst thing I have ever been through. Now I have to find some way to get out of these war zones and get back to Boston and hopefully get back to where I came from." Dave needed something to eat. After a long night of travel, he came upon a small town. His only plan was to get something to eat and continue on. He stepped down off the wagon, not sure where he was. He went into a roadhouse and proceeded to the place where they were eating. He sat down to have something to eat and drink. Not having Cole to rely on, he decided just to sit and listen. One man was talking to another and saying, "Did you hear about Burgoyne?" "No," said the other man. "Well, he surrendered, and his troops handed over their weapons." An American band struck up "Yankee Doodle" and kept playing throughout the ceremony. Red Coats no longer laughed at this tune.

Never in its long history had Great Britain lost an entire army. A London newspaper opposed to the war printed a none to funny poem. It read,

In seventeen hundred and seventy-seven
General Burgoyne set out for heaven
But as the Yankees would rebel,
He missed the route and went to hell.

In Philadelphia George Washington's eyes grew watery, and his voice broke as he gave his staff the news. Regaining his composure, he ordered a day of prayer and cannon salutes. Happy as he was, the commander in chief couldn't have known that Saratoga was the revolution's turning point. Saratoga proved to King Louis XVI that the Americans with help could win.

Dave finished his meal, got up, and left, thinking, "This is really something. I don't know what it is about this dream or whatever the hell it is, but I now know how hard it was to win this country. We read about the revolution, but living it is something else."

Dave by now was just outside Philadelphia where Washington sent his army into winter quarters. It marched to a bend in the Schuylkill River eighteen miles northwest of Philadelphia, near enough to keep an eye on the enemy yet far enough to avoid being surprised by him. The army arrived at a village of a dozen houses built near an old ironworks called Valley Forge.

The troops found no camp but a barren campsite ankle deep in mud. With winter closing in, they had to work quickly. During the following weeks, they built quite a few log cabins that were sixteen feet long by fourteen wide with a stone fireplace, earthen floor, and a roof of straw and branches. There were no windows. Life in these cabins was nasty. When it rained roofs leaked, turning floors into pools of stagnant mud. When the temperature dropped, the green wood being burned in the fireplaces filled the cabins with blinding smoke and made men cough as if their lungs would burst. Bad as they were, the cabins might have been bearable with proper food and clothing. But Washington's troops had neither. There was never enough to eat.

Dr. Albigence Waldo, First Connecticut Infantry, kept a diary during his time at Valley Forge. It wasn't pleasant reading, for there was nothing pleasant about life there:

It snows I'm sick. Eat nothing. No whiskey. No forage. Lord, Lord, Lord . . . cold and uncomfortable. I am sick, discontented and out of humor. Poor food. Hard lodging. Cold weather. Fatigue. Nasty cloths. Nasty cookery. Vomit half my time. Smoked out of my senses. The Devil is in it. I can't endure it.

Why are we sent here to starve and freeze? What sweet facilities I have left at home, a charming wife, pretty children, good beds, good food, good cookery . . . Here all confusion, smoke and cold, hunger and filthiness. A pox on my bad luck." The cry of "No meat!" Would begin at one end of camp and spread until it became a steady chorus. Day after day, men got along on fire cake (a thin paste of flour and water baked on hot stone) and water. Those lucky enough to have whiskey made "salamanders." They filled their tin cups with the raw alcohol, set it on fire, and swallowed it flames and all. Salamanders weren't very nourishing but they kept off the chill for at least a little while.

An officer found men in cabin boiling a stone. They say there's strength in a stone if you can get it out "someone" explained smiling. Even at Valley Forge there was room for a joke. Nakedness usually went along with hunger. What clothing there was had become little more than threadbare rags that gave no protection against winter's winds. The rule was share and share alike. You're your turn came for guard duty, your cabin mates lent you their clothing. Even so sentries were seen standing in their hats to keep their rag-wrapped feet out of snow.

Foreign visitors were amazed to see officers standing guard wrapped in old dressing gowns and shreds of blankets. Colonel Allen McLane poured whiskey into his boots to keep his feet from freezing. Lucky fellow: He had boots and whiskey to spare. At least twenty-five hundred men died of disease at Valley Forge more than Washington lost to enemy action during the entire Pennsylvania campaign.

Weakened by hunger and cold they fell victim to a long list of diseases: small pox, typhus, influenza, pneumonia, scurvy and lack of soap men being dirty all of the time. Dirt brought skin rashes, lice and infection. Men were covered with chilblains, purple sores caused by long exposure to cold and damp. Frostbitten toes and feet turned white, then black and had to be amputated to save the patient's life, maybe. Everything stank of dirt, damp and rot which made General Anthony Wayne prefer a battle to making a camp inspection.

Dave by now was sharing a camp that was about ready for war. He had more clothing than most of the soldiers, but it was cold, and all he wanted to do was get out of there because he had enough of war, and it looked like he was going to be in some sort of battle. He was thinking, "I don't want any part of this."

As he was walking through the snow and mud, a soldier jumped on Dave, and they both went to the ground. The man was going to kill Dave for his clothes. As they rolled around in the snow and mud, the soldier had a knife and was trying to stab Dave. However, Dave got the upper hand and stabbed the soldier to death. Dave got up and looked around. No one saw the fight, so he pulled the soldier's body off to the side and folded his arms as if he was sleeping. As he kept walking, he was asking himself, "What the hell did I do to deserve this? Why the hell did I end up in this time for Christ's sake? I am in this place fighting with George Washington. Why? I never studied him that much."

Sadly much of this misery was unnecessary. There were plenty of supplies in Pennsylvania. The problem was getting people to sell to them at fair prices. Farmers and tradesmen kept goods off the market to force up prices, not that high prices guaranteed good quality. Americans sold their own army-spoiled meat, wormy flower, and clothing that fell apart after a few days' wear. There were even those who traded with the enemy in Philadelphia. Washington dealt harshly with such people. Many a farmer lost his goods and received 250 lashes for selling to the British. Foraging parties went in search of hidden supplies, which they took or paid for with "Continentals." Near-worthless paper money issued by Congress. But men still died at Valley Forge.

Staying at Valley Forge could be harder on a man's spirit than on his body. Hundreds deserted not because of the miserable conditions but because of letters from home. The revolution often took a toll on soldiers' families as well. In small villages and isolated farms, men could not be spared for months or years at a time. There were shops to run, fields to plow, and crops to plant and harvest. Without a man to do the heavy work, wives and children might not survive. Officers reported soldiers coming to them, sobbing, with letters about how bad things were at home. Even loyal Patriots deserted rather than have their families starve. There were families, however, who believed so strongly in what their menfolk were doing that they kept their troubles to themselves.

Valley Forge was not only a winter encampment but an open air school where a balding red-faced man of forty-eight appeared at Washington's headquarters. He called himself Frederick William Augustus Henry Ferdinand, Baron von Steuben, lieutenant general in the army of King Frederick the Great of Prussia. Actually he wasn't a nobleman. His highest rank was captain, and he had not held a command for fourteen years. But he was an excellent drillmaster—exactly the man that Washington needed. Military drill was not just fancy marching in parades. Turning, about-facing, and quick stepping in columns were essential battlefield maneuvers. The ability, for example, of thousands of troops to about-face as one man might make the difference between stopping an attack from behind and defeat as on Long Island and the Brandywine.

Von Steuben turned brave fighters into disciplined soldiers. That wasn't easy for Americans who wouldn't obey orders blindly. In Europe he wrote, "You say your soldier, 'Do this,' and he doeth it. But in America I am obliged to say, 'This is the reason you ought to do that,' and he does it." If a lesson went well, he'd grin and grunt, "Ach, gut! Sehr gut!" If not, he'd let go with a mixture of German, French, and English curse words that made the troops double up with laughter. But they listened to him, and they learned.

By spring they could march and use the bayonet like professionals. Men who'd been terrified of British steel were now eager to test themselves against it. While the Continentals suffered and learned at Valley Forge, Sir William Howe decided that he'd seen enough of fighting in America and resigned his command. That was a wise decision for him personally, for Sir

Henry Clinton, who took his place, was about to face another different kind of war.

A French fleet sailed for the New World. British war planners weren't sure where they would land. But they knew they could be used against the British West Indies or to blockade New York or to close the Delaware and pin Clinton between them and Washington's army. To prevent these disasters George III personally wrote Clinton's orders. The general was to evacuate Philadelphia while there was still time and concentrate his army in New York. He must also send ships and troops to reinforce the West Indies. Clinton obeyed. And he sent three thousand Philadelphia Tories, two Hessian regiments, and most of the army's women to New York by sea. He led the army, twelve thousand troops and a wagon train twelve miles long, out of Philadelphia. The plan was to march eastward along a narrow road by way of Monmouth Courthouse, New Jersey, to Sandy Hook where ships waited to carry them the last few miles to Manhattan.

As soon as Washington heard that the British were moving, he broke up the Valley Forge encampment and went after them. This was a risk worth taking. If he could catch the enemy's main army strung out on the road, he might win a victory greater than Gates's and maybe finish the war.

The weather was cold, and Dave was trying to stay warm and wondering what was going to happen next. The wind was blowing; men were walking barefoot and ready to fight. Dave by now was saying to himself, "It was starting to get real warm. This is crazy. I am in the seventeen hundreds with George Washington's men; somehow I am caught up in history. I never studied history, so why the hell am I here?"

Just then he heard a click and turned around to be looking at a pistol aimed at him. Dave asked, "What do you want?" The answer was "I want the hell out of here. I have had enough, so I will be using your wagon to get out of here. I am sick and tired of fighting, and I want to go back home to my family."

Then they saw Washington's army moving out. Two other soldiers came up from behind. "What are you two doing here? Get the hell back to the lines; we are moving out." The soldier turned around and reluctantly said, "Yes, sir." And the other soldier looking at Dave said, "What the hell are you doing?" "Just staring." "Get that damn wagon back to the line." Dave was saying to himself, "That damn kid. If he hadn't come, I would have been well on my way out of here."

In the days that followed, the Continentals returned to places filled with painful memories. Private Joseph Plumb Martin found the country around

Princeton a wasteland. The retreating British had destroyed whatever they couldn't carry away. Cattle were shot and left to rot in the pastures. Wells were filled with garbage, houses burned, and farm tools smashed. Red Coats even chopped down trees to get at the fruit. Frugal farmers winced at such senseless destruction, imagining their own farms after an enemy visit.

The Americans caught up with their prey a little beyond Monmouth Courthouse. In the morning Washington immediately sent General Charles Lee ahead with a strike force to slow the British until he arrived with the main army. Lee, a strange man who preferred talking to dogs rather than humans, was an experienced officer who'd served in the British and Polish armies. Lee's experience didn't help him this morning. As soon as they attacked the British rear guard, Clinton turned around and counterattacked with his whole army. Lee panicked. Instead of trying to hold until Washington arrived, he ordered a retreat. The American front collapsed. Washington knew nothing of this until he met soldiers rushing to the rear. Then he met Lee doing the same thing. Washington said, "You no good son of a bitch, you bastard, you coward!" He took away his command and sent him to the rear as unfit to be near brave men. (Lee was later dismissed from the army, spending his last years alone talking to his dogs.)

Washington drew his sword and headed for the front as bullets popped overhead. He ignored them. Cannonballs tore the ground before. He kept going with soldiers following and Dave with his wagon at full speed, yelling, "What the hell am I doing here?" as bullets were flying over his head and careening off the side of his wagon. Cannonballs landing beside him, in front of him, and behind him. It was like magic. The sight of a big man on a big horse finally calmed the troops. Everywhere men stopped running. Then as von Steuben had taught them, they about-faced, straightened the line, and waited for the enemy with fixed bayonets. Red Coats and Hessians charged only to be flung back by massive volleys. These men were punished doubly. Yankee bullets were bad enough, but the heat became torture, for it was a muggy day with the temperatures nearing one hundred degrees.

Clinton's troops clad in thick wool and carrying heavy packs couldn't cope with the heat and fight at the same time. Whole squads toppled over and lay on the ground, panting. Men died of sunstroke; some poor fellows went insane. Clinton himself said he was "near going raving mad with the heat." The Americans did better, for most were still in torn rags, which gave some relief as the battlefield was a heated oven.

Dave was still in the uniform he got on ship, which was a lot cooler. The battle dragged on hour after hour. During the lulls between charges, the artillery dueled, making the soldiers more miserable if that was possible. Among the American gunners was a John Hays, a barber by profession. His wife, Mary—or Molly—had been with him during his entire enlistment. This wasn't unusual. The Continental Army, like the British and Hessian forces, were always accompanied by hundreds of women. Molly Hays, twenty-four, was a big woman who smoked, chewed tobacco, and used the most unlady-like language. The troops knew her well and treated her as an equal. At least one man owed her his life. She found him left for dead after a battle and nursed him back to health. Another time she asked a passing soldier to help her carry a pail of boiling water. He obliged so quickly that she asked his name. "George Washington," he said, bowing his head.

At Monmouth Molly brought her husband's battery crew water from a nearby stream. She carried it in a pitcher and made so many trips that thirsty men began calling her Molly Pitcher. Returning from one trip Molly noticed that her husband's gun was silent. John lay unconscious, the other crewmen dead. She dragged him into the shade and went back to the gun loading and firing it single-handedly until a relief crew arrived. (She later received a pension for "service during the Revolutionary War" and died at the age of seventy-eight.)

By late afternoon both armies were exhausted. Fighting sputtered out as each waited for the cool of night. After making his final inspection, Washington wandered among some apple trees. Under one he found a youngster asleep on the bare ground without a blanket. Quietly the commander in chief lay down beside him, spreading his cloak over himself and the Marquis de Lafayette. Sir Henry Clinton rested his troops awhile then continued his march toward Sandy Hook and safety.

The Battle of Monmouth Courthouse was a second turning point in the revolution. Before Monmouth every British commander dreamed of destroying the Continental Army in one glorious battle. Monmouth showed that this was impossible and that the Continentals were the regulars' equals in every way. It was the last big battle in the north. From then on the British didn't dare challenge Washington to an all-or-nothing fight. Their army kept behind its defenses in New York, and the action moved to other fronts.

Once back in New York, Dave was saying to one soldier, "This is where I get off. I think I have had enough."

The British were defeated in Yorktown. When news of the British surrender reached London, Lord North staggered as if he was shot. "OH GOD!" he gasped, flinging his arms apart. "It is all over!" Although the war officially continued, the armies did no more fighting after Yorktown. The only bloodshed was in the west where Tories and Indians continued to raid settlements. Lord North resigned as prime minister, and a new government was formed to make peace.

CHAPTER FIFTEEN

The Return

And now back in New York, Dave said good-bye to some soldiers he fought with. With ample provisions in his wagon, he decided to head north back to Boston thinking, "What an adventure. It is a wonder I wasn't killed with all that damn fighting." On the way back he saw a fellow on the road, stopped, and asked, "Where are you going?" "Oh," said the man, "as far as I can." Once the man was up on the wagon, Dave introduced himself. The man said, "My name is Zack." "Well," said Dave, "I guess this conflict is over." "Yeah," said Zack. "It looks that way," Dave said.

"You know, I fought in the South against a fellow named Tarleton, and after Kings Hill, I never heard about him again." "Oh, you mean Bloody Ban. Well, son, I will tell you what happened. He returned to England and fell in with the Prince of Wales and became a notorious gambler. After fleeing from gaming debts, he went to France where he wrote a history of the campaigns of 1780-1781 in the southern provinces of North America.

"Tarleton then returned to England where he was elected to parliament from Liverpool and served for twenty-two years as a representative of shipping interests. He led the reaction against social reformer William Wilberforce's antislavery movement. Tarleton was promoted to general in 1812 and made baronet in 1815."

"Son of a bitch," said Dave. "It is too bad he wasn't shot or hanged. In our day he would be up on war crimes or something." "Your day?" asked Zack. "Never mind," said Dave. "There was talk about an American traitor who at one time was a hero and then went to the British." "Oh, you mean Benedict Arnold? Well, when that bastard went to the British side, he went to New London, Connecticut, where he burned more than 150 buildings and where he also burned and raided his former neighbors. His troops massacred America militia at Fort Griswold near New London.

"In December Arnold and his family sailed to England where he advised British officials on the conduct of war. With the revolution's military conclusion and the ouster of his English political supporters, the distrusted traitor was excluded from active military service in the British army. His commercial enterprises proved unsuccessful, and for his treason he received less than one-third the money he had sought. After enduring years of British scorn, Arnold died in London in June 1801."

"You seem to know a lot," said Dave. "Well, I hear a lot," said Zack. So they continued north toward Boston. "This has been something," said Dave. "What do you mean?" asked Zack. "Well, I started out in Boston in 1984 with two other friends and somehow ended up in these years. I sure in hell don't know why. So that is why I am trying to get back to Boston and see if we can meet up." "Nineteen eighty-four?" said Zack. "Yeah," said Dave.

Finally Dave got back to Boston. Zack said, "This is where I get off, and thank you very much. I hope you meet your friends." "Yeah," said Dave, "I hope I do too." Now Dave was back in Boston. He drove his wagon by a bank looking over Boston Harbor and reached back to pick up a musket, thinking how he started out to rob a store and ending up living history. Or was it hell or purgatory or something in between?

He started toward the waterfront to see if he could find anything that looked familiar. There he saw a warehouse, drove up, and looked around. It was the craziest thing. Imagine living history. He walked into the warehouse, and there was Jim. Looking at them. It looked sort of weird. "Welcome, Dave," said Joe. "Nice to have you back."

The year was 1984, and Boston was bustling. Officers Kelly and Riley were standing by their police car, talking about the upcoming Red Sox season. There was a call that two men found something. It was about dusk, and there was a radio playing "Another Time Another Place" by Engelbert Humperdinck.

As the two policemen headed for the warehouse, the two reported that they were hanging around and just went inside. Kelly said, "You stay here." He walked in the door with his flashlight and looked around. All of a sudden he yelled, "Riley, get in here." Riley went through the door. "What are you yelling about?" "Look," said Kelly. "Holy damn," said Riley, "there are three bodies on the floor. I wonder if they are those kids that were trying to rob that store awhile ago. Damn it looks like they were here for some time." "Hey," said Kelly, "look at this, an old rifle." Riley said, "The damn thing looks like a musket that they used in the Revolutionary War." "Wow," said Kelly, "I wonder what that is worth." "Never mind," said Riley, "don't touch it until the coroner gets here."

"Let's get the call in." Finally the police came, and they put up a crime scene ribbon and waited for the coroner to get there with the rest of the police and detectives. Taking out the bodies, Riley said to Kelly, "I wonder what happened." Riley said, "I don't know." "I will say this," said Kelly. "We will leave that to the people that know those things. Let's go get some coffee."

the end

Wherever these three souls are, one thing is for sure. They will not be among "the returned."

JACK DEVINE

(Parts taken from Revolution's Privateers, spies of the Revolution, the War of independence the story of the American Revolution) Historical reference books; (Black heroes of the American revolution), (Lexington-Concord-and Bunker Hill), (First came the Indians), (Indian's Warriors and their Weapons), (Felicity's world 1774), (The American revolution, if you were there in 1776), (Revolution's Privateers Spies of the revolution), (The war of Independence the story of the American Revolution).

ABOUT THE AUTHOR

Jack Devine was born in Waterbury, Connecticut, to a family headed by a traveling salesman of the 1940s. As a result Jack's childhood was spent in many states including Minnesota, California, Arizona, and Oklahoma. Throughout the author's itinerant youth, he had two passions: golf and the American Revolution.

Jack became a golf professional in 1954 and started his golf career as the assistant pro at the Breakers Hotel in Palm Beach, Florida. In 1980 Jack became the head golf professional at the Scituate Country Club in Scituate, Massachusetts. Since moving to Scituate, Massachusetts, Jack has also worked at Widows Walk Golf Course in Scituate, Massachusetts, and the Black Rock Golf Course in Hingham, Massachusetts. Currently the author divides his work between the Halifax Country Club, the Hatherly Country Club, and coaching the Wentworth Institute Golf team in Boston, Massachusetts.

The author's second passion, colonial history and storytelling, is portrayed very nicely in his novel *The Returned*. The book starts with three punks from the streets of Charlestown, namely, Joe Davis; Jim Washington, an Afro American; and Dave Baker, robbing a store in 1984. After hiding out in a warehouse to avoid capture by the cops, the three thugs are transformed back in time to 1775. Read the thrills, challenges, and excitement these three punks encounter as they experience history in 1775. The book's narrative of the American Revolution and colonial history is factual, and the perspective of three modern-day hoods thrown back in time and surviving during the American Revolution is refreshing. The book's ending will leave you suspended, and hopefully you will appreciate the author's eight years of effort in writing *The Returned* or his view of the revolution revisited.